FilmScriptsTwo

Film Scripts Two

High Noon
Twelve Angry Men
the Defiant Ones

Edited by
GEORGE P. GARRETT
University of South Carolina

O.B. HARDISON, JR.
The Folger Shakespeare Library

JANE R. GELFMAN

IRVINGTON PUBLISHERS, INC.
NEW YORK

Distributed by
SAMUEL FRENCH TRADE
HOLLYWOOD, CALIFORNIA

Acknowledgments:
High Noon Photoplay of HIGH NOON (1952) printed by permission of John
Cunningham, National Telefilm Associates, Inc., United Artists Corporation,
and Cymo Corporation. Copyright © by John Cunningham, 1947, under the
title THE TIN STAR.
Twelve Angry Men Screenplay of TWELVE ANGRY MEN reprinted by
permission of International Famous Agency, Inc. Copyright © 1955 by
Reginald Rose.
The Defiant Ones Story and Screenplay by Nathan E. Douglas and Harold
Jacob Smith, Stanley Kramer Productions and United Artists Corporation.

First Irvington edition 1989

Distributed by
Samuel French Trade, 7623 Sunset Blvd., Hollywood, CA 90046

Library of Congress Cataloging-in-Publication Data

Film scripts/edited by George P. Garrett, O.B. Hardison, Jr.,
    Jane R. Gelfman.
        p.   cm.
    Reprint. Originally published: New York: Appleton-Century-Crofts, 1971-
        ISBN 0-8290-2275-9 (v. 1): $19.95.—
        ISBN 0-8290-2276-7 (v. 2): $19.95
        ISBN 0-8290-2277-5 (v. 3): $19.95
        ISBN 0-8290-2278-3 (v. 4): $19.95
        1. Motion picture plays. I. Garrett, George P., 1929-
II. Hardison, O.B.   III. Gelfman, Jane R.
PN1997.A1G25   1989
791.43'75—dc19   89-2004
                                                CIP

10 9 8 7 6 5 4 3 2 1

Production and design:
The Bramble Company, Ashley Falls, Massachusetts
Cover design: Peter Ermacora and Larry Bramble

Printed in the United States of America

Contents

Acknowledgments

Many people have been helpful at all stages in the task of assembling the material for *Film Scripts*. Obtaining scripts and unravelling the complexities of rights and permissions would have been impossible without the generous assistance, aid, and counsel of many of the writers and artists directly involved in the making of these pictures. Some others, whose work is not represented here, but whose interest in the book and enthusiasm for the idea behind it led them to act to make this book possible, deserve the special thanks of the editors. The editors are especially grateful for the encouragement and efforts of Michael Franklin, President of the Writers Guild of America, West, to Samuel Gelfman of the United Artists, to the distinguished producer-directors Robert Wise and Samuel Goldwyn, Jr., and to Gillon Aitken of Anthony Sheil Associates Ltd. (London).

Introduction

The first movie in the modern sense of the word was made by the Thomas A. Edison laboratories and shown in the unlikely location of West Orange, New Jersey, on October 6, 1889. It was produced by the marriage of Edison's sprocket-controlled motion picture camera with the new nitrocellulose film developed by George Eastman of Rochester, New York. Because the early Edison movies had to be viewed individually, through a peephole exhibiting device, they remained curiosities. During the early 1890s attempts were made by Major Woodville Latham, Louis and Auguste Lumière, Thomas Armat, and others to wed Edison's films to the magic lantern to permit film showings for large audiences. Armat's projector was put in regular use at Koster and Bial's music hall in New York City on April 23, 1896. In spite of a series of ills, including a disastrous fire in a Paris theater that killed some 180 spectators, legal battles by Edison over foreign patent rights, and various attempts to regulate the new industry by monopoly control, motion pictures flourished. The final step in the emergence of the modern film industry was taken by Edwin S. Porter, an Edison cameraman, in 1903. Dissatisfied with the vaudeville acts and sporting events that were the staple of early film, Porter made a narrative film crowding as many thrills as possible onto a standard thousand-foot reel. *The Life of an American Fireman* was sufficiently successful to justify a second effort, which emerged as *The Great Train Robbery* (1903). This film was the first commercially important narrative movie. When it opened in 1905 in a theater specifically designed for film showing and dubbed the *nickelodeon* on the basis of the five-cent admission price, the film industry was fairly launched on its amazing twentieth-century career.

For the first decade of the new century the movie industry was dominated by eastern producers (the Motion Picture Patents Company licensed by Edison). A group of independents using French equipment soon arose to challenge the monopoly of Edison's "movie trust." Partly as a result of competition, the independents moved to Southern California, where labor was cheap, the terrain varied, and the climate mild, an important consideration at a time when almost all movies were made outdoors. In 1911 the Nestor film company, under David Horsley, leased a studio site on Sunset Boulevard in Hollywood, and by the end of the year some fifteen companies had followed suit.

During the decade from 1910 to 1920, Hollywood became the film capital of the world. Cecil B. De Mille, Jesse Lasky, Samuel Goldwin, D. W. Griffith, Charlie Chaplin, Douglas Fairbanks, Sr., and a host of others came to Hollywood during this period and were to remain dominant for years to come, some, like De Mille and Goldwin, until after World War II. It was during this decade that movies found their audience. Regarded by intellectuals as crude popular entertainment, they quickly became the cultural staple for the unwashed millions. As success strengthened the financial position of the theater owners and Hollywood studios, movies challenged the supremacy of almost every form of popular entertainment—fiction, Victorian stage melodrama, and vaudeville—except sports. An awkward symbiosis, in some ways closer to an armed truce than peaceful coexistence, eventually developed between Hollywood and the legitimate theater, but movies badly upset the economy of stage drama. Touring companies were broken up. Smalltown theaters were everywhere converted into moving picture houses. Only the large cities—eventually, only New York—continued to support a vital stage drama. Many of the refugees from legitimate drama, of course, later found their way to Hollywood.

During the twenties and thirties movies reigned supreme in the mass entertainment field, and Hollywood was the undisputed center of world cinema. After World War I, while Europe's picture-making capacity was disrupted, the American industry quickly, and with little additional cost, peddled prints of its films abroad. By 1925, American films had captured 95 percent of the British market, 70 percent of the French, and 68 percent of the Italian; elsewhere the situation was much the same.[1]

The "Hollywood approach" was the hard sell. Hollywood producers based their work on what paid off at the box office, not on what film directors or critics claimed would make great art. They gave the public what the public wanted—slick photography, fast-paced plots, action for the men, and tear-soaked sentiment for the ladies. "Eventually two kinds of film

[1] Thomas H. Guback, *The International Film Industry: Western Europe and America Since 1945* (Bloomington: Indiana University Press, 1969), pp. 8–9; supporting references here omitted.

would dominate the screen: the peep show and the chase. As primitive tribes described them to Hortense Powdermaker, 'kiss-kiss' and 'bang-bang' stories are right for the screen." [2]

So successful was Hollywood that after 1915, the date of D. W. Griffith's *Birth of a Nation*, the film industry in England, France, Germany, and Italy never offered serious competition. But, in spite of Hollywood's unchallenged position in America as well as Europe through the twenties and thirties, the market at home still accounted for most of its income.[3] As the world's screen capital, it could afford to be as provincial and inward-looking as the country itself. To accommodate ever-larger audiences, enormous cathedrals or palaces of film were built in the major cities. The forerunner of these citadels was Mitchell Mark's Strand, opened in New York in 1914, with a seating capacity of 3,000. In the twenties the cathedral/palaces rivalled in glitter and luxury the fabled opera houses of Paris, Vienna, and Milan. The Roxy Theater in New York, for example, cost some $8,000,000 and had a seating capacity of over 6,000. But every small town had its moviehouse of some sort, and throughout America, Saturday night became almost synonymous with "going to the movies." Meanwhile, in addition to satisfying the popular craving for entertainment, movies created something like an American equivalent of European royalty. The star system fed the public on dreams of glamour, embodied in such popular idols as Theda Bara, Lillian Gish, Rudolph Valentino, Greta Garbo, William S. Hart, and others, whose exploits were followed obsessively not only on the screen but also in the gossip columns of newspapers and in the screen magazines that were by-products of the star system.

The introduction of sound in 1928 greatly increased the range of artistic effects possible in movies. At the same time it created a group of artistic problems that are still unresolved in the 1970s. Sound tended to nationalize movies. The silents spoke the universal language of visual imagery. Their few subtitles could easily be translated into French, Thai, Hindustani, or what have you, with no leakage of meaning. Talkies, however, relied heavily on rapidly spoken dialogue and often on fairly subtle vocal nuances. This was particularly true in their early years when directors tended to stress sound at the expense of image simply because sound was new, and when many Broadway plays—together with many actors—were translated bodily from the legitimate stage to film. To sell such films abroad it was necessary either to add subtitles or to dub in native-language dialogue. Neither expedient was satisfactory. Subtitles are a poor substitute for the spoken word. They can never translate more than a fraction of what is spoken in fast dialogue. And, of course, they make the unwarranted as-

[2] Roy Huss and Norman Silverstein, *The Film Experience: Elements of Motion Picture Art* (New York: Dell, 1969), p. 15; citing Hortense Powdermaker, *Hollywood: The Dream Factory* (Boston: Little, Brown, 1950), p. 14.
[3] Guback, p. 9.

sumption that the audience is literate! Dubbed dialogue, while better than subtitles, is also awkward. The actors who do the dubbing are usually poorly paid hacks. The dialogue itself is often crudely translated. Perhaps most distressing, the words on the sound track seldom correspond to the lip movements of the actors on the screen, a situation that undercuts, if it does not destroy, the dramatic illusion. Thus, in spite of the growing international character of the film industry, the serious viewer still suffers an annoying distortion and dislocation if he must experience, say, Michelangelo Antonioni's *L'Eclisse* (1961), which is set in contemporary Rome, under the amplification of an English-language sound track. Equally disturbing, on the other hand, is an encounter with the same director's *Blow-up* (1967), which is set in London of today, in any tones other than those of British English.

More fundamental, sound brought with it the unanswerable question of whether movies are a visual or a verbal art. The accident of limited technology forced the directors of the silent era to concentrate on the visual aspect of film. They explored a remarkable range of techniques for telling stories visually. In the opinion of many students of film, sound caused a regression in film technique that lasted until after World War II. Sound made it too easy to tell a story. Cinematic techniques that were commonplace to producers like Griffith and actors like Chaplin were replaced by stale devices imported from Broadway along with playscripts and actors. Not until after World War II, when a new breed of filmmakers formed by the realities of invasion, military defeat, and economic collapse made its vision felt, was Hollywood shaken out of its complacency.

While Hollywood continued to dominate world cinema between the two world wars, Europeans did produce many films that gained international attention either for their intrinsic qualities or innovative techniques. Sergei Eisenstein, the great Russian director, is a towering figure both in the art of making films and of analyzing principles of cinematography. Several of his films, notably *Potemkin* (1925), *Alexander Nevsky* (1938), and *Ivan the Terrible* (1944–46), have had worldwide influence. The silent, *The Cabinet of Dr. Caligari* (1919), by the Austrian director Robert Wiene, remains a classic of expressionism in the theater adapted to film while *The Blue Angel* (1930), a talking picture directed by Josef von Sternberg and starring Marlene Dietrich and Emil Jannings, remains a classic of harsh realism, social and psychological, which was inspired by the disillusionment that pervaded Germany in the last years of the Weimar Republic. Among the French, René Clair produced charming, socially cutting, film fantasies like *À nous la liberté* (1932) and *The Ghost Goes West* (1938); and Marcel Pagnol revealed with tender luminosity in *La Femme de boulanger* (1938) and a trilogy—*Marius* (1929), *Fanny* (1931), and *César* (1936)—complexities of feeling among the petty bourgeoisie of provincial France.

But it was not until 1945, following World War II, that European cinema began to challenge Hollywood and the economic situation for American producers began to change completely. In such films as Rossellini's *Open City* (1945), De Sica's *Shoe Shine* (1946), and his *Bicycle Thief* (1948), Italian filmmakers achieved sensitive but unsentimental renderings of the physical and emotional realities of German occupation, American liberation, and the struggle to rebuild a peacetime society with habits and outlooks conditioned by years of learning how to survive only from moment to moment. This new spirit of filmmaking, *cinéma vérité* (or direct cinema), came as a refreshing new perspective for American audiences when experienced against their own long exposure to Hollywood's vision, subsidized by our government, of a world at war. The newsreel-like verisimilitude of scenes shot on location where local inhabitants played the lesser roles was a radical break with the controlled and insulated environment of the sound studio and its professional actors.

This new and less-expensive procedure opened the door for shooting other films—from British comedies to Scandinavian psychocinedramas—out-of-doors. As the impressionists liberated painting during the last quarter of the nineteenth century by taking their canvases out of the studio and into the fields and streets, European directors led a similar revolution in filmmaking out of necessity after World War II. *Cinéma vérité* also restored to the directors some of the preeminence they had enjoyed during the silent era. They thus opened the way for such meditative, director-dominated films as *8½*, *Last Year at Marienbad* (1962), *Juliet of the Spirits* (1964), and *Blow-up*. French cinema has also been influential, though perhaps experimental, beginning with the postwar classic *Les enfants du Paradis* and extending through the *nouvelle vague* movement of the 1960s. Many isolated but major contributions have also come from Japanese and Scandinavian filmmakers, most notably Akira Kurosawa and Ingmar Bergman.

During the sixties British and American filmmakers began to draw on continental techniques. *A Hard Day's Night* (1964) is a brilliant English contribution which manages the difficult task of carrying its unorthodox techniques so lightly that they seem entirely natural expressions of the dominant tone of exuberant, uninhibited play. In the United States, as the photographic industry produced less cumbersome and expensive cameras and more light-sensitive film, a new kind of movie, one of *personal statement*, emerged. "Underground"—or "independent" as most of them preferred to be called—filmmakers could dissent "radically in form, or in technique, or in content, or perhaps in all three" from the offerings of commercial cinema, and all for an outlay of about a thousand dollars.[4] In the fifties

---

[4] Sheldon Renan, *An Introduction to the American Underground Film* (New York: Dutton, 1967), p. 17.

and sixties a subculture whose important personages included Stan Brakhage, Kenneth Anger, Stan VanDerBeek, and Andy Warhol established themselves as the heirs of an earlier generation of avant-gardists and experimentalists such as Jean Cocteau (*Le sang d'un poète*, 1930) and Luis Buñuel (*Un chien andalou*, 1928).

The response of the major American studios to the new freedom has been slow, but there are signs of change, principally in the form of more flexible use of visual strategies—jump-cuts, flash cuts (forward or backward), slow and accelerated motion, form cuts, zoom-freezes, and the like. *Petulia* (1968), *The Graduate* (1967), *The Wild Bunch* (1969), and *The Landlord* (1970) are excellent films which illustrate this tendency, and they doubtless indicate the direction of much future development. Whatever the case, the pressure on Hollywood to experiment is constant, especially (and ironically) from the screen of commercial television, which feeds heavily on Hollywood's past to keep its viewers awake and watching between plugs for automobiles, beer, and carpets. To compete, the motion picture industry, which is increasingly worldwide in every respect, must either seek a different audience from television or offer the average addict of the tube a positive inducement to leave his living room with its easy chair, ash tray, and nearby supply of cold beer for the privilege of spending from two to five dollars for a *new* movie.

The future of commercial filmmaking is now being shaped by pressures from several, and often conflicting, directions. In terms of revenues for a new feature film "just four countries in Western Europe—the United Kingdom, Italy, France, and West Germany—can yield almost half of the domestic [i.e., United States] gross for a film." [5] Indeed, as early in the postwar years as 1953, Hollywood producers conceded, through Eric Johnston, their industry spokesman, that "9 out of 10 United States films cannot pay their way on the domestic market alone." Simultaneously with greater dependence on foreign markets, other important economic shifts have occurred at home and abroad. Moviegoing in the United States, as reflected in average weekly attendance at theaters, is "but slightly more than half the 1941 figure, while population growth in the intervening years has stretched the imbalance." [6] Even though admission prices have risen steeply, they do not offset the loss of volume. In addition, the suppression of the "block-booking" system by forced separation of Hollywood's production facilities from its distribution outlets through action of the federal government (1948) early deprived major Hollywood studios of assured domestic showcases for each of their products, whatever their individual cinematic or other merits.

Since then, a number of forces are at work to push and shove the world's film capital into its future. Increasingly, "one centrally located, fully equipped permanent facility" makes little economic sense because

[5] Guback, p. 4.
[6] Guback, p. 3.

of high labor costs in the United States when compared with the rest of the world; access to remote corners of the world for airborne men and equipment becomes ever easier; an improved technology offers better and more portable cameras and more sophisticated editing equipment as well as film stock that is both more sensitive to light and less sensitive to extremes in climate; a new generation of filmmakers are as concerned about experimenting with the technical and psychological aspects of the medium as they are in exploring a variety of social themes; major studios are steadily absorbed by vast financial conglomerates which, though sensitive to costs and attentive to balance sheets, are insensitive to Hollywood's traditions and indifferent to established patterns of production.[7]

In addition to all of these pressures, American capital investment, starting in the early 1950s, has gone abroad and offered to national film industries, which welcomed aid from the United States, financial backing of production costs and the guarantees of an international distribution system for completed films. In two decades the rest of the world has, for better or worse, increasingly lost its independence. In other words, the internationalization of the film industry under American auspices has inevitably meant the diminishing of "chances for diversity and different points of view." Film, however, which is "not only a business commodity but a vehicle of communication . . . , is important not only for what it says but for what it does not say. The boundaries of human experience . . . expand or contract on the basis of what people have presented to them."[8]

The purpose of this thumbnail sketch of the history of film is not to outline or even block out a subject whose dimensions are so large that they are still partly unexplored. Rather, it is to document the basic contention of the present anthology: that film is not *an* art form of the twentieth century, it is *the* art form of the twentieth century. If sculpture was the glory of Periclean Greece, architecture of Augustan Rome, painting of Renaissance Italy, and drama of Elizabethan England, cinema has been both the major contribution of America to world culture and the dominant mode of world culture itself for the last fifty years.

In its brief history, the film has assimilated the photograph variously filtered and focused, motion near and far, sound from one or several directions, color in all of its subtle gradations, screens of great breadth both indoors and out, and lenses that give a visceral feeling of depth and movement. Within these expanding dimensions, filmmakers have elaborated techniques of transition and dislocation from frame to frame which dissolve rigidities of time and space as its audiences know them in everyday life. As a result, the tension achievable in film between order and chaos, between control and chance—which lies at the heart of every art regardless

---

[7] "Movies Leaving 'Hollywood' Behind," *The New York Times* (May 27, 1970), p. 36.
[8] Guback, pp. 203, 4; see also pp. 94–95.

of its media—is more dynamic and capable of greater complexity than in any other art. Film is far from exhausting its possibilities for artistic triumphs.

In the years since World War II a new medium and industry, television, has emerged not only to challenge established patterns of filmmaking and moviegoing but also to create intricate and reciprocal relations with cinema. Even a partial profile of the mutual impact of film and television on each other would take us too far afield from our primary concern, feature films and their scripts. But certain aspects, some of which we have already discussed, should be noted in passing. The advent of television in the United States has coincided with a reduction in selected subjects, especially newsreels and weekly serials, at moviehouses and their reintroduction in contemporary forms on home screens. Television has also relied heavily on films of the thirties through the sixties from its sister industry in order to sustain the commercial messages of its own advertisers. And, in the postwar years, while the large Hollywood production companies have redefined themselves—lost their chains of tied moviehouses, dismantled their sound stages, and dissolved the star system—commercial television has formed three major networks with affiliated stations across the country, fostered its own production facilities, and created its own stellar personalities—the hosts of its talk, news, and variety shows. At the present time, the internationalism that the film industry has gradually achieved since 1945 is only just becoming possible for television, thanks in part to the broadcast potential of transmission satellites.

The place of film in twentieth-century culture can be demonstrated in another, equally dramatic way. The average nineteenth-century child was illiterate. He was effectively isolated from the culture of the dominant class. As he matured, his entertainment, when he could afford it, consisted of dance-hall reviews, vaudeville, and, occasionally, a melodrama by Dion Boucicault or one of his imitators. Conversely, middle- and upper-class children were brought up on books. They were introduced to the world of art through the printed page. As adults they consumed a constant fare of novels, some good, most bad or indifferent. Theater and opera were significant, but the novel formed the core of the cultural life of the literate population. The modern child, by contrast, is exposed to the visual world of movies and television long before he can read. There is no class distinction in this exposure. It is experienced equally by rich and poor, and it becomes more rather than less intense as the typical modern child matures. College students read more than the general public, but it has been estimated that in the United States a typical freshman has seen twenty movies for every book he has read—and this does not include an average of some 15,000 hours of exposure to television by age 18! [9] After college, the student tends

[9] *Man and the Movies,* ed. W. R. Robinson (Baton Rouge: Louisiana State University, 1967), pp. 3–4.

to fall back into habits like those of the population in general, which means that he reads less, while his consumption of movies and television remains constant or increases. Clearly, film and television now form the cultural medium in which twentieth-century men—from the illiterate to the affluent —are immersed.

The consequences of the dominance of film and television as twentieth-century culture media have often been discussed. Marshall McLuhan feels we are being (or have been) pushed abruptly into a new phase of world culture, the post-Gutenberg era. Sounds and images, rather than printed words, shape our imaginative apprehension of the surrounding world. Sounds and images are not only far richer than printed words, they are also less "linear"—less dominated by the sequential logic of the sentence or paragraph or chapter—less constrained by the need to avoid redundancy or contradiction, and far more accessible since they do not assume literacy. McLuhan's theories imply that the printed word may be growing archaic: that some day the reading of printed books may be an antiquarian pursuit, a little like reading books written in Greek and Latin.

Whatever the future of the printed word, today's educational curricula are shaped around it to a degree that seems exaggerated on the secondary level and nearly obsessive on the college and university level. The higher-education establishment does obeisance to the printed word as devoutly as primitive tribes worship the idols of gods. While harmless in the area of the physical sciences, this behavior is questionable in the area of the humanities. Our literature departments boast of their concern for relevance—for significant examination of every aspect of modern culture. They actively encourage the study of modern fiction, modern poetry, modern drama, and modern criticism. Yet a Martian, after taking the "modern lit." curriculum at a typical American college, might emerge with no other knowledge of cinema than the vague realization that from time to time earthlings of the twentieth century went (probably furtively) to certain entertainments called movies. He might realize that plays and novels were occasionally made into movies, but he would have no inkling of the influence that movies have had on twentieth-century drama and fiction. At best, he would conclude that movies were a minor diversion appealing chiefly to the lower classes, the illiterate, the vulgar, the naive, the deviant.

Granted that film is the cultural medium characteristic of our age, that its neglect has been unfortunate, and that a proper understanding of its values and achievements would enrich studies of twentieth-century fiction, drama, and poetry, not to mention studies of modern psychology and sociology—the question remains: how does one study film?

In general, three approaches to film are possible: the technical, the historical, and the aesthetic. The technical is perhaps the most common one. Presently, some 850 courses on film are being taught at American colleges. The majority are technical in orientation. They are usually taught in departments of radio-television-film, of drama, and of speech, by individuals who are interested in how films are made.[10] Their common feature is their stress on making films—on script writing, photography, film acting, and film direction and editing. They are valuable, but they tend to be professionally oriented. In other words, they are primarily for those who hope to find a career (or, at least, an avocation) in film. They bear the same relation to the study of film that courses in creative writing bear to courses in literature and literary criticism, with the difference that, being much more technical, they are more numerous and less standardized in content.

No one who is interested in film can afford to be ignorant of the technical side of filmmaking, but the limitations of the technical approach should be recognized. One does not need to know how to write a novel in order to appreciate a good one once it is written: to respond to it, to observe its artistry, its literary relations, its form, and its thematic and historical significance. The same holds true for the study of film. Most films are made to be appreciated by audiences who could not care less about how they are made. Occasionally we have a technical *tour de force* like *The Cabinet of Doctor Caligari,* Cocteau's *Orpheus* (1949), or *Blow-up;* but the sheer cost of making a major film means that all but a few experimental directors use technique functionally—a point equally illustrated by Alfred Hitchcock's thrillers and Ingmar Bergman's meditative studies of the human psyche. Hitchcock and Bergman are both masters of film technique, and their technique is always part of their expression. Never present for its own sake, it serves as the medium of our vision, and, while we are members of an audience, we need be no more conscious of it *as technique* than the botanist examining plant cells is conscious of the complex arrangement of lenses that makes his observations possible.

The historical approach to film is also well-defined. Like the technical approach, it offers a valuable, even essential, body of information to the student. Although less common than the technical approach, it appears widely in the curriculum in the form of courses on "The History of Film," "The Silent Film Era," and the like. Historical courses are organized on analogy to the standard courses in the history of literature. Like the "surveys of English lit.," they tend to emphasize chronology, biography, and historical context, and to concentrate on early landmarks—the silent era—rather than later achievements. Their limitation is intrinsic to their approach. They are necessarily oriented toward history rather than toward the achievement of individual films.

The battle begun in the 1930s between historical scholars and the new critics of literature has given way to a generally peaceful coexistence. We recognize that there were (and are) important verities on both sides. In general, however, the basic contentions of the new critics have been established. We accept the idea that the study of literature is primarily a study

[10] *Film Study in Higher Education,* ed. D. C. Stewart (Washington, D.C.: American Council on Education, 1966), pp. 164–67.

of works of literature, not of dates, genres, influences, or biographies. This is why the old-fashioned sophomore literature survey has been replaced at most schools by courses in literary appreciation or literary masterpieces.

Surely, the same principles should apply to the study of film. It should be oriented toward our interest in ourselves and the culture within which the self is defined. The emphasis should be on individual films. Their artistic and cultural significance, rather than their technique or relation to the history of film, should receive first priority. Beyond that, if the films are considered in chronological order, the approach will take on an historical coloring; if they are considered by genres like the Western, the thriller, or the social documentary, the coloring will be formalist; if they are approached in terms of theme, the coloring will be sociological, philosophical, or theological. Some such coloration is inevitable and proper. It supplements the aesthetic approach, as long as it does not threaten to compromise examination of individual films.

To examine a film with the same care and thoroughness as a novel or a poem is difficult. The authoritative text of a film is the master print on which all prints made for commercial distribution are based. In the first place, the master print is never available. All films that are shown commercially and for educational purposes are later prints, and these are often edited silently to conform to local censorship laws, time requirements, and the like. Since many master prints have been lost, the later prints now available may or may not be edited versions, and for many early films, there is no way of knowing what the original really was.

Such bibliographical problems need not concern the average viewer. He can assume that the print of the film which he sees is reasonably close to the master print unless warned otherwise. His problem is of a different order. It stems from the fact that films are dynamic. They move. And as they move they convey more information than the human mind can retain. An experienced critic can pick up an impressive amount of detail from a single viewing of a film, but even the best observer has his limits and they are soon reached. The viewer of a film is the witness of a complex but significant series of events. We know how fallible even the most intelligent witnesses can be from the conflicting testimony that is always generated by a sensational public event. A vivid case in point is provided by the assassination of President Kennedy. We have to recognize the same propensity to error in ourselves. Yet the study of film demands accurate recall not only of what happened but what was said, how it was said, and—film being visual as well as verbal—how it was conveyed in images. That is, we certainly need to know that the hero married the heroine in the last reel. Depending on the aspect of the film that catches our interest, we may also need to know whether or not the butler was wearing gloves, whether the father drove a Ford or a Chevrolet, whether the heroine's costume in the first reel was red to foreshadow the sunset in the last, or whether there was a cut, a fade, or a dissolve from the chapel to the mountains. Moreover, if we wish to discuss our observations, we need some means of verifying them. If we disagree on the color of the heroine's costume, for example, the only way to decide who is right is to go to the film or an authoritative substitute.

Apparently, the ideal way of solving this problem is through movie archives and a viewing machine like the movieola, which permits the observer not only to see the film but to stop the action on a given frame, reverse it, and begin again. Comprehensive film archives would make it possible to document discussions of film in the same way that discussions of poems and novels are documented. An archive would have the further advantage of allowing interested critics to view films as often as necessary to refine and extend their observations.

But this solution, though ideal, is at present impracticable. No archive can accommodate the large numbers of individuals interested in film, and even if it could, the constant use of films quickly destroys them. A much more practical solution is to coordinate viewing of films with reading of scripts. Unlike reels of film, a script is easily portable; it can be read anywhere; it resists wear; notes can be written in its margins; and it is not "time bound," that is, it does not move continuously forward. If the critic comes to the last scene and wants to compare it to the first, he can simply turn back. Although a film can be reversed, the process is time-consuming, particularly if it has to be repeated several times.

Evidently, if film is to be studied as a cultural form in something of the same way that we study poetry, fiction, and drama, the script is a necessary adjunct to viewing the film. Note that it is an adjunct, not a replacement. A faithful copy of the master print must remain the final, authoritative text for the public at large. Normally, however, it is seen only once. At best it can be seen two or three times since rental schedules are fixed and viewing facilities (not to mention the time of the viewer) are limited. The script, which can be read as preparation for viewing the film, can also be annotated while the memory of the film is still fresh, reviewed easily and conveniently as often as needed, and can serve as documentation in resolving doubts about the filmmaker's intentions.

Note, too, that the importance here assigned the script does not imply that film is primarily verbal. The relative importance of image and word is a question in film aesthetics that will probably be debated as long as the question of what Aristotle meant by catharsis. The only assertion being made here is that if film is to be given its proper place in the study of modern culture, then viewing must be supplemented by use of scripts. In fact, a shooting script of the sort included in the present anthology often contains comments and revisions that call attention to effects that might otherwise be missed.

A final word may be useful concerning the scripts selected for the present volume. Silent films are not represented because they had no scripts in the modern sense of the term. Foreign films are excluded because they necessarily lead to awkward—usually misleading—compromises. Anyone who has read a translated script will be aware that its dialogue usually bears little relation to the dialogue in the film. The translator who provides subtitles works directly from the original shooting script, but within the economies of space and time in the footage. Many foreign films today are shown with dubbed-in dialogue. The alternative to a translation is thus a script transcribed from the English dialogue of a dubbed-in sound track. Such a script is next to worthless since the quality of the acting—the tonality, expression, gestures, and the like—was dictated by the nature of the *original* dialogue as well as the linguistic and cultural inheritance of the director and actor, not the words chosen by the English-language editor because they happen to fit the lip movements on the screen.

The scripts selected are entirely from the period between 1945 and 1970. The complicated legal status of prewar scripts makes permission to print difficult to obtain, and, evidently, many shooting scripts have been lost because they were not thought to have any intrinsic value. This limitation is not, however, without advantages. Hollywood's most vital periods were the silent era and the period following World War II. Postwar films are generally more serious in theme, more flexible in technique, and, of course, more directly relevant to contemporary life than their prewar forerunners. Since this anthology is intended for the study of film as an art form rather than the history or technique of film, the basis of the selection has been the quality and intrinsic interest of the film itself. Each selection attracted the serious attention of reviewers and critics when it originally appeared; and each still repays thoughtful critical analysis. Given the abundance and excellence of English and American films during the period covered, no more than a sampling of them can be offered. But an effort has been made to represent the more important types—comedy, satire, costume-movie, social criticism, psychological study, thriller, and fantasy— as well as the more important ways in which a story comes to the screen— from a novel or short story, from a drama, from television, and from an original screen play. Although every reader will inevitably miss several of his favorites, the editors believe that each film selected has a legitimate claim for inclusion.

Most of the scripts are shooting scripts; that is, they represent the written version of a story as it was available to director, actors, and cameraman before and during the making of the film itself. Because shooting scripts differ from dramatic scripts, a brief discussion of their characteristics will be helpful.

Place and Use of the Script

The true text of any film is the film itself, or, more strictly speaking it is the final negative, called the *master film*, from which all prints are made.

The relationship between a shooting script and a finished film is complex and depends upon a large number of variables, mostly upon the intentions and practices of the director. Some of the most outstanding directors, Alfred Hitchcock, for example, work with most explicit and detailed scripts and follow the script with much the same precision as a builder does the blueprints of an architect. (Hitchcock, of course, always works very closely with his writer at every step of the way in preparing his own kind of script.) Other directors prefer a loosely defined scenario so that they have a maximum amount of margin for revision and improvisation during the shooting stage. Some cineasts believe, quite wrongly, that many contemporary pictures are made without scripts. In general, this is simply not true, although the form of the script may vary widely from neatly bound scripts to pencilled scribblings done moments before shooting or even during the shooting of a scene. Granted the powerful aesthetic influence of *cinéma vérité* in our time, which some critics see as a new development in the medium and others as a return to the classical purity of improvisation that characterized the making of many of the greatest silent films, the fully developed script remains a key step in the creation of most films.

To be sure, a certain kind of film, increasingly popular and becoming well-known, dispenses with the rigidities of conventional plot and conventional story line, in favor of working out, directly before the camera, improvisations, ad lib dialogue, and even events or happenings. A conventional script obviously serves little or no purpose in such a scheme. In addition, as the old, arbitrary lines of distinction between fiction and nonfiction, fable and fact, continue to break down, even the feature-length documentary film will be affected by this new creative energy. The work of the American filmmaker Fred Wiseman is an excellent example. Using his team of cameramen to record actual people engaged in actual events, he might once have been called a documentary filmmaker, and judged by old-fashioned standards and classifications. Today he is regarded simply as a filmmaker. His *Titicut Follies* (1967), *High School* (1968), *Law and Order* (1969), and *Hospital* (1970) are, indeed, documentaries taken on the scene at particular times and places and using real people, not actors. Yet these films are also examples of advocacy reporting, designed to make strongly felt social and political points. He exercises the filmmaker's art in choosing to film the events that support his views and feelings and also in the most careful editing of the film to make "reality" coincide with his personal vision. He is thus as much a deliberate fabulator as any other filmmaker, an honest and engaged artist for whose work the old distinctions between "fiction" and "nonfiction" are largely irrelevant. But his method, at least in these films, precludes the use of any ordinary script.

Allowing for notable exceptions, however, it is still generally true that all feature films intended to be shown to audiences in theaters have a script. They may differ in form and format. The script may exist in many copies, available and known to all concerned, or it may be the private property of only a few key figures in the production process. But there is almost always a script, and that script precedes the making of the film.

The process of filmmaking and the unique nature of the medium are such that a script may be considered as raw material for the finished product. It helps to initiate the process of making, serves as a guide to director, actors, and technicians, and is then finally, to a greater or lesser degree, expendable. To the student of cinema, however, a script can be of real value. Close reading of it, in conjunction with an attentive viewing of the film, will demonstrate a great deal, which otherwise might be difficult to learn, about the nature of this twentieth-century art form. And such a procedure can offer substance for the purposes of query, discussion, and debate, the give-and-take and discovery that is learning.

The primary value of using shooting scripts in the study of films is that this method reflects honestly the first critical phase in the process of filmmaking. Although the outlines have been publicly available for a full half-century and have changed only slightly and very gradually during all that time, the process of making pictures is surprisingly little known. Or, when known, it is all too often ignored. Critics and reviewers are, for their own reasons, frequently indifferent to the process of making; or, what is perhaps less defensible, sometimes imply a very different sort of process than the one actually followed by the makers of films. Audiences, even some of the most appreciative and sophisticated, are frequently unfamiliar with the basics of the craft. This ignorance may be partially advantageous; for films, perhaps more than any other art form, depend almost as much upon sleight-of-hand, upon the magicians's art, for their effect upon the viewer as they do upon what is literally shown and seen. Often what is not shown, but is instead evoked in and imagined by the audience, is as viable as what is really shown. Good film shows us a great deal, but we perceive more than what is shown. From Eisenstein to Hitchcock to McLuhan and including the young filmmakers and cinema buffs around the world, directors and producers of films as well as critics and scholars of the art have sought to define theoretically and to name and classify the elements that combine to create the aesthetic effects of film. Their explorations, especially those of the makers of films, are a fascinating subject for research and study and are extremely important in the cultivation of a finer cinematic sensibility. The views of these men, although not to be ignored or slighted, in theory and practice, are far from definitive, whether they be interpreted singly or in any combination. The rules of the game, as even a slight reading of items listed in the bibliography will show, keep changing. One of the surest signs of vitality is the resistance of film art to every attempt at definitive classification, even the most subtle and persuasive. A rudimentary knowledge and general familiarity with the basic steps in the process of making a film should, however, at least serve to increase one's sense of appreciation, to refine one's taste and judgment rather than strip the cinematic experience of its human magic.

And that is the aim of this collection of scripts: to give the reader a means of seeing how films evolve from words to something else and, ideally, something much more than a script, namely, a complex of images, arranged in careful sequence, supported by sound and by music, dramatized by actors, and controlled by the intelligence and sensibility of a director.

Although most scripts are much transformed in the sequential processes of shooting and editing, the ideal of filmmakers, from producer to prop man, is to translate the script into the language and idiom of cinematography and to realize in doing so the script's full potential. This goal is an elusive one at best because of the nature of the process of making films and the many variables involved. All of the artists, craftsmen, and technicians who work at the making of a picture bring to it both skill and creativity. Each is a maker who seeks by his own skills to create something new and good. But even the best results have never given us "perfect" films, only truly fine films whose magic succeeds in spite of their imperfections.

A film script, even when published with care to reflect in detail the copy provided by the film's proprietors, is at best a verbal outline, a blueprint of what one sees and experiences in viewing a film. It is in no way a substitute for the actual experience of seeing a clear, unbutchered print of the film. But as an aid to memory, it helps us recall what we have already experienced as an ordering of meaningful sights and sounds.

Although the script writer is a valuable contributor to the total experience of a film, he is only one of many. Insofar as a single controlling sensibility unifies the entire process and experience, it is always that of the director. The director, of course, cannot possibly do everything himself or know in detail everything necessary to make a moving picture. But he, in the last analysis, is held responsible for all that happens or fails to happen. In recent years, especially with the decline of the large corporate producers in Hollywood, we have come to perceive this fact more clearly. The director's name rather than that of the producer or his imprint is the one we associate with a film in allotting praise or blame. In a very real sense the French critics of our time have been more accurate than innovative in naming the director of a picture its *auteur*. No full and easy analogy, however, quite explains the role of the director. His function is at once that of quarterback, orchestra conductor, building contractor, trail boss, company commander, and, sometimes, lion tamer—the latter image amusingly exploited by Fellini in 8½. The director rules, benevolently or despotically, over a little kingdom. The writer, though absolutely essential to the process and especially to the beginning of it, remains his majesty's loyal servant.

This book contains several sorts of film scripts in a variety of formats. Most are final shooting scripts, that is, examples of the very form which director, cast, and crew worked with when a film first went into production. In many cases additions and deletions and rearrangements and revisions of material take place during the period of shooting the film and, again, during the period of editing the film. Freedom and flexibility are basic characteristics of the creative process of filmmaking. The possibilities for revision are always present when a scene is being filmed, and equally so in the cutting room and laboratory as the film is being edited and polished into its finished form. The final shooting script is the first part of the production process, but it should be remembered that even in this form a script has usually been through many stages already and has been much revised.

Two scripts in this entire collection are not precisely final shooting scripts: those of *Henry V* (1944) and *The Pumpkin Eater* (1964). Each of these British scripts is designated, in British film terminology, as a *release screenplay*. That is to say, each has been more or less adjusted to conform as closely as possible to the edited film, its basic camera angles and shots, its frames and footage. These screenplays, in comparison with final shooting scripts, offer a fuller description of sound and music devices, present many more separate camera shots, and include such elements of the finished and released film as the full title and credits. Necessity requires the inclusion of these release screenplays; for, unlike their American counterparts, it is not the custom of British production companies to preserve copies of the earlier versions of scripts on file. We are most fortunate, however, thanks to the writers themselves, to have obtained rare versions of the shooting scripts of *A Hard Day's Night* (1964) and *Darling* (1965) for this collection. Yet even these release screenplays are somewhat different from and fall short of what is generally known as the *final* official form of a film script—the *combined continuity*. Created by a specialist (usually designated as *script girl*) who follows the shooting and editing of a film from beginning to end, based entirely upon the completed and commercially released form of the film, with all of the separate camera shots listed and all details of footage and running time of individual shots and scenes, etc., carefully recorded, a combined continuity is at once a sort of chart or graph of a finished film and the very last *word* of the film. Close as these two British release screenplays are to what is seen in the films, they are not combined continuities; and differences exist between them and the films. The alert student will note slight changes in each of them.

All of the other scripts in this collection are final shooting scripts. If the release screenplay comes near the end of the process of filmmaking, a final shooting script represents a true beginning. It is the demarcation point—many filmmakers would call it "the point of no return," the place where the production of the film really begins. From there on it goes first before the cameras, then, perhaps most crucially of all, into the movieola of the film editor to be cut and arranged before the finished film is to be projected upon a screen. Next to the director the film editor has, in a literal and physical sense, more control over what will be seen by an audience than anyone engaged in the making of a picture. The director remains responsible for the results and thus supervises the editing process closely. Some directors are engaged in the cutting and editing of a film in all details. Others prefer to give their film editor considerable freedom and to act in a critical capacity, viewing sections of the film in the projection room and offering general advice, suggestions, and criticism as, bit by bit, the whole film is put together. (Sometimes the screenwriter is called upon to participate at this stage as well.) The film editor, of course, is a highly professional craftsman, often an experienced artist in his own right. How he works with the director and others, and how much the actual labor is overseen and divided is a subtle matter involving diplomacy, tact, and personal relationships. Theoretically, in any event, the director has the last word in this area and is held responsible for the quality of the editing.

The Process of Filmmaking

In the beginning someone has an idea for making a picture. Once this "someone" was almost always a producer. Now, increasingly, it is a director, a writer, or occasionally a star who initiates the process. As witnessed by the scripts in this collection, the idea, the source of original inspiration for a movie, may come from almost anywhere—a novel or short story, a play for stage or television, another film old or new, something from the newspapers or magazines, or something that has captured an artist's attention and can lead to an original screenplay. However the idea may begin, it soon becomes a *property*. This term, though unfortunate in its connotations, is almost universally used by filmmakers and is used in a neutral rather than a pejorative sense. In any case, the original desire and intention to create a film becomes a matter of real property when a producer involves himself by means of an option or outright purchase of film rights.

Enter the writer (if he has not arrived already) to set about building a story and writing a script. Whether the picture is an adaptation or an original screenplay, as soon as a producer is involved, commerce begins to make its claims. The making of all pictures to be shown in theaters, where audiences buy tickets of admission, is an elaborate (and sometimes lucrative) business as well as an art. Each year the cost of making films increases. The producer must be able to raise the capital necessary to make the film from one or more sources. Perhaps, under ideal circumstances and blessed with a reputation for success, he can tentatively arrange the financing, sign options with leading actors and the right director, and gather the essential elements of the crew on the strength of the property alone. But sooner or later, and usually sooner, he will need a script to present to both potential backers and key coworkers before any firm commitments can be made, contracts signed, and a budget and production schedules devised. The writer thus comes in early. If he is lucky he stays late and sees the picture through production.

A very large number of projects, begun with high hopes and much enthusiasm, never reach the point of a workable script, one that is satisfactory to everyone who must be satisfied. A large percentage of properties never become films. And a very large number of the films we see have had more than one screenwriter and many preliminary versions and drafts of the script. Only writers whose material is actually used in the film receive *film credit*, even though a number of writers may have worked on the property earlier.

For simplicity and assuming ideal circumstances, let us imagine one writer working on a script. It should also be understood that though the stages described here are customary and conventional, they vary considerably according to the experience and reputation of the writer and his personal relationship with the producer and the director. Usually the writer will first produce a brief *synopsis* that is basically a literary outline of how he proposes to deal with the story in cinematic terms. If this proves satisfactory, he then writes a *treatment*, a much longer and detailed development of the synopsis, an extended outline of the potential script. The treatment is still more or less literary in form, descriptive rather than dramatic, though it may very well include some individual scenes done in dramatic form and with some dialogue.

Many filmmakers find the treatment a vital stage in the development of script into film. A commonplace among filmmakers says, "If it isn't in the script, it won't be in the picture." What is not meant, of course, by this aphorism is the picture's style, direction, cinematography, cutting, or any matter of filmmaking technique. What is meant is what has always been concerned writers as storytellers—structure, character, motivation, tone, etc. Some filmmakers themselves apply this rule of thumb to the treatment and swear that if a script—and hence the film—takes a wrong turn, the flaw can be found in the treatment.

Following the treatment comes the *first draft screenplay*, now employing one of the conventional formats used for film scripts. These forms, as you will see, have slight differences, but there are some general things that apply to all the shooting scripts in this collection. A script is broken down into separate units. Usually, though not always, these are numbered sequentially, and are called *master scenes*. These units may be many or relatively few in number, depending on the detail called for in order to help the translation of dialogue and action as written into camera frames, angles, depth-of-field, transitions, sound, etc. Compared to continuities all scripts are sparse in this kind of explicit direction. A master scene is, then, simply a single dramatic unit at a single location or setting. Within this unit any number of shots and camera angles may be used to shoot many feet of film—versions of the same scene from a variety of angles and points of view. Though the method is changing, the traditional one still employed by most directors requires that all actions in a given master scene be shot at least five times (sometimes the number can be as high as twelve) in order to insure proper *coverage* of the scene. The purpose here is not only to allow for different readings on the part of actors or, say, different lighting conditions, but to provide the director and the film editor with enough footage of the same basic dramatic unit so that they may cut and splice with a maximum of freedom and choice. In the cutting, which comes later, they may well use and juxtapose frames and pieces from all the separate versions of a photographed master scene. This rule does not apply easily, of course, to scenes (or entire films) based upon spontaneity and improvisation.

In addition to specifying a sequence of master scenes and calling for certain specific camera angles in the cinematography of a film, the writer may or may not specify the use of certain kinds of transitions from one unit to the next. Transitions from one scene to the next, from one piece of film to the next, are the concern of the editor. It is not properly a part of the writer's job to tell director, cameraman, or editor how to do theirs; nor will they heed his suggestions to the disadvantage of the film or the inhibition of their own talents. There are a number of reasons, however, why a writer will offer some directions, camera angles, and transitions in his script. First, he will do so in order to make clear a point within his proper area of concern—a story or plot point, a bit of characterization, a structural device, or, perhaps, an occasional suggestion as to the rhythm of a scene or sequence of shots. For the rhythm of a film is intricately wedded to its dramatic structure. Unless elapsed time, for example, is being used functionally for suspense, as in *High Noon* (1952), film is not concerned with what we call "real" time. Instead one has a sense of continual present, a sense that is created by the rhythm of the film. Context may make two scenes of approximately the same footage seem radically different. One may appear slow and lyrical whereas the other may seem jagged, jazzy, and quick. With a full awareness that his views are largely speculative suggestions and may frequently be ignored, the writer is within his rights in dealing with these elements. His views may give director, cameraman, or editor a clearer idea of the intent and inner quality of the script. He will be at fault only in persuading himself that his own visualization of the finished film ought to be binding on the director, actors, and technicians.

There is also another value in the writer's use of at least a few technical devices in his script. Although the script is mainly intended to lead towards the creation of the film, it must be read by a great many people, some very knowledgeable in cinematic technique, others less so. In addition to being examined by the cast and crew, the script is read by bankers and financial backers, by lawyers and talent agents and casting agents, by potential distributors, sometimes even by the owners of theaters, and by publishers and journalists, etc. And each of these readers must be given a sense of the finished film, enough detail to imagine, however, vaguely, the style, form, and content of the film itself. Whether or not the details are ever used as they are indicated in a shooting script depends upon many things, but clearly one function of the script writer, though it is secondary, is to produce a readable film script.

The writer writes his first draft screenplay and the drafts and versions that follow with the criticism, encouragement, and, to an increasing degree as he comes closer to the final shooting script, the collaboration of others who will be making the picture.

The *production manager* worries about the budget, tries to eliminate what seem to him unnecessary scenes and characters wherever possible. And he arranges his own *sequence* for the shooting of the picture, a sequence designed to use talent, sets, material, etc., as efficiently as possible. Almost all pictures made these days, anywhere is the world, are shot *out of sequence* because of the enormous expense of making films. The actual sequence of production and shooting thus hardly ever parallels the sequential structure of the script. Major parts, the leads, have the whole script to study and, with the help of the director, can, even out of proper order, build a character. The minor actors with bit parts are frequently given only *sides,* that is, those specific pages of the script which involve them. They are thus much more dependent on the director. Producer, director, actors, production manager, cameraman, editor, art director, set dresser, and even the prop man, these and many more all have legitimate interests and concerns, and they may exert a considerable influence before the final shooting script is ready.

Once the picture goes into production, collaboration is increased both because more people are involved at that stage and because of the necessity of meeting a fairly strict schedule, within the terms of a fixed budget. If the writer continues on the job, working through the period of production, he will make many changes on the spot to fit unforeseen circumstances. If he does not, there will be changes anyway. Like the diagram of a football play, the script, though well-conceived and planned, does not always work out on the ground exactly as anticipated.

Revision and repeated possibilities for revising, changing, and rearranging occur in every stage of the filmmaking process. Everyone involved has to make constant choices. With liberty to choose and change comes an increased responsibility. For often the choices that must be made are not clear-cut, not between good and bad, but, like many political choices, are decisions between imperfect options for the sake of expediency and in hope and faith that results may serve to justify what is finally decided.

Hence, everyone involved in the making of a film, and not least of these the writer, must always allow for the unexpected and for the possibility of change throughout the entire production. Even then, with the production finished and "in the can," the possibilities of change and (sometimes) improvement remain. Many films are slightly revised following their first previews. Some are revised even later, after their initial premiere openings and in response to reviews. One of the most famous of American filmmakers, the late Irving Thalberg (who served as the model for the producer in F. Scott Fitzgerald's last and unfinished novel, *The Last Tycoon*) is frequently quoted as describing the filmmaking process: "Pictures are not made, they are remade."

Sometime after the final shooting script is finished, the picture goes into actual production, following the shooting schedule. There are rehearsal periods (and, usually, subsequent changes) sometimes before the shooting begins, and always on the set during daily shooting. Scene by scene, the material to be shot is rehearsed until the director is ready to photograph the scene. Then, with everything in place, lighting arranged, camera and sound equipment ready to record, there is the *take*. There may be many takes before the director is satisfied and signifies that a particular take is a *print*. As the shooting schedule progresses the director and editor are regularly viewing the prints called *rushes* or *dailies* as they are delivered from the photographic laboratory. Always bearing in mind their aim of assembling the best possible scenes, they study the prints to decide if it is necessary (and possible) to reshoot sequences that seem to have failed.

When the shooting schedule has been completed and most of the cast and crew are gone, then the stage of full-scale editing commences. It is an intense time which, by traditional rule of thumb, is at least equal to the time spent shooting. All the prints must now be assembled into a single form, a sort of rough draft of the film called the *work print* or *rough cut*. Some figures will give an indication of the magnitude of the task facing the editor and the director. The average feature film runs approximately ninety minutes or, in footage, 8,100 feet of film. It is not unusual for the director and editor to have at least 200,000 feet of prints to work with, from which the film must be composed. And it is also common to have on hand another 100,000 feet of film which represent prints put aside in reserve but not yet discarded during the daily viewing of the rushes. These reserve prints are called *holds*.

Now the director and editor begin the task of composing and arranging all of this material, through constant revision, into the order and form of the rough cut. When the rough cut is ready, the director can for the first time know with some degree of accuracy how long his film, in its present stage, runs. It is not uncommon for a rough cut to be very long indeed, sometimes an hour or even several hours too long for a feature film. When this is the case, a process of cutting back and simplifying begins. In editing, whole scenes from the script can be shortened or, in some cases, ruthlessly eliminated as being, in terms of the context of the entire picture, no longer necessary. Whole scenes and even larger blocks of script material can be easily rearranged. Both sequence and structure are relatively flexible again.

When the director and the producer are satisfied with the work print, more work still remains to be done. Although this custom is changing, the services of the *composer* are called upon at this late stage. He views the work print, studies the script, then writes music for the picture, which is arranged, performed, and recorded. The contribution of music to the total experience of the film can be enormous. From the beginning, even before the advent of sound, when pianos accompanied the silent pictures in theaters, music has been an integral part of the aesthetic experience of movies. The full implications and possibilities of the use of music in support of and conjunction with all the elements of the film are only now being systematically explored and understood. At least it is clear to all that composer and musicians make a really major creative contribution to the totality of a film.

With the music ready and recorded and all the various sound effects (for example, the ringing of a doorbell, traffic noise, a jet passing overhead, train and boat whistles, etc.) on hand, then, music, dialogue and sound effects are *mixed* by a careful and complicated electronic process to become the *sound track,* a permanent part of the *negative* and, thus, of the *composite print* made from it. At that point the film is done, the picture is finished and ready to be previewed and put into release.

From this oversimplified account of the making of a film several basic generalizations can be drawn:

(a) Filmmaking is complex and collaborative to an extent beyond any of our other media or art forms.

(b) The writer has a critical part to play in the collaboration, for he makes what is at once a blueprint for and the raw material of the finished film. But nonetheless his part is only one among many.

(c) The script is only the first tentative draft text of the film. The extent to which it is followed, closely or freely, literally or with much embellishment, depends on many variable factors.

(d) The effect of the finished film as experienced by an audience is simultaneous, a happening in which all the individual parts, done separately and in bits and pieces, come together at once. Only in the film, and to a lesser extent in the shooting script from which it evolved, is this unity possible.

(e) The making of pictures is a process allowing for many stages of revision, for an extraordinary number of choices to be made. Choices, even bad choices, are exercises of reason. Filmmaking becomes, by definition, one of the most rational art forms man has known. The writer shares in this process, and there is a reason for everything in his script. But in the end, since a film must evoke emotional and imaginative responses from the audience, all the reasons of the makers of the film become means to an end, tools to accomplish a task.

Perhaps the finest picture concerned with the process of filmmaking is Fellini's 8½, in which the protagonist is a gifted director trying to make a picture. Although he fails in his intention, he does succeed in creating the picture we have seen. At the end, the next-to-last scene of the film, the director and his writer sit in a lonely car and the writer, most reasonably, tells him all of the reasons why he has failed. The writer's arguments are irrefutable. Except . . . except precisely at that point a mind reader, a kind of magician who had appeared much earlier in the film, reappears and summons the director to come and do his proper job. The characters from all of the story's episodes reappear at once and, following the instructions of the director, come together hand in hand in a beautiful dance. As they fade out and we are left to confront a dark screen, the truth brightens at the last: out of all the confusion and chaos of this collaborative enterprise, out of all the choices and reasons, good and bad, comes something marvelous, a kind of magic. All the craft of filmmaking conspires to strive towards what Alexander Pope called "a grace beyond the reach of art."

Films are the art form of our tribe, our modern cave paintings. To study the script and to see the film is only the beginning, a preliminary stage in acquiring a finer appreciation of the medium and a greater refinement of taste and judgment. It is fitting and proper to begin where the filmmakers begin, with the script, and to retrace, partly by the evidence and partly by educated surmises, their journey to the final destination of the finished film.

Film Terms in Context

The grammar and syntax of film are not verbal. In the complete cinematic experience words play a part, a very small part, in the form of dialogue. And words are important in the creation of film, beginning with the written script. But when creators, critics, and scholars speak of the *language* of film they are very seldom referring to words. Rather they are speaking of all aspects of cinematic technique as they apply to the making of films and as they are part of the aesthetic experience of the finished film. Though the language of film is essentially nonverbal, a *vocabulary* for film exists to describe the steps taken in the making of films and the effects of films upon appreciative viewers.

The terminology associated with film is complex at its best and esoteric at its worst. It is often confusing to the uninitiated when it is not apparently contradictory. A classic example is the word *montage*. Originally it was the French filmmaker's technical term for the entire process of editing. Great Russian theorists and filmmakers, notably Lev Kuleshov, Vsevolod Pudovkin, and Eisenstein, pioneers of film art, took over the term and changed its meaning. It replaced for them what they had earlier called *the American cut* and was used more strictly to describe both their theory and practice of the art of rapid cutting. (See below for definition of a *cut*.) Because the art and critical theory of these men, and others who followed, have been extremely influential and remain so today, their definitions and classifications of montage are widely used. At the same time, however, American filmmakers incorporated the term montage to describe a very different thing, and their definition is also current and is sometimes called for in scripts. They used the word to describe a series of shots rapidly *dissolving* (see below) over each other. Today the word is used in either sense. Its meaning depends upon context.

The shifting values of montage, both denotative and connotative, are typical of many words in the glossary of film. Context tends to make meaning clear even when there is disagreement about the precise definition. Critics and reviewers, looking at films from the point of view of the effect of the experience of viewing, use their own words and definitions, some of these used exclusively in this critical language. Scholars and specialists in the history of film art are often inclined to use other words, or to use more common words within the limits of special connotation. Makers of films, usually quite aware of both these "dialects," have another vocabulary to describe the technical details of making. They can communicate to each other easily enough, even across the barriers of national language, as witnessed by the fact that in our time international pictures made by multilingual casts and crews are not a novelty. A great many terms in the filmmaker's lexicon are thus more or less meaningless to all those outside of the craft. Fortunately, an appreciative student of film art need not master a very large vocabulary of technical terms at the outset to speak to the basic aspects of scripts or finished films. From an understanding of some of the elementary terms and experience with the things they signify, the student of film can go on to increase his knowledge and refine his understanding through reading the work of outstanding historians, critics, and filmmakers.

In recent years, precisely the years covered by the volumes of *Film Scripts*, it has been the custom of filmmakers to hire writers of all kinds—dramatists, novelists, poets, journalists—to write screenplays. Most of these writers at least begin their association with filmmaking without any previous experience, except for the great, common, shared experience of moviegoing. The days of great production studios, each with its building where a corps of full-time script writers was kept busy, are gone for good. A writer is generally hired to work on one particular project. The common experience of the beginner, frequently described by these writers in interviews and written accounts of their experience, has been doubt at the ability to master the form of the medium, a doubt followed by a sense of surprise and relief that the fundamentals of the vocabulary of filmmaking are not so complex as to demand years of expert experience.

The purpose here is to offer a limited glossary needed for the reading of these scripts and the viewing of the films which came from them. (A full glossary will be found in the back of the book.) Some terms have already been isolated and defined in the preceding section. Others are briefly defined and discussed below.

Those readers who wish to seek out deeper and more inclusive working definitions and examples, will find them in a number of readily accessible books.

(a) *The Filmviewer's Handbook* by Emile G. McAnany, S.J., and Robert Williams, S.J. (Glen Rock, N.J.: Paulist Press, 1965). The chapter entitled "The Language of Film" (pp. 42–69) offers excellent and precise definitions of many terms in a general introduction to the subject.

(b) *A Grammar of the Film* by Raymond Spottiswoode (Berkeley, Calif.: University of California Press, 1965). The chapter "Definitions" (pp. 42–53) offers some useful definitions, though some of his terminology is eccentric when seen beyond the context of this volume.

(c) *A Dictionary of the Cinema* by Peter Graham (New York: A. S. Barnes, 1964). Essentially a brief listing of people in films, this book does offer some definitions of film terms and, notably, some of the special terms used by British and European filmmakers.

(d) *People Who Make Movies* by Theodore Taylor (New York: Doubleday, 1967). Though intended for younger readers, this introduction is exceptionally clear and fine in its coverage of many parts of the filmmaking process. Basic terms, together with examples, are used throughout the text. A brief but accurate glossary is appended.

(e) *Behind the Screen: The History and Techniques of the Motion Picture* by Kenneth MacGowan (New York: Delacorte Press, 1965). This massive compendium of information gives examples and illustrations by a distinguished producer and deals with all aspects of picture-making. Pages 333–501, concerned in depth with technical aspects of filmmaking, present a great many useful terms with full, accurate definitions.

The scene as unit

The opening unit of the script *High Noon*, the first capitalized section, incorporating scenes 1–8 in a descriptive passage, is a useful example. Its format is conventional enough to be called standard.

1–8 EXT. OUTSKIRTS OF HADLEYVILLE–DAY

First, the numbering indicates that eight separate shorter "scenes" are here incorporated into one unit. This device, which is somewhat literary, is designed to make the script more readable at the outset, to set the tone and style before any reader contends with the difficulty of trying to visualize and imagine a large number of separate scenes, 426 in all, many of which are to be very short, individual shots. In the capitalized identification the abbreviation "EXT." establishes that the shooting of the scene is *exterior,* outdoors. The abbreviation "INT." would have established an *interior* location, a setting within some structure. Though this identification may seem so obvious as to be silly to the reader, it serves both a narrative purpose in the script and a technical purpose in making the film. A number of important members of the crew, for example the production manager and the cameraman, not to mention a host of minor functionaries, use this information at a quick glance in their preparation for a scene. Since a film can seldom be shot in the order and sequence of scenes found in the script, the production manager must devise a schedule in which exterior scenes, or nearby parts of them, can be used in a single shooting sequence. At the same time he must be ready not to lose a full day's shooting on account of weather. In the event of rain, for example, he has ready a *backup schedule,* or alternate shooting plan that uses interior sets. These sets must be in order and ready, lighting and sound facilities available, and other members of the cast alert to be called. The script and the schedule also give the cameraman and his crew or *unit* some of the basic information they need to work efficiently. Their equipment for outdoor shooting, the size and composition of the crew, will be different than for interior work.

Because the action of *High Noon* takes place within a small span of time and entirely by daylight, the convention "DAY" is not repeated after the initial heading. In other scripts, however, this traditional direction is frequently used, either regularly with each separate scene, wherever context requires it, or the information is necessary for the crew. Very often scenes supposedly set at night are photographed during the day since the illusion of darkness can be created by the use of appropriate lens and filters as well as by the type and the quality of the film. If the scene must in fact be shot at night, then the proper artificial illumination must be on hand.

Occasionally a more specific direction will be found, such as "DAWN," "TWILIGHT," or "DAY FOR NIGHT," the latter calling explicitly for the daylight shooting of a night scene. These notations tell the cameraman and his unit the kind of light qualities they must capture on film.

The scene

Generally, the breakdown of scenes, headed by the capitalized line and separated by space from other scenes, is determined not only by place, but also by the primary *setup* of the camera and other equipment necessary for shooting. Although all of this equipment cannot easily be displaced in most instances from one setting to another, within a single setting the camera is readily movable. A scene combines, therefore, the physical setting and the primary placement of camera and equipment. In all of the scripts different "scenes" occur from time to time within the larger scene. These separate units, which are part of the same setting and sequence of action, can be used to identify a new and specific setup or to isolate a particular kind of shot.

The filmmaking technique of Alfred Hitchcock is an exception to the rule. Hitchcock prepares, simultaneously with the preparation of the final shooting script, an elaborate and detailed series of sketches (rather like an oversize comic strip) visualizing the film-to-be scene by scene. These sketches are called *continuity sketches*. Script and continuity sketches together, and coordinated as to camera angles and shots, are the material upon which the production of the film is based. Many other directors use continuity sketches as a part of their working strategy, for at least parts of a film, as a guide to the shooting and editing of difficult scenes and transitions. (See "Editorial Terms" below.)

Camera shots

Many kinds of shots are possible, but basically all of them are variations upon a few standards.

Three are defined by proximity of the camera to the subject, whether literally by distance or by use of special lenses. These shots—*long, medium,* and *close*—are only relative and not specific measures. The long shot includes details of an entire setting. Its subject may be on the horizon, for example, a distant ship, the buildings of a city, an expanse of open country, or it may be as close as, say, fifty yards. In order to emphasize great distance, an *extreme long shot* is sometimes called for. A medium shot is of a distance to include, if necessary, a group of two or more people and at least part of the surroundings. A close shot, also called *closeup*, focuses closely on its subject in isolation. It may be of the face or hands of a character or of some single object. Close shots, of course, can be photographed quite separately, even at another time and place, and inserted later in the action of a sequence. For further definition close shots may be *extreme* or *tight* on the one hand or a *medium close shot*, which is indefinite in scope, but nearer at hand than a standard medium shot and at the same time not so tight as the standard closeup.

Two other shots, in which the proximity may vary, are usually included in the five basic shots. They are the *two-shot*, or *group shot* if more than two characters are involved, and the *over-shoulder* shot. The first, at whatever distance, focuses attention on two characters or the group. Sometimes the cameraman is asked in this context to center attention on one of the characters by *featuring* or *favoring*. The over-shoulder shot is, in fact, a variation of the two-shot or group shot; for, in the foreground is the back of the head of one character and in the background we see what the character sees.

Occasionally other kinds of shots are called for, which the context makes clear. For example, a *full shot* does not specify distance, merely that the shot should be fully inclusive of the subject.

In scripts the term *montage* is sometimes used to describe a shot. It then signifies a "series of rapid dissolves," which was mentioned earlier, and involves both cameraman and editor in its creation.

A *stock shot* is a shot or sequence not filmed specifically for the picture but taken from the stock of available footage of any given subject or event. A frequently used stock shot is that of a commercial jet taking off or landing.

A *process shot* is a shot in which actors in the foreground play out a scene in front of a screen that is itself filled with a photograph or movie. The most familiar conventional example occurs in traffic scenes. The characters are photographed in the shell of a stationary automobile while a film of traffic, visible through the rear window, gives the impression of movement and traffic. Process shots may also be used to give the impression of some background or setting far from the studio and set where the actors are being photographed.

Camera angles

In addition to the specific kind of shot sometimes explicitly called for in a script, camera angles may be stated. Just as in the case of shots, these suggestions by the writer will be actually followed by the director and cameraman only insofar as they are deemed valid and functional.

The camera may photograph from certain basic *angles* and, as well, it may shoot from a particular *point of view* (usually abbreviated POV). Point of view need not include the observing character, whose presence on the screen would constitute an over-shoulder shot. A character, for example, looks up; the next shot, made as if to represent what he sees, is of a buzzard in the sky.

Camera angles can be reduced to three principal types: a *regular* or standard angle, unnamed and unspecified since it is assumed to be taken from the camera as set up, straight up and down; a *high angle* (looking from above); and a *low angle* (looking up).

Occasionally the angle is assumed and the direction *shooting up* or *shooting down* is given. The high angle is sometimes simply described as a *high shot*.

Camera and movement

In shooting a camera may be either *fixed* or *moving*.

A fixed camera is set up at one spot. But a fixed camera can nevertheless be used to create a sense of movement or action.

The fixed camera can *tilt*, be moved upward or downward on its single axis while shooting.

And the fixed camera can *pan*. The word is a contraction of the original term used—*panoramic shot*. It is a pivotal movement, usually lateral, made by turning the camera on its axis from one side or part of a scene or setting to another.

Two other customary movements of a fixed camera are the *zoom* and the *whip*.

The zoom is achieved by lens adjustment during photographing so that, without any break, the camera may move (*zoom in*) to a quick closeup of a particular subject.

The whip is a variation on the pan. The camera, focused on one object in a scene, is suddenly and swiftly moved (whipped) to focus upon another subject.

But, since the earliest days, it has not been necessary to depend exclusively upon a fixed camera. The camera may be moved while shooting in what are called *moving* or *running* shots.

One method of moving the camera is by means of a *dolly*. Mounted upon a short set of tracks or a level platform with wheels, the camera can be moved along to follow action, and it can *pull back* from or *come in* on the action. A *crab dolly* is a small platform on wheels designed to move in any direction.

More extensive movement over a larger area than can be accomplished by dollying is achieved by mounting the camera on a platform on a car or truck or other moving vehicle for what are called *trucking* or *tracking* shots. A well-known example of extensive tracking, praised by some critics and censured by others, is to be seen in Olivier's direction of the Battle of Agincourt in *Henry V*.

Still another form of using a mobile camera is by means of the *crane* or *boom*. A small camera platform is set at the end of a long crane, and the crane may be moved up and down or laterally across a set.

Another basic photographic effect, increasingly popular in recent times, is most often described as the use of a *hand-held* camera. The term is most accurately used to differentiate the filmic qualities obtained by a small camera held in the hands while shooting from those created by a standard studio camera which is balanced, level, and set on its tripod, a dolly, or platform. Ironically, the results of the hand-held camera, rather like that of home movies, can be duplicated by more conventional (and more expensive) camera setups. Combined by laboratory work with grainy prints of high or low key, the camera work appears to be less smooth and even in the recording of subjects and action. What is deliberately achieved is a certain urgent and amateurish quality, associated in the minds of the contemporary audience with the verisimilitude of newsreels and documentaries and, as well, with the art films of certain prominent European directors in the immediate postwar years, the *réalismo* of Roberto Rossellini and Vittorio De Sica, for example. The effects of the hand-held camera seem more "realistic" however they are manufactured, and call attention to the cameraman's struggle and the immediacy of his work. Because of the artifice of film techniques, however, these effects may in fact be as "artificial" as those usually associated with only the highest standards of cinematography.

Editorial terms

The process of editing, which has already been mentioned, is highly technical and requires specialized study and experience. Some basic editorial techniques should, however, be understood by any student of film. One of these is the method of *transition* from one unit of film or larger sequence to another. Although the screenwriter must concern himself to some extent with the transitions, his part is marginal and limited to suggestions. For the editing of a film is exclusively the director's concern and that of his editor, or *cutter* as he is usually called by filmmakers.

There are essentially three kinds of transitions, with variations and, in some cases, different ways of accomplishing the same effect. The three forms of transition are the *cut*, the *dissolve*, and the *fade*.

The cut is, quite simply, a break or cut in the film. A sequence of images photographed from the same setup and angle is literally cut off, then spliced to another sequence. Cutting is, inevitably, continuous in a film, so frequent a pattern that we seldom notice it—unless it is the intention of the editor and the director that we should. The use of the word cut is somewhat confused by a number of other definitions of the term. For example, a cut may be used to describe a single strip of film. Many filmmakers call shots cuts, as in "Let's have a cut of the charging Indians here." And cut may mean *take out* or *add to*.

Professionals have no difficulty with this burden of possible meaning because context makes the particular case clear. But in terms of transitions, some examples may be in order. One of the most frequent cuts occurs when a character in an exterior setting starts to open a door to go into an unseen interior. We see him turn the handle of the door and start inside. The next shot will likely be a *reverse*, taken from within the interior set. The door is opening and he is coming in. Another common example of the conventional direct cut is frequently found when two characters are in conversation. At the outset we may see them both together in a two-shot. Then we cut back and forth from their separate faces as they speak to each other and react.

For the most part we do not consciously notice simple cuts. We imaginatively supply the missing connections and, so long as we are engaged in the viewing of the film, the action may seem smooth and continuous. Part of our reaction comes from experience and the habit of response; for the fundamentals of cutting have remained much the same since the days of D. W. Griffith. In *Birth of a Nation* he effectively used five-second shots, cut and joined together, in many places to establish a pattern for future editing.

Equally conventional is the use of the cut for a special effect in unexpected circumstances. An excellent example of the cut, used for humor, occurs in the fine Italian comedy *Big Deal on Madonna Street* (1959). Vittorio Gassman, arrested and awaiting trial, confidently reassures his weeping girl friend that he has an excellent lawyer and that the prosecution has no case against him. Nothing to worry about. From his smiling self-assurance there is a *direct cut* to a line of convicts, Gassman among them, marching doubletime around the yard of a penitentiary.

A *dissolve* or *lap dissolve* is a different sort of transition, sometimes called a *special effect* because it involves laboratory work. It is a process of superimposition by which one image gradually vanishes to be simultaneously replaced by another image without any perceptible fading of the light. The result is often a graceful sort of transition, traditionally used to indicate shifts of time and place without appearing to break the continuity of the film.

A variation on the dissolve is the *swish-pan*, a very swift dissolve which seems to be the result of camera movement, but is in fact a laboratory process.

A fade, used within the film as a transition, begins as a *fade out*. Both light and images fade into darkness and the screen goes (briefly) black. Following that a new image slowly *fades in*. Traditionally a fade acts as a definite break in the action of a film, somewhat analogous to the use of the curtain in the proscenium theater. It is also traditional to begin a script with the direction "Fade In" and to end it with "Fade Out."

There are a number of variations which can be used in lieu of a dissolve or fade. One is the *wipe*, in which the scene we are watching appears literally to be wiped away or erased from the screen, horizontally, vertically, or diagonally.

The *flip* is an effect in which a frame of film and its images appear to be flipped over like a card, either horizontally or vertically, to be replaced by another frame of images.

One of the oldest means of transition in the history of filmmaking, once widely used before the fade was possible, but still in use today, is the *iris*. As in fades, we *iris out* or *iris in*. The effect of irising out may occur in one of two ways. Either, within the frame, black seems to come from all sides diminishing the area of the image seen so that the image itself appears to recede or dwindle until it vanishes; or a single spot of black in the frame may appear to grow larger, going outward in all directions until the entire frame is dark. To iris in is to reverse the process.

The extent to which any of these editorial devices of transition—or, for that matter, the full variety of camera shots and angles—is employed depends, of course, on such things as current cinematic fashion and the nature and treatment of the subject of a script and a film. It also depends in large part upon the taste and aesthetic predilections of the director. On the one hand is Richard Lester, who opened up a full, rich bag of tricks, and most appropriately, to enliven *A Hard Day's Night*, whose shooting script gives very little indication of the style of the finished film. On the other hand is Billy Wilder; his scripts for *Some Like It Hot* (1959) and *The Apartment* (1960) are almost equally bare of explicit or suggested directions to cameraman or editor. Although Wilder is no stranger to the use of tricks, witness his *Sunset Boulevard* (1950), he has long been outspoken against depending too much on techniques to do the work of actors and directors. Kenneth MacGowan quotes him as saying: "If the scene is well directed from the point of view of its feelings, the camera can be set down, forgotten, and allowed to record." Wilder is, as ever, more careful than he seems at first glance. While he proposes limitations on the camera as writer-director, Wilder does not place limits upon the techniques of the editor.

Sound

Though sound as a part of motion pictures was technically possible much earlier, it did not become commercially feasible until the mid-1920s, and silent films continued to thrive until 1930. With the advent of sound as an integral part of the film art, this element became a part of the editor's general responsibility. In preparing the sound track, he has a number of technicians to help him. A *sound crew*, which works during the shooting of the picture, usually consists of a *mixer*, a *recordist*, and a *sound boom man*. Once the editing process begins a *sound effects editor* and a *music editor* are usually on hand in addition to a number of mixers who work on the final synchronization of all sounds and images in creating the composite print.

For a beginning, the editor has at his disposal the sound crew's original recordings taken during shooting. When synchronized with the rough cuts these recordings comprise the *wild track*. Where dialogue needs correction and better quality, which is often the case, the actors redo their lines in a controlled sound studio where *off-screen* or *voice over* dialogue is also added. This process of recording in synchronization with the film is called *dubbing* or *looping*. The opposite procedure, the deletion of sound effects or unwanted noises, is called *dialing out*.

The technical resources and possibilities of filmmaking, as even this brief glossary makes clear, are enormous. The greatest problem facing all of a film's creators is to choose among all of the possibilities the most efficient and most suitable means. The director, aided and advised by other artists, bears final responsibility for the choices made.

The writer's special responsibility is to create a script which, whatever its format, speaks to the needs of all the cast and crew, points directions by suggestion, and yet leaves each artist and technician free to create within the framework of his own competence. Within this context the technical terms of filmmaking should be understood. The value in application can be measured only by close viewing of films.

A Note on the Text of These Scripts

In preparing *Film Scripts* for publication, the editors have tried to present, as closely as is reasonable and possible, the version of each script acquired in the form in which it originally came to them. Because no two are precisely the same in all details, the special characteristics of each are mentioned in the appropriate headnote.

All of the American scripts included here are final shooting scripts. Some were more "finished" and "clean" than others; some contained pencilled revisions, made on the spot during the process of making.

In order to facilitate comparative study of word and image, the following conventions have been observed in reproducing facsimile versions of the scripts:

Deletions (of a passage, line, speech, direction, etc.) are indicated by asterisks plus any end punctuation.

New passages are underlined with dashes. Where there was a deletion involved this is likewise indicated by asterisks.

Deleted material is given in the form of annotation at the foot of the page. Large brackets have been placed around each continuous deletion. Small brackets are used to indicate changes in material that was later discarded.

The purpose here is not to provide a description or analysis of bibliographical changes; for the true bibliography of a film would chiefly be concerned with the text of the film—the master film and the prints made from it. But since revisions, even of the final shooting script, are parts of the process of making a film, these changes are indicated where evidence of them in the script was decipherable.

The most important revisions and changes, however, are manifest in the difference between the script and the finished film. The reader, who should also be a viewer, may wish to keep his own notes, perhaps in the margin of the text, on the basis of his own seeing of the film. This anthology can thus lead the reader/viewer to a better and more detailed understanding of the process of filmmaking. For, by having the script in handy and readable form, he not only has points of reference for testing his own memory of a screening but also, at least in a number of cases, a base line for questioning the possible function and purpose of some of the filmmaker's visions and revisions.

High Noon

Director Fred Zinnemann
Script Carl Foreman
1952—A Stanley Kramer Production;
released by United Artists
Source John M. Cunningham, "The Tin Star" in *Western
Writers of America: Bad Men and Good*, foreword
by Luke Short (New York: Dodd, Mead & Co., 1953)
Stars Gary Cooper, Grace Kelly, Thomas Mitchell, Lloyd Bridges

High Noon, which is as intense a study in unity of time as *Twelve Angry Men* is in unity of place, both announces the importance of time in its title and identifies the deadline. The dominant image is the clock, whose face registers 10:40 A.M. when the movie opens. As the action proceeds, the hands move inexorably toward noon. The time of the movie is thus identical to "real time" as measured by the watches of the audience. This effect, which could have been merely clever, remains subordinate because Fred Zinnemann keeps the story in the foreground. Although we are keenly aware of the irreversible passing of time, we never have the sense of watching a clever exercise in film technique. The subject is not the running out of time but of lives. The intense suspense generated by the movement of the clock occurs because we are interested in the characters and their problems. In contrast, a film like Ingmar Bergman's *Wild Strawberries* (1959), for example, reflects the human experience of time itself as an object of narrative interest; here time's passing, and the reliving of time past, is not charged with suspense. The major difference between the two films is one of mode and illustrates the enormous range of effects possible in movies. *High Noon* is a drama that approximates the kind of one-to-one correspondence between drama and life that was the impossible ideal of Corneille and Racine; *Wild Strawberries* is an introspective film in the tradition of Coleridge and Freud.

All Westerns depend to some degree on time. The genre is built around the convention of the showdown, which is both the payoff of the suspense and the moment of truth when the issues posed in the plot are resolved by a six-gun. The audience knows this and anticipates it from the first reel. The unique feature of *High Noon* is that it moves more urgently and relentlessly toward the final showdown and shootout than other Westerns. Beyond this crucial difference, the film shares the standard situations and character types of the genre—the quiet man whose courage is forced on him by events, the frightened woman, the demoralized, corrupt town symbolizing the weakness of collective Man in contrast to the strength of the Individual, the villains who have all the cards stacked in their favor, and the ending in which right triumphs over wrong. The film does not reject these conventions any more than Shakespeare rejected the conventions of the revenge play. Rather, it accepts them and attempts to infuse them with deeper meaning through exploration of social and psychological issues raised by the events it narrates. Thus, while the movie retains the decorum of a formal genre with mythic overtones, it shows that the genre can be opened to accommodate more introspection than is typically permitted. Normally, the Western concludes not only with the defeat of evil but with the resolution of social conflict as well. The hero, previously a loner, decides to marry and take over the job of marshal. Or, if he rides off to further adventures, he at least leaves on friendly terms with the town he has saved. This pattern is one of comedy and romance, from which *High Noon* departs radically. In so doing, it veers in the direction of bitter satire. Evil is defeated in one form, but the town is not liberated from its own corruption. The townspeople are shamed and humbled by their experience, not purged. The hero leaves in disgust after scornfully throwing the tin star that symbolizes justice in the dust of the street.

In general, *High Noon* was recognized by American reviewers as a classic Western. Philip Hartung, writing in *Commonweal* (July 25, 1952), compared it to what is by general agreement the best of the Westerns of the thirties: "*High Noon*," he wrote, "wins a place next to *Stagecoach* as a firstrate Western, and for its intelligent themes, social significance and high entertainment values, it is outstanding in any category." Another common subject for praise was Dimitri Tiomkin's "High Noon Ballad," which established the vogue for similar ballads in a score of Westerns of the fifties and sixties. The effect of the ballad is that of a leitmotif. Although the lyrics are not particularly distinguished, they announce the subject of the film, while the melody, recurring at critical moments from beginning to end, cooperates effectively with the clock motif to emphasize the film's unity.

Fred Zinnemann's career extends from work as a cameraman in Paris and Berlin and a bit part in *All Quiet on the Western Front* (1930) to direction of *A Man for All Seasons* (1966). For an interesting statement of his critical views, see "Zinnemann Talks Back," *Cinema* 2, iii (October-November, 1964), 20ff. See also Richard Griffith, *Fred Zinnemann* (New York, 1958). The best survey of the Western as a genre is George N. Fenin and William K. Everson, *The Western: From Silents to Cinerama* (New York, 1962).

The Script The script opens with "Some Notes About This Story" that are somewhat more detailed than the notes for *Twelve Angry Men*. The extent of the revisions preceding this version can be estimated by the scene numbers: "23A" for example represents a scene added, while "25–36" indicates condensation resulting from elimination of scenes.

Credits Producer, Stanley Kramer; Director, Fred Zinnemann; Author, John M. Cunningham; Screenplay, Carl Foreman; Art Direction, Rudolph Sternad; Music, Dimitri Tiomkin; Photography, Floyd Crosby; Editor, Elmo Williams.

Cast	Will Doane:	Gary Cooper
	Jonas Henderson:	Thomas Mitchell
	Harvey Pell:	Lloyd Bridges
	Helen Ramirez:	Katy Jurado
	Amy Doane:	Grace Kelly
	Percy Mettrick:	Otto Kruger
	Martin Howe:	Lon Chaney
	William Fuller:	Ian MacDonald
	Mildred Fuller:	Eve McVeagh
	Cooper:	Harry Shannon
	Jack Colby:	Lee Van Cleef
	James Pierce:	Bob Wilke
	Ben Miller:	Sheb Woolley
	Sam:	Tom London

Awards The 1952 Film Critics' Poll voted Fred Zinnemann "Outstanding Director" and Floyd Crosby "Outstanding Photographer" for their work on *High Noon*. The film was first on *Film Daily's* "Ten Best Pictures" list of 1952. Gary Cooper received an Academy Award as "Best Actor" for the role of Will Doane; and Dimitri Tiomkin and Elmo Williams received awards for their music and editing respectively.

SOME NOTES ABOUT THIS STORY

THE TIME is about 1870 or 1875.

THE PLACE is HADLEYVILLE, population around 400, located
in a Western territory still to be determined, a town just old
enough to have become pleasantly aware of its existence, and to
begin thinking of its appearance.
There is one street, a rambling, crooked affair that
begins at the railroad station, meanders along through the town,
ends a little way past the relatively new Commercial Hotel, and
then becomes a narrow and disappearing path into the prairie. Most
of the people in town, particularly those in better circumstances,
have built houses away from the street, and some of them even have
small lawns and flower patches, most of them rather pathetic.
Between the station and the hotel are to be found the
majority of the settings for the action of the story: the Marshal's
office and the courtroom, the Ramirez Bar, the barber shop, the
general store, the livery stable. Other establishments that should
be indicated but will not be used (as of this writing) will be in
tune with the place and period: a bank, restaurants, rooming houses,
a millinery shop, a hand laundry, etc. Almost all the buildings
along the street have some kind of structures behind them, such as
outhouses or sheds or, in some cases, living quarters.
Not so long ago, Hadleyville, like many other frontier
towns that were at the mercy of nearby feudal barons, had been
terrorized by Gil Jordan and his retainers. From his ranch, Gil
Jordan had ruled Hadleyville, and ruled it ruthlessly and cruelly.
There are still men -- and women, too -- who bear the physical marks
of Jordan's maniacal rages. Five years ago, however, Marshal Will
Doane, backed by a half a dozen hard-riding deputies, had broken
the Jordan gang and arrested Jordan for murder. At his trial, he
had been sentenced to hang, but Jordan's influential friends in the
territorial capital had had his sentence commuted to life imprison-
ment. Now, five years later, Hadleyville is a safe place for women
and children. Law and order have been so firmly established that
Doane now has only two deputies.

THE PEOPLE are MARSHAL WILL DOANE, HELEN RAMIREZ,
AMY DOANE, HARVEY PELL and others.

WILL DOANE is in his middle thirties. Adequately
educated, he is a second-generation westerner in a land that is
still spreading out. Like most of the other citizens of Hadleyville,
he is not a native of the town. He is direct, practical, not too

articulate. His approach to the job of peace officer is matter-of-fact, unromantic, but in the five years that he has been town marshal he has always liked it. He has enjoyed the prestige it has given him, and the knowledge that he is respected and liked by the townspeople. Now that he is being married, he is leaving the job and the town with some regret, but secure in the feeling that he is doing the sensible thing in moving to another town, where a general store should do good business.

He is, certainly, not an average man, but a very human one. Some two years ago he had a somewhat lengthy affair with: HELEN RAMIREZ. She is two or three years older than Doane, a victim of an era and environment with rigid social standards. To begin with, Helen is half Mexican, and thus neither acceptable to the "pure" American women of the region, nor eligible for a "good" marriage. Consequently, in addition to being intelligent, shrewd and strong-willed, she is also hard and resentful. Physically, she is handsome, full-breasted, passionate. More, she has style, personality.

Some years ago, Helen had married Ramirez, the local saloon-keeper. After his death she had become Gil Jordan's mistress. With Jordan in jail for life, Helen had herself selected Will Doane as his successor, and Helen still cannot forgive Doane for ending the liason, for this is a priviledge she reserves for herself. Recently, she has allowed herself to drift into an affair with Harvey Pell, Doane's friend and deputy. A good business women, she has long since disposed of her interest in the Ramirez saloon, and is a silent partner in the town's general store.

AMY DOANE is, without knowing it, one of the new women of the period, women who are beginning to rebel against the limitations and restrictions of the Victorian epoch. Young, attractive, intelligent, strong-willed, Amy is determined not to be a sheltered toy-wife but a full partner in her marriage, and it is she who has planned their future. More, Amy has strong emotional and intellectual convictions against any form of violence, because her father and brothers were killed while taking part in Vigilante action, and she has since embraced the Quaker faith. Marriage to Doane would have been unthinkable had he remained a peace officer.

HARVEY PELL is younger than Doane, his deputy and friend. But beneath that friendship is a nagging sense of inferiority and an envy of Doane. Thus, although he has secretly taken Doane's place as Helen's lover, he has a feeling that he has not really replaced Doane. In addition, Harvey is ambitious, anxious to prove his manhood and importance. He has hoped to be appointed Marshal in Doane's place, and he has expected that Doane would secure the position for him. Since the promotion has not taken place, he is resentful towards Doane for this as well. Yet, with all this, there is a remnant of the old liking. Doane, however, is unaware of the change in Harvey's feelings toward him.

OTHERS ARE: PERCY METTRICK, Justice of the Peace;
JONAS HENDERSON, WILLIAM FULLER and MARTIN HOWE, selectmen; MILT
JORDAN, PIERCE and COLBY, remnants of the Jordan gang; SAM, Helen's
elderly retainer; TOBY, Doane's other deputy; and a surprising
number of other bits.

METTRICK is urbane, cultured, cynical, unmarried,
middle-aged.

HENDERSON AND FULLER, and their WIVES, are in the same
age category, and very solid citizens.

MART HOWE is about sixty, a bachelor. He has been a
peace officer all his life, but age and the arthritis that has
crippled his hands have caused his retirement some years before.

MILT JORDAN, Gil's younger brother, JAMES PIERCE and
JACK COLBY are all that remain of the Jordan bunch. Milt is handsome,
wild, with cruel eyes and a quick, meaningless smile. Colby is
dour, remote, indrawn. Pierce, the oldest and the leader, is a
chronically sour-tempered man, nervous and irritable.

SAM is a thin, leathery, taciturn man about Martin Howe's
age. He looks as if he has known a considerable amount of violence
and hard-living (and probably lawlessness) in his time, from which --
like Mart Howe -- he has retired, but in his own way. Helen Ramirez
is the only person in town -- and perhaps the world -- for whom he has
any feeling. You sense that he is intensely loyal and devoted, that
he understands and admires her, and that he is content to be her
watch-dog.

DR. MAHIN, the minister, is a sincere, devout, unworldly
man, who has his share of human weakness.

TOBY, Doane's other Deputy, is about Harvey Pell's age.
Lacking Harvey's tense drive, he is good-natured, easy-going,
dependable in a fight.

Other characters will be described as we go along. However, while we are here, we may as well describe the settings for
some of the scenes to follow.

These are: (1) the Commercial Hotel, (2) Helen Ramirez'
rooms, (3) the courtroom, (4) the Marshal's office, (5) the Ramirez
Bar, (6) the Barbershop, (7) the livery stable, (8) the Church,
(9) the railroad station, (10) Martin Howe's home, (11) William
Fuller's home, (12) the general store, and (13) Mendosa's place.

The COMMERCIAL HOTEL would seem to be about six years
old. It is a two-story building. The desk is in the center hall,
on one side of which is the small lobby, and on the other, cut off
from view by curtains or swinging doors, the dining room. From the
hall, a stairway leads up to the second floor, where all rooms are
entered from the hall.

HELEN RAMIREZ occupies two connecting rooms on the
second floor of the hotel, toward the front. One is her bedroom
and the other has been furnished as a kind of sitting room or what

was called a front room then. The front room overlooks the street. Her taste is fairly expensive, feminine and good.

WILL DOANE'S OFFICE, which he shares with Judge Mettrick, is a one-story building on the main street. On one side of the office is the COURTROOM and on the other the jail. The court-room is still a somewhat makeshift affair, but the bench, witness stand, jury box, attorney tables and spectators' section can be recognized. We will probably not see the jail. The Doane-Mettrick office should be large enough to contain two desks, chairs, etc. The "Gun-Fighter" had a very good marshal's office.

The RAMIREZ BAR is a typical small saloon of the period -- a bar and some tables, but no dance floor, no stage, no glittering gambling layouts.

THE CHURCH has a capacity of about 200, a small wooden structure. It has a small organ, or whatever they were called then, and behind the pulpit there hangs a large painted replica of the Ten Commandments.

THE BARBER SHOP has one chair and a round card table. The window bears the following legend; BARBER SHOP AND DENTIST. HOT BATHS. Then lower down, and in smaller letters: DIGNIFIED UNDERTAKING. H. LeSIEUR, PROP. Behind the shop are living quarters and space designed for Mr. LeSieur's other activities, but we will see none of these except the shed where coffins are built and stored.

MART HOWE'S HOME is small, simple, almost barren reflecting his bachelorhood. WILLIAM FULLER'S HOME is larger, more affluently furnished in the taste of the period, and fussy, showing the hand and taste of his wife. Although we will use both exteriors, we will probably see only the living-room of each house.

THE LIVERY STABLE fronts on the main street, but the stable part, where the horses are stalled, is at the rear, and out of sight and hearing from the street.

THE RAILROAD STATION, for our purposes, is one small building. Part of this is waiting room, and part has been partitioned off to be the Station-Master's Office. The office windows look out to the track and to a large bench outside. It is presently planned to play the material with Milt Jordan, Pierce and Colby outside the station house.

THE GENERAL STORE is a typical store of the period. If possible, it should be indicated that the store is a prosperous one. It shouldn't be too large, though.

MENDOZA'S PLACE is a stopping-off place some five or ten miles from town, containing rude accomodations for horses and humans. For our purposes, we will probably see only the corral, the exterior of the building and the interior of the combined bar and eating space -- in other words, one large room containing a bar, tables, a large fire-place, etc. It is not a fancy place. For a good picturization of this kind of establishment, you should see "Stage-Coach."

"HIGH NOON"

FADE IN:

1-8.   EXT. OUTSKIRTS OF HADLEYVILLE -- DAY. It is not yet eleven
       A.M., and the sun is high and hot in a clear sky. Near a
       landmark of some kind -- a tree or an out-cropping of rock --
       a Man on horseback waits. In the distance, another Rider
       appears, riding toward the waiting Man. Now, the MAIN
       and CREDIT TITLES APPEAR. Behind them, the Rider reaches
       the Man who is waiting. They recognize each other, wave
       briefly, wait together. The distant bells of an o.s.
       Church begin to toll. From ANOTHER ANGLE, a Third Rider
       gallops toward them. He reaches them. The First Man
       takes out his watch as the FINAL CARD APPEARS AND FADES.
       We are in CLOSE to the three Men now, close enough to see
       that they are travel-weary and grim, men who seem to be
       driven by a mixture of hatred and hunger. In the order
       of their appearance, they are JAMES PIERCE, JACK COLBY
       and MILT JORDAN. Pierce snaps his watch-case shut, puts
       it away, nods briefly to the others. He spurs his horse,
       and they follow him. CAMERA PANS and HOLDS as they ride
       out of scene in the direction of a church spire that can
       be seen above screening trees.

9-11. EXT. CHURCH. Its bell tolls calmly and unhurriedly, and
       the people going into it move torpidly, hot and uncomfor-
       table in their Sunday best. Along the road that winds past
       the church, Jordan, Pierce and Colby appear and ride by.
       They are too far from the church to be recognized by any
       of the people going in, and when they pass the CAMERA as
       they ride away from it they seem oblivious to it. Although
       they are only cantering, they ride with purpose, and it is
       as if the church and the people do not even impinge them-
       selves on their consciousnesses. As they move out of
       scene, they pass a wagon which has come to a stop in the
       f.g. A Man and his Wife are in the wagon, and as the Man
       starts to climb down, he sees the Three Riders. He looks
       after them thoughtfully.

12.   EXT. MAIN STREET. It bakes in the sun, a rather crooked
       and winding street that seems deserted now in the Sunday
       calm. Jordan, Pierce and Colby canter into the scene and
       ride away from CAMERA.

13.   EXT. FIRE-HOUSE. A Volunteer Fireman, his Sunday coat off,
       is lovingly polishing the bright new engine. As he pauses

to pour himself a glass of beer from a nearby can, the
Three Riders pass. He looks after them with frowning
recognition.

14.   CLOSE SHOT --ANOTHER MAN -- staring o.s. at the passing
       riders. Troubled, he wipes his dripping forehead.

15.   HEAD-ON TRUCK SHOT -- on Jordan, Pierce and Colby. They
       keep their eyes focused ahead of them, almost contemp-
       tuously easy in their saddles but unwaveringly purposeful.

16.   EXT. STREET -- SHOOTING TOWARD THE HOTEL -- far up the
       street, as the three men approach it. The shutters of
       a second-story window open, and the figure of a Woman
       can be seen.

17.   MED. CLOSE SHOT -- HELEN RAMIREZ -- through the window into
       her sitting-room. She is in negligee, still languorous
       from sleep, her long black hair cascading down over her
       shoulders. She stretches luxuriously. There is the o.s.
       SOUND of the approaching horses. HARVEY PELL enters the
       scene from behind her, and draws her back into the room.

18.   INT. HELEN'S FRONT ROOM. Harvey draws Helen into his arms,
       and she accepts the familiar embrace. The purely physical
       attraction each has for the other is obvious. But the sound
       of the approaching horses comes nearer. Helen's gaze strays
       to the window. She recognizes the Three Riders below. She
       frowns, detaching herself from Harvey, moves back to the
       window. Harvey cranes his neck to follow her gaze.

                         HARVEY
                  Who's that?

                         HELEN
                    (abstracted)
                  You don't know them . . .

       She follows the o.s. Riders with her eyes.

19.   EXT. HAY AND GRAIN STORE. The Storekeeper, in his Sunday
       best, is locking the door as Jordan, Pierce and Colby ride
       by. He, too, recognizes them. He stares after them.

19A.   EXT. STREET. An Elderly Mexican Woman is carrying a
       market basket, the CAMERA MOVING WITH her. As the Three
       Men ride by, she recognizes them and stops. Unselfcon-
       sciously, she crosses herself.

20.   EXT. MARSHAL'S OFFICE -- as Jordan, Pierce and Colby ride
      by. Milt Jordan reins up, looking toward the Marshal's
      office, then deliberately rears his horse. The others
      have stopped.

                         PIERCE
                       (angrily)
                   You in a hurry?

                         MILT
                       (smiling)
                   I sure am . . .

                         PIERCE
                   You're a fool! Come on --

      He kicks his horse. Milt shrugs, grins.

21.   INT. COURTROOM -- SHOOTING TOWARD the street. A wedding
      is in progress. WILL DOANE and AMY, behind them the
      HENDERSONS, the FULLERS and MARTIN HOWE, face JUDGE
      METTRICK. Most of the men are perspiring. Mrs. Henderson,
      a woman conscious of her own importance in this community,
      and Mrs. Fuller, a motherly-looking woman, make futile
      motions with their handkerchiefs. In the street beyond
      and unseen by the group, the three riders pass from view.
      Judge Mettrick finds his place in his book, looks down at
      Amy and Will with benign good humor, and begins.

                         METTRICK
                   Will Doane and Amy Fowler, you have
                   come before me in my capacity as
                   Justice of the Peace of this town-
                   ship . . .

22.   LOW TRUCK SHOT -- of the Three Men as they ride toward
      CAMERA. They continue down the street, grim, implacable,
      deadly.

23.   EXT. RAMIREZ BAR. Four Men, loafing in front of the bar,
      are staring o.s. GILLIS, who owns the bar, turns excitedly
      to the others.

                         GILLIS
                   Did you see what I saw?
                       (to one of the Men)
                   Open 'er up, Joe! We're going
                   to have a big day today --

Grinning, he hands JOE the key.

23A.   EXT. STREET. On a bench in the f.g., a little barefoot
       Mexican boy lies asleep. PAST him, the Three Men ride
       in and out of the scene. Above the waist they are out
       of frames, but their holster-guns and the rifles secured
       to their saddles are in plain and emphatic view. The
       little boy sleeps on.

24.   INT. BARBERSHOP -- SHOOTING TO STREET. The Barber is
       shaving a man.

                         BARBER
              Hot? You call this hot? . . .

He sees the Three Men ride by, and stops amazed.

                         BARBER
              Well, I'll be -- !

                         MAN
              What's the matter?

                         BARBER
              Thought I saw Milt Jordan . . .

                         MAN
              He's down in Texas, somewheres.

                         BARBER
              I know . . .
                   (he resumes work)
              Looked like Pierce and Colby, too.
              Couldn't be, though . . .
                   (he shrugs)

25.   INT. HELEN'S FRONT ROOM. Harvey is in an easy chair,
       lighting a cigar. Near him, Helen is combing her hair
       before a mirror on the wall.

                         HARVEY
              I thought they were all split up . . .
              I heard Milt Jordan got killed down
              in Texas . . .

                         HELEN
                   (matter-of-factly)
              Too bad he wasn't.

He looks at her speculatively, then rises and goes to her.
He leans against the wall, and, with almost unconscious
fascination, reaches over and fingers the ends of her long
hair.

> HARVEY
> (carefully)
> Ever hear from his brother?
> From Guy?

He lets go as Helen stops, looks at him briefly, then
continues.

> HELEN
> (with finality)
>
> No.

Harvey senses that the discussion is closed. He puffs his
cigar, then smiles suddenly.

> HARVEY
> Hey, maybe it's a good thing
> Doane's leaving town today.

> HELEN
> (idly)
> Maybe . . .

Harvey looks at her shrewdly. He reaches for a tendril of
hair again. Unaware, Helen tosses her mane, and he withdraws his fingers.

26.   INT. STATIONMASTER'S OFFICE. The Station-Master, a small
citified-looking man, is taking down a telegram. The
ticker stops. He reads what he has written.

> STATIONMASTER
> (shocked)
> My goodness gracious -- !

Then, looking up, he sees -- through the window -- the Three
Men. Dismounted, they are hitching their horses to the rail.

> STATIONMASTER
> (really upset now)
> Oh, my goodness!

Now, to his increasing dismay, the three men turn and

approach him. Instinctively, he turns the message face down.

27. EXT. STATIONMASTER'S OFFICE. A weather-faded sign is nailed near the window. It reads:

> THROUGH TRAIN -- 2 WHISTLES.
> STOP TRAIN   -- 3 WHISTLES.
>
> -o-
>
> IF STATION-MASTER NOT IN OFFICE,
> BUY TICKET FROM CONDUCTOR.

Pierce, Jordan and Colby move stiffly to the window. They get there.

> PIERCE
> (wiping his forehead
> with his sleeve)
> Noon train on time?

> STATIONMASTER
> (nervously)
> Oh, yes, sir! . . . At least I think so, sir. Don't know any reason why it shouldn't be, Mr. Pierce . . . How are you, Mr. Pierce? . . . Mr. Jordan, Mr. Colby . . . ?

They stare him down, then turn and move toward a bench. They sprawl on it, remembering they are hot and tired, as they reach for tobacco. Pierce looks at his watch again.

28. INT. STATIONMASTER'S OFFICE. The Stationmaster watches them. When he is sure that he is unobserved, he slips furtively out by the rear door, carrying the telegram with him.

29- INT. COURTROOM -- as Mettrick concludes the ceremony.
30.

> METTRICK
> (to Doane)
> Do you, Will Doane, take Amy to be your lawful wedded wife, to have and to hold from this day forward, until death do you part?

                         DOANE
              I do . . .

                         METTRICK
              And do you, Amy, take Will to be
              your lawful husband, to have and
              to hold from this day forward,
              until death do you part?

                         AMY
              I do . . .

                         METTRICK
              The ring, please.

Doane gets it from Henderson, slips it on Amy's finger.

                         METTRICK
              Then, by the authority vested in
              me by the laws of this territory
              I pronounce you man and wife.

There is the usual brief, tentative pause, with Doane very
much aware of the others, and then he takes Amy in his
arms and kisses her, rather briefly. The tension breaks.
As the Men crowd around Doane and the Women surround Amy,
Mettrick smilingly moves to Amy.

                         METTRICK
              I can't speak for the rest of
              you men, but I claim an ancient
              privilege . . .

There is laughter as he kisses her.

31.   EXT. STREET -- as the Stationmaster, clutching the telegram,
      hurries up the street, his passage occasioning curious
      stares from loafers and passerby.

32.   MED. CLOSE SHOT -- The Two Old Men, sitting in the shade.
      They watch the Station-Master pass.

                         FIRST OLD MAN
              Moving mighty fast for a Sunday . . .

33-   INT. MARSHAL'S OFFICE. The door leading to the courtroom
36.   is open, and Doane is leading Amy through it. He shuts it
      firmly behind him.

                    AMY
            (embarrassed but amused)
     Will -- !

                    DOANE
            All those people . . .

He leads her away from the doorway toward his desk, where
his holster and guns hang from a hook.

                    DOANE
               (as they move)
            Seems to me people ought to be
            alone when they get married . . .

He is half-serious, and Amy understands his urge
to be away from the others.

                    AMY
            I know . . .

They are facing each other now, their eyes holding, very
conscious of each other.

                    DOANE
                (awkwardly)
            Amy, I'm going to try . . . I'll
            do my best . . .

He is brushing aside the formal vows of the ceremony with
his own promise, Amy understands.

                    AMY
                (softly)
            I will, too . . .

Their awareness of each other grows. This time, when they
kiss, there is a healthy passion in the embrace, and they
are both a little shaken when they part. The knock on the
door startles them. Henderson opens the door and leans
through.

                    HENDERSON
                (grinning)
            The honeymoon is officially over --
                (he turns and calls
                over his shoulder)
            Come on, everybody! . . .

> HENDERSON (Cont'd.)
> (as the others come
> through the doorway)
> And don't look so shocked, ladies.
> A man's entitled to some privacy
> on his wedding day --

> METTRICK
> That's debatable, Jo. However,
> one more ceremony, and Will's a
> free man. More or less . . .
> (he turns to Doane)
> Marshal, turn in your badge . . .

Laughing, smiling, the group has converged on Will and
Amy at the desk. Doane understands Mettrick's reference,
and his hand goes up to his badge, then falls away. Unconsciously, he stalls a little.

> DOANE
> I was hoping Harvey and Tobe'd
> be here . . .
> (he grins)
> A man ought to be able to make
> a final speech to his deputies.
> And here they don't even show
> up for his wedding . . .

> METTRICK
> They'll be along before you leave.

Amy is watching Doane with quiet understanding.

> DOANE
> I guess so . . .
> (he reaches for his badge
> again, then stops)
> Tell the truth, I kind of hate to
> do this without your new marshal
> being here . . .

> HENDERSON
> (with mock solemnity)
> Will, Sam Fuller and Mart Howe and
> I are the entire board of selectman
> of this community. We are, also,
> your very good friends. And you've
> done such a fine job here, that I

                    HENDERSON (Cont'd.)
          feel completely free to say -- and
          the Judge will bear me out --
                    (he grins jovially
                    for his punch line)
          that this town will be perfectly
          safe until tomorrow! . . .

Doane joins in the general laughter. His eyes meet Amy's
and when he speaks it is to her.

                    DOANE
                    (ruefully)
          You win.
                    (to the others)
          But don't ever marry a Quaker.
          She'll have you running a store . . .

                    FULLER
          Can't quite picture you doing that,
          Will . . .

                    AMY
                    (quietly)
          I can . . .

                    HOWE
                    (soberly)
          So can I. And a good thing, too.

                    AMY
                    (smiling at him)
          Thank you, sir.

Doane looks at Howe quizzically.

                    DOANE
          You didn't talk that way when
          you were wearing a star . . .

He shakes his head with mock sadness, and then a wicked
glint comes into his eyes.

                    DOANE
          Alright, it's coming off, but
          I got to be paid first.

Swiftly he sweeps Amy off her feet and holds her aloft.

                              AMY
                      Will, let me down!

                              DOANE
                      Not till you kiss me --

                              AMY
                           (laughing)
                      Let me down, you fool!

Then she gives in, and Doane lets her down. Grinning, he
takes off his badge and pins it to his holster on the
wall. The street door opens loudly, and as they turn to
it, the Stationmaster hurries in.

                           STATIONMASTER
                           (breathless)
                  Marshal -- ! Telegram for you --
                      (as he hands it to Doane)
                  It's just terrible . . . ! It's shocking!

The others stare as Doane reads it.

                              DOANE
                           (unbelievingly)
                  They -- they pardoned Guy Jordan . . .

                              AMY
                  What is is, Will?

                           HENDERSON
                  I don't believe it!
                      (he takes the wire
                       from Doane)
                  A week ago, too . . . Nice of them
                  to let you know . . .

                           STATIONMASTER
                  That ain't all. Milt Jordan's
                  down at the depot with Jim Pierce
                  and Jack Colby. . . . They asked about
                  the noon train . . .

                              DOANE
                           (still dazed)
                  Noon train . . . ?

He turns to look at the wall clock, and the others follow

his gaze. It is twenty to eleven.

> HENDERSON
> You get out of here, Will! You
> get out of town this minute!

The others join him as he hustles Doane and Amy to the door.

> AMY
> What is it? What's the matter -- ?

> HENDERSON
> Never mind -- there's no time --

The office empties. There is a silence. Suddenly it is broken by the <u>Sound</u> of a lusty snore. CAMERA PANS TO the cell at the rear of the office. A DRUNK is sleeping it off on the cell cot. He sleeps on.

37.   EXT. MARSHAL'S OFFICE -- as the group emerges, and Doane helps Amy up into the buckboard at the hitching rail. He turns to the others.

> HENDERSON
> Go on --

> FULLER
> Yes, go on, Will!

Mart Howe has already unhitched the two horses and turned them to the street. Doane hesitates, then turns and climbs up into the buckboard.

> HENDERSON
> Good luck, boy, and hurry!

He slaps one of the horses on the rump. They start and move into a gallop. Henderson and the others wave anxiously, as the wagon moves o.s.

38.   EXT. STREET. Pedestrians react as the buckboard rattles by, Doane whipping the horses with the reins.

39.   INT. HELEN'S FRONT ROOM. Harvey Pell is at the window, staring into the street. There is the o.s. rush and clatter of Doane's wagon rolling past.

                    HARVEY
                   (aloud)
             That's funny . . .

                    HELEN'S VOICE
         What?

She comes into the scene and to the window.

                    HARVEY
             You can't see now, Doane and
             his new wife took off in a big
             hurry.

                    HELEN
                  (not amused)
             What's so funny?

                    HARVEY
             I mean a <u>big</u> hurry. . . . Hey, you
             don't suppose Doane's scared
             of those three gunnies?

Helen looks at him skeptically.

                    HARVEY
                  (irritated)
             Well, you didn't see him. I
             never saw him whip a horse
             that way.

Helen stares at him. Obviously, he is telling the truth.
She frowns, then goes to the door, opens it.

40.   INT. HALL -- as Helen comes out, goes to the room next
      door, knocks.

                    HELEN
             Sam -- ?

                    SAM'S VOICE
             Come on in, Helen --

She opens the door and goes in.

41.   INT. HALL. In his shirtsleeves, SAM is seated at a table,
      cleaning a rifle. He looks up at Helen's entrance.

                         HELEN
                       (quietly)
                 Milt Jordan's in town. He's
                 got two of the old bunch with
                 him.

Sam looks at her unwinkingly, then gets up slowly.

                         SAM
                       (simply)
                 I guess I'll take a look around.

He starts to put on his coat.

42.   EXT. STREET -- on the Stationmaster hurrying back to the
      station. As he reaches the Barber Shop, the Barber comes
      out, razor in hand.

                         BARBER
                 What's going on, Oliver?

                         STATIONMASTER
                       (not without pleasure
                        in his role)
                 Guy Jordan's been let go . . .

                         BARBER
                       (amazed)
                 No! . . . Then that <u>was</u> Milt I seen
                 just now --

                         STATIONMASTER
                 It sure was -- and Pierce and
                 Colby, too . . .

                         BARBER
                 You don't say! . . . Where's Doane?

                         STATIONMASTER
                 He's left . . .

                         BARBER
                 That's a smart man . . .

They part, the Stationmaster going on down the street, the
Barber returning into his shop.

                        BARBER
                 (as he goes in)
        Now, Mr. Thompson, didn't I tell you -- ?

CAMERA HOLDS on window of the shop.

43-   EXT. PRAIRIE -- MED. LONG SHOT -- on the buckboard as it
48.   careens over the uneven plain, Doane keeping the horses
       at a wild gallop. But, then, gradually, as the wagon
       approaches the CAMERA, Doane begins to rein up.

49.   EXT. PRAIRIE -- BUCKBOARD -- as Doane brings it to a halt.
       He is frowning with thought, struggling with himself.
       Amy stares at him.

                          AMY
                 Why are you stopping?

                         DOANE
                      (finally)
                 It's no good. I've got to go
                 back, Amy . . .

                          AMY
                 Why?

                         DOANE
                 This is crazy. I haven't even
                 got any guns.

                          AMY
                 Then let's go on -- hurry!

                         DOANE
                 No. That's what I've been thinking.
                 They're making me run. I
                 never run from anybody before.

                          AMY
                      (frantic)
                 Who? . . . I don't understand any
                 of this.

                         DOANE
                    (taking out his watch)
                 I haven't got time to tell you.

                    AMY
          Then don't go back, Will . . .

                    DOANE
          I've got to. That's the whole
          thing . . .

He whips the horses and turns them back toward the town.

50.   EXT. RAILROAD STATION. Milt Jordan, Pierce and Colby are
      on the bench. Milt is drinking from an almost depleted
      whiskey bottle. He hands it to Colby, who takes a swallow,
      and returns it. Milt offers it to Pierce, who shakes his
      head angrily.

                    PIERCE
          I thought you'd grew up by now.

                    MILT
          I thought your disposition might've
          sweetened a little down in Abiline. . . .
          Guess we were both wrong.

He takes another drink.

50A. INT. SALOON. Six more Men have joined the others. Gillis,
      flushed with drink and anticipation, is in the centre of a
      group at the bar. He pounds on it with his open hand for
      emphasis and attention.

                    GILLIS:
          Hit the bar, all of you! I'm
          settin' 'em up!

They move to the bar in acceptance of his largesse.

51.   INT. HELEN'S FRONT ROOM. Helen and Harvey are facing Sam.

                    HELEN
          How could they pardon Guy? He
          was in for life --

                    SAM
               (shrugging)
          He's out . . .

                    HARVEY
               (a glint of triumph

> HARVEY (Cont'd.)
> in his eyes)
> So that's why Doane run away . . .

Helen looks at him, starts to say something, then stops.
There is the o.s. CLATTER of hoofbeats in the streets.
They turn to the window.

51A.   EXT. STREET -- from Helen's point of view. Doane's buckboard
can be seen clattering PAST TOWARD his office.

51B.   BACK TO SCENE 51. Helen turns to the others and looks
quizzically at Harvey. He scowls under the amusement
in her eyes.

52.   EXT. MARSHAL'S OFFICE -- as the buckboard pulls up before it.

53.   INT. BARBERSHOP. The Barber is finishing with his
Customer. An Elderly Man (FRED) hurries in.

> FRED
> (excited)
> Doane's back . . . !

The Customer sits up.

> BARBER
> Don't believe it!

> FRED
> Just seen him . . .

The Barber looks at the clock. It is ten minutes to
eleven.

> BARBER
> How many coffins we got?

> FRED
> Two . . .

> BARBER
> We're gonna need at least two
> more, no matter how you figure
> it. You better get busy, Fred.

Fred nods and hurries out through a rear door. The Barber
remembers his customer, and removes the cloth with a flourish.

                    BARBER
        All finished, Mr. Thompson.
        You look just fine! . . .

54-55. OUT.

56-   INT. MARSHAL'S OFFICE. Amy and Doane come in, and Doane
60.   goes quickly to where his guns hang on the wall. Amy
        watches him as he buckles them on. His mind is already
        in the future, and she knows it. Nevertheless, she
        perseveres.

                    AMY
            Please, Will -- !

        Doane looks at her, then goes on.

                    AMY
                (desperately)
            If you'd only tell me what this
            is all about . . .

                    DOANE
                (checking his guns)
            I sent a man up five years ago for
            murder. He was supposed to hang,
            but up north they commuted it to
            life. Now he's free -- I don't
            know how. Anyway, it looks like
            he's coming back.

                    AMY
            I still don't understand --

                    DOANE
                (choosing his words
                 carefully)
            He's a . . . he was always wild --
            kind of crazy. . . . He'll probably
            make trouble . . .

                    AMY
            That's no concern of yours -- not
            anymore!

                    DOANE
            I'm the one who sent him up.

                              AMY
                That was part of your job. That's
                finished now. They've got a new
                marshal -- !

                              DOANE
                Won't be here till tomorrow. Seems
                to me I've got to stay a while.
                    (he reaches for his star)
                Anyway, I'm the same man -- with or
                without this . . .

He pins it on.

                              AMY
                That isn't so.

                              DOANE
                    (patiently)
                I expect he'll come looking for
                me. Three of his old bunch are
                waiting at the depot . . .

                              AMY
                That's why we ought to go . . .

                              DOANE
                    (still patient)
                They'll just come after us. . . .
                Four of them, and we'd be all
                alone on the prairie . . .

                              AMY
                We've got an hour!

They both look at the clock. It shows nine minutes to
eleven.

                              DOANE
                What's an hour? . . .

                              AMY
                We could reach --

                              DOANE
                    (cutting in)
                What's a hundred miles, even?
                We'd never be able to keep that

                    DOANE (Cont'd.)
          store, Amy. They'd come after
          us. We'd have to run again.
          Long as we live . . .

                    AMY
          No, we wouldn't -- not if they
          didn't know where to find us!

Doane's face tightens. He starts toward the door. Amy
stops him.

                    AMY
          Will, I'm begging you -- please! . . .
          Let's go . . . !

                    DOANE
          I can't . . .

                    AMY
               (angry)
          Don't try to be a hero! You don't
          have to be a hero -- not for me!

                    DOANE
               (losing his temper)
          I'm not trying to be a hero! If
          you think I like this, you're crazy!
               (he masters himself)
          Amy, look. This is my town. I've
          got friends here. Toby and Harvey'll
          be here. I'll swear in a bunch of
          special deputies. With a posse
          behind me, maybe there won't even be
          any trouble . . .

                    AMY
               (defeated)
          You know there'll be trouble.

                    DOANE
          Then it's better to have it here. . . .
          I'm sorry, honey. I know how you
          feel about it --

                    AMY
               (harshly)
          Do you?

                    DOANE
                  (awkwardly)
          Of course I do. I know it's against
          your religion and all -- Sure I know
          how you feel about it.

                    AMY
                  (bitterly)
          But you're doing it just the same.

                    DOANE
                  (helplessly)
          Amy . . .

Amy comes to him, her heart in her eyes, deliberately
throwing all she has of magnetism and sex at him.

                    AMY
          Will, we were married just a few
          minutes ago -- doesn't that mean
          anything to you? We've got our
          whole lives ahead of us. . . .
          * * * Doesn't that mean anything
          to you.

With an effort, Doane gently pushes her aside. Amy is
shattered.

                    DOANE
          Amy, you know I've only got an
          hour . . . I've got things to do . . .
          You stay at the hotel till it's
          over.

With his hand at her elbow, he starts toward the door.
Amy holds her ground.

                    AMY
          No! You're asking me to wait an
          hour to find out if I'm going to
          be a wife or a widow, and I say
          it's too long to wait! I won't
          do it!

---

60.   [You want me, Will, or you wouldn't have
                    married me. . . . If you love me, Will—]

                    DOANE
                  (stunned)
          Amy . . .

                    AMY
          I know -- you think I'm just
          saying it -- because I'm angry.
          But I mean it! If you won't go with
          me now -- I'll be on that train
          when it leaves here . . .

Their eyes meet and hold.

                    DOANE
                  (finally)
          I've got to stay, Amy . . .

Amy tries to mask her hurt. Chin high, she moves past
him to the door, and out. Doane stares after her a
moment, then follows her out.

61-   EXT. MARSHAL'S OFFICE. Judge Mettrick is tying his horse
63.   to the hitching rail as Amy emerges. Too blinded by tears
        of hurt and anger to see him, she climbs into the buckboard.
        Mettrick looks on impassively, first at Amy and then at
        Doane when the Marshal comes out. The two men watch as
        Amy turns the horses toward the station and whips them
        out of scene. Then, as Mettrick takes down his saddle-
        bags, Doane comes toward him, his face lightening with
        relief.

                    DOANE
          I'm glad you got here, Perce . . .

                    METTRICK
                  (evenly)
          Are you?

Carrying the bags, he walks deliberately past Doane and
into the office. Surprised, Doane follows him.

64.   INT. MARSHAL'S OFFICE. Mettrick strides quickly across
        the room into the courtroom. Doane continues after him,
        puzzled.

65-   INT. COURTROOM. Mettrick goes to the desk that serves
68.   as the bench, and quickly begins to stuff the saddle-

bags with papers, his gavel, and other belongings.
During the course of the scene, he will also pack his
legal books, and when the bags are full he will stack
and tie the remainder of his books with rawhide thongs.
Watching from the doorway, Doane stares at him with
sick understanding. Mettrick is very much aware of
Doane's eyes on him. Finally, he pauses in his work.

                    METTRICK
                  (sharply)
          Are you forgetting I'm the man who
          passed sentence on Guy Jordan?

Doane shakes his head numbly. Mettrick resumes his
hurried packing.

                    METTRICK
          You shouldn't have come back.   It
          was stupid . . .

                    DOANE
          I figured I had to.   I figured it
          was better to stay.

                    METTRICK
          You figured wrong.

                    DOANE
          I can deputize a posse.   Ten,
          twelve guns is all I'd need.

                    METTRICK
          My intuition tells me otherwise.

                    DOANE
      Why?

Mettrick looks up at the wall clock.   It is seven
minutes to eleven.

                    METTRICK
                  (bitterly)
          There's no time for a lesson
          in civics, my boy.

On the wall behind the bench are an American flag of
the period and a picture of Justice, with scales and
blindfold. The Judge goes to them and starts to

take down and fold up the flag. Almost helplessly,
he begins to talk.

                    METTRICK
               (taking down the flag)
          In the fifth century B.C., the
          citizens of Athens -- having
          suffered grievously under a
          tyrant -- managed to depose and
          banish him. However, when he
          returned after some years with
          an army of mercenaries, these
          same citizens not only opened
          the gates to him, but stood by
          while he executed the members
          of the legal government. . . . A
          similar thing took place about
          eight years ago in a town called
          Indian Falls. I escaped death
          only through the intercession of
          a lady of somewhat dubious reputa-
          tion, and at the cost of a handsome
          ring that once belonged to my
          mother . . .
               (he shrugs)
          Unfortunately, I have no more rings . . .

He has neatly folded up the flag by now and has placed
it in one of the saddlebags. He turns to the picture
of Justice and takes it down.

                    DOANE
          But you're a judge --

                    METTRICK
          I've been a judge many times in
          many towns. I hope to
          be a judge again.

                    DOANE
               (giving up)
          I can't tell you what to do . . .

                    METTRICK
               (harshly)
          Will, why must you be such a fool!
          Have you forgotten what he is? Have
          you forgotten what he's done to people?

METTRICK (Cont'd.)
Have you forgotten that he's <u>crazy</u>?

He points to the vacant chair near the defense table.

METTRICK
Don't you remember when he sat in
that chair there and said --

69.   CLOSE SHOT -- VACANT CHAIR

METTRICK'S VOICE
(over)
You'll never hang me! I'll be
back! I'll kill you, Doane!
I swear it, I'll kill you!

70.   BACK TO SCENE. Doane and Mettrick stare at each other.

DOANE
(after a pause)
Yeah. . . . I remember . . .

71.   CLOSE UP -- WHISKEY BOTTLE as it shatters loudly on the
railroad track, and the shards and splinters tumble and
glitter in the sunlight. Then the CAMERA TILTS UP to
REVEAL Jordan, Pierce and Colby in the b.g. Colby is
staring at the broken glass with childlike interest.
Pierce is scowling angrily at Milt, who is looking
innocently off.

72-   INT. STATIONMASTER'S OFFICE -- AMY AND THE STATIONMASTER.
74.   Separated by the counter, they are both staring through
the window at the three men on the platform outside,
Amy with fascinated loathing, the Stationmaster worried.
Then they exchange a quiet look, and the Stationmaster
goes back to what he has been doing. He stamps Amy's
ticket and hands it to her.

STATIONMASTER
(soberly)
Here you are, ma'am. This'll
take you to St. Louis . . .

AMY
Thank you.

She starts to turn away to sit down, then realizes that
she will have to share the station with Jordan, Pierce
and Colby for the next hour. The Stationmaster senses
her predicament.

> STATIONMASTER
> (kindly)
> Maybe you'd rather wait somewheres
> else, ma'am? Like at the hotel,
> maybe. We'll get three whistles if
> the train's going to stop, and you'll
> have plenty of time to get down here.

> AMY
> (puzzled)
> If the train stops?

> STATIONMASTER
> (he is embarrassed)
> Yes, ma'am. It don't always,
> little town like this. I'd
> hate to tell you how many times
> she's just run right through my
> flag, 'specially if she's late.
> But she will stop to let off
> passengers . . .

> AMY
> I see. . . . Thank you . . .

She turns and starts out.

> STATIONMASTER
> (sincerely)
> I'm awful sorry about this, Mrs.
> Doane. . . . But the Marshal can handle
> himself alright.

> AMY
> (wryly)
> Thank you very much . . .

She goes out of scene.

75.   EXT. PLATFORM -- GROUP SHOT -- JORDAN, PIERCE AND COLBY.
      Milt is looking off, and when Amy appears in the b.g.
      and goes to the buckboard, he follows her with his eyes.

> MILT
> (lightly)
> That wasn't here five years
> ago . . .

> PIERCE
> So what?

> MILT
> (smiling)
> Nothing. . . . Yet. . . . Maybe . . .

His smile broadens as Pierce's irritation mounts, and
he continues to watch Amy until she is out of sight.

76.   INT. HELEN RAMIREZ' SITTING ROOM. The table has been
set, and Helen and Harvey are eating breakfast. Helen
looks at the clock. It is five minutes to eleven.

> HELEN
> (quietly)
> Don't you think Doane will be
> looking for you about now?

> HARVEY
> (carelessly)
> Yeah . . .

He continues eating. Helen watches him.

> HELEN
> (mildly)
> You're really sore at him . . .

> HARVEY
> (pausing)
> Wouldn't you be, if you were me?

> HELEN
> (gently)
> I suppose I would -- if I were you . . .

Harvey looks at her, not quite certain of her meaning.
Then he goes back to his food. Helen resumes eating.
They eat in silence for a while. Then an idea begins
to grow in him, and he smiles suddenly. He wipes his
mouth and pushes away from the table.

> HARVEY
> I'll be back in a while --

Grinning now, he gets his hat and goes. Helen looks
after him speculatively.

77.   INT. HALL. Harvey comes out of the room. Down the
      hall Sam's door is open, and Sam can be seen sitting
      quiet guard in the doorway. He looks at Harvey with-
      out expression and without warmth or liking. But
      Harvey is too pleased with himself to care. Whistling
      softly, he goes to the stairs.

78.   INT. STAIRWAY -- as Harvey comes down the stairs.

79.   INT. LOBBY. The Hotel Clerk watches Harvey come down,
      cross the lobby and go out.

80-   EXT. HOTEL. Harvey comes out and walks down the street.
81.   Two SMALL BOYS in their Sunday best run into the scene,
      to Harvey.

> FIRST BOY
> Hey Harvey -- !

Harvey turns to see them, grins.

> SECOND BOY
> You gonna shoot it out with Guy
> Jordan, Harvey? Are you?

> FIRST BOY
> You gonna kill him, Harvey?

> HARVEY
> (ruffling his hair)
> I sure am.

Amy's buckboard clatters into the scene and past. Harvey,
puzzled, watches her stop before the hotel and climb down.

> SECOND BOY
> (tugging at Harvey's shirt)
> Hey, Harvey --

> HARVEY
> Go on, go on, you ought to be
> in church -- the both of you.

He throws a final look at the hotel, which Amy has entered, and walks off.

82-
83.   INT. HOTEL LOBBY -- at desk.   The Clerk is staring at Amy.

                    AMY
          May I wait here for the noon
          train?
                    (as the Clerk continues
                    to stare at her)
          I said may I wait in the lobby
          until noon?

                    CLERK
                    (unabashed)
          Sure, lady.

                    AMY
                    (turning away)
          Thank you.

                    CLERK
          You're Mrs. Doane, ain't you?

                    AMY
          Yes.

                    CLERK
          And you're leaving on the noon
          train?

                    AMY
                    (sharply)
          Yes.

                    CLERK
                    (skeptically)
          But your husband ain't?

                    AMY
                    (studying him)
          No. Why?

                    CLERK
                    (coolly)
          No reason. But it's mighty
          interesting. . . . Now me, I wouldn't
          leave this town at noon for all

                    CLERK (Cont'd.)
            the tea in China.
            (he smiles vindictively)
            No sir. It's going to be quite
            a sight to see . . .

    Amy stares at him, puzzled by his hostility, then goes
    to a chair near the window.

84-   EXT. MARSHAL'S OFFICE -- at hitching rail. Doane watches
86.   the Judge make his saddlebags and books secure. Mettrick
        gives the straps a final tug, hesitates, then turns to
        face Doane.

                    METTRICK
            Goodby, Will . . .

                    DOANE
                (flatly)
            Goodby . . .

    Mettrick is horribly ashamed. Doane tries to hide his
    own sick, still somewhat dazed, shock and disappointment.

                    METTRICK
            You think I'm letting you down,
            don't you?

                    DOANE
            No.

                    METTRICK
            Look, this is just a dirty little
            village in the middle of nowhere.
            Nothing that happens here is
            really important. . . . Get out!

                    DOANE
            There isn't time . . .

                    METTRICK
                (staring at him)
            What a waste . . .
                (gently)
            Good luck.

    He turns, mounts, rides off. Doane looks after him a
    moment, then turns to go into his office. He sees a

Boy of about fifteen who has been lounging curiously
nearby, trying to overhear.

> DOANE
> (calling him)

>Johnny --

Johnny comes over to him. His wide eyes make it obvious
that he knows what is going on.

> DOANE

>Why aren't you in church?

> JOHNNY

>Why ain't you?

Doane raises his arm in a mock threat, then drops it.

> DOANE

>Do something for me. Find Joe
>Henderson, Mart Howe and Sam
>Fuller, and tell 'em I want 'em
>here. And then go find Harve
>Pell --

> HARVEY'S VOICE

>Don't have to do that -- here I
>am . . .

Doane's face lights up as he turns and sees Harvey
approaching them. Johnny takes off. Doane senses
that Harvey needs no explanation.

> DOANE
> (with gruff warmth)

>Where you been?

> HARVEY
> (lightly)

>Busy . . .

Doane is able to smile. He knows what being 'busy'
usually means for Harvey, and even at this moment
his paternal feeling for the younger man can break
through the situation. then he sobers.

> DOANE

>You know what's doing?

                    HARVEY
        Sure.

                    DOANE
        Come on. Lots to do . . .

He starts to go into the office, but Harvey stops him
gently and leans against the door jamb.

                    HARVEY
            Hold up a second.
            (as Doane stares
             at him)
            This ain't really your job, you
            know.

                    DOANE
            (almost absently)
            That's what everybody keeps telling
            me . . .

He starts in again, but Harvey bars his way with his arm.

                    HARVEY
            Yeah, but when I tell you it
            means something. So you can
            listen a second.

                    DOANE
            (humoring him)
            Alright, I'm listening.

                    HARVEY
            Now, the way I see it, if you'd
            gone, and with the new marshal
            not due till tomorrow, I'd be
            in charge around here. Right?

                    DOANE
            (patiently)
        Right.

                    HARVEY
            Well, tell me this then. If I'm
            good enough to hold down the job
            when there's trouble, how come
            the city fathers didn't trust me
            with it permanent?

Doane stares at him, beginning to be disturbed.

>   DOANE
> I don't know.

>   HARVEY
>   (thinly)
> Don't you?

>   DOANE
>   (flatly)
> No.

>   HARVEY
> That's funny. I figured you
> carried a lot of weight.

>   DOANE
> Maybe they didn't ask me. . . . Maybe
> they thought you were too young.

>   HARVEY
> You think I'm too young, too?

Doane's irritation and his liking for Harvey struggle
with each other. His liking wins.

>   DOANE
> You sure act like it sometimes!
> Come on!

Grabbing Harvey, he shoves him inside ahead of him.

87-   INT. MARSHAL'S OFFICE.   Doane propels Harvey into the room.
89.

>   HARVEY
>   (triumphantly)
> Now here's what I want you to do,
> Will. When the old boys come, you
> tell 'em you want me to be Marshal,
> and tomorrow they can tell the new
> man they're sorry but the job's
> filled.

>   DOANE
>   (stopping) .
> You really mean it, don't you?

                    HARVEY
Sure.

                    DOANE
Well, I can't do it.

                    HARVEY
Why not?

                    DOANE
If you don't know, there's no
use me telling you.

                    HARVEY
You mean you won't do it.

Doane looks at him helplessly, then turns away from him
and goes toward the desk. The clock on the wall reads
one minute to eleven.

                    DOANE
Have it your way . . .

                    HARVEY
                 (flaring)
Alright. The truth is you probably
talked against me from the start.
You been sore about me and Helen
Ramirez right along, ain't you?

                    DOANE
                 (surprised)
You and Helen Ramirez? I don't --
                 (he begins to
                  understand)
It so happens I didn't know, and
it don't mean anything to me one
way or another. You ought to
know that.

                    HARVEY
Yeah? You been washed up for
more than a year -- you go out
and get yourself married -- only
you can't stand anybody taking
your place there, can you?
Especially me!

                        DOANE
                    (overwhelmed)
            You're --

He cannot find words. He turns and looks at the clock.
It is two minutes after eleven.

                        DOANE
            I haven't got time, Harvey . . .

                        HARVEY
            Okay! Then let's get down to
            business. You want me to stick,
            you put the word in for me like
            I said.

                        DOANE
                    (quietly)
            Sure. I want you to stick, but
            I'm not buying it. It's got to
            be up to you . . .

They look at each other as if across a chasm. Harvey
sees that Doane means it. He cannot quite believe it,
but he is committed now. He goes to the desk, takes
off his gun belt and badge, puts them down, turns and
goes out. Doane stares after him, sick at heart.

                                    QUICK DISSOLVE TO:

90.   EXT. COUNTRYSIDE -- MED. LONG SHOT -- on Two Riders
        galloping single-file toward CAMERA.

91.   EXT. COUNTRYSIDE. The Two Riders near the CAMERA. The
        Man in front (ED PETERSON) reins up. The other rider,
        who wears a star, pulls up beside him. This is TOBY,
        Doane's second deputy. Toby looks at Peterson warily.

                        PETERSON
            How about resting a minute?

                        TOBY
            I'm in a hurry.

                        PETERSON
            I ain't.

                    TOBY
          I know. . . . Goldarn you, I ought
          to be kissing a bride about
          now instead of riding herd on
          a mean old polecat like you.

                    PETERSON
          Come on -- how about a smoke?

He raises his arms, and we see now that his wrists are
bound by a rawhide thong.

                    TOBY
          You gonna be a good boy?

                    PETERSON
          You know me, Toby.

                    TOBY
          Sure, I know you . . .

He takes out a knife and cuts the leather strap.   Peterson
reaches for his tobacco.

                    TOBY
          Make it a quick one. I want to
          get to that wedding before it's
          over.

                                        QUICK DISSOLVE TO:

92-   INT. HELEN'S FRONT ROOM -- CLOSE SHOT -- HARVEY. He is
96.   red-faced, baffled. There is the o.s. sound of Helen's
       laughter.

                    HARVEY
          What's so funny?

CAMERA PULLS BACK to INCLUDE Helen. She pulls herself
together somewhat.

                    HELEN
          You didn't really think you could
          put that over on Doane, did you?

                    HARVEY
          Why not?

                    HELEN
          When are you going to grow up?

                    HARVEY
                 (angrily)
          I'm getting tired of that kind
          of talk.

                    HELEN
                 (lightly)
          Then grow up.

Harvey is increasingly irritated and confused under the
goad of the almost maternal pity in her laughter and
manner.

                    HARVEY
               Cut it out!

                    HELEN
                 (gently)
               Alright . . .

She pats his cheek placatingly, but Harvey shoves her
hand away. Under her level look, he starts to pace
angrily.

                    HARVEY
          Why shouldn't he have gone for
          it? He needs me. He'll need
          me plenty when Jordan gets here.

                    HELEN
                 (watching him)
          That's possible.

                    HARVEY
          He should've had me made marshal
          to begin with. He's just sore, is
          all. He's sore about you and me.

                    HELEN
                 (frowning)
          Is he?

                    HARVEY
               Sure . . .

                    HELEN
                 (quietly)
          You told him?

                    HARVEY
                 (unaware of his danger)
          Sure.

                    HELEN
                 (with controlled rage)
          You're a fool.

                    HARVEY
                 (reacting to her tone)
          Why? Didn't you want him to know? . . .
                 (with a blind impulse
                  to hurt her)
          Say, who did the walking out anyway,
          you or him?

                    HELEN
                 (flatly)
          Get out, Harvey.

Harvey begins to realize that he has made a fatal blunder.

                    HARVEY
          I might just do that.

                    HELEN
                 (and she means it)
          Then do it.

                    HARVEY
          You don't mean that.

                    HELEN
          You think not?

                    HARVEY
                 (beginning to
                  bluster)
          You're going to talk different
          when Guy Jordan gets in. You
          might want somebody around you
          when you're explaining to him
          about Doane.

> HELEN
> I can take care of myself.

> HARVEY
> Sure. Only from what I've heard,
> you might not be so pretty when
> he gets through with you.

Helen looks at him with cold disgust, then goes to the
the door and opens it.

> HARVEY
> (his last attempt)
> I won't be back.

> HELEN
> (quietly)
> Good.

He slams the door as he goes. Alone, Helen paces the
floor. She looks at the clock. It is five after eleven.
She comes to a decision, goes to the door, opens it.

97.   INT. HALL. In his room, Sam looks up as Helen's door
opens.

> HELEN
> Sam --

He rises and goes to her.

> HELEN
> I think I have to talk to Mr.
> Weaver . . .

> SAM
> You're getting out?

> HELEN
> Yes.

He considers her answer, accepts it.

> SAM
> You want me to give Doane a
> hand?

Helen thinks it over, almost but not quite disguising her

inner struggle. Then she makes her decision.

                    HELEN
                  (flatly)
          No.

Sam nods, turns and goes.

98.   INT. HELEN'S FRONT ROOM. She shuts the door, stands there
       a moment, thinking, then walks unhurriedly toward her
       bedroom. CAMERA PANS WITH her. Reflected in her dresser
       mirror, we can see her beginning to change.

99-   INT. MARSHAL'S OFFICE. Doane is at his desk, lost in
101.   thought. There is the SOUND of his door opening, and
       he jerks into awareness and turns. A solidly-built,
       normally pleasant-looking, Man now scowling with
       indignation is coming in. His name is BAKER.

                    BAKER
          Will -- I just heard -- !

                    DOANE
                  (rising)
          Hello, Herb --

                    BAKER
          You can count on me. You know
          that, don't you?

                    DOANE
                  (his spirits rising)
          I figured I could.

                    BAKER
          Why, you cleaned this town up --
          you made it fit for women and
          children to live in, and neither
          Jordan or nobody else is going
          to drag it down again!

                    DOANE
          I was hoping people'd feel that
          way . . .

                    BAKER
          What other way is there?
                  (as Doane shrugs)

                              BAKER (Cont'd.)
                    How many men you got lined up?

                              DOANE
                    None, yet . . .

          Baker looks at the clock. It is seven after eleven.

                              BAKER
                    You better get going, man.
                         (he starts out)
                    I'll be back in ten minutes --
                         (he grins)
                    -- loaded for bear . . .

          Doane looks after him, touched and encouraged. He looks
          up at the clock, then frowns as he remembers his scene
          with Harve Pell. He takes a wanted poster from a desk
          drawer, and on its back he writes:

                    "BACK IN FIVE MINUTES --

                    DOANE."

          He props this up on his desk, and goes out.

102.   EXT. SALOON. Harvey Pell, still seething, strides toward
          the saloon. He passes Two Indians lounging before the
          saloon, and goes in.

103.   INT. SALOON. It is crowded now, with an almost holiday
          atmosphere. Harvey comes in and goes to the bar. His
          entrance gains considerable attention. Some of the Men
          nod, and Harvey returns the gesture briefly. The Bar-
          tender comes to him with a bottle and glass, and Harvey
          pours himself a drink. Gillis, the owner, leaves the
          group he is with and comes over to the bar next to
          Harvey. Harvey ignores him as he drinks.

                              GILLIS
                    Hi, Harve --

                              HARVEY
                    How are you . . .

                              GILLIS
                    Where's the tin star?

                              HARVEY
                I turned it in. I quit . . .

                              GILLIS
                Smart move.

                              HARVEY
                I didn't ask for your opinion.

           He takes the bottle and moves to a vacant table.
           Gillis looks after him wisely.

104.   EXT. STREET. Doane walks steadily toward the hotel. The
           street seems empty except for him, but Doane has the feeling
           that eyes are watching him.

105.   INT. ROOM OVERLOOKING STREET. A Man and a Woman, townspeople,
           are looking out of the window at Doane as he passes.

106.   EXT. STREET -- TRUCK SHOT WITH Doane. The Two Little Boys
           we have seen before dash into the scene, one in pursuit
           of the other. The pursuer extends his arm and shoots.

                              FIRST BOY
                Bang! Bang! -- You're dead,
                Doane! . . .

           He turns and runs headlong into Doane, who holds and
           steadies him. The Boy looks up and recognizes Doane.
           His mouth goes wide in dazed panic. Then he jerks out
           of Doane's grasp and runs away, as the other Boy disappears
           as well. Doane continues up the street.

107.   EXT. DEPOT -- JORDAN, PIERCE AND COLBY. Colby is playing
           a western folk tune on his harmonica. Milt takes a deep
           drag of his cigarette, then flips the butt away sharply
           and gets to his feet. Pierce watches him narrowly.
           Milt stretches.

                              MILT
                You know what? Think I'll go
                get some liquor.

                              PIERCE
                You have to have it?

                              MILT
                Yep.

                          PIERCE
                  If you're going after that
                  woman --

                          MILT
                  I said I was going for liquor . . .

He starts to walk away.

                          PIERCE
                  You keep away from Doane! . . .

                          MILT
                  Sure. . . . I can wait . . .

He saunters on.

108.   EXT HOTEL. As Doane nears the hotel, he sees the
        buckboard hitched before it. His face brightens
        and his pace quickens.

109-   INT. HOTEL LOBBY. Amy, sitting near the window, sees
110.   Doane approaching. Believing he is coming to her, she
        is overjoyed. Rising, she hurries to the door, and is
        there waiting for him when he comes in. Doane takes
        her arms in his happily.

                          DOANE
                  Amy, you changed your mind --

Amy stares up at him, the joy ebbing out of her eyes as
she begins to understand him. She disengages her arms.

                          AMY
                        (dully)
                  I'd thought you had changed
                  yours. . . . No, Will, I have my
                  ticket . . .

                          DOANE
                        (brought down)
                  I see . . .

He looks at her, his disappointment suddenly boiling
over into anger, then turns from her and goes toward
the desk. The Clerk is leaning on it, watching him
come. There is no sympathy in his eyes. As Doane
nears the desk, an Elderly Chambermaid comes in with

mop and pail, and reaches the desk at the same time
as he does. Ignoring Doane, the Clerk gets a key
and tosses it on the counter toward the Chambermaid.

> CLERK
> Open 19, and clean it up good.
> (deliberately)
> Mr. Jordan's very particular . . .

As she takes the key and goes, he looks at Doane calmly.
Doane's face tightens.

> DOANE
> Helen Ramirez in?

> CLERK
> Guess so . . .

Doane looks at him, turns and goes to the stairs.

> CLERK
> (meaningly)
> Think you can find it alright?

Doane doesn't answer. He starts up the stairs. The
Clerk grins. Amy is watching Doane as he goes, puzzled.

111. INT. STAIRWAY -- on Doane as he mounts the stairs.

112. INT. HALL -- on Doane as he comes to the landing and
goes to Helen's door. He knocks.

113. INT. HELEN'S BEDROOM. She is packing as she hears
Doane's knock.

> HELEN
> Come --

114. INT. HELEN'S FRONT ROOM -- as Doane enters, looks around,
sees no one, waits.

115. INT. HELEN'S BEDROOM. She stops, puzzled, then goes
to the front room.

116- INT. HELEN'S FRONT ROOM. Helen enters the room, stops
119. short as she sees Doane. Their eyes meet and hold. The
silent tension grows, seeming to fill the room as with
an explosive gas. It is Helen who breaks the silence.

                    HELEN
                  (quietly)
          What are you looking at? You
          think I've changed?

                    DOANE
          No.

All the long-pent fury of her baffled anger and wounded
pride overflows.

                    HELEN
          Well, what do you want? You
          want me to help you? You want
          me to ask Guy to let you go?
          You want me to beg for you?
          Well, I won't do it. I won't
          lift a finger for you! You're
          on your own!

Doane has been waiting patiently for the storm to subside.

                    DOANE
                  (gently)
          I came to tell you he was coming.
          I should've figured you'd know
          about it.

Helen has pulled herself together, angry and ashamed with
herself.

                    HELEN
          I know about it.

                    DOANE
          I think you ought to get out of
          town. I might not be able to --
          Well, anything can happen . . .

                    HELEN
                  (quietly)
          I'm not afraid of him.

                    DOANE
          I know you're not, but you know
          how he is.

           HELEN
        (dully)
I know how he is . . .

She turns away from him, goes to the window. They are
both silent for a moment.

           HELEN
     (without hope)
Maybe he doesn't know . . .

           DOANE
He probably got letters.

           HELEN
Probably . . .
     (she smiles without
      humor)
Nothing in life is free. . . . I'm
getting out -- I'm packing now.

           DOANE
That's good.

He hesitates, then turns to the door. Hearing him, she
turns. Again, their eyes meet and hold.

           HELEN
     (in Spanish)
It's been more than a year . . .

           DOANE
     (also in Spanish)
Yes. I know . . .

There is a pause. Then, unable to help herself. Helen
goes on, still in Spanish.

           HELEN
Do you want to kiss me goodby?
     (but as Doane hesitates,
      she cuts in sharply, in
      English)
Never mind! Goodby . . .

           DOANE
Goodbye, Helen . . .

He turns to the door again.

                    HELEN
                 (flatly)
            Doane --
                 (as he looks at her)
            If you're smart, you'll get out
            yourself.

                    DOANE
            I can't.

                    HELEN
            I didn't think you would.

He goes out. Helen stares after him. For a moment her
heart and soul are in her eyes, going after him.

                    HELEN
                 (to herself, in Spanish)
            Do you want to kiss me goodby . . . ?

She grimaces with self-contempt. Then, herself again,
she turns and goes to her bedroom.

120.   INT. HOTEL LOBBY. Amy, back at the window, and the
        Clerk, behind the desk, listen to Doane's footsteps
        as he comes down the steps. As he reaches the landing,
        his eyes go to the clock. It is 11:11. Deliberately, the
        Clerk takes his watch out, checks it with the clock,
        apparently adjusts it and then starts to wind it. Doane
        looks at him, then turns and goes to the door. As he
        passes her, Amy averts her head. Without breaking stride,
        Doane goes out.

121.   EXT. SALOON. Milt Jordan approaches the saloon and
        goes inside.

122.   INT. SALOON. The murmur of conversation and cards
        stops as the men recognize Milt. Unconcerned, he
        goes to the bar, takes out a silver dollar.

                    BARTENDER
                 (obsequiously)
            How are you, Milt?

                    MILT
            Alright. Give me a bottle.

                         BARTENDER
            Sure thing!

He turns away to get one. Gillis has sidled up to
the bar.

                         GILLIS
            It's been a long time, Milt!

Milt looks at him dryly.

                         GILLIS
            Yes, sir! . . . How's Guy?

The Bartender returns with the bottle.

                         MILT
            He's not complaining.

                         GILLIS
                (jovially)
            Well, there'll be a hot time in
            the old town tonight, hey, Milt?

Milt looks at him, then grins suddenly.

                         MILT
            I wouldn't be surprised.

123.   INT. HOTEL LOBBY. Amy is still at the window, her face
        mirroring her inner struggle. Then, giving in, she
        turns and goes to the desk. The Clerk waits coolly for
        her approach.

                         AMY
                (trying to cover her
                 embarrasment)
            May I ask you something?

                         CLERK
            Sure.

                         AMY
            Who is Miss Ramirez?

                         CLERK
                (enjoying himself)
            Mrs. Ramirez. . . . She used to be a

                    CLERK (Cont'd.)
          friend of your husband's a while
          back. Before that, she was a
          friend of Guy Jordan's . . .

                    AMY
               (off balance)
          I see. . . . Thank you --
               (she starts to go back
               to her place, stops)
          You -- don't like my husband, do
          you?

                    CLERK
          No.

                    AMY
          Why?

                    CLERK
          Lots of reasons. . . . One thing, this
          place was always busy when Guy
          Jordan was around. I'm not the
          only one -- there's plenty people
          around here think he's got a
          comeuppance coming. . . . You asked
          me, ma'am, so I'm telling you.

                    AMY
               (quietly)
          Thank you.

     She goes back to the window thoughtfully.

124. CLOSEUP-- CLOCK IN MARSHAL'S OFFICE. It reads 11:16.
      CAMERA PANS DOWN to reveal the empty room and the
      note still on Doane's desk. Then Doane enters, looks
      around and realizes that no one has come yet. He
      looks up at the clock worriedly. Then, frowning, he
      gets the note, goes back to the door, spikes the
      note on a nail on the outside of the door and goes
      out, closing the door behind him.

125. EXT. STREET -- TRUCK SHOT -- DOANE -- as he comes out
      and starts down the street. He approaches the
      saloon, hesitates, then goes on. He changes his
      mind, crosses the street and goes to the saloon.
      As he reaches the door and is about to go in, it

swings out and Milt Jordan emerges. Both men are
taken off balance for an instant, and then they
achieve control. Their eyes hold for a long moment.
Then Milt's lips curl in a confident grin. Shifting
his grip on his quart of whiskey, he turns and
deliberately walks away, whistling softly. Doane
looks after him, tight-lipped, then takes a deep
breath, and pushes the door open. There is a burst
of laughter from within.

126-   INT. SALOON. Doane's entrance is unnoticed at first
130.   except by those near the door. Gillis is in a small
        group, his back to the door.

                    GILLIS
                   (loudly)
          I'll give you odds Doane's dead
          five minutes after Guy gets off
          the train!

                    MAN
          That's not much time . . .

                    GILLIS
          That's all Guy'll need --
          because --

He becomes aware that everyone is looking past him to
the entrance, turns and sees Doane standing there.
The room has gone silent. Doane starts over slowly
toward Gillis, his face tight. He has had enough.
When he reaches Gillis, he stops, then swings from
the hip. Gillis goes down to the floor. No one moves
as he lies there a moment, then sits up dazedly, wiping
the blood from his lips.

                    GILLIS
                   (thickly)
          You carry a badge and a gun,
          Marshal. You had no call to
          do that.

Doane slumps, suddenly and obscurely ashamed.

                    DOANE
          You're right . . .

He starts toward Gillis to help him up and Two Men step

out for the same purpose. But Gillis shoves the Marshal's
proffered hand out of the way, and lets himself be helped
by the others on his feet and to a table. The Bartender
pours a drink for him and brings it to him. The customers
wait silently for Doane to make his move. Doane looks
at them. At his table near the window, Harvey is watching.
Doane's eyes meet Harvey's, then move away.

> DOANE
> (to all of them)
> I guess you all know why I'm
> here. I need deputies. I'll
> take as many as I can get.

He waits. There is no response.

> GILLIS
> (suddenly)
> I ain't saying I'd've helped
> you before, but I sure ain't
> gonna now.

> DOANE
> (ignoring him)
> Some of you were special deputies
> when we broke this bunch. I need
> you again -- now . . .

The Men in the room remain silent. One or two seem
affected, but they look at the others, waiting for
a lead. Doane waits, his heart sinking. The clock
ticks loudly in the silence. Doane looks at it.
Some of the other Men follow his eyes. It is 11:19.

> DOANE
> (finally)
> Well? . . .

> MAN AT BAR
> Things were different then, Doane.
> You had six steady deputies to
> start off with -- everyone a top
> gun. You ain't got but two now.

> SECOND MAN
> You ain't got two. Harve Pell
> here says he quit. Why?

Everyone turns to look at Harvey. He stares them down.

> DOANE
> That's between the two of us.

> FIRST MAN
> And where's Toby?

> DOANE
> He's on his way in. He'll be
> here.

> SECOND MAN
> That's what you say. You're asking
> a lot, Doane, all things considered . . .

He turns to look at a Man alone at a table, and the
others follow his glance. The Man at the table looks
up. He is bleary-eyed, an obvious alcoholic, and he
has a livid whip-lash scar across one eye and across
his face.

> DOANE
> Alright, we all know what Jordan's
> like. That's why I'm here. . . . How
> about it?

> GILLIS
> (suddenly)
> You must be crazy, coming in
> here to raise a posse. Guy's
> got friends in this room -- you
> ought to know that!

Doane ignores him, waits. The room is silent. The
Two Men who have seemed to be disposed to join him
shrink back among the others. Doane realizes there
is nothing here. The Men watch him go in silence.

131.   EXT. SALOON. The Two Indians have been listening from
the outside door. They give way for Doane. He comes
out, looks across the street toward his office.

132.   EXT. MARSHAL'S OFFICE-- from Doane's point of view.
There are no horses at the rail, and Doane's note
can be seen fluttering on the door.

133.   EXT SALOON. Doane turns and starts down the street,
moving out of scene. The Indians watch him go. The
Young Indian turns to the Older Indian and looks at
him inquiringly. The Older Man shrugs.

134-   INT. CHURCH. It is well-filled, and the choir -- composed
138.   of six Men and six Women -- is singing a hymn. Sam comes
        in unobtrusively and unnoticed and searches the room with
        his eyes. Finally he sees the man he is looking for,
        WEAVER the storekeeper, singing in the choir. Their eyes
        meet, and Weaver gets the almost imperceptible signal
        Sam sends him with his lifted eyebrows. Weaver frowns with
        annoyance and worry, but when the hymn ends and
        while the rest of the choir is finding its seats again,
        he leans over to his pompous Wife, whispers to her, and
        slips out through the rear door. She, too, is puzzled
        and annoyed, but she covers his exit by dropping and
        retrieving her hymnal. With his usual impassivity, Sam
        turns and gets out as quietly as he came.

139.   EXT. MART HOWE'S HOUSE. It is a small house, rather
        shabby in appearance, as if its owner is unwilling or
        unable to keep its paint and trim and flower beds in
        order, or perhaps just doesn't care. Doane enters the
        scene and walks to the door, sweating freely under the
        glare of the high sun. He knocks and waits. The door
        is opened by a stout Indian Woman well past middle age.
        She recognizes Doane wordlessly, and lets him in.

140-   INT. MART HOWE'S HOUSE. This main room of the house,
144.   which serves as both living and dining room, is fairly
        clean and well kept, but like the exterior it is barren,
        unloved. Two large, old-fashioned guns hang on the wall
        beneath a badge mounted on a leather base. Mart Howe
        is sitting in the one comfortable chair in the room,
        staring at the floor. The Indian Woman goes to the
        chair at the eating table and resumes what she was doing
        before Doane's interruption -- rolling cigarettes by hand
        and mouth and adding them to the small pile already on
        the table. Doane goes toward Howe and stops, looking
        down at him. Howe finally looks up at him, his face
        wooden, his eyes hopeless.

                          DOANE
                I sent a kid to find you. Didn't
                he come?

                          HOWE
                        (heavily)
                He was here . . .

        Doane stares down at him unbelievingly, turns away
        helplessly, then to him again.

                    DOANE
                (finding words)
            You been my friend all my life. You
            got me this job! You made them send
            for me . . .

Howe's bent frame droops, but he remains silent.

                    DOANE
            From the time I was a kid I
            wanted to be like you. . . .
            Mart, you been a law man your
            whole life -- !

                    HOWE
                (bitterly)
            Yeah . . . yeah, my whole life.
            A great life. You risk your
            skin catching killers and the
            juries let them go so they can
            come back and shoot at you again.
            If you're honest, you're poor
            your whole life, and in the end
            you wind up dying all alone in
            a dirty street. For what? For
            nothing. A tin star . . .

The Indian Woman picks up the handful of cigarettes she
has made, comes over and puts them on the small table
near Howe's chair, takes some wooden matches out of a
pocket of her apron and puts them down alongside, then
turns and shuffles out of the room. With difficulty,
Howe picks up a cigarette in his gnarled fingers and
strikes a match to it. Doane looks at him.

                    DOANE
            Listen! The Judge left town.
            Harvey's quit. I'm having
            trouble getting deputies . . .

                    HOWE
            It figures. . . . It's all
            happened too sudden. People
            have to talk themselves into law
            and order before they do anything
            about it. . . . They don't care.
            They really don't care.

The room goes silent. The two men look at each other.
All barriers are down now. It is a time for complete
honesty, for they will never again be this close to
each other, this intimate.

> DOANE
> What should I do, Mart?

> HOWE
> I was hoping you wouldn't come
> back.

> DOANE
> You know why I came back.

> HOWE
> But not to commit suicide.

> DOANE
> Sometimes prison changes a
> man . . .

> HOWE
> Not him. . . .
> (despairingly)
> It's all planned, that's why
> they're all here. . . . Get
> out, Will! Get out! . . .

Doane turns away, wrestling it out with himself. Howe
watches him for a moment, then averts his eyes. Finally
Doane draws a deep, almost shuddering breath, and shakes
his head. Howe understands that Doane has fought back.

> DOANE
> Will you go down to that station
> with me?

> HOWE
> (dully)
> No . . .
> (his cigarette drops
> to the floor, and after
> only a momentary hesita-
> tion he rubs it out under
> his shoe)
> You know how I feel about you, but

                    HOWE (Cont'd.)
          I won't go with you.
                (he looks at his
                 twisted fingers)
          Seems like a man that already had
          busted knuckles didn't need ar-
          thritis, too, don't it?
                (he shrugs hopelessly)
          No. . . . I couldn't do anything
          for you. You'd be worried about
          me. You'd get yourself killed
          worrying about me. It's too
          one-sided the way it is . . .

                    DOANE
                (tired)
          So long, Mart . . .

                    HOWE
          So long.

Doane turns and goes out.

                    HOWE
                (hopelessly)
          It's for nothing, Will. It's all
          for nothing . . .

But Doane's footsteps continue to fade in the distance.
Howe looks at the clock. It is 11:26.

145-   EXT. HOWE'S HOUSE. Doane is walking steadily away from
147.   the house.

                    VOICE
                (O.S.)
          Doane -- !

Doane stops, turns. The Scarred Drunk from the saloon
hurries into the scene and to the Marshal. Doane waits,
surprise struggling with his impatience.

                    DOANE
          What's the matter, Jimmy?

The Drunk is sweaty and breathless, but he carries
himself with the deceptive steadiness of the confirmed
alcoholic.

                         DRUNK
               Nothing. . . . I been looking for
               you. . . . I want a gun. I want
               to be with you when that train
               comes in . . .

Doane stares at him.

                         DOANE
               Can you handle a gun?

                         DRUNK
               Sure I can. I used to be good.
               Honest . . .

                         DOANE
               But why?

The Drunk is all too conscious of Doane's eyes searching
his face, seeing the patch. His own fingers go up to it.

                         DRUNK
               It ain't just getting even, no! . . .
               It's a chance, see? It's what I
               need. . . . Please, Doane . . . let
               me get in on this. . . !

In his urgency he has reached out and clutched Doane's
arm. Doane looks down at the hand gripping his forearm,
sees the Drunk's fingers and arm trembling. The Drunk
follows Doane's eyes. He pulls his hand away and tries
desperately to stop the trembling. But his fingers
continue to quiver until, in an agony of helplessness,
he covers them with his other hand. Then his eyes meet
Doane's again, bleak, shamed and hopeless but with a
last tiny spark of pleading.

                         DOANE
                      (gently)
               Alright, Jim . . . I'll call you if
               I need you. . . .
                      (he reaches in his pocket
                      for a silver dollar)
               Get yourself a drink, meanwhile --

He forces the coin into the Drunk's hand, tries to
bring sincerity into his smile, and turns and goes.

> DRUNK
> (dully)
> Thanks . . . Will . . .

148. CLOSE TRUCK SHOT -- DOANE -- as he continues away, his face
still set in the empty, meaningless smile. Then his lips
tighten with helpless anger.

149. OUT.

150- INT. HELEN'S FRONT ROOM. She is standing in the doorway
151. to her bedroom as Sam comes in and closes the door behind
him.

> HELEN
> Where is he?

> SAM
> Coming up the back way. . . .
> (he allows himself the
> ghost of a smile)
> That's a careful man . . .

There is the sound of approaching footsteps in the hall,
and Sam nods. He turns and opens the door, catching
Weaver as he is about to knock.

> HELEN
> Come in, Mr. Weaver.

Awkwardly, the storekeeper comes in, and Sam closes the
door after him. Throughout the scene the business man
is quite respectful towards Helen.

> WEAVER
> Anything wrong, Mrs. Ramirez?

> HELEN
> No.

> WEAVER
> Then why did you send for me?

> HELEN
> I'm leaving town. I want to sell
> my half of the store. You want
> to buy me out?

                    WEAVER
              (covering his surprise)
       How much did you want?

                    HELEN
       Two thousand. I think that's fair.

                    WEAVER
       Oh, it's fair alright, Mrs.
       Ramirez. But I couldn't raise
       that much right now.

                    HELEN
       How much can you raise?

                    WEAVER
       About a thousand . . .

                    HELEN
       Alright. You can pay Sam, here,
       the rest in six months, and he'll
       get it to me. A deal?

                    WEAVER
              (pleased)
       Yes, ma'am.

                    HELEN
              (dismissing him)
       Alright, Mr. Weaver . . .

                    WEAVER
              (somewhat embarrassed)
       Well, I'd like to thank you, Mrs.
       Ramirez -- for everything. . . .
       I mean, when you first called me
       in and put the deal to me -- about
       staking me in the store and being
       the silent partner -- my wife thought --
              (he realizes he is on
              dangerous ground)
       Well, what I really mean is, you've
       been real decent to me right along.
       And I want you to know I've been
       honest with you.

                    HELEN
       I know you have. Goodby, Mr. Weaver.

                         WEAVER
          Goodby . . .

He turns to the door, stops and turns back to her.

                         WEAVER
                      (meaningly)
          And good luck to you . . .

Helen nods. Weaver and Sam go out.

152.   MED. LONG SHOT -- EXT. FULLER HOUSE. Doane is walking
       steadily toward the house, a larger, more-imposing, better-
       cared-for place than Mart Howe's. It has been painted
       recently, and the picket fence and flower beds are in good
       order. Doane nears the house.

153-   INT. FRONT ROOM -- FULLER HOUSE. Sam Fuller is peering out
157.   through the window.

                         FULLER
                      (agitated)
          Mildred -- ! Mildred! . . .

Mrs. Fuller hurries into the room. A simple woman, she
knows the reason for his agitation, but she is bewildered,
troubled.

                         FULLER
                   (leaving the window)
          He's coming. . . . I knew he would . . .
          Now you do like I told you! I'm
          not home -- don't let him in! No
          matter what he says, I'm not home! . . .

                        MRS. FULLER
          Sam, he's your friend --

                         FULLER
          Don't argue with me! He'll be
          here in a second!

                        MRS. FULLER
          He won't believe me. He'll know
          I'm lying --

                         FULLER
          You do like I tell you -- !

Doane's footsteps can be heard on the porch approaching
the door. Then he knocks. Fuller points a tense finger
at his wife, then tiptoes to the bedroom and closes the
door behind him. Doane knocks again. Frightened, wretched,
Mrs. Fuller goes to the door and opens it about halfway.

> MRS. FULLER
> (with tremendous effort)
> Oh . . . hello, Will . . .

Surprised at first by her manner and the unmistakable lack
of welcome in the partly opened door, Doane quickly sees and
understands her tension.

> DOANE
> Hello, Mrs. Fuller. Sam in?

> MRS FULLER
> No. . . . No, he isn't . . .

Doane stares at her, convinced she is lying.

> DOANE
> (quietly)
> Do you know where he is, Mrs.
> Fuller? It's important to me
> that I find him.

> MRS. FULLER
> (in agony)
> I think he's in church, Will --
> he's gone to church --

> DOANE
> Without you?

> MRS. FULLER
> I'm going in a little while -- as
> soon as I dress --

For a moment anger surges up in Doane, and then he checks
it.

> DOANE
> (gently)
> Thanks, Mrs. Fuller. . . . Goodby . . .

He turns and lets her shut the door after him.

158.   EXT. FULLER HOUSE -- as Doane steps down the porch steps,
       stops a moment to stare up at the merciless sun. He wipes
       his face wearily, then continues down the steps and along
       the walk, his face grim.

159.   INT. FRONT ROOM -- FULLER HOUSE. Mrs. Fuller has crept to a
       chair, where she slumps miserably. Fuller is at the window,
       watching Doane go. He turns finally, and looks at her
       stricken face.

                         FULLER
                     (shame-ridden)
               Well, what do you want? You
               want me to get killed? You
               want to be a widow? Is that
               what you want?

       Mrs. Fuller raises her eyes to his. She is torn,
       bewildered, miserable.

                         MRS. FULLER
               No, Sam. . . . No . . .

160.   EXT. RAILROAD STATION -- CLOSE SHOT -- MILT -- as he drinks
       from the whiskey bottle. There is the O.S. MUSIC of
       Colby's harmonica, as he plays "Blue-Tail Fly." CAMERA
       PULLS BACK to INCLUDE Pierce and Colby. Milt wipes his
       lips and then deliberately offers the bottle to Pierce,
       and grins as the latter looks at him darkly. Milt extends
       the bottle to Colby, who takes it and drinks. Pierce
       turns and looks down the track.

161.   EXT. RAILROAD TRACK. The parallel lines of the track merge
       in the hazy distance.

162.   GROUP SHOT. Pierce frowns to himself, takes out his watch,
       and looks at the time. Colby finishes his drink, hands the
       bottle back to Milt, then resumes his playing. Pierce gets
       up and goes over to the window in the b.g. The Station-
       master comes up to it.

                         PIERCE
               Anything on the train?

                         STATIONMASTER
               It's on time, far as I know. . . .
                     (as Pierce turns away)
               If it don't stop, there's no more

STATIONMASTER (Cont'd.)
southbounds till tomorrow --

Pierce looks at him coldly, then turns and comes back to
the group, sits down and starts to roll a cigarette. Milt
whistles softly to Colby's playing.

QUICK DISSOLVE TO:

163.   EXT. PRAIRIE -- MED. LONG SHOT -- on Toby and Peterson as
their horses gallop along the faint trail. Toby keeps
his horse steadily at Peterson's flank.

164.   MED. TRUCK SHOT -- on Toby and Peterson. Peterson's hands
are still free. Toby moves up alongside Peterson and
points o.s. They change direction and ride out of scene.

165-   EXT. WATERHOLE. Toby and Peterson appear in the b.g., and
175.   ride down to the waterhole. They are both tired, hot,
dusty. They dismount near the hole and lead their horses
to the water. The horses drink greedily. Peterson looks
over at Toby thoughtfully, then around him, sees a stone
near his feet. Behind the cover of his horse, he bends
quietly and picks it up. When Toby draws his horse from
the water, then goes upstream a little way, Peterson
follows suit, hiding the stone behind his back. Toby
bends down and starts to drink. Peterson tenses and
starts to swing the stone down on Toby's head. Almost in
time, but not quite, Toby sees his reflection in the water,
and tries to dodge. Peterson's fist and stone come down
in a glancing blow on Toby's head and Toby goes face
forward into the water. Peterson goes in after him. Toby
manages to get to his feet before Peterson can wrestle
him down into the water, and the two men begin swinging
at each other. The horses rear and retreat from the
waterhole. Toby and Peterson fight fiercely and soundlessly,
except for their panting and choking breath. When they are
on their feet they are waist-deep, but more often than not
both men are out of sight in the roiling and threshing
water. Finally, Peterson manages to knock Toby down, and he
is on top of him in an instant, hitting him and ducking him
until Toby goes limp and sinks under water. Peterson lets
him go and scrambles breathlessly out and to his horse.
Toby comes to, and with tremendous effort takes out after
him. Peterson has trouble getting his frightened horse to
stand still enough to mount, and Toby catches him from
behind and drags him down. They roll over and over into a
rocky growth and a right hand from Toby sends Peterson's

head back against a rock. He is hurt. Toby continues to
bang Peterson's head against the stone until he caves in.
Toby rolls off and lies there, trying to recapture his breath
and strength. Finally, he is able to get up. He pulls
Peterson to his feet, turns him around, and kicks him toward
the waterhole. Peterson staggers forward and falls. Toby
picks him up again and kicks him all the way to the hole,
where Peterson finally falls face down at the edge of the
hole. Toby looks down at the waterhole. The water is
muddy and thick with silt.

>   TOBY
>   (glaring at Peterson)
>   Now see what you went and done!
>   That water won't be fit to drink
>   for hours --

Disgusted, he whistles for his horse.

                                        QUICK DISSOLVE TO:

176.   INT. HOTEL LOBBY. The front door bangs open, and Harvey
        strides in, liquor-flushed. Again Amy has looked up hope-
        fully. She recognizes Harvey, but he is too full of his
        errand to see her. Ignoring the Clerk as well, he goes
        across the lobby and up the stairs.

>   CLERK
>   (drily)
>   There's another one of Mrs.
>   Ramirez's friends . . .

>   AMY
>   (puzzled)
>   Oh? . . .

>   CLERK
>   (grinning)
>   Yep. . . . I'd say she's got some
>   explaining to do when that
>   train gets in . . .

Amy looks at him with increasing dislike, but she is very
thoughtful as she turns away.

177-   INT. HELEN'S FRONT ROOM. She is putting the final touches
182.   to her packing as a knock sounds on the door.

> HELEN
> Come in, Sam --

The door opens and Harvey enters. He is stunned when he
sees the suitcases. Then Helen looks up and sees him.
She braces herself for the unpleasantness to come.

> HARVEY
> You leaving town -- ?

Helen looks at him, but does not bother to answer. She
fastens the last buckle.

> HARVEY
> Where you going?

> HELEN
> I don't know yet.

She moves past him, checking the room for things she may
have forgotten to pack. Baffled and frustrated by her
manner, Harvey follows her.

> HARVEY
> That doesn't make much sense.

Helen shrugs.

> HELEN
> I'll think of somewhere, once
> I'm on the train.

> HARVEY
> You're afraid, huh? You're
> afraid of Jordan . . .

> HELEN
> (honestly)
> No . . .

> HARVEY
> Sure you are, or you wouldn't
> be running. You got nothing to
> be afraid of as long as I'm
> around -- you know that. I'm not
> scared of Jordan. I'll take him
> on any time!

                    HELEN
                (matter-of-fact)
        I believe you . . .

She goes to the window now and looks out. Harvey stares
sullenly at her insolent back, his rage mounting.

                    HARVEY
            Then why are you going?
                (as Helen shrugs)
            Are you cutting out with Doane?

Helen turns and looks at him. She smiles with weary
contempt.

                    HELEN
            Oh, Harvey . . .

                    HARVEY
            Then why are you going?

                    HELEN
            What difference does it make?

                    HARVEY
                (furiously)
            It's Doane, it's Doane! I know
            it's Doane!

                    HELEN
            It isn't Doane!
                (she stops, then
                  goes on)
            But I'm going to tell you some-
            thing about you and your friend
            Doane. You're a nice looking boy.
            You have big wide shoulders. But
            he's a man. . . . It takes more than
            big wide shoulders to make a man,
            Harvey. And you've got a long way
            to go. . . . You know something? I
            don't think you'll ever make it . . .

She turns away from him. Exploding, Harvey comes after
her, grabs her and turns her to him. Helen is passive
in his arms.

                    HARVEY
                  (huskily)
          Now I'll tell you something.
          You're not going anywhere --
          you're staying here with me --
          It's going to be just like before --

He kisses her brutally. Helen remains completely and
coolly unresponsive, unresisting, untouched. Harvey
lets her go uncertainly.

                    HELEN
                  (quietly)
          You want to know why I'm getting
          out? Then listen. . . . Doane will be
          a dead man in half an hour, and
          nobody is going to do anything
          about it. Don't ask me how I know.
          I know. And when he dies, this
          town dies, too. It smells dead to
          me already. And I'm a widow. I'm
          all alone in the world. I have to
          make a living. So -- I'm going
          somewhere else. That's all . . .
                  (she studies him a moment,
                   then goes on softly)
          And as for you -- I don't like
          anybody to put their hands on me
          unless I want them to. . . . And I
          don't want you to . . . anymore --

Stung, Harvey reaches for her. She slaps him sharply,
viciously.

183.   MED. LONG SHOT -- EXT. CHURCH. Doane can be seen climbing
       the hill toward the church. The distant strains of a
       small organ can be heard.

184.   MED. SHOT -- EXT. CHURCH -- as Doane walks through the
       churchyard to the church. The organ music within comes
       to a stop. Doane opens the doors.

185-   INT. CHURCH. The Minister is beginning his sermon.
195.
                    MINISTER
          Our text today is from Malachi,
          chapter four . . .

Doane enters and stands near the doorway.

                    MINISTER
               (reading from the bible)
          . . . For, behold, the day cometh,
          that shall burn as an oven; and
          all the proud, yea, and all that
          do wickedly shall be as --

He has looked up, seen Doane, and stopped. The congregation,
seeing him stare, turns toward the entrance. There is a
rustle, a shuffle, a whispering, and then silence. Some
of the people seem aware of Doane's mission, others are
puzzled. Jo Henderson seems honestly surprised to see Doane.

                    MINISTER
               (to Doane, frowning)
          Yes?

                    DOANE
               (awkwardly)
          I'm sorry, parson. I don't want
          to disturb the services --

                    MINISTER
               (irritated)
          You already have . . .
               (now he gives away the
               real cause of his anger)
          You don't come to this church very
          often, Marshal. And when you got
          married today, you didn't see fit
          to be married here. What could be
          so important to bring you here now?

                    DOANE
          I need help.

He strides up front to the pulpit.

                    DOANE
               (to Minister)
          It's true I haven't been a church-
          going man, and that's maybe a bad
          thing. And I wasn't married here
          today because my wife's . . .
               (he suddenly remembers
               Amy with a pang of pain)

                         DOANE (Cont'd.)
              my wife's a Quaker. . . . But I've
              come here for help because there
              are people here . . .

The Minister, a good man who already regrets his display
of temper, has been staring at him with growing shame.

                         MINISTER
              I'm sorry, Marshal. Say what
              you have to say.

Doane turns to the people.

                         DOANE
              Maybe some of you already know.
              If you don't, it looks like Guy
              Jordan's coming back on the noon
              train. I need as many special
              deputies as I can get.

There is a momentary pause, as those to whom this is news
take it in. The Minister is shocked. He hasn't known.
Then a Man (SCOTT) in a rear pew rises.

                         SCOTT
              What are we waiting for? Let's
              go! . . .

He starts toward the aisle and to Doane. There seems to be
a fairly general movement to follow him. Then Another Man
(COOPER) near the rear of church, rises and yells
through the jumble of voices.

                         COOPER
              Hold it! Hold it a minute! . . .

The crowd is held. They turn to him.

                         COOPER
              That's right -- hold it! Before
              we go rushing out into some-
              thing that ain't going to be so
              pleasant -- let's be sure we know
              what this is all about . . .

The room is silent. Some of the Men sit down. Doane is
watching Cooper, frowning.

                         COOPER
              What I want to know is this --
              ain't it true that Doane ain't
              the Marshal anymore? And ain't
              it true that there's personal
              trouble between him and Jordan?

Men jump to their feet. There is a jumble of outcries,
some in protest, some in agreement. But Cooper's charge
has had its effect. Jo Henderson hurries up front and
comes beside Doane.

                         HENDERSON
                      (over the crowd)
              Alright, alright! . . . Quiet,
              everybody -- !

Henderson commands the crowd's attention. The noise
subsides.

                         HENDERSON
              If there's difference of opinion,
              let everybody have his say. . . . But
              let's get all the kids out of
              the building . . .

Men on their feet find seats. Parents push their children
toward the aisles. One Boy about twelve, highly intrigued,
tries to hang back. Hia Father jerks him to his feet and
helps him along with a slap on the behind. There is a
movement of children to the doors. Henderson puts his
hand on Doane's arm, and Doane looks at him gratefully.

196.   EXT. RAILROAD STATION. Pierce is pacing tensely. Milt is
        sprawled lazily. Colby is playing his harmonica. Pierce
        stares out into the distance.

197.   EXT. TRACKS. They stretch out emptily.

198-   INT. CHURCH. Scott is speaking.
208.
                         SCOTT
                      (angrily)
              I say it don't matter if there
              is anything personal between
              Jordan and the Marshal here.
              We all know who Jordan is and

SCOTT (Cont'd.)
what he is! What's more, we're
wasting time! . . .

Doane, Henderson and the Parson are listening and watching
intently. From outside, there is the SOUND of children's
voices, singing. Hands shoot up as Scott finishes.
Henderson recognizes another Man.

                    HENDERSON
          Alright, Coy --

                    COY
               (rising)
          Yeah, we all know who Jordan is,
          but we put him away once. Who
          saved him from hanging? The
          politicians up north. This is
          their mess -- let them take care
          of it . . .

He sits. There are more hands. Henderson recognizes
another Man.

                    HENDERSON
          Sawyer --

                    SAWYER
               (rising)
          What I got to say is this -- we've
          been paying good money right along
          for a marshal and deputies. But
          the first time there's trouble, we
          got to take care of it ourselves!
          What we been paying for all this
          time? I say we're not peace officers
          here! This ain't our job . . .

There are cries of assent and disagreement. A Man (LEWIS)
jumps to his feet.

                    LEWIS
               (over noise)
          I been saying right along we ought
          to have more deputies! If we did,
          we wouldn't be facing this now! . . .

                              HENDERSON
                            (loudly)
                    Just a minute now -- let's keep it
                    orderly! Everybody, quiet down! . . .
                            (as they do)
                    You had your hand up, Ezra . . .

The Man named Ezra gets up, quivering with indignation.

                              EZRA
                    I can't believe I've heard some of
                    the things that've been said here.
                    You all ought to be ashamed of your-
                    selves. Sure, we paid this man, and
                    he was the best marshal this town
                    ever had. And it ain't his trouble,
                    it's ours. I tell you if we don't
                    do what's right, we're going to have
                    plenty more trouble. So there ain't
                    but one thing to do now, and you all
                    know what that is!

Another Man shoots his hand into the air. Henderson nods
to him.

                              HENDERSON
                    Go ahead, Kibbee --

                              KIBBEE
                            (stupidly)
                    Been a lot of talk about what our
                    duty is. . . . Well, this is Sunday,
                    and I don't hold with no killing on
                    the Sabbath . . .

He sits down, highly satisfied with himself. Doane stares
at him in amazement. Henderson hides a wry smile.

209-   EXT. CHURCH. Some of the older children are trying to
212.   peer in through a window. The rest are playing a game
          brought out from Kentucky and Tennessee by the early
          pioneers. They have formed a circle, and hand in hand
          they are passing under a bridge formed by the raised
          arms of two taller children, a Boy and a husky, rawboned
          girl. They are the Captains. As the circle revolves,
          they sing these words:

"The needle's eye that does supply
The thread that runs so true,
Many a beau I have let go
Because I wanted you.
Many a dark and stormy night
When I went home with you,
I stumped my toe and down I go
Because I wanted you. . . ."

The Captains let their arms drop around one of the Boys in
the circle, stopping it. They take him away from the circle.

> BOY CAPTAIN
> What you going to be, injun or
> white man?

> LITTLE BOY
> Injun . . .

They return to the others. The Boy and Girl form the bridge
again, the Little Boy standing behind the taller Boy. The
children in the circle form hands again and resume the game.

213-
228.   INT. CHURCH.   A Man (TRUMBULL) is on his feet, talking.

> TRUMBULL
> . . . This whole thing's been handled
> wrong. Here's those three killers
> walking the street bold as brass.
> Why didn't you arrest them, Marshal?
> Why ain't they behind bars? Then
> we'd only have Jordan to worry about,
> instead of the four of 'em! . . .

> DOANE
> (simply)
> I didn't have nothing to arrest 'em
> for, Mr. Trumbull. . . . They haven't
> done anything. There's no law
> against them sitting on a bench at
> the depot . . .

A Woman (MRS. SIMPSON) jumps to her feet.

> MRS. SIMPSON
> (excited)
> I can't listen to any more of this!
> What's the matter with you people?

                    MRS. SIMPSON (Cont'd.)
          Don't you remember when a decent
          woman couldn't walk down the street
          in broad daylight? Don't you re-
          member when this wasn't a fit place
          to bring up a child? How can you
          sit here and talk -- and talk and
          talk like this?

Another Woman, (MRS. FLETCHER) older, rises.

                    MRS. FLETCHER
          That's easy for you to say, Mrs.
          Simpson -- your husband's a hun-
          dred miles away. . . . Still, I
          ain't saying you're wrong. Only,
          those fellows are mighty bad. We
          need the strongest men we've got --
          young men --

A Very Young Woman, sitting beside her Young Husband,
bursts out.

                    YOUNG WOMAN
          Sure, let the young men do it!
          It's always the young men who
          have to do it, have to go out
          and do the killing and get
          killed before they do any living!
          Why don't the old men do it for
          once? They're king of walk when
          things are good! . . .

There is an outburst of sound. A Man leaps to his feet.

                    MAN
               (over)
          What are we all getting excited
          about? How do we know Jordan's
          on that train, anyway?

                    HENDERSON
               (quietly)
          I think we can be pretty sure
          he's on it. . . .
                    (he takes out his
                     watch, looks at it)

                    HENDERSON (Cont'd.)
              Time's getting short.
                (he turns to the Minister)
              Parson, you got anything to say?

                    MINISTER
                 (slowly)
              I don't know. . . . The Commandments
              say: Thou shalt not kill. . . . But
              we hire men to do it for us. . . .
              The right and the wrong seem pretty
              clear here, but if you're asking me
              to tell my people to go out and kill
              and maybe get themselves killed --
              I'm sorry -- I don't know what to
              say . . . I'm sorry . . .

The room is quiet. Finally Ezra raises his head.

                    EZRA
                 (to Henderson)
              What do you say, Jonas?

                    HENDERSON
              Alright, I say this -- What this
              town owes Will Doane here, you
              could never pay him with money,
              and don't ever forget it. Yes,
              he is the best marshal we ever
              had, maybe the best we'll ever
              have.

Doane listens gratefully.

                    HENDERSON
                 (continuing)
              Remember what this town was like
              before Will came here? Do we want
              it to be like that again? Of
              course we don't! So Jordan's
              coming back is our problem, not his.

The Men and Women listen intently.

                    HENDERSON
                 (continuing)
              It's our problem because it's our
              town. We built it with our own

                    HENDERSON (Cont'd.)
     hands, from nothing. . . . And if
     we want to keep it decent, keep it
     growing, then we got to think
     mighty clear here today -- and we
     got to have the courage to do the
     right thing, no matter how hard it
     is. . . . Alright. There's going
     to be a fight when Doane and Jordan
     meet, and somebody's going to get
     hurt, that's for sure. . . . Now,
     there's people up north who've
     been thinking about this town,
     and thinking mighty hard. They've
     been thinking about sending money
     down here -- to put up stores,
     build factories. . . . It'd mean a
     lot to this town, an awful lot.
     But when they read about shooting
     and killing in the streets, what
     are they going to think then? I'll
     tell you. They'll think this is
     just another wide open town, that's
     what. And everything we worked for
     is going to be wiped out in one day.
     This town is going to be set back five
     years, and I say we can't let that
     happen. . . . Mind you, you know how
     I feel about this man. He's a mighty
     brave man, a good man. He didn't
     have to come back today . . . and for
     his sake and the town's sake I wish
     he hadn't. Because if he's not here
     when Jordan comes in, my hunch is
     there won't be any trouble, not one
     bit. Tomorrow we'll have a new
     marshal, and if we all agree here
     to offer our services to him, I think
     we can handle anything that comes
     along. To me, that makes sense. To
     me, that's the only way out of this . . .

Almost without exception, the people are persuaded.

                    HENDERSON
                 (turning to Will)
     Will, I think you ought to go while
     there's still time. It's better

                              HENDERSON (Cont'd.)
                    for you -- and better for us . . .

Doane is staring at him, stunned. Then he looks out at
the silent people, reads the answer in their eyes, in
their averted or guarded faces. He turns from Henderson
and walks out of the church.

229.   EXT. CHURCH. The game has reached its climax as Doane
       emerges from the church. There are now two rows of
       children, each with their arms around the child in front.
       With the two Captains in the middle, a tug of war is going
       on. Doane stares at the screaming children for a moment,
       then goes wearily on, out of scene. The Girl-Captain's
       team pulls the other line of children over until it breaks.
       The game ends in a melee of breathless laughter and shouting.

230.   EXT. RAILROAD STATION. Jordan and Colby are removing their
       spurs. Pierce looks at his watch, then follows suit.

231-   CLOSEUP -- SALOON CLOCK. The time is 11:44. CAMERA PANS
233.   DOWN to Gillis and Two Men at the bar, looking up at the
       clock.

                              GILLIS
                            (finally)
                    Well, I got no use for him, but
                    I'll say this -- he's got guts . . .

The other Men nod their agreement. Harvey is alone at a
table near the window with a bottle and glass. Drink has
obviously not cooled his seething rage. Now, he hears
what Gillis has said, and reacts to it with a mixture of
anger and shame. He drinks. Of the Two Men beside Gillis,
we remember one of them as seeming sympathetic to Doane
in Scs. 126-130. He now picks up the conversation.

                         SYMPATHETIC MAN
                            (dryly)
                    That's mighty broadminded, Joe . . .

Gillis looks at him doubtfully, but the Sympathetic Man's
face is blandly innocent. Gillis' look slides away from
him and focuses on Harvey. He goes toward Harvey's table.

                              GILLIS
                    Now you, Harve -- I always figured
                    you for guts, but I never give you

>   GILLIS (Cont'd.)
>   credit for brains . . . till now . . .

Harvey doesn't know how to take this. Is Gillis accusing
him of cowardice?

>   HARVEY
>   What does that mean?

>   GILLIS
>   (sitting)
>   Nothing . . . only it takes a smart
>   man to know when to back away . . .

>   HARVEY
>   If I can't pick my company when
>   I drink in here, I ain't coming
>   here anymore.

>   GILLIS
>   (losing his smile)
>   Okay . . .

He gets up with bad grace and goes angrily back to the bar.
Harvey watches him go. Once back among his friends, however, Gillis' aplomb returns. He whispers something to a
Man at the bar, and the Man smiles quietly. Seething,
Harvey looks at the other occupants at the bar and sees
only blank faces, wise faces, shrewd eyes, unspoken amusement or contempt. But no one says anything. Furious,
Harvey turns away and pours himself a drink with fingers
trembling with rage. Then, as he drinks, his glance moves
to the window, and he sees something far down the street.

234.   LONG SHOT -- DOANE -- From Harvey's point of view. His
        figure is tiny but recognizable as he walks slowly up
        the quiet street.

235-   INT. SALOON. Harvey, in the foreground, reacts with blind
237.   rage to the sight of Doane. PAST him, the swinging door
        opens, and the Drunk comes in and goes directly to the bar.

>   DRUNK
>   (to Bartender)
>   I want a bottle.

The Bartender and those nearby stare at him.

                              DRUNK
                 I got the money . . .

He opens his hand and lets the silver dollar Doane has
given him fall on the bar. Surprised, the Bartender
gets a bottle and shoves it toward him. He takes it
and walks out.

                              GILLIS
                 Well, I'll be . . .

Harvey, staring through the window, is unaware of the
incident. He continues to watch Doane.

238.   EXT. STREET -- MED. FULL SHOT. Doane is continuing up
       the street. A man going in the opposite direction sees
       him, hesitates, then crosses the street to avoid meeting
       him. As the Man comes into CLOSER CAMERA VIEW, his face
       reveals his mixture of shame and relief.

239.   MED. CLOSE TRUCK SHOT -- DOANE -- as he realizes that he
       has been avoided, and his face, already drawn and sick,
       goes tighter.

240.   MED. TRUCK SHOT -- DOANE -- as he continues up the street,
       past the Two Oldsters, whom he passes in mutual silence,
       and then past the General Store. Through the window,
       altho Doane does not pause to look inside. Weaver and
       Sam can be seen at the safe in the rear. Doane continues
       to the end of the block. Almost without thinking, he
       stops there, staring almost blankly up the quiet street.

241.   FULL SHOT -- EXT. STREET -- from Doane's point of view.
       It stretches out, empty and dusty under the sun.

242.   MED. CLOSE SHOT -- DOANE. He becomes conscious of the
       sweat rolling down his forehead, and wipes his face
       with his handkerchief. Then, walking very slowly, he
       turns the corner, the CAMERA TRUCKING WITH him.

243.   INT. SALOON. Harvey has been watching Doane through the
       window. Now, he gets up suddenly, his face tight with
       decision, and goes out of the saloon.

244.   EXT. LIVERY STABLE. Doane approaches the entrance to the
       stable. It is closed. A crude sign on the door reads
       "GONE TO CHURCH." Doane goes around toward the rear of
       the stable.

245-
255.

INT. STABLE. A half-dozen horses are standing quietly in
their stalls as Doane enters the stable. He stands there
a moment, accustoming his eyes to the cool, quiet semi-
twilight after the harshness of the sunlight. Then,
slowly, he goes over to one of the stalls and looks at
the horse in it. It is a strong, fast animal, and the
CAMERA FOLLOWS Doane's eyes as they roam over the sleek
body and powerful legs. This horse could make a race of
it across the plains.

> HARVEY'S VOICE (o.s.)
> Put a saddle on him, Doane . . .

Surprised, Doane turns quickly, sees that Harvey has
come into the stable behind him. Harvey comes toward
him, his old confidence surging back into him.

> HARVEY
> Go on, saddle him. He'll go a
> long way before he tires. . . . That's
> what you were thinking, ain't it?

> DOANE
> Kind of . . .

Harvey studies his face with almost greedy curiosity.

> HARVEY
> You scared?

> DOANE
> I guess so.

> HARVEY
> (triumphantly)
> I knew it. It stands to reason. . . .
> (brushes past him)
> Come on, I'll help you --

He sees a saddle hanging nearby, takes it down and goes
to put it on the horse.

> HARVEY
> (almost feverishly)
> You've wasted a lot of time, but
> you still got a start. Milt and
> the others've been doing a lot of
> drinking. It might slow 'em up . . .

Doane has been watching Harvey as he throws the saddle
on the horse. He shrugs wearily.

>   DOANE
>   (smiling wryly)
>   Seems like all everybody and his
>   brother wants is to get me out
>   of town.

>   HARVEY
>   Well, nobody wants to see you
>   get killed.

Tiredly, Doane turns and starts out of the stable. Harvey
hears him, and turns quickly.

>   HARVEY
>   Hold it -- where you going?

>   DOANE
>   (dully)
>   I don't know. Back to the office,
>   I guess.

>   HARVEY
>   Oh, no! You're getting on that
>   horse and you're getting out!

Doane turns away from him. Harvey grabs his arm and turns
him back to face himself.

>   HARVEY
>   What's the matter with you? You
>   were ready to do it yourself --
>   you said so!

>   DOANE
>   Look, Harve, I thought about it
>   because I was tired. You think
>   about a lot of things when you're
>   tired -- when people cross the
>   street so they won't have to look
>   at your face. . . . And with everybody
>   telling me I ought to get out, for
>   a minute there I began to wonder
>   if they weren't right. . . . But I
>   can't do it . . .

                    HARVEY
              (almost frantic)
    Why?

                    DOANE
              (honestly)
    I don't know . . .

                    HARVEY
         Get on that horse, Will.

                    DOANE
         Why's it so important to you?
         You don't care if I live or die.

                    HARVEY
         Come on --

He starts to shove Doane toward the horse. Doane stands
his ground.

                    DOANE
         Don't shove me, Harve. I'm tired
         of being shoved. . . . I don't know
         what I'm going to do, but whatever
         it is it's going to be my way.

                    HARVEY
              (frantic now)
         You're getting out of town if I
         have to beat your brains out and
         tie you to that horse!

Doane jerks loose from him and starts out. Harvey swings
at him and connects to the back and side of his jaw, and
Doane goes face down to the stable floor. Harvey hurries
to him, grabs him and starts to drag him toward the horse.
He has started to lift Doane on the horse when Doane comes
to. He jerks out of Harvey's grasp. Disappointed, Harvey
launches himself at him. Doane sets himself as quickly as
he can, but Harvey's momentum lets him get the first blows
in, hard blows that send Doane reeling. Then Doane fights
back. They punish each other mercilessly, nothing barred.
The horses, becoming nervous, rear and whinny in their
stalls. Doane goes down again, then Harvey. They roll
and tumble under the rearing hooves of the horses. Once,
Doane is knocked down under a horse, and narrowly escapes

being trampled. As the fight reaches a climax, the horses
go completely wild. Then, finally, Doane connects with a
series of crushing blows, and Harvey goes down and out.
Doane stands over him, panting and dazed. Then, almost
staggering, he goes to a bag of feed, slumps exhaustedly
down on it, and sits there, his breath whistling through
his bruised lips.

256.   INT. HOTEL LOBBY. Amy is staring up at the clock. The
time is ten to twelve. Behind his desk, the Clerk is
whistling softly as he goes about his work. Amy comes
to a decision. She rises and goes to the desk.

> AMY
> (quietly)
> Excuse me --
> > (then, as the Clerk
> > looks at her)
> What is Mrs. Ramirez' room
> number?

The Clerk looks at her. Then a glitter of amusement comes
into his eyes.

> CLERK
> Three . . .

> AMY
> (maintaining her poise)
> Thank you.

She turns from him and goes to the stairs.

257.   INT. HOTEL STAIRWAY -- on Amy as she mounts the stairs.

258.   INT. HALLWAY -- on Amy as she reaches the second floor and
looks about uncertainly. Then she moves doubtfully down
the hall in the direction of Helen's rooms, and sees the
number on Helen's door. She pulls herself together and
knocks.

259-   INT. HELEN'S FRONT ROOM. Helen and Sam are facing each
262.   other across the table, on which lies a small stack of
money. They react to Amy's knock.

> HELEN
> Come in --

The door opens, and Amy stands in the doorway. Helen
and Sam stare at her in surprise, and Amy remains rooted
there, confused by Sam's presence and her first sight of
Helen. Helen recovers first.

> HELEN
> Yes -- ?

> AMY
> Mrs. Ramirez?
> (as Helen nods)
> I'm Mrs. Doane . . .

> HELEN
> I know.

> AMY
> May I come in?

> HELEN
> If you like . . .

Sam takes his cue and goes out silently as Amy comes into
the room. Now that she has come this far, she is confused
and uncertain again. The two women take each other in for
a long moment. Finally, Helen breaks the strained silence.

> HELEN
> Sit down, Mrs. Doane . . .

> AMY
> No, thank you . . .

> HELEN
> (sharply)
> What do you want?

Amy realizes that Helen has misunderstood her refusal.

> AMY
> Please . . . it's just that I'm
> afraid if I sat down I wouldn't
> be able to get up again.

> HELEN
> Why?

> AMY
> It wasn't easy for me to come here . . .

                        HELEN
                    (unrelenting)
            Why?

                        AMY
                    (meeting the issue)
            Look, Mrs. Ramirez . . . Will and I
            were married an hour ago -- we
            were all packed and ready to
            leave. . . . Then this thing happened,
            and he wouldn't go. I did every-
            thing -- I pleaded. I threatened
            him -- I couldn't reach him.

Helen has been listening intently, watching Amy's face.

                        HELEN
            And now?

                        AMY
                    (quietly)
            That man downstairs -- the clerk --
            he said things about you and Will. . . .
            I've been trying to understand why
            he wouldn't go away with me. Now
            all I can think of is that it's got
            to be because of you.

                        HELEN
                    (deliberately)
            What do you want from me?

                        AMY
            Let him go! He's still got a
            chance -- let him go!

There is a pause. Helen has a brief inner struggle, then
decides to be honest.

                        HELEN
                    (flatly)
            I can't help you.

                        AMY
            Please . . .

                        HELEN
            He's not staying for me. I

                    HELEN (Cont'd.)
              haven't spoken to him for a
              year -- until today. I told
              him to go. I'm leaving on
              the same train you are . . .

Amy stares at her, believing her. But with belief, her
confusion returns.

                         AMY
              Then what is it? Why?

                        HELEN
              If you don't know, I can't explain
              it to you . . .

                         AMY
                       (dully)
              Thank you . . . anyway. You've been
              very kind.

She turns and starts out.

                        HELEN
                 (lashing out at her)
              What kind of a woman are you? How
              can you leave him like this? Does
              the sound of guns frighten you that
              much?

Amy has turned and waited her out.

                         AMY
                 (quietly, with great
                  dignity)
              No, Mrs. Ramirez. I've heard
              guns. My father and my brother
              were killed by guns. They were
              on the right side, but it didn't
              help them when the shooting
              started. My brother was nineteen.
              I watched him die. . . . That's when I
              became a Quaker -- because every
              other religion said it was alright
              for people to kill each other at
              least once in a while. . . . I don't care
              who's right or wrong! There's got to
              be some better way for people to live! . . .

She starts out again.

> HELEN
> (gently)
> Just a minute. . . .
> (as Amy turns)
> Are you going to wait for the train
> downstairs?
> (as Amy nods)
> That man down there can't be much
> company. Why don't you wait here?

> AMY
> (reacting to the sympathy
> in her tone)
> Thank you. I will . . .

She comes forward into the room again, sees the chair Helen
has offered her before, hesitates an instant, then sits
down. Helen takes another chair. For a moment the silence
is strained again. Amy looks down at the arms of the chair
she is sitting in, realizing that Will must have sat here
many times in the past. Her eyes go about the room, and
finally reach Helen. Helen is aware of what Amy is thinking.
She nods in quiet affirmation. Amy takes it.

263. INT. STABLE. Doane has recovered and is on his feet now.
His face is still marked and bloodstained, but he is
attempting with his battered hands to bring some semblance
of order to his clothing. Finished, he looks down at his
bruised knuckles and fingers, then starts out. Seeing a
bucket of water, he stops, looks back where Harvey is still
lying unconscious on the stable floor, picks up the bucket,
goes to Harvey and douses his limp body with it. Then he
tosses the bucket aside and goes out.

264. EXT. STABLE -- TRUCK SHOT -- on Doane as he comes out of the
stable and moves wearily up the street to the main street,
and turns the corner into it.

265. EXT. BARBER SHOP. Doane approaches it and goes in.

266- INT. BARBER SHOP. The Barber, alone in the shop, is putting
268. his instruments in a cupboard as Doane comes in. There is
the SOUND of hammering from the rear.

> DOANE
> You got some clean water I can use?

The Barber turns and recognizes him.

                    BARBER
            Why, sure, Marshal --
                (then, looking at
                 him more closely)
            Sure, sure . . .
                (he motions to
                 the chair)
            Sit down --

Doane goes over to it and sinks into it. The Barber draws
some water, staring over his shoulder at Doane. He gets a
towel and soaks it in the water.

                    BARBER
            Run into some kind of trouble,
            Marshal?

                    DOANE
            No trouble . . .

He becomes conscious of the hammering. The Barber comes
over with the wet towel.

                    DOANE
            What are you building?

The Barber is embarrassed and ashamed.

                    BARBER
            Just -- just fixing things up
            out back. . . .
                (recovering)
            Now take it easy, Mr. Doane.
            Just settle back --

Doane relaxes and closes his eyes. The Barber carefully
wraps the wet towel about his face, then hurries to the
rear door.

                    BARBER
                (sharply)
            Fred -- !
                (as the hammering
                 continues)
            Fred! . . . Hold it a while,
            will you?

The hammering stops.

> FRED'S VOICE
> (puzzled)
> Hold it?

> BARBER
> (cutting in)
> You just stop until I tell you
> to start again -- !

He turns from the doorway, gets a basin and fills it
with water. He takes it to Doane, sets it in his
lap, then takes Doane's battered hands and puts them
in the basin, looking at the bruised knuckles with
curiosity as he does so. He stares at Doane's hidden
face for a moment, then looks up at the clock. CAMERA
PANS UP to it. It is seven minutes to twelve.

269-270. OUT

271. EXT. RAILROAD STATION. Jordan, Pierce and Colby are
      checking their guns, carefully reloading them and
      adjusting their belts and holsters. Beside Milt there
      is an extra gun-belt holding two guns.

272. INT. STABLE. Harvey is straightening his clothes. The
      fine patina of confidence and conceit is gone and he
      looks utterly crushed and defeated. He goes wearily out.

273. INT. BARBER SHOP. The Barber watches Doane as he adjusts
      his coat, takes a final look at his face in the mirror,
      and starts out.

> DOANE
> Thanks --

He goes on to the door.

> BARBER
> You're welcome, Marshal.

Doane stops at the door, reaches into a pocket, fishes
out a coin.

> BARBER
> Oh, no charge, Marshal --

Doane looks at him, untouched by his eagerness to please.
Deliberately, he flips it to the Barber, who catches it.

> DOANE
> (and he knows what he
> is talking about)
> You can tell your man to go back
> to work now . . .

He goes out. The Barber stares after him as he passes
the window. Then he shrugs helplessly, and goes to the
rear door.

> BARBER
> (calling out)
> Alright, Fred. Go ahead . . .

274. EXT. MARSHAL'S OFFICE. Doane approaches the office,
eyes narrowed against the glare of the sun. He sees
that his note still flutters on the door. He rips it
off, starts in, then stops and looks up at the sky.

275. FULL SHOT -- SKY. The glaring white-hot ball of fire is
almost exactly at its zenith. It hangs there, baleful,
merciless.

276. MED. CLOSE SHOT -- DOANE. He squints, rubs his eyes,
goes into his office.

277-
280.   INT. MARSHAL'S OFFICE. Baker, armed, is pacing the floor
tensely. In a corner of the room, almost hidden in the
shadow, the Boy Doane had sent to find the selectmen is
standing. Baker turns quickly as Doane comes in and
tries to accustom his eyes to the change in light.

> BAKER
> Will --

Doane stares at him with relief and remembrance.

> DOANE
> I guess I forgot about you, Herb.
> I'm sure glad you're here.

He goes to his desk.

> BAKER
> I couldn't figure out what was

                    BAKER (Cont'd.)
          keeping you. Time's getting
          short.

Doane looks up at the wall clock. It is five to twelve.

                    DOANE
          Sure is . . .

                    BAKER
          When are the other boys going to
          get here? We got to make plans . . .

                    DOANE
          The other boys?

He realizes that Baker does not know. He turns to face him.

                    DOANE
          There aren't any other boys, Herb.
          It's just you and me . . .

                    BAKER
          You're joking . . .

                    DOANE
          No. I couldn't get anybody.

                    BAKER
          I don't believe it! This town
          ain't that low --

                    DOANE
          I couldn't get anybody . . .

Baker stares at him. Then, suddenly, full realization
of the situation comes to him.

                    BAKER
          Then it's just you and me?

                    DOANE
          I guess so.

In his corner, forgotten by Baker and unseen by Doane,
the Boy looks on, fascinated.

                    BAKER
You and me, against Jordan and --
all four of 'em . . .

                    DOANE
That's right. . . . You want
out, Herb?

                    BAKER
          (writhing inwardly)
Well, it's not that I want out, no.
But . . . I'll tell you the truth. . . .
I didn't figure on anything like this,
Doane. Nothing like this --

                    DOANE
          (smiling mirthlessly)
Neither did I . . .

                    BAKER
          (with growing terror)
I volunteered. You know I did.
You didn't have to come to me.
I was ready. . . . I'm ready now!
But this is different. This
ain't like what you said it was
going to be. . . . This is just plain
committing suicide, that's what
it is! And for what? Why me?
I'm no law-man -- I just live here! . . .
I got nothing personal against
anybody -- I got no stake in this!

                    DOANE
          (harshly)
I guess not . . .

                    BAKER
There's a limit how much you can
ask a man! -- I've got a wife and
kids! . . . What about my kids?
It's not fair -- you ain't got the
right to ask it --

                    DOANE
Go home to your kids, Herb . . .

Baker grabs up his rifle and starts toward the door.

He stops, striving for a remnant of decency.

> BAKER
> You get some other fellows, and
> I'll still go through with it,
> Doane --

> DOANE
> (harshly)
> Go on home, Herb!

Baker hurries out. The door slams loudly behind him.
Doane stares into nothing for a moment, turns and sits
down automatically. Then his control gives way, and
the tide of bitterness and anger overflows in him. He
pounds his battered fists on the desk top brutally,
almost sobbing his outrage. The surge of emotion ebbs.
Gradually, Doane reclaims his hold on himself. In the
corner, the Boy looks on, wide-eyed and frightened.
Doane straightens, wipes his face and eyes, turns his
chair and sees the Boy.

> DOANE
> (brusquely)
> What do you want?

> BOY
> (frightened)
> I found 'em, Marshal, like you
> wanted me to -- all but Mr.
> Henderson.

Doane is fully himself now.

> DOANE
> (wryly)
> I found him. . . . Thanks . . .

> BOY
> Oh, you're welcome --

He hesitates, afraid to say what he has in mind. Doane
looks at him quizzically. He comes to him.

> BOY
> (eagerly)
> Marshal - listen -- let me fight
> with you! I'm not afraid!

              DOANE
No.

              BOY
Please, let me, Marshal!

              DOANE
You're a kid. You're a baby . . .

              BOY
I'm sixteen! And I can handle a
gun, too. You ought to see me --

              DOANE
You're fourteen. . . . What do you
want to lie for?

              BOY
Well, I'm big for my age. . . .
Please, Marshal . . .

              DOANE
No!
        (he rises and goes
        to him)
You're big for your age, alright. . . .
But you get out of here --

              BOY
Aw, please . . .

              DOANE
Go on, go on . . .

He turns away. The Boy starts unhappily to the door.
Doane stops, turns back to him.

              DOANE
        (gently)
Johnny . . .

Johnny turns to him, his eyes brimming over.

              DOANE
        Thanks . . .
He gives a little wave, as when a man says goodby to a
friend. Johnny manages to muster a kind of a smile and
returns the gesture. Then he is gone. Doane looks after

him, almost smiling, the rage and bitterness in him
leavened a little. Then he goes to his desk, sits down,
takes his guns out of their holsters and checks them
methodically. His bruised fingers are clumsy. He puts
his gun down and looks down at his hands ruefully. He
rubs and kneads his fingers, then picks up the gun again.

281.   CLOSEUP -- GUN IN DOANE'S HAND. It looks deadly.

282.   BACK TO SCENE. Doane stares down at the gun. His hand
turns the barrel upward, pointing toward his face. For
an instant it almost seems as if he is weighing the
benefits of a quick, more merciful self-inflicted death.
He presses the trigger. The safety catch is on. It
clicks harmlessly. He picks up the other gun in his
left hand and works the trigger on it. Then, putting
down both guns, he opens a drawer, takes out a box of
bullets and stuffs bullets into his coat pockets.

283.   EXT. RAILROAD STATION. Jordan and the others have moved
down to the track. Jordan is pacing tensely. Pierce
and Colby are staring down the gleaming track. There is
no sign of the train in the distance.

284.   INT. CHURCH. The congregation is singing a hymn.
Henderson, as he sings, takes out his watch and looks
at it. He shakes his head slightly, returns his watch,
and keeps on singing.

285-286. OUT.

287.   CLOSE SHOT -- WOODEN SIGN. Weatherbeaten and so faded
that it is difficult to read, it says:

"STAGE STATION"

288.   EXT. CORRAL. We see now that the sign is over the corral
gates. Near the gates, Toby has Peterson tied hand and
foot in a sitting position, and he is now tying him to
one of the fence rails. In the b.g., MARTINEZ, a middle-
aged Mexican, has tethered the horses. He comes out of
the corral and looks on as Toby finishes and straightens.

                    MARTINEZ
                  (interested)
          What he do?

                    TOBY
      Oh, he's a bad boy. . . . Very bad . . .

He turns and starts for the low house past the corral,
and Martinez falls in alongside, the CAMERA TRUCKING
WITH them.

>   TOBY
>   How's the beer?

>   MARTINEZ
>   How is my cerveza?

He shrugs contemptuously.

>   TOBY
>   Cold?

>   MARTINEZ
>   Like weel water . . .

Toby smiles happily. They have reached the house.

289- EXT. MARTINEZ HOUSE. Toby sprawls on the porch step, as
293. Martinez goes on into the house. Toby lets himself go,
      stretching his tired and aching muscles, then starts to
      roll a cigarette. Martinez comes out with a copper
      pitcher and two mugs. He starts to pour beer for Toby
      and himself.

>   TOBY
>   How's business?

>   MARTINEZ
>   It will be better when the stage
>   runs again.

>   TOBY
>   That stage ain't never going to
>   run again. Ain't you heard? We
>   got a railroad now.

>   MARTINEZ
>   (shrugging)
>   Railroad . . .

Toby looks down at his beer with delight, then takes a
long drink. He sighs happily.

>   MARTINEZ
>   I go to the horses now. You
>   wish your friend to drink?

Toby hesitates, then his good nature gives in.

                    TOBY
          Give him beer. . . . But be careful.
          Muy malo . . .

Martinez shrugs again, pours a mugful of beer, sets the
pitcher down and goes out of scene. Toby takes another
drink. A pretty young Mexican Girl comes out. She
recognizes him.

                    MEXICAN GIRL
          Look who's here. Wild Bill
          Hickock . . .

                    TOBY
          Ah, Chicquita. . . . Come esta?

It is obvious that they know each other well.

                    MEXICAN GIRL
          If you really want to know, you
          come by once in a while.

                    TOBY
          I been busy . . .

                    MEXICAN GIRL
          Sure. You're a big man. Very
          busy. Very important . . .

Grinning, Toby shoves over his empty mug. Carelessly,
she moves it back with her toe.

                    MEXICAN GIRL
          What happened to your clothes?

                    TOBY
          I been swimming.

                    MEXICAN GIRL
          In your clothes?

                    TOBY
          Sure . . .

                    MEXICAN GIRL
          You're crazy.

>   TOBY
>   I got a crazy job.

He flicks the mug closer to her. Again she inches it
back to him with an insolently provocative toe-nudge.

>   MEXICAN GIRL
>   You going to stay a while?

>   TOBY
>   I got to go. I got a prisoner.
>   Besides, I'm invited to a
>   wedding . . .

>   MEXICAN GIRL
>   If you stay a while, I'll wash
>   your shirt . . .

Their eyes meet and hold. Toby turns and looks out to
where Peterson is sprawled near the fence. Then he
takes out his large old-fashioned watch, looks at it,
puts it to his ear, shakes it, puts it to his ear again.
He shrugs.

>   TOBY
>   What do you know. Must have
>   stopped when I went swimming --

He puts the watch away, his eyes meeting the Girl's again.

>   TOBY
>   Ah -- I probably missed that
>   wedding anyway . . .

Smiling, the Girl bends and gets his mug and starts to
fill it with beer.

294.   CLOSEUP -- CLOCK IN MARSHAL'S OFFICE. The time is two
        minutes to twelve. CAMERA PANS DOWN to Doane, writing
        at his desk.

295.   INSERT -- DOANE'S HAND -- as it writes:

>   LAST WILL AND TESTAMENT

As he crosses the last "T" he pauses. In the silence the
loud ticking of the clock can be heard. Deliberately, he
draws a line under the words.

296.   INT. SALOON. All the Men are silently watching the clock.

297-   INT. HELEN'S FRONT ROOM. Amy is still in the chair, lost
300.   in her thoughts. Helen is standing at the window, looking
        down into the street.

                    HELEN
          Where are you going when you
          leave town?

                    AMY
          Home. St. Louis . . .

                    HELEN
              (turning to her)
          All that way alone?

                    AMY
          That's the way I came. . . . My family
          didn't want me to marry Will in
          the first place. . . . I seem to make them
          unhappy no matter what I do. Back
          home they think I'm very strange.
          I'm a feminist. You know, women's
          rights -- things like that. . . .
              (she looks up at Helen)
          Where will you go?

Helen shrugs.

                    AMY
          Why are you going? Are you afraid
          of that man?

                    HELEN
          Not afraid, no. . . . There are
          very few men who cannot be managed,
          one way or another . . .

They each think of Doane, and look at each other.
Then Helen goes on.

                    HELEN
          I'm just tired. . . .
              (she starts to pace)
          I hate this town. I've always hated
          it. To be a Mexican woman in a town
          like this. . . .
              (she shakes her head)

HELEN (Cont'd.)
I married Ramirez when I was sixteen.
He was fat and ugly, foolish. When
he touched me, I would feel sick.
But he had money. When he died, I
had money. . . . I sold the saloon.
I bought the biggest store in town.
Nobody knew. I hired a big citizen
to run it for me. Nobody knew that
either. Big citizens do many things
for money. . . . And all the fine ladies,
who never saw me when they passed me
on the street, they paid me their
money and they never knew. . . . I
enjoyed it for a while. But now . . .
    (she shrugs again)

AMY
    (after a pause)
I understand . . .

HELEN
You do? That's good. I don't
understand you. . . .
    (as Amy looks at her)
No matter what you say, if Doane
was my man, I'd never leave here.
I'd get a gun -- I'd fight . . .

AMY
    (deliberately)
Why don't you?

HELEN
He's not my man . . .

She turns suddenly and goes to one of her bags, opens
it quickly, rummages in it, comes up with a gun.

HELEN
Here. Take this. You're his wife . . .

AMY
    (sharply)
No! If I did I'd be saying my
whole life up to now was wrong!

HELEN
Right, wrong, what's the difference?
He's your man --

AMY
(rising)
Is he? What made him my_man? A
few words spoken by a Judge? Does
that make a marriage? . . . There's
too much wrong between us -- it
doesn't fit! Anyway, this is what
he chose . . .

There is an instant of complete silence, which is
shattered suddenly by the distant but loud, hoarse scream of
a train whistle. Involuntarily, both women react physically.

301.   INT. MARSHAL'S OFFICE. The train whistle continues OVER.
Doane has been sitting at his desk, writing. He sits
there, frozen.

302.   EXT. STREET. The Two Old Men listen. The Train whistle
continues OVER.

303.   INT. SALOON. Train whistle OVER. The Men are rooted in
their places.

304.   INT. ROOM. Harvey is sprawled on the rumpled bed. There
is a bottle nearby. He hears the whistle.

305.   EXT. RAILROAD STATION. Train whistle OVER. Jordan,
Pierce and Colby are standing at the tracks. The train
is not yet visible. Then the whistle stops. They look.

306.   EXT. COUNTRYSIDE -- TRAIN TRACKS. In the distance a small
cloud of smoke can be seen.

307.   INT. MARSHAL'S OFFICE -- on Doane -- as he waits. Then
there is the sound of the SECOND WHISTLE.

308.   INT. CHURCH. The Congregation is on its feet, Henderson
in the f.g., but no one is singing as the train whistle
continues OVER.

309.   MED. CLOSE SHOT -- ORGANIST. He is working the keys but
the music emerges with the sound of the whistle.

310.   INT. FULLER LIVING ROOM. Train whistle OVER. Fuller and
his wife listen.

311.   INT. MARTIN HOWE'S HOUSE. Train whistle OVER. Howe sits
       in his chair, listening.

312.   INT. SALOON. Train whistle OVER. The Men listen.

313.   INT. HELEN'S FRONT ROOM. Train whistle OVER. Helen and
       Amy listen. The whistle dies.

314.   INT. DOANE'S OFFICE. He waits.

315.   EXT. STATION. Jordan, Pierce and Colby wait. There is
       still no sign of the train. They look at each other
       tensely.

316.   INT. STATIONMASTER'S OFFICE. He stands rooted, waiting.

317.   INT. HELEN'S FRONT ROOM. Amy and Helen look at each other,
       their eyes asking the question they are afraid to speak.

318.   INT. SALOON. The Men begin to look at each other wonder-
       ingly.

319.   INT. MARSHAL'S OFFICE. Doane waits.

320.   EXT. COUNTRYSIDE -- on the moving train.

321.   INT. MARSHAL'S OFFICE. On Doane waiting. He starts to
       put down the pen he has been holding, and now, louder
       than before, the third whistle blasts OVER the scene.
       Doane quivers. The breath he has been holding escapes
       in a long soundless sigh.

322.   EXT. RAILROAD STATION. Jordan, Pierce and Colby look at
       each other in triumph. In the distance, the train becomes
       visible.

323.   INT. SALOON. As the whistle dies, the Men stampede out.
       The saloon is empty. From outside, we hear the click of
       Gillis' key in the lock, see the knob turn as he tries it.

324.   INT. HELEN'S FRONT ROOM. Helen and Amy are both on their
       feet, and Sam has Helen's bag. They move numbly toward
       the door.

                          HELEN
                        (quietly)
                   Can I ride with you to the
                   station?

                          AMY
                Of course . . .

        They start out.

325.   INT. MARSHAL'S OFFICE. Doane signs his name to what he
        has written, folds it, then writes on it:

                TO BE OPENED IN THE EVENT OF
                        MY DEATH.

        He places the folded testament in the center of his desk,
        and then puts the cartridge box on it for a paper-weight.
        He rises, takes a deep breath.

326.   EXT. HOTEL. The Clerk is closing the metal shutters.
        They clang into place.

327.   SERIES OF SHOTS -- of shutters, windows and doors being
        closed all over town.

328.   EXT. RAILROAD STATION. Jordan, Pierce and Colby watch
        as the approaching train draws nearer. The noise of
        its engine and wheels can be heard plainly now.

329.   INT. MARSHAL'S OFFICE. Doane takes a last look around
        the office and goes out.

330.   EXT. MARSHAL'S OFFICE -- as Doane emerges into the sunlight.
        He looks around.

331.   EXT. STREET -- FROM DOANE'S POINT OF VIEW. It is completely
        deserted. CAMERA PANS to other extreme of the street.
        It, too, is empty.

332.   CLOSE SHOT -- DOANE. He smiles mirthlessly. Suddenly,
        there is the SOUND of horses' hooves, and he turns.

°333.   EXT. STREET. The buckboard, Amy driving and Helen beside
        her, comes down the street toward Doane.

334.   CLOSE SHOT -- DOANE -- as he sees and recognizes them.

335.   MED. CLOSE SHOT -- AMY AND HELEN -- as they see Doane.

336.   CLOSE SHOT -- DOANE -- as he watches them approach.

337.   CLOSEUP -- HELEN. She is at her best. Her eyes are
        looking directly toward Doane, and there is a faint

smile on her lips.

338. CLOSEUP -- AMY. She has never looked more beautiful.
Her eyes avoid Doane's.

339. CLOSEUP -- DOANE -- as he stares o.s. at life itself.

340. EXT. MARSHAL'S OFFICE -- as the buckboard sweeps past
Doane. We see that Sam is sitting in the back among
the luggage. It passes out of scene.

341. MED. CLOSE SHOT -- DOANE -- as he looks after the buckboard.
Then, with an effort, he pulls himself together, takes
out his watch and looks at the time.

342-
343. EXT. RAILROAD STATION. The train pulls in. Conductors
alight. Jordan, Pierce and Colby wait impatiently. Then,
one of the car doors opens, and a moment later GUY JORDAN
steps out into the sunlight. He is a big man, pale, but
dangerous looking, implacable. The three men hurry to
him. Smiling, they extend their hands to him. Jordan is
not surprised to see them. He shakes hands unsmilingly,
then moves off to a more secluded portion of the platform.
They follow him.

344. EXT. STATION -- ANOTHER ANGLE -- as the buckboard drives
into the station yard and stops near the tracks. Sam
jumps down and begins to unload the luggage, and Amy
and Helen climb down.

345. GROUP SHOT. Jordan extends his hand inquiringly to
Milt. Smiling, Milt hands him two guns. Guy takes no
chances. He checks both guns. Then, looking up, his
glance goes o.s. and is caught there.

346. EXT. RAILROAD CAR. Sam is helping Amy up the steps.
As she goes in and he extends an arm to Helen, she
looks off toward Guy.

347. MED. CLOSE SHOT -- GUY JORDAN -- as his eyes meet Helen's.

348. MED. CLOSE SHOT -- HELEN. Her eyes meet Guy's calmly.
Then, taking her time, she climbs the steps into the car.

349. GROUP SHOT. Guy watches her disappear without expression.
Nothing can interfere with the business at hand. He nods
to the others, and starts out of the station. They follow
him.

350.   INT. RAILROAD CAR. Amy is sitting by the window, pale,
       tense. Helen is beside her on the aisle, Sam putting away
       the last of the luggage. He comes to Helen and they look
       at each other in silence. It is a difficult parting for
       both of them.

                            SAM
                         (finally)
                   So long, Helen . . .

                            HELEN
                   Good-by, Sam. . . . You'll hear
                   from me . . .

                            SAM
                         (nodding)
                   Take care . . .

       Sam's tight, weather-beaten face breaks into something
       like a smile, and he goes out quickly. There is the
       sudden o.s. blast of the train whistle.

351.   EXT. MARSHAL'S OFFICE. Doane reacts to the whistle. He
       feels for his guns, then starts slowly but firmly down the
       street.

352.   EXT. STREET -- on Jordan and the others as they come up the
       middle of the street.

353.   EXT. TOWN -- HIGH SHOT of the main street. We see the
       small figures approaching each other, hidden from each
       other by the bend of the street.

354.   MED. CLOSE TRUCK SHOT -- DOANE. As he continues, keeping
       along the sidewalk.

355.   CLOSE TRUCKING GROUP SHOT -- on Jordan and the others.

356.   CLOSE TRUCK SHOT -- DOANE -- going on.

357.   EXT. STREET -- on Jordan and the others. Suddenly Milt
       stops, his attention caught by a shop window. As he darts
       over to it, the others stop, startled. Milt reaches the
       shop. It has women's hats of the period on display.
       Deliberately, Milt smashes the window with his gun butt,
       reaches in and takes out a hat. Guy Jordan's grim face
       tightens.

> GUY JORDAN
> (angrily)
> Can't you wait?

> MILT
> Just want to be ready . . .

He stuffs the hat under his shirt and hurries to rejoin them. They continue up the street.

358. EXT. STREET -- on Doane as he continues. He reaches the bend, pauses, then takes shelter in the space between two houses. He waits there.

359. MED. CLOSE SHOT -- DOANE. As he waits tensely.

360. EXT. STREET. Jordan and the others come into scene. They pass Doane's hiding place and continue on. Doane lets them go about twenty feet, then draws his guns.

> DOANE
> (calling)
> Jordan -- !

The other men turn, drawing as they do. Milt is the first to shoot. His shot misses Doane, but Doane does not miss him. Milt whirls and goes down. Bullets from the other three pockmark the wall behind Doane. He returns the fire, then runs for it.

361. INT. RAILROAD CAR -- AMY AND HELEN. They sit tensely, as the SOUND of the gun fight comes OVER. Then, suddenly, the firing stops, and there is a dead silence. Helen slumps a little, believing the fight is over and Doane is dead. Amy stares at her, and then, beside herself, leaps to her feet, brushes past Helen and runs wildly to the door.

362. EXT. RAILROAD STATION. Amy climbs down the steps and runs wildly out of the station. In the b.g., the Stationmaster is the centre of a curious group composed of the train crew and passengers.

363. EXT. MAIN STREET. On Amy as she runs up the deserted street.

364. EXT. STREET -- SHOOTING PAST Milt's body toward the bend in the street. In the b.g., Amy's figure runs into view, then stops short as she sees the body.

365.   CLOSE SHOT -- AMY as she sees Milt's body and thinks that
       it is Doane's. CAMERA PANS with her as she runs toward it.

366.   EXT. STREET -- Milt's body in the f.g., the hat he has stolen
       lying beside him. Amy runs toward CAMERA, finally crumples
       to her knees at Milt's body. To her amazement and relief,
       she sees that it is not Doane. There is a fusilade of o.s.
       shots, and she realizes that the gunfight is still going on.

367.   EXT. BACK ALLEY -- on Doane as he runs, bent low. There is
       a shot from ahead, and he ducks into the shelter of a shed.
       He peers in the direction of the shot.

368.   EXT. ALLEY -- FROM DOANE'S POINT OF VIEW. Colby is at the
       other end of the alley, behind shelter.

369.   INT. SHED. Doane goes to the other side of the shed, peers
       through a crack. Through it, the figures of Guy Jordan and
       Pierce can be seen coming into the other end of the alley.
       Doane fires at Jordan, misses, and they duck out of sight.
       There is a burst of shots from Colby and an answering burst
       from the other two. Doane throws himself on the ground. He
       surveys his situation, realizing he is caught in a cross-fire.

370.   EXT. STREET. Amy is on her feet now, hearing the o.s.
       SHOTS. She starts uncertainly up the street.

371.   INT. SHED. Doane crawls to the door of the shed, and looks
       out.

372   EXT. STABLE -- from Doane's point of view. Its wide door,
       diagonally across the alley from Doane, is open.

373.   INT. STABLE. Doane makes up his mind to try for it. He
       gets to his feet, crouches, launches himself out.

374.   EXT. ALLEY -- as Doane's crouched body cannonballs across
       the alley, untouched.

375.   INT. STABLE. Doane's body hurtles into the stable and
       hits the floor. He lies there, struggling for breath.
       The horses whinny and rear nervously.

376.   EXT. ALLEY. Jordan, Pierce and Colby move cautiously
       toward the stable.

377.   INT. STABLE. Doane gets up, looks around, climbs up to
       the loft.

378. INT. LOFT. Doane goes toward a large opening in the loft
wall. From here, he and the CAMERA have a good high view
of the alley. Jordan and Pierce at their end and Colby at
his end are both in view. Doane takes aim at Colby, but
misses. Colby and the others duck out of sight. Pierce
dashes across the alley, Doane firing but missing him.

379. EXT. STABLE -- as Pierce crawls around to the rear of the
stable and takes shelter. He begins to fire into the stable.

380. EXT. ALLEY -- COLBY -- as he fires.

381. EXT. ALLEY -- GUY JORDAN -- as he fires.

382. INT. LOFT -- as bullets from all three directions hit into
the loft. There is a scream of pain from one of the horses
below. Bullets continue into the loft. Doane crawls to
the ladder and climbs down.

383. INT. STABLE. Doane comes down into the stable. The horses
are mad with fear. Doane goes to them. In one of the stalls,
one of the horses had been hit and is down. Doane hurries
to the stable door and slides it shut. He finds some small
shelter behind some bags of feed, and painfully begins to
load his guns.

384. EXT. ALLEY -- JORDAN. He studies the situation, as o.s.
shots come from Colby and Pierce. Looking around, he
sees that he is behind the general store. He gets an
idea, goes to the rear door and deliberately kicks it
in. He disappears inside and returns in a moment carrying
three oil lamps. Coming back to his place, he takes aim
and throws one.

385. EXT. STABLE -- as the lamp flies against the stable door
and smashes against it, spattering oil against the door.

386. INT. STABLE -- Doane as he reacts to the sound of the
lamp as it lands. Then he hears another lamp smashing
on the stable wall.

387. EXT. ALLEY -- ON JORDAN SHOOTING TOWARD STABLE -- as Jordan
flings the third lamp toward the stable. It takes a high
arc and lands near the stable. Then Jordan takes careful
aim, and fires. We see one of the lamps explode, bouncing
crazily against the stable and splattering fire against it.
Jordan fires again, misses his target, fires again, hits it.

There is another explosion, and another splash of oil and fire on the stable door.

388.   EXT. STABLE -- LAMP IN FOREGROUND. There is the SOUND of JORDAN'S o.s. shot, and we see the lamp explode and carom off the ground against the stable. Another sheet of flame falls on the wooden stable wall. Flames begin to spread along the front of the stable.

389.   INT. STABLE -- ON DOANE -- as he realizes what is happening. The horses are increasingly mad with fear.

390.   INT. MARSHAL'S OFFICE. Amy comes in, breathless, confused, terrified. Exhausted now, she can go no further; indeed she does not know where to go. She sees Doane's testament on the desk, goes to it, reads the inscription. There is the o.s. WHISTLE of the train.

391.   INT. STABLE. Fire is eating away at the door, and smoke is beginning to fill the stable. Doane goes to one of the stalls and leads out the maddened horse. One by one he leads all the horses out of their stalls, pulls them toward the door, manages with a mighty effort to slide the door open, and then sends the rearing, screaming horses out into the alley.

392.   EXT. ALLEY -- as the horses burst out into the alley and scatter wildly. At their opposite ends of the alley, Jordan and Colby take cover. Doane slips out of the stable and around it.

393.   EXT. RAILROAD STATION. The train is pulling out, the faces of the passengers pressed against the windows.

394.   EXT. WOODED AREA -- as Doane passes the CAMERA on the run. A moment later, the three men enter the scene, fanned out and firing from cover. The fading train whistle comes OVER.

395.   EXT. BURYING-GROUND. Doane runs into the scene, and takes cover behind a marker. In the b.g., the three men enter the scene, still fanned out. SHOOTING FROM cover, they gradually move in on him.

396.   INT. CHURCH. The congregation is huddled together in terror, the Minister standing with head bowed, praying silently at the pulpit.

397. EXT. CEMETERY. On Doane as Colby exposes himself. Doane
      shoots, and brings him down.

398. INT. MARSHAL'S OFFICE. Amy is slumped at Doane's desk,
      past tears now, Doane's open testament crumpled in her
      hands. The SOUND of o.s. firing begins to come closer.
      Sensing it, she rises and hurries to the window. Through
      it, she now sees Doane running into the street.

399. EXT. STREET. Doane is zigzagging down the street. Pierce
      appears at the far end of the street behind him, and then
      suddenly Jordan comes into view in the f.g. They have him
      in a cross-fire again.

400. EXT. SALOON. Doane heads for it, bangs against the door.
      It is locked. Bullets pockmark the door around him. With
      a supreme effort, he charges the door and smashes it in,
      falling inside.

401. CLOSE SHOT -- AMY -- as she sees what is happening.

402. MED. CLOSE SHOT -- JORDAN -- as he fires.

403. MED. CLOSE SHOT -- PIERCE -- as he fires.

404. INT. SALOON. Doane squats on the floor, exhausted.

405. EXT. STREET. Pierce makes his way carefully along the
      street, firing as he goes. He reaches the Marshal's
      office, and shoots toward the saloon.

406. INT. MARSHAL'S OFFICE. Amy looks on in horror as she sees
      Pierce through the window, a scant few feet from her, shooting
      at the saloon. She looks about wildly, beside herself, then
      sees Harvey's guns hanging on the wall. Then, deliberately,
      she goes to them, takes down a gun, and goes to the window.
      Pierce's back is only two or three feet away past the window.
      Amy lifts the gun, holds it steady with both hands.

407. EXT. STREET -- on Pierce, with Amy visible in the b.g.
      Pierce shoots, takes aim again. Then Amy's gun goes
      off, and Pierce tumbles face forward to the ground.

408. INT. MARSHAL'S OFFICE. Amy reels and clings to the
      shattered window for support.

409. INT. SALOON. Doane, at the window, now, stares out into the
      street in surprise. He cannot see into his office, but

Pierce's body is plainly visible. Still, it may be a ruse.

410. EXT. STREET -- ON JORDAN -- as he stares off toward Pierce's
body. Then he dashes toward the alley.

411. EXT. ALLEY. Jordan runs up the alley.

412. EXT. REAR OF MARSHAL'S OFFICE. Jordan goes stealthily to
a window, sees Amy and that she is alone. He goes to the
door. It is open. He opens it quietly and leaps in.

413. INT. MARSHAL'S OFFICE. Amy looks up with a start as Jordan
jumps into the room, his gun ready. Exhausted, she can only
stand there as Jordan darts across the room, dashes the gun
from her hand and grabs her. Holding her in front of him,
he pushes her out toward the street.

414. INT. SALOON. SHOOTING PAST Doane into the street, as he sees
Jordan, with Amy as a shield, come out of the office and
toward him.

415. EXT. STREET -- on Jordan and Amy.

                    JORDAN
                   (yelling)
          Alright, Doane, come on out!
          Come out -- or your friend
          here'll get it the way Pierce
          did -- !

416. INT. SALOON. -- as Doane stares out, shocked.

                    DOANE
          I'll come out -- let her go!

417. EXT. STREET -- on Jordan and Amy.

                    JORDAN
          Soon as you walk through that
          door! Come on -- I'll hold
          my fire! . . .

He waits, holding Amy tightly. Amy is half-fainting with
terror.

418. INT. SALOON. Doane starts slowly toward the door, then
hesitates. He stops, picks up a large chair and heaves
it through the doorway.

419-
421.

EXT. STREET. As the chair hurtles through, Jordan fires a burst of shots. Wildly, Amy reaches up with her free hand and claws at his face and eyes. Jordan flings her away from him and she lands in the street. Doane steps quickly out of the saloon, firing as he comes. Jordan brings his other gun up. Doane staggers from a bullet in the shoulder, but keeps shooting, and Jordan goes down, his guns slipping from his fingers. For a moment, Doane leans tiredly against the building. Then he goes to Amy. He helps her up, and they cling to each other silently.

422.

FULL SHOT -- STREET. From everywhere, people begin to appear in the street, more and more of them. They look at Doane and Amy in silence.

423-
425.

EXT. STREET. Doane and Amy become aware of the people. Doane pulls himself together. He drops his guns in the street, takes off his gun-belt and lets it fall. Deliberately, he takes off his badge and drops it to the dust. The Drunk enters the scene, pulling the buckboard horses. Seeing the buckboard, Doane guides Amy to it, helps her in, then climbs up after her. He nods to the Drunk, who steps away, then takes the reins and starts the horses. The crowd gives way.

426.

FULL SHOT -- STREET. Without a backward glance, Doane and Amy ride out of town, the buckboard growing smaller in the b.g. The crowd remains silent. The buckboard passes out of view.

Twelve Angry Men

1957—Orion-Nova Productions
Director Sidney Lumet
Script Reginald Rose
Source A 1954 television script by Reginald Rose; see also
the stage version, adapted by Sherman L. Sergel
(Chicago: Dramatic Publishing Co., 1955)
Stars Henry Fonda, Lee J. Cobb

If the most obvious freedom of cinema is its ability to ignore time and space, to move abruptly from one time or location to another or to move from panoramic scenes like the charge of the French cavalry in *Henry V* to closeups of individuals or even intimate facial expressions, another and rarely explored freedom is the ability to give the illusion of movement and action within the narrowest limitations of time and space. The action of *Twelve Angry Men,* which takes place within twenty-four hours, is confined almost entirely to a small jury room. No neoclassical tragedy observes the unity of space more strictly than Sidney Lumet's movie, yet the spectator never has the sense, so oppressive in all but the greatest neoclassic dramas, of action being stifled by impossibly artificial limitations. The success stems equally from Lumet's direction and Boris Kaufman's fine camera work.

The subject of *Twelve Angry Men* associates it with crime pictures. Any jury movie involves the quest for truth, which is also a basic theme in detective movies like *The Big Sleep.* The differences, however, are all-important. *Twelve Angry Men* is not a thriller but an attempt to examine realistically the working of a social institution designed specifically to elicit truth, or as much of it as is possible in a given situation. Its vitality stems from its demonstration that truth is rarely the simple factual kind "discovered" by detectives like Raymond Chandler's Philip Marlowe. In a real situation there are only versions of truth, and hence justice is an extremely complex, often unsatisfactory, matter. The ambiguity in *Twelve Angry Men* stems partly from the ambiguity of the evidence, but this is only the beginning. The jurors' inability to recognize that the evidence is ambiguous is the real story. Their failure is not a function of the evidence but of the prejudices, guilts, secret desires, and hostilities that each juror carries within him. In short, it is a function of the psychological flaws of the twelve human beings, who were assembled from a random *venire* list to pass judgment on a stranger.

The value of the situation is its typicality. The jury system is as traditional in Anglo-Saxon culture as is the common law itself. It is widely considered one of the most fundamental of our democratic institutions. Reginald Rose further universalizes the situation by refusing names to his jurors. Numbered but not named, they comprise a cross-section of American society. Their value as social representatives rather than individuals is clear from the brief character descriptions that introduce the script.

One of the more curious reviews of the movie, which appeared in *Cahiers du Cinéma* (December, 1957), admitted the intelligence of the original idea but attacked the script for failing to achieve adequate differentiation among the jurors and added the mystifying observation that the unity of action gives a feeling "not of something done but of something in the process of doing." British and American reviewers, perhaps because of their greater familiarity with the American legal system, were more positive. The acting of Lee J. Cobb, of the lesser jurors, and (less unanimously) of Henry Fonda was generally praised. Several reviews pointed to the special virtues of tight structure and rapid development, which the film derived from its origin as a television play. Some reviewers speculated that the film was intended as an attack on the jury system, but most of them interpreted it as a tribute to this system. The viewer will, of course, decide for himself. What is undeniable is that the film retains its interest and grows in stature over the years.

The Script   Note the character sketches of the jurors that precede the script proper. The fact that the jurors are numbered rather than named is an integral part of the concept of the film. The script has no revisions. It is divided into master scenes with many instructions for the camera, a by-product of the need to give the illusion of movement in a film limited for the most part to a single set, the jury room.

Credits   Producers, Henry Fonda, Reginald Rose; Director, Sidney Lumet; Author, Reginald Rose; Script, Reginald Rose; Art (no listing); Music, Kenyon Hopkins; Photography, Robert Markell; Editor, Carl Lerner.

Cast	Juror #8:	Henry Fonda
	Juror #3:	Lee J. Cobb
	Juror #10:	Ed Begley

Juror #4:	E. G. Marshall
Juror #7:	Jack Warden
Juror #1:	Martin Balsam
Juror #2:	John Fiedler
Juror #5:	Jack Klugman
Juror #6:	Edward Binno
Juror #9:	Joseph Sweeney
Juror #11:	George Voskovec
Juror #12:	Robert Webber

Awards   None.

NOTE: The notes on characters are extremely brief, since it is felt that what they are and who they are will be revealed in their dialogue and actions during the course of the film.

FOREMAN: 35 years old. Assistant high school football coach. A small, petty man who is at first wary of, and then impressed with the authority he has. Handles himself quite formally. Not overly bright, but dogged.

Juror #2: 38 years old. Bank clerk. A meek, hesitant man who finds it difficult to maintain any opinions of his own. Easily swayed and usually adopts the opinion of the last person to whom he has spoken.

Juror #3: 40 years old. Head of messenger service. A very strong, very forceful, extremely opinionated man within whom can be detected a streak of sadism. A humorless man who is intolerant of opinions other than his own, and accustomed to forcing his wishes and views upon others.

Juror #4: 50 years old. Stockbroker. A man of wealth and position. A practised speaker who presents himself well at all times. Seems to feel a little bit above the rest of the jurors. His only concern is with the facts in this case and he is appalled with the behavior of the others. Constantly preening himself, combing his hair, cleaning his nails, etc.

Juror #5: 25 years old. Mechanic. A naive, very frightened young man who takes his obligations in this case very seriously but who finds it difficult to speak up when his elders have the floor.

Juror #6: 33 years old. Housepainter. An honest, but dull-witted man who comes upon his decisions slowly and carefully. A man who finds it difficult to create positive opinions, but who must listen to and digest and accept these opinions offered by others which appeal to him most.

Juror #7: 42 years old. Salesman. A loud, flashy, glad-handed salesman type who has more important things to do than to sit on a jury. He is quick to show temper, quick to form opinions on things about which he knows nothing. He is a bully, and, of course, a coward.

Juror #8: 42 years old. Architect. A quiet, thoughtful, gentle man. A man who sees many sides to every question and constantly seeks the truth. A man of strength tempered with compassion.

Above all, a man who wants justice to be done, and will fight to see that it is.

Juror #9: 70 years old. Retired. A mild, gentle old man, long since defeated by life, and now merely waiting to die. A man who recognizes himself for what he is, and mourns the days when it would have been possible to be courageous without shielding himself behind his many years. From the way he takes pills whenever he is excited, it is obvious that he has a heart condition.

Juror #10: 46 years old. Garage owner. An angry, bitter man. A man who antagonizes almost at sight. A bigot who places no values on any human life save his own. A man who has been nowhere and is going nowhere and knows it deep within him. He has a bad cold and continually blows his nose, sniffs a benzedrine inhaler, etc.

Juror #11: 48 years old. Watchmaker. A refugee from Europe who has come to this country in 1941. A man who speaks with an accent and who is ashamed, humble, almost subservient to the people around him, but a man who will honestly seek justice because he has suffered through so much injustice.

Juror #12: 30 years old. Advertising man. A slick, bright advertising man who thinks of human beings in terms of percentages, graphs and polls, and has no real understanding of people. A superficial snob, but trying to be a good fellow. Throughout the film he doodles on a scratch pad.

AND

THE JUDGE

THE COURT CLERK

THE GUARD

THE TWO ALTERNATE JURORS

AND   (IF DESIRED)

THE COURT STENOGRAPHER

FADE IN:

1. EXT.   LONG SHOT   N. Y. COURT OF GENERAL SESSIONS   DAY

A large, imposing building, gray, impressive as a background for the comings and goings of a number of ordinary people on an ordinary day. Camera holds on steps and building front from a distance and then dollies in slowly.

DISSOLVE TO:

2. LONG SHOT   THE LOBBY

Seething with activity, people of all kinds walking swiftly, purposefully to and from elevators, newsstands, etc., others standing, waiting. Guards stationed at various posts. Camera pans across lobby, and then dollies into a bank of elevators. A number of people crowd into one. The door closes.

DISSOLVE TO:

3. LONG SHOT   A LONG CORRIDOR UPSTAIRS

The elevators on left. Many doorways to various courtrooms on right. Each door marked with a hanging sign. The first sign reads "Court of General Sessions. Part I". The second sign reads "Court of General Sessions. Part II" etc. An elevator door opens and a number of people exit and walk down the corridor. Other people, men and women, stand in the corridor talking. The whole feeling is one of movement, activity, intense concentration. Everyone has a purpose. Camera dollies down the corridor, following group of people who exited from elevator. People peel off from the group at various doors. At each door stands a guard. People move in and out of the doors. Camera reaches the door marked "Part VI", and pans around to face the door. A guard stands in front of it, impassively. No one else is in front of the door, as compared to the knots of whispering people in front of all the other doors. The case going on in "Part VI" obviously has very little general interest. Through the glass window of the door we can see, far in the background, the judge at his bench. He is facing to his left, and talking. We hear nothing. He stops and turns to his right. He raises his hand as if calling a waiter.

DISSOLVE TO:

4. CLOSE UP   AN EMPTY WATER GLASS ON A TRAY

From the noise of the corridor we are now in the deathlike stillness of a courtroom. A hand places a freshly-filled pitcher of water on the tray. A pair of hands fills a glass from the pitcher. Camera pans with glass as it is raised. Camera holds on close-up of judge, drinking the water. He finishes, puts the glass down,

and turns to his left again. He clears his throat. Then he begins
to speak.

> JUDGE
> Pardon me, gentlemen.
> (Gravely)
> To continue, you've heard a long
> and complex case. Murder in the
> first degree . . . premeditated
> homicide . . . is the most serious
> charge tried in our criminal courts.

5. MEDIUM SHOT   THE JURY

From judge's angle. Seated in the jury box, listening intently to
the judge. We see the 14 members of the jury. This includes the
two alternates who sit on the far right side of the jury, one behind the other. The jury sits in numerical order reading from left
to right: the foreman through #6 in the front row, #7-#12 in the
rear row. As the judge speaks, camera dollies slowly in, still
holding on jury but excluding the alternates.

> JUDGE
> You've listened to the testimony, and
> you've had the law read to you and
> interpreted as it applies to this case.
> It now becomes your duty to sit down to
> try and separate the facts from the
> fancy. One man is dead. The life of
> another is at stake. I urge you to
> deliberate honestly and thoughtfully.

Camera is now in close on #'s 1, 2, 7 and 8. It begins to pan
slowly right. #7 fidgets endlessly. #10 sniffs as if he has a
cold. #3 looks coldly off in the direction in which the defendant
sits. All other jurymen watch the judge, listening intently. As
the judge finishes his lines, camera is on #'s 5, 6, 11 and 12.

> JUDGE
> If there is a reasonable doubt in your
> minds as to the guilt of the accused . . .
> a reasonable doubt . . . then you must
> bring me a verdict of not guilty. If,
> however, there is no reasonable doubt,
> then you must, in good conscience find
> the accused guilty. However you decide,
> your verdict must be unanimous. In the
> event you find the accused guilty the

                                JUDGE (cont.)
                    bench will not entertain a recommenda-
                    tion for mercy. The death sentence is
                    mandatory in this case.

The judge pauses for a moment. There is a stillness in the room.

6. CLOSE UP   JUDGE, ENTIRE JURY IN BACKGROUND

The judge's profile fills the left side of the frame. In right
background we see the jury box.

                                JUDGE
                    I don't envy you your job. You are faced
                    with a grave responsibility. Thank you,
                    gentlemen.

There is a pause. The judge turns away from the jury and nods in
another direction.

7. CLOSE UP   THE FACE OF THE COURT CLERK

                                CLERK
                    The alternate jurors are excused.

8. MEDIUM SHOT   THE JURY

All of their heads turn to camera right. Self-consciously the two
alternates rise and move awkwardly out of the jury box. When they
are gone, we hear the clerk.

                                CLERK
                    The jury will retire.

The members of the jury look hesitantly at each other, each reluc-
tant to be the first to stand. Finally #3 stands up. Then the
others begin to rise and file slowly off left until the jury box is
empty.

8A. MEDIUM SHOT   THE JURY

They file through a long corridor, then through one door, then
another. They are silent, serious. All we hear is the sound of
their footsteps. Credits are superimposed over this scene. As
credits end:

                                                    DISSOLVE TO:

9. MEDIUM SHOT   THE JURY ROOM

The room is empty, silent save for the sounds of traffic twelve
floors below. In center of room is a large scarred table and
twelve chairs. There are four other chairs against the wall opposite the windows. Along one wall are three windows through which
we can see the New York skyline. On the opposite wall is an electric clock and an electric fan. At one end of the Jury room is a
coat rack, on either side of which is a door, one lettered "men"
and the other lettered "women". Against the fourth wall is an
old-fashioned water cooler. There are pencils, pads, ashtrays on
the table. Nothing else. The room is drab, bare, in need of a
painting. Camera holds on room and then dollies in toward the door
as we hear footsteps outside. The door is opened by a uniformed
guard. On the door are lettered the words "Jury Room". The guard
stands against the door, holding it open, as the members of the
jury file into the room. He holds a clip-board and pencil, and we
can see his lips moving, counting the jurymen as they enter. Four
or five of the jurymen light cigarettes immediately. They move
into the room. Juror #2 goes to the water fountain. Juror #9,
the old man, enters hastily and goes toward the men's room. Juror
#7 enters the room last. The guard steps into the room and closes
the door. Again he begins to count the jurors. Camera slowly pans
with #7 as he walks across the room toward the windows. The foreman has seated himself at the head of the table. #11 and #4 also
sit at the table. #11 begins to make notes in a little pad. #4
reads the newspaper. The others move awkwardly about the room.
They are ill at ease, do not really know each other to talk to,
wish they were anywhere but here. There is no conversation for a
moment. #7 reaches the window. Camera is on him and #6 who looks
out at the skyline. #7 offers a stick of gum to him. He shakes
his head. #7 offers the gum to #8 who also looks out window. #8
smiles.

>   #8
>   No thanks.

#7 mouths the gum, and mops his brow.

>   #7
>   (To #6)
>   Y'know something? I phoned up for
>   the weather this morning. This is
>   the hottest day of the year.

#6 nods and continues to look out window.

>   #7
>   You'd think they'd at least air
>   condition the place. I almost

                    #7 (cont.)
           dropped dead in court.

He reaches over and opens the window wider.

10. MEDIUM SHOT   CENTERED ON GUARD

He has finished counting them.

                    GUARD
           Okay, gentlemen. Everybody's here.
           If there's anything you want I'm
           right outside. Just knock.

He exits, closing the door as camera dollies back to include juror
#5, the youngest juryman, who watches the door. We hear the lock
click. #5 half grins, self-consciously.

                    #5
           I never knew they locked the door.

                    #10
           Sure they lock the door. What'd
           you think?

                    #5
           I don't know. It just never oc-
           curred to me.

#10 gives him the look of a professional know-it-all, and then
turns and takes off his jacket. He walks across room to coat rack,
camera dollying with him. He passes the Foreman who stands at the
head of the table tearing up little slips of paper for ballots,
and he stops.

                    #10
           Hey, what's that for?

                    FOREMAN
           Well I figured we might want to
           vote by ballots.

                    #10
                (Grinning)
           Great idea! Maybe we can get him
           elected senator.

#10 laughs until he begins to cough. He moves off to the coat

rack, coughing. The Foreman laughs, not appreciatively, and stops
as #10 walks off. Camera holds on him as he continues to tear
slips. He looks at his watch now, and then up at the wall clock,
comparing times.

11. CLOSE UP   THE CLOCK

It reads 4:35. Camera pans down from clock. #2 sits in a chair
against the wall, thinking about the trial. #3 passes by him
carrying a paper cup of water from water cooler. He stops in front
of #2 and looks around the room, sipping the water. #2 looks at
him a bit self-consciously. #3 looks down at him. #2 smiles and
nods.

> #3
> How'd you like it?

> #2
> (Mildly)
> I don't know, it was pretty in-
> teresting.

> #3
> (Pleasantly)
> Yeah? I was falling asleep.

> #2
> I mean I've never been on a jury before.

> #3
> Really? I don't know. I've sat on juries,
> and it always kind of amazes me the way
> these lawyers can talk, and talk and talk,
> even when the case is as obvious as this
> one. I mean, did you ever hear so much
> talk about nothing?

> #2
> Well, I guess they're . . . entitled.

> #3
> Sure they are. Everybody deserves a
> fair trial.

He balls up his paper cup and flips it at the water cooler.

> #3
> That's the system. Listen, I'm the last

#3 (cont.)
one to say anything against it, but I'm
telling you sometimes I think we'd be
better off if we took these tough kids and
slapped 'em down hard <u>before</u> they make
trouble, you know? Save us a lot of time
and money.

#2 looks at him nervously, nods, gets up and walks to the water
cooler, camera dollying with him. He pours himself a drink and
stands alone sipping it. We hear movement in the room during all
of this, and quiet ad lib conversation.

12. MEDIUM SHOT   THE ROOM FROM #2'S ANGLE

#2 big in foreground, sipping his water. #3 is hanging up his
jacket. #6 and #8 are looking out windows. #4, #11 and the
Foreman are seated at table. #7 and #10 are at far end of room,
talking quietly. #7 lets out a raucous laugh. #9 is still in
men's room. #5 walks toward water cooler. #12 is walking over to
windows. Camera dollies in on #12. As camera nears #12, #7 calls
out to Foreman. #12 stops walking.

#7
Hey, how about getting started here.

#3
Yeah, let's get this over with. We've
probably all got things to do.

FOREMAN
Well I was figuring we'd take a five
minute break. I mean one gentleman's
in the bathroom. . . .

#7 shrugs, and turns back to #10. #5 walks over to the Foreman as
#12 continues over to #8 at the window, camera moving with him. #3
continues business of hanging up his jacket, and goes to sit at
table.

#5
(Hesitantly)
Are we going to sit in order?

FOREMAN
(Looking up)
What? I don't know. I suppose so.

Camera moves in tight on #8 and #12. #8 is thinking hard, biting
his fingernail. #12 looks out the window over his shoulder.

                          #12
              Not a bad view.

#8 nods.

                          #12
              What'd you think of the case?

#8 looks at him questioningly.

                          #12
              It had a lot of interest for me. No dead
              spots, know what I mean? I'll tell you
              we were lucky to get a murder case. I
              figured us for a burglary or an assault or
              something. Those can be the dullest. Say,
              isn't that the Woolworth Building?

                          #8
              That's right.

                          #12
              Funny, I've lived here all my life and
              I've never been in it.

#8 looks out the window. #12 looks at him for a moment and then
walks away. Camera holds on #8 for a moment. He stares out the
window. We hear #7 laugh again.

                          #7
              Yeah! And what about the business with
              the knife. I mean asking grown-up people
              to believe that kind of bushwash.

#8 turns during these lines to look at #7.

13. MEDIUM SHOT   #7 AND #10

#10 sits in a chair not at table, #7 stands over him mopping his
brow.

                          #10
              Well look, you've gotta expect that.
              You know what you're dealing with.

                          #7
              Yeah, I suppose.

#10 blows his nose vigorously.

                          #7
              What's the matter, you got a cold?

                          #10
              And how. These hot weather colds can
              kill you.
                   (He tilts his head back slightly)
              I can hardly touch my nose. Know what
              I mean?

#7 nods sympathetically.

                          #7
              I just got over one.

There is an awkward pause. #7 looks at his watch. Then he looks
up at Foreman, who is standing at head of table.

                          #7
              What d'ya say, Mr. Foreman?

14. MEDIUM SHOT   #7, #10, FOREMAN, #3, #4, FROM ANOTHER ANGLE

Foreman big in foreground, standing at head of table. #7, #10 in
background. #3, #4 seated at left at table. Foreman looks around
at the wall clock. #3 leans over to scan #4's newspaper.

                          #3
              Anything exciting going on?

#4 looks up at him.

                          #3
                   (Smiling)
              I didn't get a chance to look at the
              papers today.

                          #4
              I was just wondering how the market closed.

                          #3
                   (Pleasantly)
              I wouldn't know. Say, are you on the

                  #3   (cont.)
Exchange or something.

                     #4
I'm a broker.

                     #3
Well that's very interesting. Listen, maybe
you can answer a question for me. I have
an uncle who's been playing around with
some Canadian stuff. . . .

The foreman turns around and, as if it is an effort, calls out
loudly to the others.

                  FOREMAN
All right, gentlemen. Let's take seats.

There is a slow movement towards the table. #3 shrugs at #4 and
turns to the Foreman.

                    #7
This better be fast. I got tickets to a
ball game tonight. Yanks-Cleveland. We
got this new kid, Modjelewski, or whatever
his name is, going. He's a bull, this kid!

He shoots his hand forward and out to indicate the path of a curve
ball.

                    #7
Shhhooooom. A real jug handle.
        (To Foreman)
Where d'ya want us to sit?

15. CLOSE UP   FOREMAN

When he gets used to this minor authority he will enjoy it. Right
now he is still nervous.

                  FOREMAN
Well, I was thinking we ought to sit in
order, by jury numbers.
        (He points with each number)
Two. Three. Four, and so on. If that's
okay with you gentlemen.

#10
What's the difference?

#4
I think it's reasonable to sit according
to number.

#10
Let it be.

Foreman has looked back and forth a bit anxiously at this exchange.
Now he relaxes and sits down. Camera holds. Now, where Foreman's
head had been in closeup, we see #2 in medium shot, sitting in
sideline chair. He gets up and camera pans with him to his seat at
the table. Camera pans down table from #2. #3, #4, #5 are seated.
#6 is hanging his coat on the coat rack. #7 is draping his over
the chair. #8 still stares out the window. #9 is in bathroom.
#10 is walking toward his seat, mopping his brow. #11, #12 are
seated.

#12
(To #11)
What was your impression of the
prosecuting attorney?

#11 looks at him.

#11
(German accent)
I beg pardon?

#12
I thought he was really sharp. I
mean the way he hammered home his
points, one by one, in logical sequence. It takes a good brain to
do that. I was very impressed. . . .

16. MEDIUM SHOT   FOREMAN'S END OF TABLE

From side, shooting towards window. #8 stares out window, thinking.

#11
(To #12)
Yes, I think he did an expert job.

#12
I mean, he had a lot of drive too.

                    #12   (cont.)
        Real drive.

                        #7
                    (Calling, off)
        Okay, let's get this show on the
        road.

                      FOREMAN
                  (Standing, to #8)
        How about sitting down.

16A. CLOSE UP   #8

    #8 doesn't hear the Foreman. He stares out window.

                      FOREMAN
              The gentlemen at the window

    #8 turns, startled.

                      FOREMAN
            How about sitting down.

                        #8
            Oh. I'm sorry.

16B. MEDIUM SHOT   CENTERING ON #11

    #8 heads for a seat.

                        #10
                  (Across table to #4)
            It's pretty tough to figure, isn't
            it? A kid kills his father. Bing!
            Just like that.

                        #12
                  (Butting in)
            Well, if you analyze the figures. . . .

                        #10
                  (Ploughing ahead)
            It's the element. I'm tellin' you
            they let those kids run wild up
            there. Well, maybe it serves 'em
            right. Know what I mean?

This is an annoying characteristic of #10's, this forcing an answer with "know what I mean?", as if he is saying "listen, you
better answer me, because I'm somebody, see?" #4 reacts by looking
squarely at #10, nodding and turning back to his paper. #8 has sat
down quietly by this time. #11 has looked curiously from #10 to
#12 during this exchange.

16C. CLOSE UP   FOREMAN

FOREMAN

Is everybody here?

17. MEDIUM SHOT   #'S 4, 5, 6, 7

#6
(Gesturing towards bathroom)

The old man's inside.

FOREMAN

Would you knock on the door.

#6 gets up and starts for the bathroom, camera panning with him.

#7
(To #5 as #6 goes by)

Hey, you a Yankee fan?

#5

No. Baltimore.

#7

Baltimore! Oh, the suffering! That's
like being hit in the head with a
crowbar once a day! Listen, who they
got. . . .

Camera has stayed with #6. He reaches the bathroom door and is
about to knock when #9 opens the door.

#6
(Apologetically)

I was just coming to get you.

#7
(Off)

I'm asking you, who they got besides
great groundskeepers?

                         FOREMAN
                    (Off)
             We'd like to get started.

                        #9
             Forgive me gentlemen.   I didn't mean
             to keep you waiting.

He begins to walk toward his seat as does #6.

                               #7
                    (Off)
             Baltimore!

18. CLOSE UP   FOREMAN

He is still standing. He looks around. This is the moment for
his big speech.

                         FOREMAN
                    (Nervously)
             All right. Now you gentlemen can
             handle this any way you want to.
             I mean, I'm not going to make any
             rules. If we want to discuss it
             first and then vote, that's one way.
             Or we can vote right now to see how
             we stand.

He pauses and looks around.

                         FOREMAN
             Well . . . that's all I have to say.

19. MEDIUM SHOT   CENTERED ON #4

                        #4
             I think it's customary to take a
             preliminary vote.

                        #7
                    (Off)
             Yeah, let's vote. Who knows, maybe
             we can all go home.

20. LONG SHOT   CENTERED ON FOREMAN

From opposite end of the table.

> FOREMAN
>
> It's up to you. Just let's remember
> we've got a first degree murder
> charge here. If we vote guilty we
> send the accused to the electric
> chair. That's mandatory.

> #4
> I think we all know that.

> #3
> Come on, let's vote.

> #10
> Yeah. Let's see who's where.

> FOREMAN
> Anybody doesn't want to vote?

He looks around the table. There is no answer.

> FOREMAN
> All right. This has to be a twelve-
> to-nothing vote either way. That's
> the law. Okay, are we ready? All
> those voting guilty raise your hands.

Seven or eight hands go up immediately. Several others go up more
slowly. Everyone looks around the table as the Foreman begins to
count hands. #9's hand goes up now, and all hands are raised,
save #8's.

> FOREMAN
> . . . nine . . . ten . . . eleven. That's
> eleven for guilty. Okay, Not guilty.

21. CLOSE UP   #8

He slowly raises his hand.

> FOREMAN
> One. Right. Okay, eleven to
> one, guilty. Now we know where
> we are.

#8 lowers his hand.

#10
(Off)
Boy-oh-boy. There's always one.

#8 doesn't look in his direction.

#7
So what do we do now?

#8
Well, I guess we talk.

#10
Boy-oh-boy.

22. CLOSE UP   #3

#3
(Leaning across to #8)
Well look, do you really think he's
innocent?

23. CLOSE UP   #8

#8
I don't know.

24. CLOSE UP   #3

#3
(Smiling)
I mean let's be reasonable. You
sat right in court and heard the
same things we did. The man's a
dangerous killer. You could see it.

25. CLOSE UP   #8

#8
He's nineteen years old.

26. CLOSE UP   #3

#3
Well, that's old enough. He knifed his
own father. Four inches into the chest.

27. MEDIUM SHOT   CENTERING ON #6

#6
(To #8)
It's pretty obvious. I mean I was
convinced from the first day.

28. CLOSE UP #3

#3
Well, who wasn't?
(To #8)
I really think this is one of those open
and shut things. They proved it a dozen
different ways. Would you like me to list
them for you?

29. CLOSE UP #8

#8
No.

#10
(Off, annoyed)
Then what do you want?

#8
Nothing. I just want to talk.

30. ELIMINATED

31. MEDIUM SHOT #'S 7, 8, 9, 10.

#7
Well what's there to talk about?
Eleven men in here agree. Nobody
had to think about it twice, except
you.

#10
(Leaning over toward #8)
I want to ask you something. Do you
believe his story?

#8
I don't know whether I believe it or
not. Maybe I don't.

#7
So what'd you vote not guilty for?

                    #8
          There were eleven votes for guilty.
          It's not so easy for me to raise my
          hand and send a boy off to die with-
          out talking about it first.

                    #7
          Who says it's easy for me?

                    #8
               (Turning)
          No one.

32. CLOSE UP   #7, #8 FROM ANOTHER ANGLE

                    #7
          What, just because I voted fast? I
          think the guy's guilty. You couldn't
          change my mind if you talked for a
          hundred years.

                    #8
          I'm not trying to change your mind.
          It's just that we're talking about
          somebody's life here. I mean, we
          can't decide in five minutes. Sup-
          posing we're wrong?

There is a pause. #7 looks at #8

                    #7
          Supposing we're wrong! Supposing
          this whole building fell on my head.
          You can suppose anything.

                    #8
          That's right.

                    #7
          What's the difference how long it
          takes? We honestly think he's guilty.
          So supposing we finish in five minutes?
          So what?

                    #8
          Let's take an hour. The ball game
          doesn't start till eight o'clock.

#7 looks angrily at him for a moment, and then suddenly breaks
into a smile as if to say, "What am I heating myself up over you
for?" #7 makes the curve ball motion with his hand again.

>   #7
>   (Smiling)
>   Shhhooom!

He settles back in his chair, smiling.

33. LONG SHOT   TABLE FROM #7'S ANGLE CENTERED ON FOREMAN

No one says a word for a moment.

>   FOREMAN
>   (Hesitantly)
>   Well who's got something to say?

He looks at #2. #2 shrugs.

>   #2
>   Not me.

Foreman looks around the table. Some of them shrug, others merely
sit. He looks at #9.

>   #9
>   I'm willing to sit for an hour.

>   #10
>   Great.
>   (A pause)
>   I heard a pretty good story last
>   night. . . .

>   #8
>   (Sharply)
>   That's not what we're sitting here
>   for.

34. MEDIUM SHOT   CENTERED ON #9

#10 and #8 speak across #9, who turns from one to the other.
Camera shoots over shoulders of #'s 4 and 5.

>   #10
>   All right, then you tell me. What
>   are we sitting here for?

#8 looks at him, trying to phrase the following. They wait.

#8

>   Maybe for no reason. I don't know.
>   Look, this boy's been kicked around
>   all his life. You know, living in a
>   slum, his mother dead since he was
>   nine. He spent a year and a half in
>   an orphanage while his father served
>   a jail term for forgery. That's not
>   a very good headstart. He's a wild,
>   angry kid and that's all he's ever been.
>   You know why he got that way? Because
>   he was knocked on the head by somebody
>   once a day, every day. He's had a pretty
>   terrible nineteen years. I think maybe
>   we owe him a few words. That's all.

He looks around the table. #9 nods slowly.

#10

>   I don't mind telling you this, mister.
>   We don't owe him a thing. He got a
>   fair trial, didn't he? What d'you
>   think that trial cost? He's lucky he
>   got it.
>   (Turning to #11)
>   Know what I mean?
>   (Now looking across table
>   at #'s 3, 4, 5)
>   Look, we're all grown-ups in here. We
>   heard the facts, didn't we?
>   (To #8)
>   Now you're not going to tell us that
>   we're supposed to believe that kid,
>   knowing what he is. Listen, I've
>   lived among 'em all my life. You
>   can't believe a word they say. You
>   know that.
>   (To all)
>   I mean they're born liars.

There is a pause.

#9

>   (Slowly)
>   Only an ignorant man can believe that.

                             #10
                    Now listen. . . .

                             #9
                      (To #10)
                    Do you think you were born with a
                    monopoly on the truth?
                      (To all)
                    I think certain things should be
                    pointed out to this man.

35. CLOSE UP   #3

     He is annoyed at this argument.

                             #3
                    All right. It's not Sunday. We
                    don't need a sermon in here.

36. MEDIUM SHOT   #'S 8, 9, 10

                             #9
                      (To all)
                    What he says is very dangerous. . . .

                             #10
                      (Loudly)
                    All right, that's enough!

     He glares at #9. #9 half rises, but then feels #8's hand firmly
     on his arm, gently pulling him down. He sits down, turns away
     from #10 and looks briefly at #8. #8 looks calmly, firmly back,
     and in his look there is understanding and sympathy.

                             #4
                      (Off)
                    I don't see any need for arguing like
                    this. I think we ought to be able
                    to behave like gentlemen.

                             #12
                    Right!

37. MEDIUM SHOT   #'S 4, 3, 2, FOREMAN

                          #4
                      (Calmly)
            If we're going to discuss this case
            let's discuss the facts.

                      FOREMAN
            I think that's a good point. We have
            a job to do. Let's do it.

#2 rises and walks around end of table. Camera pans with him till
it reaches #'s 11 and 12. Foreman is still on camera. #2 goes
off to his jacket to get a package of cough drops, and returns
during the next lines. #12 doodles steadily on his pad. #11
watches him. He draws a cereal box.

                      FOREMAN
            Maybe if the gentleman who's disagree-
            ing down there could tell us why. You
            know, tell us what he thinks, we could
            show him where he's probably mixed up.

#12 looks at #11 and sees him watching his doodling. He holds up
his drawing for him to see.

                          #12
                  (To #11 confidentially)
            Rice Pops. It's one of the products
            I work on at the agency. "The Break-
            fast With The Built-In Bounce". I
            wrote that line.

#11 smiles in spite of himself.

                          #11
            It's very catchy.

                      FOREMAN
                  (Annoyed, to #12)
            If you don't mind.

                          #12
            I'm sorry. I have this habit of
            doodling. It keeps me thinking
            clearly.

                      FOREMAN
            We're trying to get someplace here.
            Y'know we can sit here forever. . . .

#12
Well look, maybe this is an idea.
I'm just thinking out loud, but it
seems to me it's up to us to con-
vince this gentleman
        (Indicating #8)
that we're right and he's wrong.
Maybe if we each took a minute or
two. Mind you, this is just a quick
idea. . . .

                    FOREMAN
No, I think it's a good one. Supposing we go once around the table.

38.   CLOSE UP   #7

                    #7
Anything. Let's start it off.

                    FOREMAN
        (To #7)
Okay. How about you going first?

                    #7
Not me. I think we oughta go in
order.

He takes his gum out of his mouth and looks for a place to throw
it. Finally he lets fly. We hear a thin clank. He seems satisfied.

39.   MEDIUM SHOT   FOREMAN, #2, #3

                    FOREMAN
That sounds all right. In order, a
coupla minutes apiece.
        (To #2)
I guess you're first.

                    #2
Oh. Well. . . .
        (He pauses nervously)
Well it's hard to put into words.
I just . . . think he's guilty. I
thought it was obvious from the
word go. I mean nobody proved
otherwise.

40.   CLOSE UP   #8

#8
(Quietly)
Nobody has to prove otherwise. The
burden of proof is on the prosecution. The defendant doesn't have
to open his mouth. That's in the
Constitution. You've heard of it.

41.   CLOSE UP   #2

#2
(Flustered)
Well sure I've heard of it. I know
what it is. I . . . what I meant . . .
well the man is guilty. I mean somebody saw him do it. . . .

He looks around helplessly, and then looks down. Camera pans over
to #3 who has been watching #2, waiting his turn. #2, now in
close up, turns to the others.

#3
Okay. Now here's what I think, and I
have no personal feelings about this.
I'm talking about facts. Number one:
let's take the old man who lived on
the second floor right underneath the
room where the murder took place. At
ten minutes after twelve on the night
of the killing he heard loud noises in
the apartment upstairs. He said it
sounded like a fight. Then he heard
the kid shout out, "I'm gonna kill
you." A second later he heard a body
fall, and he ran to the door of his
apartment, looked out, and saw the
kid running down the stairs and out
of the house. Then he called the
police. They found the father with a
knife in his chest. . . .

42.   MEDIUM SHOT   CENTERED ON FOREMAN

FOREMAN
And the coroner fixed the time of
death at around midnight.

43.   MEDIUM SHOT   OVER #3'S SHOULDER TOWARD #8

#3
Right. I mean there are facts for
you. You can't refute facts. This
boy is guilty. I'm telling you.
Look, I'm as sentimental as the next
guy. I know the kid is only nineteen,
but he's still got to pay for what he
did.

#7
(Off)
I'm with you.

FOREMAN
All right. Next.

44.   MEDIUM SHOT   CENTERING ON #4

#'s 3 and 5 listen closely to this quiet, imposing, meticulous man.
He takes off his eyeglasses, waving them as he talks.

#4
It was obvious, to me anyway, that
the boy's entire story was flimsy.
He claimed he was at the movies during
the time of the killing and yet one
hour later he couldn't remember what
films he saw, or who played in them.

#3
That's right. Did you hear that?
(To #4)
You're absolutely right.

#4
No one saw him going in or out of the
theatre. . . .

45.   CLOSE UP   #10 AND PART OF #11

#10

Listen, what about that woman across
the street? If her testimony don't
prove it, nothing does.

                    #11
          That's right. She was the one who
          actually saw the killing.

46. CLOSE UP   FOREMAN

                    FOREMAN
          Let's go in order here.

47. MEDIUM SHOT   CENTERED ON #10

#10 rises, handkerchief in hand.

                    #10
          Just a minute. Here's a woman. . . .

He blows his nose.

                    #10
          Here's a woman who's lying in bed
          and can't sleep.

He begins to walk around the table, wiping his tender nose and
talking. Camera follows him around the table.

                    #10
          She's dying with the heat. Know what
          I mean? Anyway, she looks out the
          window and right across the street
          she sees the kid stick the knife into
          his father. The time is 12:10 on the
          nose. Everything fits. Look, she's
          known the kid all his life. His win-
          dow is right opposite hers, across
          the el tracks, and she swore she saw
          him do it.

#10 is now standing behind #6 and looking across table at #8.
Camera shoots over #8's shoulder. #10 wipes his nose.

                    #8
          Through the windows of a passing ele-
          vated train.

                    #10
               (Through the handkerchief)
          Right. This el train had no passengers
          on it. It was just being moved downtown.

#10 (cont.)
The lights were out, remember? And they
proved in court that at night you can
look through the windows of an el train
when the lights are out and see what's
happening on the other side. They
proved it!

48. CLOSE UP   #8

#8
(To #10)
I'd like to ask you something. You
don't believe the boy. How come you
believe the woman? She's one of "them"
too, isn't she?

49. CLOSE UP   #10

He is suddenly angry.

#10
You're a pretty smart fellow, aren't
you?

He takes a step towards #8.

50. FAST CLOSE UP   #8

Sitting calmly there.

51. LONG SHOT   ENTIRE TABLE FROM BEHIND FOREMAN

#10 strides toward #8. The Foreman rises in his seat. #'s 3 and
5 jump up and move toward #10.

FOREMAN
(Nervously)
Hey, let's take it easy.

52. MEDIUM SHOT   #'S 3, 5, and 10 STANDING BEHIND #7

#'s 3 and 5 have reached #10 who looks angrily at #8. #3 takes
#10's arm.

#10
(Angrily)
What's he so wise about? I'm telling
you. . . .

> #3
> (Strongly)
> Come on. Sit down.

He begins to lead #10 back to his seat, camera panning with them.

> #3
> What are you letting him get you
> all upset for? Relax.

> FOREMAN
> (Off)
> Let's calm down now. I mean we're
> not gonna get anywhere fighting.

#'s 3 and 10 reach #10's seat. #10 sits down. #3 remains stand-
ing now. Until his next lines he walks around the room, takes a
drink at the fountain, etc.

53. MEDIUM SHOT   CENTERED ON FOREMAN

He is standing.

> FOREMAN
> Okay. Let's try to keep it peaceful
> in here.

He looks down the table.

> FOREMAN
> Whose turn is it?

> #12
> (Pointing at #5, who is
> off camera)
> His.

> FOREMAN
> Okay. You've got two minutes.

54. CLOSE UP   #5

He looks around nervously.

> #5
> I'll pass it.

                         FOREMAN
                    (Off)
          That's your privilege. How about the
          next gentleman?

Camera pans to close up of #6.

                          #6
          I don't know. I started to be con-
          vinced, uh . . . you know, very early
          in the case. Well, I was looking for
          the motive. That's very important.
          If there's no motive where's the
          case? So anyway, that testimony from
          those people across the hall from
          the kid's apartment, that was very
          powerful. Didn't they say something
          about an argument between the father
          and the boy around seven o'clock that
          night? I mean, I can be wrong.

55. MEDIUM SHOT   #11, #10, #9, #8   FROM ACROSS TABLE

                         #11
          It was eight o'clock. Not seven.

                          #8
          That's right. Eight o'clock. They
          heard an argument, but they couldn't
          hear what it was about. Then they
          heard the father hit the boy twice,
          and finally they saw the boy walk
          angrily out of the house. What does
          that prove?

56. CLOSE UP #6

Any time he is working on his own ideas he feels himself on un-
steady ground, and is ready to back down. He does so now.

                          #6
          Well it doesn't exactly prove any-
          thing. It's just part of the pic-
          ture. I didn't say it proved any-
          thing.

57. MEDIUM SHOT   CENTERING ON #'S 6, 7, 8

>   #8
>   You said it revealed a motive for
>   this killing. The prosecuting at-
>   torney said the same thing. Well,
>   I don't think it's a very strong
>   motive. This boy has been hit so
>   many times in his life that violence
>   is practically a normal state of
>   affairs for him. I can't see two
>   slaps in the face provoking him into
>   committing murder.

58. MEDIUM SHOT   #4

>   #4
>   (Quietly)
>   It may have been two too many. Every-
>   one has a breaking point.

59. CLOSE UP   #8

Looking across at #4, and realizing instantly that this will probably be his most powerful adversary. #4 is the man of logic, and
a man without emotional attachment to this case.

60. LONG SHOT   ENTIRE TABLE FROM BEHIND FOREMAN

>   FOREMAN
>   (To #6)
>   Anything else?

>   #6
>   No.

#6 gets up and walks a few paces from the table to stretch. #3
is standing at the water fountain, listening. All others are
seated.

>   FOREMAN
>   (To #7)
>   Okay. How about you?

>   #7
>   Me?

He pauses, looks around, shrugs, then speaks.

>   #7
>   I don't know, it's practically all

#7 (cont.)
said already. We can talk about it
forever. It's the same thing.

61.   CLOSE UP   #7 WITH #8 AT RIGHT SIDE OF FRAME.

#7
I mean this kid is five for oh. Look
at his record. He was in children's
court when he was ten for throwing a
rock at his teacher. At fifteen he
was in reform school. He stole a car.
He's been arrested for mugging. He
was picked up twice for knife-fighting.
He's real swift with a knife, they said.
This is a very fine boy.

#8
Ever since he was five years old his
father beat him up regularly. He
used his fists.

#7
(Indignantly)
So would I! A kid like that.

Camera dollies back now to show #3 walking over from the water
fountain toward #7. He stands behind #7, talks to #8.

#3
And how. It's the kids, the way they are
nowadays. Listen, when I was his age I
used to call my father "sir". That's
right. Sir! You ever hear a boy call his
father that anymore?

#8
Fathers don't seem to think it's important
any more.

#3
No? Have you got any kids?

#8
Three.

#3
Yeah, well I've got one, a boy twenty-two

#3 (cont.)
years old. I'll tell you about him. When
he was nine he ran away from a fight. I
saw him. I was so ashamed I almost threw
up. So I told him right out. I'm gonna
make a man outa you or I'm gonna bust you
in half trying. Well I made a man outa him
all right. When he was sixteen we had a
battle. He hit me in the face! He's big,
y'know. I haven't seen him in two years. . .
Rotten kid. You work your heart out. . . .

He stops. He has said more than he intended and more passionately
than he intended it. He is embarrassed. He looks at #8, and then
at all of them.

#3
(Loud)
All right. Let's get on with it.

He turns and walks angrily around the table to his seat, camera
panning with him. He sits down. Camera now covers #'s 3, 4, 5.
#4 looks at #3 and then across the table.

#4
I think we're missing the point here.
This boy, let's say he's a product of
a filthy neighborhood and a broken
home. We can't help that. We're here
to decide whether he's guilty or innocent,
not to go into the reasons why he
grew up this way. He was born
in a slum. Slums are breeding
grounds for criminals. I know it.
So do you.

62. CLOSE UP #5

He reacts to the following.

#4
It's no secret. Children from slum
backgrounds are potential menaces to
society. Now, I think. . . .

#10
(Interrupting)
Brother you can say that again. The

>   #10 (cont.)
>   kids who crawl outa those places are
>   real trash. I don't want any part
>   of them, I'm telling you.

Camera pans over to close up of #5. His face is angry. He tries
to control himself. His voice shakes.

>   #5
>   I've lived in a slum all my life. . . .

63. CLOSE UP   #10

He knows he has said the wrong thing.

>   #10
>   Oh, now wait a second. . . .

64. CLOSE UP   #5

>   #5
>   (Furious)
>   I used to play in a back yard that
>   was filled with garbage. Maybe it
>   still smells on me.

65. CLOSE UP   #10

>   #10
>   (Beginning to anger)
>   Now listen, sonny. . . .

66. LONG SHOT   ENTIRE TABLE OVER FOREMAN'S SHOULDER

Foreman has risen.

>   FOREMAN
>   (#5)
>   Now let's be reasonable.   There's
>   nothing personal. . . .

#5 shoots to his feet.

>   #5
>   (Loud)
>   There is something personal!

He looks around at the others, all looking at him. Then, suddenly

he has nothing to say. He sits down, fists clenched. #3 gets up
and walks to him, pats him on the back. #5 doesn't look up.

>   #3
>   Come on now. He didn't mean you,
>   feller. Let's not be so sensitive.

67. MEDIUM SHOT   #'S 11, 12, FOREMAN   SHOOTING OVER #'S 3, 4

>   #11
>   (Softly)
>   This sensitivity I can understand.

The Foreman looks at #11, and his face shows distaste for him in
spite of himself. #12 gets up and walks to the window.

>   FOREMAN
>   All right, let's stop all this arguing.
>   We're wasting time here.
>   (Pointing to #8)
>   It's your turn. Let's go.

68. MEDIUM SHOT   #'S 8, 9, 10.

>   #8
>   Well, I didn't expect a turn. I
>   thought you were all supposed to be
>   convincing me. Wasn't that the idea?

>   #12
>   Check. That was the idea.

68A. CLOSE-UP   FOREMAN

>   FOREMAN
>   I forgot about that. He's right.

68B. CLOSE-UP   #10

>   #10
>   (Annoyed with #12)
>   Well, what's the difference! He's
>   the one who's keeping us in here.
>   Let's hear what he's got to say.

68C. MEDIUM SHOT   #'S 10, 11, 12, FOREMAN

>   FOREMAN
>   Now just a second. We decided to do

FOREMAN (cont.)
it a certain way. Let's stick to what
we said.

#10
(Disgusted)
Ah stop bein' a kid, willya!

FOREMAN
A kid! Listen, what d'you mean by
that?

#10
What d'ya think I mean? K-I-D, Kid!

FOREMAN
What, just because I'm trying to keep
this thing organized? Listen. . . .

He gets up.

FOREMAN
You want to do it? Here. You sit
here. You take the responsibility.
I'll just shut up, that's all.

#10
Listen, what are you gettin' so hot
about? Calm down, willya.

FOREMAN
Don't tell me to calm down! Here!
Here's the chair.
(Gesturing toward his
empty chair)
You keep it goin' smooth and everything.
What d'ya think it's a snap? Come on,
Mr. Foreman. Let's see how great you'd
run the show.

#10 turns to #11.

#10
(Grinning helplessly)
Did y'ever see such a thing?

FOREMAN
(Loud)
You think it's funny or something?

#12 walks over to him from the window.

                    #12
          Take it easy. The whole thing's
          unimportant.

68D. CLOSE UP   FOREMAN

He glares up at #12.

                    FOREMAN
          Unimportant? You want to try it?

                    #12
          No. Listen, you're doing a beautiful
          job. Nobody wants to change.

The Foreman turns away from #12 and looks at the rest of the jury.
He is embarrassed now. For a moment he tries to think of something
to say. Then, abruptly he sits down. Camera holds on him. He
looks down at the table.

68E. MEDIUM SHOT   #'S 8, 9, 10

They all look in direction of Foreman. There is a pause. Then:

                    #10
          All right. Let's hear from somebody.

There is another pause.

                    #8
          Well, it's all right with me if you
          want me to tell you how I feel about
          it right now.

68F. CLOSE UP   FOREMAN

He looks down at table.

                    FOREMAN
                   (Softly)
          I don't care what you do.

68G. MEDIUM SHOT   #'S 8, 9, 10

#8 waits for a moment, and then begins. As he speaks, #12 walks
into shot, stands behind #9.

#8

All right. I haven't got anything
brilliant. I only know as much as
you do. According to the testimony
the boy looks guilty. Maybe he is.
I sat there in court for six days
listening while the evidence built
up. You know everybody sounded so
positive that I started to get a
peculiar feeling about this trial.
I mean nothing is that positive. I
had questions I would have liked to
ask. Maybe they wouldn't have meant
anything. I don't know. But I
started to feel that the defense
counsel wasn't conducting a thorough
enough cross-examination. He let too
many things go. Little things.

#10

What little things? Listen, when
these guys don't ask questions that's
because they know the answers already,
and they figure they'll be hurt.

#8

Maybe. It's also possible for a
lawyer to be just plain stupid,
isn't it? It's possible.

69. CLOSE UP #6

#6

You sound like you met my brother-in-
law once.

A few of the jurors laugh.

70. CLOSE UP #8

#8

I kept putting myself in the place of
the boy. I would have asked for
another lawyer I think. I mean if I
was on trial for my life I'd want my
lawyer to tear the prosecution witnesses to shreds, or at least to try.

#8 (cont.)
Look, there was one alleged eye-witness
to this killing. Someone else claims
he heard the killing and then saw the
boy running out afterward. There was
a lot of circumstantial evidence, but
actually those two witnesses were the
entire case for the prosecution.
We're dealing with a human life here.
Supposing they were wrong?

71. CLOSE UP   #12

He stands behind #8 and looks down at him.

#12
What do you mean supposing they were
wrong? What's the point of having
witnesses at all?

72. MEDIUM SHOT   #'S 8, 9, 12

#12 stands behind #8. #8 is turned to look up at him. #9 listens
carefully.

#8
Could they be wrong?

#12
They sat on the stand under oath.
What are you trying to say?

#8
They're only people. People make mis-
takes. Could they be wrong?

#12
I. . . . No! I don't think so!

#8
Do you know so?

#12
Well now listen, nobody can <u>know</u> a
thing like that. This isn't <u>an</u>
exact science. . . .

73. CLOSE UP   #8

As he turns away from #12, satisfied.

> #8
> (Quietly)
> That's right. It isn't.

74. LONG SHOT   ENTIRE TABLE FROM BEHIND #7

There is silence for a moment. #12 walks back to his seat.   #3
gets up angrily and strides down to a position behind #5.

> #3
> (To #8)
> All right. Let's try to get to the point
> here. What about the switch-knife they
> found in the father's chest?

75. CLOSE UP   #2

> #2
> (Nervously)
> Well, wait a minute. I think we
> oughta. . . . There are some people who
> haven't talked yet. Shouldn't we . . .

76. MEDIUM SHOT   #3 STANDING BEHIND #5

> #3
> (To #2)
> Look, they can talk whenever they like.
> Now just be quiet a second, willya please.

77. FLASH CLOSE UP   #2

Wounded at being slapped down by #3, he looks down at table.

78. MEDIUM SHOT   #'S 3, 5, 6, 7 SHOOTING OVER #8'S SHOULDER

> #3
> (To #8)
> Okay what about the knife? You know,
> the one that fine upright boy admitted
> buying on the night of the murder.
> Let's talk about that.

79. MEDIUM SHOT   #'S 7, 8, 9 SHOOTING OVER #3'S SHOULDER

#8 appears just a bit pleased at this turn of conversation.

                         #8
              All right. Let's talk about it.
              Let's get it in here and look at it.
              I'd like to see it again.
                    (He turns toward Foreman)
              Mr. Foreman?

80. MEDIUM SHOT   CENTERED ON FOREMAN

He looks at #8 for a moment.

Then he gets up and moves to the door, camera panning with him.

                         #3 (Off)
              We all know what it looks like. I
              don't see why we have to look at it
              again.

The Foreman knocks on the door. The door opens and the guard
pokes his head into the room.

81. MEDIUM SHOT   #'S 3, 4, 5

#3 still stands behind #5. He looks at door where Foreman stands
Whispering to the guard. Then #3 turns to table.

                         #3
              What are we gonna get out of seeing
              the knife again?

                         #5
                    (Looking up)
              You brought it up.

                         #3
                    (Giving him a look and
                    then turning to #4)
              What do you think?

                         #4
              The gentleman has a right to see
              exhibits in evidence.

#3 shrugs and turns away.

                         #4
                    (Across to #8)
              The knife, and the way it was bought,

#4 (cont.)
is pretty strong evidence. Don't
you think so?

82. CLOSE UP   #8

#8
I do.

83. MEDIUM SHOT   CENTERED ON #4, SHOOTING PAST #8'S PROFILE

#4
Good. Now supposing we take these
facts one at a time. One. The boy
admitted going out of his house at
8 o'clock on the night of the murder
after being punched several times by
his father.

#8
He didn't say punched. He said hit.
There's a difference between a slap
and a punch.

#4
(Doggedly)
After being hit several times by
his father. Two. The boy went
directly to a neighborhood junk shop
where he bought a . . . what do you call
these things. . . .

SIMULTANEOUSLY   #3   #4
Switch-knives.   a switch-blade knife.
                    (To #3)
                    Thanks.

#4
Three. This wasn't what you'd call an
ordinary knife. It had a very unusual
carved handle. Four. The storekeeper
who sold it to him identified it and
said it was the only one of its kind he
had ever had in stock. Five. At oh,
about 8:45 the boy ran into some friends
of his in front of a tavern. Am I
correct so far?

#8
Yes, you are.

#3
(To #8)
You bet he is.
(To all)
Now listen to this man. He knows
what he's talking about.

#4
The boy talked with his friends for about
an hour, leaving them at about 9:45.
During this time they saw the switch-
knife. Six. Each of them identified
the death-weapon in court as that same
knife. Seven. The boy arrived home at
about 10 o'clock. Now this is where
the stories offered by the boy and the
state begin to diverge slightly.

84. CLOSE UP   #8

He listens quietly, patiently, waiting his turn.

#4
He claims that he stayed home until
11:30 and then went to one of those
all-night movies. He returned home
at about 3:15 in the morning to find
his father dead and himself arrested.

85. MEDIUM SHOT   CENTERED ON #4

#4
Now, what happened to the switch-
knife? This is the charming and
imaginative little fable the boy
invented. He claims that the knife
fell through a hole in his pocket
sometime between 11:30 and 3:15 while
he was on his trip to the movies, and
that he never saw it again. Now
there is a tale, gentlemen. I think
it's quite clear that the boy never
went to the movies that night. No
one in the house saw him go out at
11:30. No one at the theatre

> #4 (cont.)
> identified him. He couldn't even
> remember the names of the pictures
> he saw. What actually happened is
> this. The boy stayed home, had another
> fight with his father, stabbed him to
> death with the knife at ten minutes
> after twelve and fled from the house.
> He even remembered to wipe the knife
> clean of fingerprints.

86. MEDIUM SHOT   THE DOOR

It opens. The guard enters carrying a curiously designed knife
with a tag hanging from it. #4 walks into the shot and takes the
knife from the guard. He turns and moves back to his seat as the
guard exits. He stands behind his seat holding his knife. Camera
is now at an angle which includes #'s 4, 5, 8, 9.

> #4
> (Leaning over to #8)
> Everyone connected with the case
> identified this knife. Now are you
> trying to tell me that it really
> fell through a hole in the boy's
> pocket and that someone picked it
> up off the street, went to the boy's
> house and stabbed his father with it
> just to be amusing.

> #8
> No. I'm saying that it's possible
> that the boy lost the knife, and
> that someone else stabbed his father
> with a similar knife. It's possible.

87. CLOSE UP   #4

He flicks open the blade of the knife and jams it into the table.
Camera dollies back to show knife in table. Jurors #2, 5, 10, 11,
12 get up and crowd around to get a better look at it.

> #4
> Take a look at that knife. It's a very
> unusual knife. I've never seen one like
> it. Neither had the storekeeper who sold
> it to the boy. Aren't you trying to make
> us accept a pretty incredible coincidence?

88.   CLOSE UP   #8

                              #8
                    I'm not trying to make anyone accept it.
                    I'm just saying that it's possible.

89.   CLOSE UP   #3

Standing next to #4, is suddenly infuriated at #8's calmness. He
leans forward.

                              #3
                          (Shouting)
                    And I'm saying it's not possible.

90.   CLOSE UP   #8

He stands for a moment in the silence. Then he reaches into his
pocket and swiftly withdraws a knife. He holds it in front of his
face, and flicks open the blade. Then he leans forward and sticks
the knife into the table next to the other.

91.   BIG CLOSE UP   THE TWO ORNATELY CARVED KNIVES

Stuck into the table, side by side, each exactly alike. There is
an immediate burst of sound in the room.

                              #7
                    (What is this?
                    (
                    (#12
        Simultaneous(Where'd that come from?
                    (
                    (#6
                    (What is it?
                    (
                    (#2
                    (How d'you like that!

92.   MEDIUM SHOT   THE JURORS, CLUSTERED AROUND KNIVES

#8 is standing away from the table, watching. #3 looks up at him.

                              #3
                          (Amazed)
                    What are you trying to do?

#10
(Loud)
Yeah! What's going on here? Who do
you think you are?

93. CLOSE UP #6

In the group of faces. He has taken the knife out of the table and
is holding it.

#6
Look at it! It's the same knife!

94. CLOSE UP #8

Watching them closely, a few steps back from the group. The ad lib
hubbub still goes on.

#4
Quiet! Let's be quiet!

The noise begins to subside.

95. MEDIUM SHOT CENTERED ON #4

He takes the knife from #5's hand and speaks to #8, who stands at
left of frame.

#4
Where'd you get it?

#8
I was walking for a couple of hours last
night, just thinking. I walked through
the boy's neighborhood. The knife comes
from a little pawnshop three blocks from
his house. It cost two dollars.

#4
It's against the law to buy or sell
switch-blade knives.

#8
That's right. I broke the law.

#3 pushes in next to #4. He is much too angry for the situation.
Others look at him peculiarly as he speaks.

>   #3
>   Listen, you pulled a real bright trick
>   here. Now supposing you tell me what
>   you proved. Maybe there are ten knives
>   like that. So what?

96. CLOSE UP   #8

>   #8
>   Maybe there are.

97. MEDIUM SHOT   #'S 3, 4, 7, 11, 5.

#3 is silent for a minute. He knows that a tiny dent has been
made in the case. He splutters.

>   #3
>   So what does that mean? What do you
>   think it is? It's the same kind of
>   knife. So what's that? The dis-
>   covery of the age, or something?

>   #11
>   (Quietly)
>   This does not change the fact that it
>   would be still an incredible coinci-
>   dence for another person to have made
>   the stabbing with the same kind of
>   knife.

>   #3
>   That's right! He's right.

>   #7
>   The odds are a million to one.

98. CLOSE UP   #8

>   #8
>   It's possible.

99. CLOSE UP   #4

#4 looks calmly at #8, and speaks quietly.

>   #4
>   But not very probable.

100. CLOSE UP   #8

Looking steadily at #4.

> FOREMAN
> (Off)
> Listen, let's take seats. There's
> no point in milling around here.

101. LONG SHOT   THE JURYMEN

As they begin to move back to their seats. #4 flips the knife
back into the table and sits down. There is quiet ad libbing as
most of the jurors take seats. #8 stays on his feet, watching
them.

102. MEDIUM SHOT   FOREMAN, #2, #3

#2 turns to the Foreman with a nervous half-smile.

> #2
> It's interesting that he'd find a
> knife exactly like the one the boy
> bought. . . .

> FOREMAN
> (Ignoring him, speaking
> to all)
> Okay. Now what?

> #3
> (To #2)
> What's interesting?   You think it
> proves anything?

> #2
> Well, no.   I was just. . . .

> #3
> (Turning away)
> Interesting!

103. MEDIUM SHOT   #8, STANDING BEHIND #9, SHOOTING OVER #3'S SHOULDER

#3 suddenly has an idea.   He points at #8.

> #3
> Listen, how come the kid bought the

                    #3   (cont.)
          knife to begin with?

                    #8
          Well, he claims that. . . .

                    #3
          I know. He bought it as a present
          for a friend of his. He was gonna
          give it to him the next day, because
          he busted the other kid's knife
          dropping it on the pavement.

                    #8
          That's what he said.

                    #7
               (Off)
          Boloney!

                    #9
          The friend testified that the boy
          did break his knife.

                    #3
          Yeah. And how long before the kill-
          ing? Three weeks. Right? So how
          come our noble lad bought this knife
          one half hour after his father
          smacked him, and three and a half
          hours before they found it shoved
          up to here in the father's chest?

104. CLOSE UP   #7

                    #7
               (Grinning)
          Well, he was <u>gonna</u> give the knife to
          his friend. He just wanted to use it
          for a minute.

     There is scattered laughter.

105. MEDIUM SHOT   #8, BEHIND #9

     #8 waits till the laughter dies down.

                              #8
                        (To #3)
              Look, maybe you can answer this. It's
              one of the questions I wanted to ask
              in court. If the boy bought the knife
              to use on his father, how come he
              showed what was going to be the murder
              weapon to three friends of his just a
              couple of hours before the killing?

106. LONG SHOT   THE ENTIRE JURY

     There is silence. The silence holds for a minute.   #8 watches
     them, and then walks to the window and looks out. The following
     speeches are simultaneous.

                              #10
                   (So maybe he decided to knife his
                   (old man when he got home.
     Simultaneous(
                   (FOREMAN
                   (He never told his friends he bought
                   (the thing as a present.

107. CLOSE UP   #3

     He gets to his feet.

                              #3
                         (Angry)
                   Listen, all of this is just talk.
                   The boy lied and you know it.

108. MEDIUM SHOT   #8 AT WINDOW

     He turns, waits a beat, and then walks toward table.

                              #8
                   He may have lied.

     He reaches #10 and puts his hand on #10's shoulder.

                              #8
                   Do you think he lied?

                              #10
                   Now that's a stupid question. Sure
                   he lied!

109. MEDIUM SHOT   #'S 8, 10, 11, SHOOTING BETWEEN #'S 4 AND 5

>   #8
>   (To #4)
>   Do you?

>   #4
>   You don't have to ask me that.   You
>   know my answer.   He lied.

>   #8
>   (To #5)
>   Do you think he lied?

110. CLOSE UP   #5

He can't answer immediately.   He looks around nervously.

>   #5
>   Well . . . I don't know. . . .

111. MEDIUM SHOT   #3, STANDING

>   #3
>   Now wait a second!

He starts to stride around table past #'s 4, 5, 6

>   #3
>   What are you, the kid's lawyer or
>   something?   Who do you think you are
>   to start cross-examining us?   Listen,
>   there are still eleven of us in here
>   who think he's guilty.

#3 is standing behind #7 now.

>   #7
>   Right!   What do you think you're
>   gonna accomplish?   You're not gonna
>   change anybody's mind.   So if you
>   want to be stubborn and hang this
>   jury go ahead.   The kid'll be tried
>   again and found guilty sure as he's
>   born.

112. MEDIUM SHOT   #8

Camera pans with him as he walks back to his seat. He stands behind it. #'s 3, 7, 9 are included in the shot, #3 standing behind
#7's seat.

                    #8
          You're probably right.

                    #7
          So what are you gonna do about it?
          We can be here all night.

                    #9
          It's only one night. A boy may die.

#7 glares at #9, but has no answer. #8 sits down.

                    #7
          Brother! Anybody got a deck of
          cards?

There is silence. #3 starts a walk over to the coat rack to get
some cigarettes from his jacket. Camera holds centered on #8 for
a moment. The room is quiet.

113. MEDIUM SHOT   CENTERED ON #2, SHOOTING OVER #10 AND #11

                    #2
               (To Foreman)
          I don't think he ought to joke about
          it.

                  FOREMAN
               (Annoyed)
          What do you want me to do?

#2 would like to say something to #7, but daren't. #10 slams his
hand down on the table.

                    #10
          Listen, I don't see what all this
          stuff about the knife has to do
          with anything. Somebody saw the
          kid stab his father. What more do
          we need? You guys can talk the
          ears right offa my head. Know what
          I mean? I got three garages of mine
          going to pot while you're talking!
          Let's get done and get outa here!

                        #11
                   (Mildly)
              The knife was very important to the
              district attorney. He spent one
              whole day. . . .

                        #10
                   (Mad)
              He's a fifteenth assistant, or some-
              thing. What does he know?

#10 blows his nose loudly. #11 shifts in his seat away from #10.
#10 glares at him over the handkerchief.

                   FOREMAN
              Okay. I think we oughta get on with
              it now. These side arguments only
              slow us up.

He leans down to #8.

                   FOREMAN
              What about it?

114. CLOSE UP   #8

He sits in his seat quietly.

                        #6
                   (Off)
              You're the only one.

#8 nods. He still sits silently, thinking. Then he looks slowly
around the table for a moment. Finally he seems to have made his
decision.

                        #8
              I have a proposition to make to all
              of you.

115. CLOSE UP   #5

Listening closely.

                        #8
              I want to call for a vote. I'd like
              you eleven men to vote by secret
              written ballot.

116. CLOSE UP   #9

 Listening closely.

>   #8
> I'll abstain. If there are still
> eleven votes for guilty I won't
> stand alone. We'll take a guilty
> verdict in to the judge right now.

117. CLOSE UP   #2

 Listening closely.

>   #8
> But if anyone votes not guilty we'll
> stay and talk this thing out.

118. CLOSE UP   #11

 Listening closely. There is a pause.

>   #8
> Well that's all. If you want to
> try it, I'm ready.

>   #7
> Okay. Let's do it.

119. LONG SHOT   ENTIRE JURY SHOOTING FROM HIGH OVER HEAD OF FOREMAN

>   FOREMAN
> That sounds fair. Is everyone agreed?

 Some of the jurors nod their heads.

>   FOREMAN
> Anyone doesn't agree?

 There is silence.

>   FOREMAN
> Okay. Pass these along.

The Foreman begins to pass out slips of paper. #8 gets up and
walks over to the window. He stands with his back to it. Camera
moves higher, so that it is shooting almost directly down on
table. The jurors pass the slips along. And finally each of them
begins to write.

120. CLOSE UP   #8

Watching, waiting.

121. LONG SHOT   ENTIRE JURY, FROM ABOVE

Writing. Now some of them begin to fold up their slips, and pass
them back to the Foreman. As the passing back begins, camera begins to move down, centering on entire jury. By the time all the
slips are back the camera is shooting over shoulder of Foreman.
He stacks the slips on the table next to him. Then he looks over
at #8.

122. CLOSE UP   #8

Looking back at Foreman, waiting.

123. CLOSE UP   FOREMAN

He looks from #8 down to table. He picks up the first slip, opens
it, and reads.

                    FOREMAN
          Guilty.

The Foreman opens another slip and reads it.

                    FOREMAN
          Guilty.

124. CLOSE UP   #2

And now camera begins a long slow pan around the table, catching a
close up of each face as the Foreman reads off the slips. No one
moves. Each man waits tensely.

                    FOREMAN
          Guilty.
               (A pause)
          Guilty.
               (A pause)
          Guilty.
               (A pause)
          Guilty.
               (A pause)
          Guilty.
               (A pause)

                              FOREMAN   (cont.)
          Guilty.
                    (A pause)
          Guilty.
                    (A pause)

The camera is now on #10. He waits anxiously.

                              FOREMAN
          Not guilty.

#10 shows instant anger. We hear a quick babble of shots. A hand
slams down on the table.

125. CLOSE UP   #8

He seems to relax a bit. He starts back for his seat.

126. MEDIUM SHOT   #'S 10, 11, 12, FOREMAN

The foreman reads off the last ballot.

                              FOREMAN
          Guilty.

                              #10
                    (Angry)
          Boy! How do you like that!

                              #7
                    (Off)
          And another chap flips his wig!

                              #10
          All right, who was it? Come on, I
          want to know!

                              #11
                    (Looking at #10)
          Excuse me. This was a secret ballot.
          We agreed on this point, no? If the
          gentleman wants it to remain secret. . . .

127. MEDIUM SHOT   CENTERED ON #3

                              #3
          Secret? What d'ya mean, secret?

                        #3   (cont.)
          There are no secrets in a jury room!
          I know who it was!

He stands up and walks over to #5's seat, camera panning with him.
#5 turns and looks up at him. #3 stares down at #5.

                        #3
          Brother, you're really something! You
          come in here and you vote guilty like
          everybody else, and then this golden-
          voiced preacher over here starts to
          tear your heart out with stories about
          a poor little kid who just couldn't
          help becoming a murderer. So you
          change your vote. If that isn't the
          most sickening. . . . Why dontcha drop a
          quarter in his collection box?

#5 listens to this, his face growing darker and angrier. Toward
the conclusion of the speech he begins to rise to his feet, facing
#3.

                        #5
          Now wait a minute!

But #3 turns his back on him and starts to walk away. Camera
holds on #5. Then he starts out after #3.

                        #5
          (Angry)
          Who d'ya think you are to talk
          like. . . .

#3 has his back to #5. #5 reaches out and takes his shoulder.

                        #5
          Who d'ya think you are. . . .

#3 shakes him off angrily, and turns to face him. #4 is on his
feet swiftly now, and slips in between them. He takes #5's arm.

                        #4
          (Calmly)
          All right, let's calm down. . . .

                        #5
          Who does he think he is?

#4 leads #5 back to his seat, camera panning with him.

                    #5
          I mean did you see him?

                    #4
                 (Softly)
          Just sit down. He's very excitable.
          Forget it. It doesn't matter.

128. MEDIUM SHOT   #3 STANDING BEHIND #2

                    #3
          Excitable! You bet I'm excitable.
          We're trying to put a guilty man
          into the chair where he belongs, and
          all of a sudden somebody's telling
          us fairy tales . . . and we're listening!

#2 leans back.

                    #2
                 (Mildly)
          Take it easy.

                    #3
          What do you mean take it easy! D'you
          feel like seeing a proven murderer
          walking the streets? Why don't we
          give him his knife back? Make it
          easier for him!

He indicates #5 with a wave of his hand.

                    #3
          Where does he have the right. . . .

129. MEDIUM SHOT   #'S 10, 11, 12, FOREMAN

                    FOREMAN
          Okay, let's stop the yelling.

                    #11
          Please. I would like to say something
          here. I have always thought that a
          man was entitled to have unpopular
          opinions in this country. This is
          the reason I came here. In my own
          country, I am ashamed to say. . . .

                              #10
                    What do we have to listen to now, the
                    whole history of your country?

#11 subsides into silence, embarrassed. #10 glares at him.

130. MEDIUM SHOT   #'S 5, 6, 7, 8.

                              #7
                    Yeah, let's stick to the subject.

He turns to #5.

                              #7
                    Now I'm talking facts. What made
                    you change your vote?

131. MEDIUM CLOSE UP   #9, #8

#9 speaks softly. #8 watches him as if he had known all along.

                              #9
                    There's nothing for him to tell you.
                    He didn't change his vote. I did.

132. CLOSE UP   #7

He reacts to this with obvious disgust.

133. MEDIUM CLOSE UP   #'S 7, 9

                              #9
                       (To #7)
                    Would you like me to tell you why?

134. CLOSE UP   #7

                              #7
                       (Turning away)
                    No, I wouldn't like you to tell me why.

135. CLOSE UP   #9

                              #9
                    Well, I'd like to make it clear anyway,
                    if you don't mind.

136. MEDIUM SHOT   FOREMAN, #12, #11, #10

#10
Do we have to listen to this?

FOREMAN
(Tough, to #10)
The man wants to talk.

#10 looks angrily at him and then turns away. The Foreman looks proudly down at #9.

137. MEDIUM SHOT   #9, #8, #7

#9
(In foreman's direction)
Thank you.
(To #7)
This gentleman
(Indicating #8)
has been standing alone against us. He
doesn't say the boy is not guilty. He
just isn't sure. Well, it's not easy to
stand alone against the ridicule of others,
even when there's a worthy cause.

#7 raises his eyes to heaven, shakes his head in disgust, and gets up. He turns his back on #9 and heads for the men's room. #9 stands up and speaks spiritedly to his back.

#9
So he gambled for support, and I gave
it to him. I respect his motives.
The boy on trial is probably guilty.
But I want to hear more. Right now
the vote is ten to two.

The bathroom door slams shut. #9 takes one step toward it, furious at #7's arrogance.

#9
(Shouting)
I'm talking here! You have no right
to. . . .

But he is stopped by #8's hand on his shoulder. He turns to #8.

#8
(Gently)
He can't hear you. He never will.

                         #8   (cont.)
              Let's sit down.

#9 nods and slowly takes his seat, spent with his effort. #8
remains standing, looking down at him.

138. MEDIUM SHOT   FOREMAN, #2, #3

                         #3
              Well if the speech is over, maybe
              we can go on.

                      FOREMAN
              I think we ought to take a break.
              One man's inside there. Let's wait
              for him.

The Foreman stands up and camera pans with him as he walks around
the table to where the two knives are stuck into table. He plucks
the tagged one out, and closes it. #4 opens up his newspaper and
begins to read it. #3 gets up and, standing behind his chair,
stretches. We hear murmured ad lib conversations, and the sound
of several other jurors getting up. The Foreman goes to the door,
camera holding on him. He knocks. The door opens and the guard
pokes his head in. The Foreman hands him the knife. The guard
closes the door. Foreman walks back to his seat camera dollying
back with him. #2 sits at table cleaning his glasses. Camera
dollies back of #'s 11 and 12, still seated. Their heads are
turned toward each other. Camera is at their backs. In background, #3 stands near door, thinking. He watches #5, and while
we hear following dialogue between #'s 11 and 12, #3 watches as #5
gets up, crosses in front of him, and goes to far end of room. #3
obviously wants the right opportunity to talk with him alone.

                        #12
              Looks like we're really hung up here.
              I mean that thing with the old man
              was pretty unexpected.

#11 nods and shrugs.

                        #12
              I wish I knew how we could break this
              up.
                   (Suddenly smiling)
              Y'know in advertising . . . I told you
              I worked at an agency, didn't I?
                   (#11 nods)

#12   (cont.)
Well there are some pretty strange
people . . . not strange really . . . they
just have peculiar ways of expressing
themselves, y'know what I mean?
    (#11 nods again)
Well it's probably the same in your
business, right? What do you do?

#11
I'm a watchmaker.

#12
Really? The finest watchmakers come
from Europe I imagine.
    (#11 bows slightly)
Anyway, I was telling you, in the
agency, when they reach a point like
this in a meeting, there's always
some character ready with an idea.
And it kills me, I mean it's the
weirdest thing in the whole world
sometimes the way they precede the
idea with some kind of phrase. Like . . .
Oh, some account exec'll say,
"Here's an idea. Let's run it up the
flagpole and see if anyone salutes
it."
    (#12 laughs)
I mean it's idiotic, but it's funny . . .

Camera dollies past them in on #3 now as he walks over to #5 who
stands at the water fountain. #5 looks up at him over a cup of
water.

#3
Look, I was a little excited. Well,
you know how it is, I . . . I didn't
mean to get nasty or anything.

#5 finishes the water and tosses the cup in the basket.

#3
I'm glad you're not the kind who lets
these emotional appeals influence him.

#10 walks into the shot, stands next to #5, sniffing.

#3
I'm telling you there's always someone who wants to give a proven
criminal another chance.
          (Thumbing in #8's direction)
Like this guy. . . .

#10
They're old women. Waddya expect?
          (To #5)
Look, nobody meant anything before
y'know? It's just sometimes ya get
heated up. Listen, intelligent
people gotta stick together here to
see that justice is done. That's the
most important. You stay with us,
hear?

#10 claps #5 on the back, and looks off across the room.

139. MEDIUM SHOT   #8

Standing alone against the window at far end of room, watching
#'s 3, 5, 10. He watches for a moment and then turns and walks
toward men's room, camera following. #7 is at sink drying his
hands and face on a paper towel, his back to camera. He looks up
into the mirror now, and we see his face in mirror, looking at #8
whose back is also to camera. #7 turns and steps away from sink.
#8 goes to sink and runs water. #7, still drying, watches him.

#7
Say, are you a salesman?

#8
          (Looking at him in mirror)
I'm an architect.

#7
You know what the soft sell is?

#8, his face dripping now, looks at him again in the mirror.

#7
You're pretty good at it. I'll tell ya.
I got a different technique. Jokes.
Drinks. Knock 'em on their tails. I
made twenty-seven thousand last year sell-
ing marmalade. That's not bad.

#8 bends to rinsing his face. #7 watches him for a moment.

> #7
> What are ya getting out of it, kicks?

#8 looks up at him.

> #7
> The boy is guilty, pal. Like the nose
> on your face. So let's go home before
> we get sore throats.

#8 turns off the water, and turns to #7. #7 hands him a paper
towel and waits. #8 starts to dry his face, watching #7.

> #8
> (Through the towel)
> What's the difference whether you get
> it here or at the ball game?

#7 looks at him narrowly, and then smiles.

> #7
> No difference, pal. No difference at all.

#7 exits, letting the door slam. #8 slowly dries his face. A
moment later the door opens. We hear a loud laugh from outside.
#6 enters the bathroom. The door closes. #6 walks over to the
sink, turns on the water. During this next exchange he lets it
run over his wrists.

> #6
> (Sarcastically)
> Nice bunch of guys.

> #8
> I guess they're the same as any.

> #6
> That loud, heavy-set guy, the one who was
> tellin' us about his kid . . . the way he was
> talking . . . boy, that was an embarrassing
> thing.

> #8
> (Smiling)
> Yeah.

#8 stands watching #6 cool his wrists.

> #6
> What a murderous day.

He looks at #8 in the mirror.

> #6
> (Pointedly)
> You think we'll be much longer?

> #8
> I don't know.

> #6
> He's guilty for sure. There's not a doubt
> in the whold world. We shoulda been done
> already.

#8 doesn't answer him.

> #6
> Listen, I don't care, y'know. It beats
> workin'.

He laughs, and #8 smiles. Then #6 pointedly looks at #8. His
smile vanishes.

> #6
> You think he's not guilty?

> #8
> I don't know. It's possible.

> #6
> (Friendly)
> I don't know you, but I'm bettin' you've
> never been wronger in your life. Y'oughta
> wrap it up. You're wastin' your time.

> #8
> Supposing you were the one on trial?

#6 looks at him seriously. There is a pause. He takes a towel
and dries his hands.

> #6
> I'm not used to supposing. I'm just a

#6 (cont.)
working man. My boss does the supposing.
But I'll try one. Supposing you talk us
all outa this, and the kid really did
knife his father?

#6 looks at #8, and then exits. #8 stands there alone for a few moments, and we know that this is the problem which has been tormenting him. He doesn't know, and never will. Finally he exits.

* * *

#8
I don't know if there are any more
to make. I just have a feeling. . . .

#9
Well . . . I think the boy is probably
guilty. But you go ahead and see
what comes out. For the time being
it's a little less onesided. That's
all. My vote is only temporary. It's
all the support I'm equipped to give.

#8 smiles, and nods understandingly.

                    FOREMAN
          (Off)
     Okay. Let's take seats.

141. LONG SHOT   THE ENTIRE JURY

As they move for their seats. Finally all are seated. Camera dollies in on #2 as he settles his glasses on his nose and turns to look up at the wall clock. He turns to Foreman.

                    #2
     Looks like we'll be here for dinner.

---

140. [A page or part of a page of the only existing copy of the final shooting script is missing here. This situation is not unusual; many of the shooting scripts to be found in the libraries or the files of major studios and production companies have missing material, a fact which illustrates clearly the expendability of the shooting script once the true text, the film itself, is created. Rather than transcribing from the film or using the descriptive continuity, we have chosen to leave this break as we found it. It is remarkable that so much material in the form of shooting scripts has survived time and indifference. In large part we owe the preservation of shooting scripts to their possible value as legal documents in a litigious industry.—THE EDITORS.]

142. CLOSE UP   FOREMAN

He scowls at #2, then turns and addresses the group.

> FOREMAN
> Okay. Let's get down to business.
> Who wants to start it off?

There is a pause.

143. MEDIUM SHOT   #'S 4, 5, 6

#'s 4 and 6 start to speak at the same time.

> (SIMULTANEOUS)

#6	#4
Well, I'd like to make a point. . . .	Maybe it would be profitable if we. . . .
(To #4)	(To #6)
Pardon me.	I'm sorry, go ahead.

> #6
> I didn't mean to interrupt. . . .

> #4
> No. Go ahead. It's all right.

> #6
> Well . . . I was going to say, well
> this is probably a small point,
> but anyway. . . .
>   (Across to #8)
> The boy had a motive for the killing.
> You know, the beatings and all. So
> if he didn't do it, who did? Who else
> had the motive? That's my point. I
> mean nobody goes out and kills someone
> without a motive, not unless he's
> just plain nuts. Right?

He sits back rather proudly.

144. CLOSE UP   #8

> #8
> As far as I know we're supposed to
> decide whether or not the boy on
> trial is guilty beyond a reasonable

#8 (cont.)
doubt. We're not concerned with
anyone else's motives here. That's
a job for the police.

145. MEDIUM CLOSE UP   #4, #3

#4
Very true. But we can't help letting
the only motive we know of creep into
our thoughts, can we? And we can't
help asking ourselves who else might
have had a motive. Logically, these
things follow.
(Nodding at #6)
This gentleman is asking a reasonable
question. Somebody killed him. If
it wasn't the boy, who was it?

#3
(Grinning)
Modjelewski.

146. CLOSE UP   #7

#7
(Mock indignance)
You're talking about the man I
love! The world's fastest rookie. . . .

147. MEDIUM CLOSE UP   #'S 3, 4

#3
(Still grinning)
He's got a rubber arm!

We hear a few laughs off.

#4
(Angry)
I don't see what's funny about this.
If you haven't got anything to add
besides jokes I suggest you listen.

#3
(Still grinning)
Okay. It's just letting off steam.
I'm sorry. Go ahead.

#3, as always, shows real respect for #4. The grin fades from his face.

#4
(Across to #8)
Well maybe you can answer me. Who
else might have killed the father?

148. MEDIUM SHOT CENTERED ON #8

#8
Well I don't know. The father
wasn't exactly a model citizen.
The boy's lawyer brought this out
pretty clearly, I thought. He
was in prison once. He was known
to be a consistent horse better.
He spent a lot of time in neighborhood bars and he'd get into fist
fights sometimes after a couple of
drinks. One of them was over a
woman no one could seem to remember.
He was a tough, cruel, primitive
kind of a man who never held a job
for more than six months in his
life. So here are a few possibilities.
He could have been murdered by any
one of many men he served time with
in prison. By a bookmaker. By a
man he'd beaten up. By a woman he'd
picked up. By anyone of the characters
he was known to hang out with. . . .

149. CLOSE UP #10

#10
(Blustering)
Boy-oh-boy, that's the biggest
load 'a tripe I ever. . . . Listen,
we know the father was a bum!
So what has that got to do with
anything?

150. MEDIUM CLOSE UP #'S 8, 9

#8
I didn't bring it up. I was asked
who else might have killed him.

#8 (cont.)
I gave my answer.

#9
(Mildly, pointing
across table)
That gentleman over there asked a
direct question.

151. CLOSE UP   #10

#10
Everyone's a lawyer!

152. CLOSE UP   #3

He points down at #9

#3
Listen, as long as you've joined
the discussion, supposing you answer
this question. The old man. . . .

153. MEDIUM SHOT   #'S 8, 9

#8
(Firmly)
There's no need to be sarcastic.

He looks unwaveringly at #3.

154. MEDIUM SHOT   CENTERED ON #3

#3's face hardens. He stares at #8.

#3
(Controlled now)
Would you please answer
this question for me. . . .
(Then, sarcastically)
Sir. . . .
(He pauses)
The old man who lived downstairs
heard the kid yell out "I'm going
to kill you". A split second later
he heard a body hit the floor. Then
he saw the kid run out of the house.
Now what does all that mean to you?

155. MEDIUM SHOT   CENTERED ON #9, SHOOTING OVER #3'S SHOULDER

#8 is still standing. He looks down at #9. #9 doesn't have an
answer, obviously. He looks up at #8, then down at table. #8
looks across at #3.

> #8
> I was wondering how clearly the old
> man could have heard the boy's voice
> through the ceiling.

> #3
> He didn't hear it through the ceiling.
> His window was open and so was the
> window upstairs. It was a hot night,
> remember?

> #8
> The voice came from another apartment.
> It's not that easy to identify a
> voice, especially a shouting voice.

156. CLOSE UP   FOREMAN

> FOREMAN
> He identified it in court. He picked
> the boy's voice out of five other
> voices, blindfolded.

157. LONG SHOT   ENTIRE JURY, SHOOTING FROM BEHIND FOREMAN

> #8
> That's not the same. He knows the
> boy's voice very well. They've lived
> in the same house for years. But to
> identify it positively from the apart-
> ment downstairs. Isn't it possible
> that he was wrong . . . that maybe he
> thought the boy was upstairs, and
> automatically decided that the voice
> he heard was the boy's voice?

> #4
> I think that's a bit far-fetched.

> #10
> You said a mouthful!
> (To #8)

#10 (cont.)
Look. He heard the father's body
falling, and then he saw the boy
run out of the house 15 seconds
later. He saw the boy!

#12
Check. And don't forget the woman
across the street. She looked right
into the open window and saw the boy
stab his father. I mean, isn't
that enough for you?

#8
Not right now. No, it isn't.

158. CLOSE UP   #7

#7
(Exasperated)
How do you like him? It's like talk-
ing into a dead phone!

159. MEDIUM SHOT   CENTERED ON #4, SHOOTING BETWEEN #'S 8 AND 9

#4 appears to be a bit impatient now. He gestures with a nail
clipper with which he has been clipping his nails. #3 gets up
during these lines and strides restlessly around the table.

#4
The woman saw the killing through the
windows of a moving elevated train.
The train had six cars and she saw it
through the windows of the last two
cars. She remembered the most insig-
nificant details.

160. MEDIUM SHOT   #3, STANDING BEHIND #12, SHOOTING OVER #4'S SHOULDER

#4
I don't see how you can argue with
that.

There is silence for a moment. #3 looks down at #8. #12 doodles
busily on a scrap of paper.

#3
(In #8's direction)
Well, what have you got to say about
it.

161. CLOSE UP   #8

#8
(Doggedly)
I don't know. It doesn't sound
right to me.

162. MEDIUM SHOT   #3, BEHIND #12, SHOOTING OVER #4'S SHOULDER

#3
Well supposing you think about it.

He looks down at #12, who has drawn a crude picture of an elevated
train. Camera dollies in on them.

#3
Lend me your pencil.

#12 gives it to him. #3 bends over #12 and starts to draw a tic-
tac-toe pattern on the same sheet of paper upon which #12 has
drawn the train.

#5
(Off)
Y'know I don't think he would've
shown the knife to his friends that
time. . . .

#7
(Off)
Listen, what difference does that
make?

#3 has finished the tic-tac-toe pattern. He fills in an X, hands
the pencil to #12.

#3
Your turn. We might as well pass
the time.

163. MEDIUM SHOT   CENTERED ON #8

He watches this tic-tac-toe business, suddenly angry for the first
time.

#5
(Off, to #7)
Well I don't know if it makes a
difference or not. Listen, this
boy. . . .

And #8 is up on his feet, walking fast toward #12's seat, camera
panning with him. #12 has just finished making an O and is hand-
ing pencil to #3. #8 reaches down and snatches the paper off the
table. #3 whirls around.

#3
(Furious)
Wait a minute.

#8
(Hard)
This isn't a game!

#3
(Shouting)
Who do you think you are?

He lunges at #8, but is caught by #'s 11 and 12. The Foreman
hops into it, taking him by the arm. #8 stands calmly near him,
watching. Camera dollies back, as the three jurors move #3
around the table toward his seat. Other jurors are on their feet
suddenly, watching, some crowding around. #3 is furious.

#12
(To #3)
All right, let's take it easy.

FOREMAN
(To #3)
Come on, sit down now. . . .

#3 is urged around the table. He shakes off #'s 11 and 12.

#3
I've got a good mind to walk around
the table and belt him one!

FOREMAN
Now please. I don't want any fights
in here.

He reaches for #3's arm. #3 shakes him off.

                              #3
              Did you see him? The nerve! The
              absolute nerve!

                              #10
              All right. Forget it. It's not im-
              portant. Know what I mean?

                              #3
              This isn't a game. Who does he think
              he is?

164. MEDIUM SHOT   #8

     Standing calmly alone, holding the paper he has snatched from #12,
     looking steadily at #3.

165. CLOSE UP   #3

     Glaring angrily at #8. Then, finally he sits down in his seat.

                           FOREMAN
                         (Off)
              Come on now. It's all over. Let's
              take our seats.

166. LONG SHOT   THE ENTIRE JURY FROM ABOVE

     Slowly moving to their seats, save #8. #8 looks at the paper in
     his hand, and suddenly something seems to click for him. He be-
     gins a walk around the table toward #3's seat. Camera dollies
     down and in on him. When he reaches #3's seat, #3 is busy fixing
     his tie. #8 stands behind him, looking at the paper. Then sud-
     denly he leans over #3 and throws the paper in front of him onto
     the table. #3 half rises, angry again. #4 puts a hand on his
     arm. He sits down. Camera is close on him and #8.

                              #8
              Take a look at that sketch.

167. CLOSE UP   THE SKETCH

                              #8
                         (Off)
              I wonder if anybody has an idea how
              long it takes an elevated train
              going at medium speed to pass a given
              point?

168. MEDIUM SHOT   #'S 3, 4, 5, 8

> #4
> What has that got to do with anything?

> #8
> How long?   Take a guess.

> #4
> I wouldn't have the slightest idea.

> #8
> (To #5)
> What do you think?

> #5
> I don't know. About ten or twelve
> seconds maybe.

> #3
> What's all this for?

> #8
> (Ignoring #3)
> I'd say that was a fair guess. Any-
> one else?

169. MEDIUM SHOT   #'S 10, 11

> #11
> That sounds right to me.

#10 looks at him and then across at #8, off.

> #10
> Come on, what's the guessing game for?

170. MEDIUM SHOT   #'S 2, 3, 4, 8

> #8
> (To #2)
> What would you say?

> #2
> (Shrugging)
> Ten seconds is about right.

                              #4
                    All right. Say ten seconds. What are
                    you getting at?

                              #8
                    This. A six-car el train passes a
                    given point in ten seconds. Now say
                    that given point is the open window
                    of the room in which the killing
                    took place. You can almost reach
                    out of the window of that room and
                    touch the el tracks. Right?

     #2 nods.

171. MEDIUM SHOT   FROM BEHIND FOREMAN'S BACK   FOREMAN, #'S 2, 3, 8,
     4, 5, 6, 7

                              #8
                    All right. Now let me ask you this.
                    Has anyone here ever lived right
                    next to the el tracks?

                              #6
                    Well I just finished painting an
                    apartment that overlooked an el
                    line. I'm a house-painter, y'know.
                    I was there for three days.

                              #8
                    What was it like?

                              #6
                    What d'ya mean?

                              #8
                    Noisy?

                              #6
                    Brother! Well it didn't matter.
                    We're all punchy in our business
                    anyway.

     #6 laughs and is joined by others.

                              #8
                    I lived in a second-floor apartment
                    next to an el line once. When the

#8 (cont.)
window's open and the train goes by
the noise is almost unbearable. You
can't hear yourself think.

#3
Okay. You can't hear yourself think.
Will you get to the point!

172. CLOSE UP #8

#8
I will. Let's take two pieces of
testimony and try to put them together. First, the old man in the
apartment downstairs. He says he
heard the boy say "I'm going to kill
you", and a split second later he
heard the body hit the floor. One
second later. Right?

#2
(Off)
That's right.

173. MEDIUM SHOT #8 BEHIND #3

#8
Second, the woman across the street
claimed positively that she looked
out of her window and saw the killing
through the last two cars of a passing elevated train. Right? The last
two cars.

#3
All right, what are you giving us here?

#8
Now, we agreed that an el takes about
10 seconds to pass a given point.
Since the woman saw the stabbing
through the last two cars we can assume that the body fell to the floor
just as the train passed by. Therefore, the el had been roaring by the
old man's window for a full ten seconds
before the body hit the floor.

174. CLOSE UP   #8

                        #8
            The old man, according to his own tes-
            timony, "I'm going to kill you", body
            falling a split second later, would
            have had to hear the boy make this
            statement while the el was roaring
            past his nose. It's not possible that
            he could have heard it!

175. LONG SHOT   THE ENTIRE JURY

    There is silence as they digest this. Then #3 angrily turns
    around in his chair.

                        #3
            That's idiotic. Sure he could have
            heard it.

                        #8
            Do you think so?

175A. CLOSE UP   #3

                        #3
            He said the boy yelled it out. That's
            enough for me.

                        #8
                    (Off)
            If he heard anything at all, he still
            couldn't have identified the voice
            with the el roaring by. . . .

    #3 shoots to his feet, camera moving up with him. He glares at
    #8.

                        #3
                    (Furious)
            You're talking about a matter of
            seconds here. Nobody can be that
            accurate!

    #3 stands next to #8 now.

                        #8
                    (Quietly)
            Well, I kind of think that testimony

#8 (cont.)
which could put a human being into
the electric chair should be reasonably
accurate.

#3 moves away from #8 down towards #5. Camera holds on him in
background, #8 in foreground. #5 turns around in his seat.

#5
I don't think he could have heard it.

#6
(Turning around)
Maybe he didn't hear it. I mean with
the el noise. . . .

Camera moves in slowly on #3.

#3
What are you people talking about?

#5
Well it stands to reason. . . .

#3
You're crazy! Why would he lie?
What's he got to gain?

176. CLOSE UP   #9

#9
(Softly)
Attention, maybe.

177. CLOSE UP   #3

#3
You keep coming up with these bright
sayings. Why don't you send one in
to a newspaper? They pay three dollars!

178. CLOSE UP   #9

He seems to shrink in his seat. He looks down at the table.

178A.MEDIUM SHOT   #'S 5, 6, 3

#3 stares at the old man. #5 looks at #3. #6 rises, and faces

#3. He stares at him with frank disgust. He looks ready for almost any trouble #3 can name. He speaks quietly, but with great strength, heightened by his slow-witted sincerity. This is a man who is rarely aroused, but when he is, is afraid of nothing.

> #6
> What're ya talking to him like
> that for?

#3 looks at him and then turns disgustedly away. #6 reaches out and turns #3 firmly around by the arm, looks into his face.

> #6
> A guy who talks like that to
> an old man oughta really get
> stepped on, y'know.

> #3
> Get your hands off me.

#5 rises and makes a move toward #6. #6 looks at him briefly. He stops. #6 looks back to #3.

> #7
> (Off)
> Hey let's not get into any fist
> fights in here.

> #6
> (Riding over #7's
> lines)
> You oughta have some respect,
> mister.

> #3
> I said let go of me. . . .

#6 pulls #3 firmly, strongly towards him. #3 helplessly stands there.

> #6
> (Very low)
> If you say stuff like that to him
> again . . . I'm gonna lay you out.

#6 releases #3 and steps away from him. #3 continues to stare harshly at him. #6 quietly turns in the direction of #9.

                         #6
                      (Softly)
          Go ahead. You can say anything you
          want. Why do you think the old man
          might lie?

179. ELIMINATED

180. CLOSE UP   #9, #10 AT EDGE OF FRAME

    #9 looks up and seems to take strength. #10 shows disgust.

                         #9
          It's just that I looked at him
          for a very long time. The seam
          of his jacket was split under the
          arm. Did you notice it? I mean
          to come into court like that.

    #9 pauses, and #10 deliberately yawns.

                         #9
          He was a very old man with a torn
          jacket, and he walked very slowly
          to the stand. He was dragging
          his left leg, and trying to hide
          it because he was ashamed. I think
          I know him better than anyone here.
          This is a quiet, frightened, in-
          significant old man who has been
          nothing all of his life, who has
          never had recognition, his name
          in the newspapers. Nobody knows him,
          nobody quotes him, nobody seeks his
          advice after seventy-five years.
          That's a very sad thing, to be
          nothing. A man like this needs to
          be recognized, to be listened to,
          to be quoted just once. This is
          very important.

181. MEDIUM SHOT   #'S 3, 6, 7, 8.

    All listening to #9. Only #8 shows pity. #6 half understands.
    #3 is furious, #7 incredulous.

                         #9
          It would be so hard for him to

                              #9   (cont.)
                    recede into the background when
                    there's a chance to be. . . .

                              #7
                           (Superior)
                    Now wait a minute. Are you trying
                    to tell us he'd lie just so that
                    he could be important once?

182. MEDIUM SHOT   #7, #9

                              #9
                    No. He wouldn't really lie. But
                    perhaps he'd make himself believe
                    that he'd heard those words and
                    recognized the boy's face.

182A. CLOSE UP   #3

     #3 looks at #6, and then turns to #9

                              #3
                    Well that's the most fantastic
                    story I've ever heard! How can
                    you make up a thing like that?
                    What do you know about it?

183. CLOSE UP   #9

                              #9
                           (Softly)
                    I speak from experience.

     He lowers his head, embarrassed.

184. CLOSE UP   #3

     His jaw hangs open. He stares at #9. There is absolute silence,
     punctuated only by the honking of a horn in the street. Then,
     abruptly #3 whirls about and, as camera pans with him, he stalks
     back to his seat.

185. LONG SHOT   THE ENTIRE JURY

     Frozen for a moment now as #3 sits down. #2 clears his throat,
     and begins to unwrap a cough drop. #12 lights a cigarette. #6
     begins to tap the dottle out of his pipe. But no one speaks.

186. MEDIUM SHOT   #10, #9

#9 sits with head bowed. #10 looks at him as if he were a bug on a pin.

>   #10
>   (Shaking his head)
>   Boy-oh-boy. That's what I call a
>   hot one!

He lets out a short, mocking laugh.

187. CLOSE UP   #5

Looking at #10, wishing he could crack him across the mouth.

>   FOREMAN
>   (Off)
>   Okay. Is there anything else?

#5's spell of contained anger is broken. He looks in the direc-
tion of the Foreman as camera dollies back to include #4 in shot.

>   #5
>   (Hesitantly)
>   Yeah, I'll tell you, I was figuring
>   I'd like to. . . .

>   #4
>   (Interrupting)
>   Listen! I think it's about time we
>   stopped behaving like kids in here.
>   We can't continue to allow these
>   emotional outbursts to influence us.
>   Gentlemen, this case is based on a
>   reasonable and logical progression
>   of facts. Let's keep it there.

188. MEDIUM SHOT   CENTERED ON #11

>   #11
>   Facts are sometimes colored by the
>   personalities of the people who
>   present them. . . .

189. MEDIUM SHOT   #'S 2, 3, 4

#4 gives #11 a somewhat sour look. There is silence for a moment.

Then, #2 haltingly breaks the silence.

                         #2
            Anybody . . . want a . . . cough drop?

190. LONG SHOT   THE ENTIRE JURY

There is an awkward silence again. #2 holds out the cough drops
to the Foreman. The Foreman looks away, annoyed. The only man
standing is #8. He walks from his position behind #6 toward #2,
obviously thinking of something. He reaches #2.

                         #8
            I'll take one.

#2 almost gratefully offers him the box. He pops a cough drop
into his mouth.

                         #8
            Thanks.

Then he continues his walk around the table, sucking the cough
drop.

                         #12
                    (Embarrassed)
            Say what you like, I still don't see
            how anybody can think he's not guilty.

He looks around, and his statement hangs emptily in the air. He
looks around for confirmation, and then begins to doodle again.
Camera moves in on #8, he stands near the windows. #10 gets up
and begins a cross which will leave him behind #3 for his next
lines. He blows his nose gingerly as he walks.

                         #8
            There's another thing I wanted to
            talk about for a minute. I think
            we've proved that the old man
            couldn't have heard the boy say,
            "I'm going to kill you," but sup-
            posing. . . .

191. CLOSE UP   #10

                         #10
                    (Interrupting)
            You didn't prove it at all. What

#10 (cont.)
are you talking about?

192. MEDIUM SHOT   CENTERED ON #8

Standing near the windows.

#8
(Steadily)
But supposing he really did hear it.
This phrase, how many times has each
of us used it. Probably hundreds.
"I could kill you for that, Darling".
"If you do that once more, Junior,
I'm going to kill you". "Come on
Rocky, kill him!" We say it every
day. It doesn't mean we're going to
kill someone.

193. MEDIUM SHOT   CENTERED ON #3

#3
(Angry)
Wait a minute. What are you trying
to give us here? The phrase was,
"I'm going to kill you," and the
kid screamed it out at the top of
his lungs. Don't tell me he didn't
mean it. Anybody says a thing like
that the way he said it, they mean
it.

#2
(Hesitantly)
Well gee, I don't know. I remember
I was arguing with the guy I work
next to at the bank a couple of
weeks ago, so he called me an idiot,
so I yelled at him. . . .

#3
(Interrupting)
Now listen, this guy
(Indicating #8)
is making you believe things that
aren't so. The kid said he was
going to kill him, and he did kill
him!

194. MEDIUM SHOT   #8

> #8
> Well let me ask you this. Do you
> really think the boy would shout
> out a thing like that so the whole
> neighborhood would hear it? I don't
> think so. He's much too bright for
> that.

195. CLOSE UP   #10

> #10
> (Exploding)
> Bright? He's a common ignorant slob.
> He don't even speak good English!

196. CLOSE UP   #11

> #11
> (Quietly)
> He <u>doesn't</u> even speak good English.

197. CLOSE UP   #10

He glares at #11 furiously. There is silence for a moment.

198. CLOSE UP   #5

#5 looks anxiously around the table for a moment. Then he clears
his throat.

> #5
> I'd like to change my vote to not
> guilty.

> #7
> (Off)
> You what?

#5 turns his head toward #7 and looks firmly at him.

> #5
> You heard.

199. MEDIUM SHOT   FOREMAN, #'S 2, 3, 4, 5, AND 10

#3 starts to get up, trying to control his anger. #4 stares at

#5. #5 sits stiffly, waiting to be bombarded.

> FOREMAN
> Are you sure?

> #5
> Yes. I'm sure.

> FOREMAN
> The vote is 9 to 3 in favor of
> guilty.

#3 stalks off past #5 on his way around to the windows. Camera
pans with him. As he passes #7, #7 speaks, two beats after
Foreman finishes above line.

> #7
> Well if that isn't the livin' end!

Camera continues to pan with #3, as #7 speaks. He reaches the
windows and finds himself next to #8. #8 is calm, #3 furious but
controlled. They exchange one look, and it is as if at that moment this entire room has become a battleground for these two
men, who have never known each other before. This is the battle
of good against evil, of compassion against brutality. #3 turns
away from #8, and looks out the window. During all of this #7
speaks.

> #7
> (Off)
> What are you basing it on? Stories
> this guy made up! He oughta write
> for Amazing Detective Monthly. He'd
> make a fortune.

200. CLOSE UP #7

> #7
> (To #5)
> Listen, there are facts staring you
> right in your face. Every one of
> them says this kid killed his old
> man. For cryin' out loud his own
> lawyer knew he didn't stand a chance
> right from the beginning. His own
> lawyer. You could see it!

201. CLOSE UP   #8

                         #8
It's happened before that a lot of
facts somehow fall into place and
all of a sudden it looks like a
murderer has been caught. But
every once in a while you read
about a convict who's freed ten
years after the crime because someone else has confessed.

202. MEDIUM SHOT   #'S 7, 8, 9, 3 -- SHOOTING OVER #5'S SHOULDER

#'s 7. and 9 in their seats, #3 at window, #8 standing behind #9.

                         #7
                   (To #8)
I'm talkin' to him.
                   (Indicating #5)
Not to you!
                   (To all)
Boy, this guy is really something.
                   (To #8)
Listen, the kid had a lawyer, didn't
he? The lawyer presented his case,
not you. How come you've got so
much to say?

                         #5
Lawyers aren't infallible.

#7 swings around to #5, gives him a look.

                         #8
He was court-appointed.

#7 swings back to #8.

                         #7
So what does that mean?

                         #8
Well it could mean a lot of things.
It could mean he didn't want the
case. It could mean he resented
being appointed. It's the kind of
case that brings him nothing. No
money. No glory. Not even much

                    #8 (cont.)
          chance of winning. It's not a very
          promising situation for a young
          lawyer. He'd really have to believe
          in his client to make a good fight.
          As you pointed out a minute ago,
          he obviously didn't.

                    #7
          Sure he didn't! Who in the heck
          could, except God come to earth or
          somebody.

203. CLOSE UP   #8

     He looks calmly at #7.

204. CLOSE UP   #7

     He evades #8's eyes. He looks down at his watch and then up at
     the clock.

                    #7
          Come on already! Look at the time!

205. MEDIUM CLOSE UP   #11

     He shows disgust with #7's concern for the time. Then he looks
     down at the table at some notes he has made on a scrap of paper.
     Camera dollies back to show paper, and shot now includes #10, who
     is back in his seat.

                    #11
          Pardon me, but I have made some notes
          here. I would like please to say
          something.

     He picks up the scrap of paper, and, finding himself hampered by
     a lighted cigarette in his hand, looks for an ashtray in which to
     put it. The ashtray is in front of #10. He looks at #10, and
     then reaches over for the ashtray. #10 looks at him with obvious
     distaste.

                    #10
          Wait a minute! Here.

     #10 slides the ashtray over to him.

#11
Thank you.

He puts out the cigarette, and looks at his notes.

#11
I have been listening very closely,
and it seems to me that this man
(Indicating #8)
has some very good points to make.
From what was presented at the
trial the boy looks guilty, on the
surface. But maybe if we go deeper. . . .

#10
Come on, willya. . . .

#11
(More firmly)
There is a question I would like to
ask. We assume that the boy committed
murder. He stabbed his father in the
chest, and ran away. This was at ten
minutes after twelve. Now, how was
he caught by the police? He came
home at three o'clock or so, and was
captured by two detectives in the
hallway of his house. My question
is, if he really had killed his father,
why would he come back home three hours
later? Wouldn't he be afraid of being
caught?

206. MEDIUM SHOT   #3

He stands at window, listening.

#3
(As if talking to a child)
Look . . . he came home to get his knife.
It's not nice to leave knives around
sticking in people's chests.

#7
(Off)
Yeah, especially relatives.

#3 looks off in his direction and grins appreciatively.

207. MEDIUM SHOT   CENTERED ON #11, SHOOTING OVER #4'S SHOULDER

                         #4
                 (In #7's direction)
         I don't see anything funny about it.
                 (To #11)
         The boy knew that there were people
         who could identify the knife as the
         one he had just bought. He had to
         get it before the police did.

                         #11
         But if he knew the knife could be
         identified, why did he leave it
         there in the first place?

                         #4
         Well I think we can assume he ran
         out in a state of panic after he
         killed his father, and then when he
         finally calmed down he realized that
         he had left his knife there.

                         #11
         This then depends on your definition
         of panic. He would have had to be
         calm enough to see to it that there
         were no fingerprints on the knife.
         Now where did his panic start and
         where did it end?

#3 walks up behind #11, annoyed.

                         #3
         Look, you can forget all that other
         stuff. He still came home to dig
         out his knife, and get rid of it.

                         #11
         Three hours later?

                         #3
         Sure three hours later!

                         #11
         If I were the boy and I had killed
         my father I would not have come home
         three hours later. I would be

                    #11 (cont.)
           afraid that the police would be
           there. I would stay away, knife
           or no knife.

208. CLOSE UP   #3

                    #3
           Listen, you voted guilty, didn't
           you? What side are you on?

209. CLOSE UP   #11

                    #11
           I don't believe I must be loyal
           to one side or the other. I am
           simply asking questions.

210. MEDIUM SHOT CENTERED ON #11

      He looks at his notes. #12 clear his throat.

                    #12
           Well this is just off the top of
           my head, but if I were the boy, and
           I'd, you know, done the stabbing and
           everything, I'd take a chance and
           go back for the knife. I'll bet he
           figured no one had seen him and that
           the body probably wasn't even dis-
           covered yet. After all, it was the
           middle of the night. He probably
           thought no one would find the body
           till the next day.

                    #11
           Pardon. Here is my whole point.
           The woman across the street testified
           that a moment after she saw the
           killing, that is, a moment after the
           el train went by, she screamed, and
           then went to telephone the police.
           Now, the boy must certainly have
           heard that scream, and known that
           somebody saw something. I don't
           think he would have gone back, if
           he had been the murderer.

211. MEDIUM SHOT   CENTERED ON #4

                        #4
        Two things. One, in his state of
        panic he may not have heard the
        scream. Perhaps it wasn't very
        loud. Two, if he did hear it, he
        may not have connected it with his
        own act. Remember, he lived in a
        neighborhood where screams were
        fairly commonplace.

212. MEDIUM SHOT   #'S 8, 9, 10, 11, 12, 3

#'s 9, 10, 11, 12 seated. #3 behind #11, #8, near his seat, be-
gins a walk toward #11.

                        #3
            Right! There's your answer!

                        #8
        Maybe. Maybe he did stab his father,
        didn't hear the woman's scream, did
        run out in a panic, did calm down
        three hours later and come back to
        try and get the knife, risking being
        caught by the police. Maybe all of
        those things are so. But maybe
        they're not. I think there's enough
        doubt to make us wonder whether he
        was there at all during the time the
        murder took place.

#10 stands up furiously, turns to #8.

                        #10
                    (To #8)
        What d'ya mean doubt? What are you
        talking about? Didn't the old man
        see him running out of the house.

He turns to all the others.

                        #10
        He's twisting the facts! I'm telling
        you!

He turns to #11, who is still seated.

                  #10
        Did or didn't the old man see the
        kid running out of the house at
        12:10?

#11 turns away from him. #10 moves around to the other side of
him.

213. MEDIUM CLOSE UP   #'S 10 AND 11

                  #10
           (Harshly)
        Well did or didn't he?

                  #11
        He says he did.

                  #10
        Says he did!
           (To all)
        Boy-oh-boy. How do you like that.
           (Bending to #11)
        Well did or didn't the woman across
        the street see the kid kill his
        father?

He stands up and answers for #11, mocking him.

                  #10
        She says she did.
           (To #11)
        You're makin' out like it don't
        matter what people say.

#11 gets up and begins a walk to the water cooler. #10 looks
angrily after him and then starts to pursue him, still talking.
Camera pans with them, shooting at their backs.

                  #10
        What you want to believe, you be-
        lieve, and what you don't want to
        believe, so you don't. What kind
        of way is that?

#11 is at the cooler now. #10 has stopped halfway.

214. LONG SHOT   #'S 11, 10 IN FOREGROUND   REST OF JURY IN BACKGROUND

Shooting from water cooler. #11 takes a cup and begins to pour some water.

                    #10
          What d'ya think these people get up
          on the witness stand for, their
          health?

#10 turns to the table.

                    #10
          I'm telling you men the facts are
          being changed around here. Witnesses
          are being doubted and there's no
          reason for it.

                    #5
          Witnesses can make mistakes.

                    #10
               (Loud)
          Sure, when you want 'em to, they do!
               (He turns to #3)
          Know what I mean?

                    FOREMAN
          Okay. Let's hold the yelling down.

215. CLOSE UP   #11 AT WATER COOLER

    He slowly sips, and listens as #10 goes to Foreman.

                    #10
               (Off)
          You keep saying that. Maybe what we
          need is a little yelling in here.
          These guys are going off every which
          way. Did hear the scream, didn't
          hear the scream. What's the differ-
          ence?

216. MEDIUM SHOT   #8, #10, #11

    #8 standing quietly by in foreground, watching #11 at water cooler
    in background as #10, halfway between them talks on.

                    #10
          You people are only talking about

                         #10 (cont.)
                    the little details. You're for-
                    getting the important stuff. I
                    mean all of a sudden here every-
                    body. . . .

                             #8
                         (Quietly)
                    I'd like to call for another vote.

                             #10
                          (Angry)
                    Listen I'm talking here!

#8 turns his back on #10 and walks out of shot toward his seat.
#10 is visibly annoyed at this. He takes one step after #8, then
stops.

                          FOREMAN
                         (Off)
                    There's another vote called for.

#10 burns.

                          FOREMAN
                         (Off)
                    How about taking seats.

#10 starts for his seat.

217. MEDIUM SHOT   FOREMAN #'S 2, 3, 4, 5. SHOOTING OVER #11'S EMPTY
      SEAT.

Foreman stands at his seat. The others who are standing head for
seats.

                             #3
                    What are we gonna gain by voting
                    again?

                          FOREMAN
                    I don't know. The gentleman asked. . . .

#11 sits in his seat.

                             #3
                    I never saw so much time spent on
                    nothing.

#2
(Mildly to #3)
It only takes a second.

#3 gives him a look, then turns away.

218. LONG SHOT   ENTIRE JURY, FROM ABOVE AND BEHIND FOREMAN

FOREMAN
Okay. I guess the fastest way is
to find out who's voting not guilty.
All those in favor of not guilty
raise their hands.

There is a great deal of looking around the table as #'s 5, 8 and
9 raise their hands.

FOREMAN
Still the same. One, two, three not
guilty's. Nine guilty's.

219. CLOSE UP   #11

He is in the process of making a very difficult decision.

#7
(Off)
So now where are we? I'm telling you,
we can yakity-yak until next Tuesday
here. . . . Where's it getting us?

There is a pause.

#11
(Quietly)
Pardon.

He slowly raises his hand.

#11
I vote not guilty.

#7
(Off)
Oh brother!

#3
(Off)
Oh now listen, what are you talking

                         #3 (cont.)
          about? I mean we're all going
          crazy in here or something. This
          kid is guilty! Why dontcha pay
          attention to the facts!

220. MEDIUM SHOT   #'S 2, 3, 4.

                         #3
                     (To #4)
          Listen, tell him, will ya?

#4 shrugs.

                         #3
          This is getting to be a joke!

He gets up and starts a walk down toward #7. Camera pans with
him.

                      FOREMAN
                     (Off)
          The vote is eight to four, favor of
          guilty.

                         #3
                  (Over #5's shoulder
                   toward #11)
          I mean everybody's heart is starting
          to bleed for this punk little kid
          like the President just declared it
          Love Your Underprivileged Brother
          week, or something. Listen I'd like
          you to stand up and tell me why you
          changed your vote. Come on, give me
          reasons!

221. CLOSE UP   #11

He looks straight at #3, and speaks strongly.

                        #11
          I don't have to defend my decision to
          you! I have a reasonable doubt in my
          mind.

222. MEDIUM SHOT   #'S 3, 5, 6, 8, 9 SHOOTING ACROSS TABLE FROM BEHIND
     #3

#3 stands behind #5 who is turned, looking at him. #3 looks off
at #11 angrily.

> #3
> What reasonable doubt? That's
> nothing but words!

He leans over the table, pulls the switch knife out of the table,
and holds it up.

> #3
> Here, look at this! The kid you
> just decided isn't guilty was <u>seen</u>
> ramming this thing into his father!
> Well, look at it, Mr. Reasonable
> Doubt!

#3 flicks it angrily into the table. It quivers in the wood.

> #9
> (Mildly)
> That's not the knife. Don't you
> remember?

#3 whirls and stares at him. #9 regards him steadily. #8 smiles
openly.

223. CLOSE UP   #3

Burning, but controlled.

> #3
> Brilliant!

224. MEDIUM SHOT   #'S 3, 5, 6, 7, 8

#3 stares at #9 for another moment and then walks around past #7
and off camera. His next lines will be taken at the window.
There is a pause. #7 looks around.

> #7
> I'm tellin' ya, this is the craziest!
> (To #8)
> I mean you're sittin' in here pulling
> stories outa thin air! What're we
> supposed to believe?
> (To all)

                    #7 (cont.)
        I'm telling ya if this guy
              (Indicating #8)
        sat ringside at the Dempsey-Firpo
        fight, he'd be tryin' to tell us
        Firpo won!
                  (To #8)
        Look, what about the old man? Are
        we supposed to believe that he
        didn't get up and run to his door
        and see the kid tearing down the
        stairs fifteen seconds after the
        killing? He's only saying he did
        to be important, right? I mean
        what's the point of the whole. . . .

                       #5
                (Interrupting)
        Hold it a second.

                       #7
                (Looking at #5 and doing
                a Clem McCarthy)
        And the Baltimore rooter is heard
        from! And pop-ups are falling for
        base hits wherever we look. I tell
        you. . . .

                       #5
                (Interrupting)
        Did the old man say he ran to the
        door.

                       #7
        Ran. Walked. What's the difference?
        He got there.

                       #6
        He said he ran to the door. At least
        I think he did.

                       #5
        I don't remember what he said. But
        I don't see how he could run.

225. MEDIUM SHOT   #'S 4, 5, 6, 7, SHOOTING FROM BEHIND #8

                       #4
        He said he went from his bedroom to

                    #4 (cont.)
          the front door. That's enough, isn't
          it?

                    #8
          Where was his bedroom again?

226. MEDIUM SHOT   #'S 7, 8, 9, 10

                    #10
          Down the hall somewhere. I thought
          you remembered everything. Don't
          you remember that?

                    #8
          No. Mr. Foreman, I'd like to take
          a look at the diagram of the apart-
          ment.

                    #7
               (To #8)
          Why don't we have them run the trial
          over just so you can get everything
          straight?

                    #8
               (Ignoring him)
          Mr. Foreman. . . .

227. MEDIUM SHOT   FOREMAN, #12, #11 AND #3 IN BACKGROUND AT WINDOW

                    FOREMAN
          I heard you.

     He rises, and walks out of shot towards door. #3, standing at
     windows glares at #8. Camera dollies in on #3. We hear business
     of door opening and closing during next lines.

                    #3
          All right, what's this for? How
          come you're the only one in the
          room who wants to see exhibits all
          the time?

                    #5
               (Off)
          I want to see this one too.

     #3 starts a walk from the windows which will lead him to a position directly behind #8. Camera pans with him.

> #3
> And I want to stop wasting time!

> #4
> (Off)
> If we're going to start wading through
> all that nonsense about where the
> body was found. . . .

#3 is standing behind #8 now. Camera is in medium close up on
them both. #8 leans across table toward #4's position.

> #8
> We're not. Not unless someone else
> wants to. I'd like to see if a very
> old man who drags one leg when he
> walks because he had a stroke last
> year can get from his bed to his
> front door in fifteen seconds.

> #3
> He said twenty seconds!

> #8
> He said fifteen.

> #3
> Now I'm telling you he said twenty!
> What're you trying to distort. . . .

> #11
> (Off)
> He said fifteen.

> #3
> (Turning in that
> direction)
> How does he know how long fifteen
> seconds is. You can't judge that
> kind of a thing!

Camera dollies back slightly to include #9. He looks up at #3.

> #9
> He said fifteen seconds. He was
> very positive about it.

#3
(Down to #9,
furiously)
He's an old man. You saw him.
Half the time he was confused!
How could he be positive about . . .
anything?

Camera moves in for big closeup of #3. He looks around angrily,
unable to cover up his blunder. Then he walks out of the closeup,
and stalks around the table. Camera pans with him. The others
watch. As he gets to his seat the door behind him opens. The
guard enters carrying a large pen and ink diagram of the apartment. Foreman crosses to guard.

GUARD
This what you wanted?

FOREMAN
That's right. Thanks.

The guard nods and exits. Foreman holds up the diagram and, looking at it, crosses back toward his seat, camera panning with him.
#8 rises from his seat and walks toward Foreman's seat. During
these crosses we hear the following.

#4
I don't see what we're going to
prove here. The man said he saw
the boy running out.

#8
(Walking to Foreman)
Well let's see if the details bear
him out. As soon as the body fell
to the floor, he said, he heard
footsteps upstairs running toward
the front door. He heard the upstairs
door open and the footsteps start
down the stairs. He got to his front
door as soon as he could. He swore
that it couldn't have been more than
fifteen seconds. Now, if the killer
began running immediately. . . .

Camera is now on medium shot of #8 standing next to Foreman at
head of table.

#12
(Interrupting)
Well maybe he didn't.

#8
The old man said he did!

228. LONG SHOT   ENTIRE JURY FROM BEHIND FOREMAN AND #8.

#7
(To #8)
Brother, I crown you king of the hair-
splitters.

#10 laughs at this.

#6
(Mildly, to #7)
Listen, why don't you stop making
smart remarks all the time.

#7
My friend, for your three dollars a
day you've gotta listen to everything.

There is a silence for a moment. #6 has no answer, but he hasn't
liked what he heard.

#10
(To #8)
Well now that you've got that thing
in here, what about it?

#8
(To Foreman)
May I?

He takes the chart, and holds it up on a corner of the table so
that everyone can see it.

229. MEDIUM SHOT   #8 WITH DIAGRAM

Also included in shot are #12, and #11 and Foreman. During #8's
lines, #'s 2, 5, and 6 also crowd around diagram. The diagram
itself is a layout of a railroad flat. A bedroom faces the el
tracks. Behind it is a series of rooms off a long hall. In the
front room is an X marking the spot where the body was found. At
the back of the apartment we see the entrance into the apartment

hall from the building hall. We see a flight of stairs in the
building hall. Each room is labeled, and the dimensions of each
room are shown.

> #8
> This is the apartment in which the
> killing took place. The old man's
> apartment is directly beneath it, and
> exactly the same.
> (Pointing)
> Here are the el tracks. The bedroom.
> Another bedroom. Living room. Bath-
> room. Kitchen. And this is the
> hall. Here's the front door to the
> apartment. And here are the stairs.
> (Pointing to front bedroom)
> Now, the old man was in bed in this
> room. He says he got up, went out
> into the hall, down the hall to the
> front door, opened it and looked out
> just in time to see the boy racing
> down the stairs. Am I right so far?

230. CLOSE UP   #3

He stands at his chair, watching.

> #3
> That's the story, for the nineteenth
> time.

231. MEDIUM SHOT   #8 (SAME AS 229)

> #8
> (Ignoring this)
> Fifteen seconds after he heard the
> body fall.

> #11
> Correct.

> #8
> His bed was at the window. It's --
> (Looking closely at
> diagram)
> 12 feet from his bed to the bedroom
> door. The length of the hall is
> 43 feet 6 inches. Now, he had to

                    #8 (cont.)
            get up out of bed, walk 12 feet,
            open the bedroom door, walk 43 feet
            and open the front door . . . all in 15
            seconds. Do you think he could have
            done it?

#10, standing behind #8, barks out.

                    #10
            Sure he coulda done it!

                    #11
                 (To #10)
            He can only walk very slowly. They
            had to help him into the witness
            chair.

232. MEDIUM SHOT   #3, #4

                    #3
            You make it sound like a long walk.
            It's not!

233. MEDIUM SHOT   #8   (SAME AS 229)

He looks in #3's direction, and then, laying down the diagram,
begins a walk around to the other side of the table, camera panning with him. As he walks, #9, who had been standing near #8,
answers #3.

                    #9
            For an old man who had a stroke
            it's a long walk.

#8 has walked directly to the empty chairs of #2 and #3. He takes
one in each hand now, and swings them out into the middle of the
floor, placing them side by side. #3 strides into the shot.

                    #3
            What are you doing?

                    #8
            I want to try this thing. Let's see
            how long it took him.

                    #3
            What d'you mean you want to try it?

#3 (cont.)
Why didn't the kid's lawyer bring
it up if it's so important?

The other jurors have begun to crowd into the shot.

#5
Well maybe he just didn't think of it.

#10
What d'ya mean didn't think of it!
You think the man's an idiot or some-
thing? It's an obvious thing.

#5
Did you think of it?

#10 moves a step or two towards #5.

#10
(Angry, to #5)
Listen, smart guy! It don't matter
whether I thought of it.

FOREMAN
(Worried)
Okay, now. . . .

#10
He didn't bring it up because he
knew the answer'd hurt his case.
Now what d'ya think of that?

FOREMAN
Okay. . . .

#8
It's possible that he didn't bring
it up because it would have meant
badgering and bullying a helpless
old man, something that I don't think
sits very well with a jury. Most
lawyers avoid that kind of thing if
they can.

#7
(Loud)
So what kind of a bum is he then?

                              #8
                          (Quietly)
                  That's what I've been asking.

#7 shuts up, sorry that he's spoken.

                              #8
                  All right, let's say these chairs
                  are the old man's bed. I'm going
                  to pace off 12 feet, the length of
                  the bedroom.

He begins to do this, camera staying with him.

                              #3
                  You're crazy. You can't recreate a
                  thing like that.

                              #11
                  I'd like to see it.

                              #3
                  It's a ridiculous waste of time!

                              #6
                  Let him do it.

#8 has now paced off his 12 feet. He stands on the spot.

                              #8
                  Someone hand me a chair.

#6 picks up a chair and brings it to him. #8 puts it down where
he is standing. Camera moves in for medium shot of #8.

                              #8
                  All right, this is the bedroom door.

He looks around.

                              #8
                  The hall is a little over 43 feet
                  long. I'll pace over to that wall
                          (Pointing)
                  and back again.

He starts to do it, counting his steps silently as he paces. He
passes #10 after a dozen steps.

#10
Look, this is absolutely insane. What's
the idea of wasting everybody's time
here.

#8
(Interrupting his counting)
Sixteen.

He stops pacing, turns to #10.

#8
According to you it'll only take 15
seconds. We can spare that.

He resumes his pacing, counting to himself. He reaches the wall.
Everyone watches silently. He turns and paces back, counting off
the rest of the 43 steps.

#8
(Aloud)
Thirty-nine, forty, forty-one, forty-
two, forty-three. Okay, pass me
another chair please.

#2 hands him a chair. He places it down.

#8
This is the door to the outside hall
and stairway. It was chain-locked
according to testimony.

#5
Right.

#8 now walks over to the two chairs he placed side by side,
camera dollying in close on him. He sits down.

#8
Who's got a watch with a second hand?

#2
I have.

#8
When you want me to start, stamp your
foot. That'll be the body falling.
Time me from there.

He lies down on the two chairs.

                    #7
            Anyone for charades?

                    #3
               (Exasperated)
            I've never seen anything like this in
            my whole life!

                    #8
            Okay. I'm ready.

He lies down on the chairs. They all watch carefully. #2 stares
at his watch, waiting. There is a tense silence.

                    #2
               (Apologetically)
            I want to wait till the second
            hand reaches sixty.

They wait, silent, tense. Suddenly #2 stamps his foot. #8 rises
to a sitting position, swings his legs to the floor. He stands
up. #2 keeps his eyes on the watch. #8 begins to hobble, dragging one leg, toward the chair which serves as the bedroom door.
He reaches it, pretends to open it. He turns now and begins to
hobble along the simulated 43 foot hallway.

                    #10
            Come on. Speed it up. He walked
            twice as fast as that!

#8 continues to walk.

                    #11
            This is, I think, even more quickly
            than the old man walked in the
            courtroom.

                    #8
               (Still hobbling)
            If you think I should go faster,
            I will.

He speeds up his pace slightly, reaches the wall and turns. He
heads for the second chair, the chair simulating the door to the
outer hallway.

>   #3
>   Come on, willya! Let's get this
>   kid stuff over with!

They watch as #8 reaches the last chair. Camera is now on medium close up of him. He pretends to open an imaginary chain lock, and then opens the imaginary door.

>   #8
>   Stop!

>   #2
>   Right.

>   #8
>   What's the time?

Camera is on #8 in foreground, and #2 in background, surrounded by four or five of the jurors.

>   #2
>   Fifteen . . . Twenty . . . Thirty . . . Thirty-
>   three seconds exactly.

>   #6
>   Thirty-three seconds!

The other jurors around #2 ad lib their surprise.

>   #8
>   I think this is what happened. The
>   old man had heard the fight between
>   the boy and his father a few hours
>   earlier. Then, while lying in bed
>   he heard a body hit the floor in the
>   boy's apartment, and he heard the
>   woman scream from across the street.
>   He got up, tried to get to the door,
>   heard someone racing down the stairs,
>   and assumed it was the boy.

>   #6
>   I think that's possible.

234. CLOSE UP   #3

Standing, furious.

#3
(Shouting)
Assumed? Now listen to me, you
people! I've seen all kinds of
dishonesty in my day . . . but this
little display takes the cake!

235. MEDIUM SHOT   #8 IN FOREGROUND, #3 IN BACKGROUND. #'S 2, 4, 5, 6
ALSO IN SHOT

#3 strides swiftly toward #8. He reaches him, waves his hand in
#8's face.

#3
You come in here with your heart
bleeding all over the floor about
slum kids and injustice, and you
make up some wild stories, and all
of a sudden you start getting through
to some of these old ladies in here!
Well you're not getting through to
me! I've had enough!
(To all)
What's the matter with you people?
Every one of you knows this kid is
guilty! He's got to burn! We're
letting him slip through our fingers
here!

236. MEDIUM SHOT   #8, AND BEHIND HIM #'S 11, 12 9, FOREMAN

#8
(Calmly)
Slip through our fingers? Are you
his executioner?

237. MEDIUM SHOT   #3, AND BEHIND HIM #'S 2, 4, 5, 6, 7, 10

#3
(Furious)
I'm one of 'em.

238. MEDIUM SHOT   SAME AS 236

#8
Maybe you'd like to pull the switch. . . .

239. MEDIUM SHOT   SAME AS 237

                          #3
                      (Shouting)
            For this kid?   You bet I'd like to
            pull the switch!

240. MEDIUM SHOT   SAME AS 236

                          #8
            I'm sorry for you. . . .

                          #3
                      (Off)
            Don't start with me now!

                          #8
            What it must feel like to want to
            pull the switch!

241. CLOSE UP   #3

                          #3
                      (Raging)
            Listen, you shut up!

                          #8
                      (Baiting him)
            Ever since we walked into this room
            you've been behaving like a self-
            appointed public avenger!

                          #3
                      (Loud)
            I'm telling you now!   Shut up!

242. CLOSE UP   #8, OVER #3'S SHOULDER

                          #8
            You want to see this boy die because
            you personally want it, not because
            of the facts.

                          #3
                      (Roaring)
            Shut up!

                          #8
            You're a sadist. . . .

242A.MEDIUM SHOT   #3, #8 -- AND THE REST OF THE JURY GROUPED AROUND
         THEM

                              #3
                          (Roaring)
               Shut up!

And he lunges wildly at #8. #8 holds his ground as #3 is caught
by many hands and held back. He strains against the hands, his
face dark with rage.

                              #3
                  Let me go! I'll kill him! I'll
                  kill him!

243. CLOSE UP   #8

                              #8
                          (Calmly)
                  You don't <u>really</u> mean you'll kill
                  me, do you?

244. MEDIUM SHOT   THE ENTIRE JURY

#3 stops struggling with the jurors who are restraining him.
Still held, he stares bitterly at #8. Then, finally, he shrugs
off the many hands on him, adjusts his jacket and walks around the
group of silent, watching men to the window, camera moving up high,
and holding on him and the entire jury. He stands at the window
and there is not a sound for a moment. Then we hear the sound of
the door being opened. Some of the jurors turn their heads in
that direction.

245. MEDIUM SHOT   GUARD IN THE DOORWAY

                          GUARD
                  Is there anything wrong, gentlemen?
                  I heard some noise.

246. MEDIUM SHOT   FOREMAN AND OTHERS

                          FOREMAN
                  No. There's nothing wrong.

He walks toward the door, picking up the diagram of the apartment
on the way. He reaches the door. Camera holds on shot of Foreman
and guard.

                         FOREMAN
            Just a little argument. Everything's
            okay.

He hands the guard the diagram.

                         FOREMAN
            We're finished with this.

The guard takes it, looks carefully around the room and then
exits. The Foreman turns to the others.

247. LONG SHOT   ENTIRE JURY, FROM ABOVE

     #3 stands at the windows. A few of the jurors walk back to their
     seats. The others stand watching #3. He turns to look at them.

                          #3
                       (Angry)
            Well what are you looking at?

Embarrassed, they turn away. He stands there for a moment and
then begins the long walk back to his seat. After a moment the
other jurors begin to take their seats. There is a stiffness in
the room which had not been there before. The jurors sit at the
table without a sound. The Foreman clears his throat. #10 blows
his nose. They are each waiting for some one else to break the
silence. Camera moves slowly in on table.

                          #12
                      (Tentatively)
            Well . . . I suppose someone has to . . .
            start it off again . . .

Again there is a pause. #2 turns elaborately in his chair and
cranes his neck for a look at the wall clock. Camera is on medium
shot of him now.

                          #2
            It's getting late.
                     (To Foreman)
            What do they do, take us out to a
            restaurant for supper?

                         FOREMAN
            How do I know?

                                    #2
                        I wonder if they let us go home in case we
                        can't finish tonight. I've got a boy with
                        mumps.
                            (He smiles self-consciously,
                            gesturing with his hands around his
                            jaws to indicate a swelling)
                        He's out to here. The wife says he looks
                        like Mussolini.

Camera holds on him as he subsides into embarrassed silence. No
one laughs.

248. MEDIUM SHOT   #'S 2, 3, 4, 5, 6, 7

Sitting silently, each trying to think of some way to break out of
his own personal embarrassment. The room begins to darken per-
ceptibly now. No one notices it.

249. MEDIUM SHOT   #'S 8, 9, 10, 11, 12, FOREMAN

And now #11 clears his throat slightly and leans forward. Camera
closes in on him as he talks.

                                   #11
                        Pardon. This fighting. This is not why
                        we are here, to fight. We have a responsi-
                        bility. This, I have always thought, is a
                        remarkable thing about democracy. That we
                        are, uh, what is the word?
                            (A pause)
                        notified. That we are notified by mail to
                        come down to this place and decide on the
                        guilt or innocence of a man we have never
                        heard of before. We have nothing to gain
                        or lose by our verdict. This is one of
                        the reasons why we are strong. We should
                        not make it a personal thing.

Now fearing perhaps that he has forced his views on others a bit
too passionately, #11 sits back, somewhat embarrassed.

                                   #11
                               (Humbly)
                        Thank you.

Again there is a silence. Camera is on #11, #12, and Foreman.
#12 leans forward into the silence.

>   #12
>   (Brightly)
>   Um, if no one else has an idea I may have
>   a cutie here. I mean I haven't put much
>   thought into it. Anyway, lemme throw it
>   out on the stoop and see if the cat licks
>   it up.

>   FOREMAN
>   See if the cat licks it up?

>   #12
>   (Insisting)
>   Yeah! Now, if the boy arrived home . . .

The Foreman laughs and then #12 realizes that he has fallen into
the trap he set for himself earlier. He stops in mid-sentence.
#11 joins in the laughter. The edge is off the tension now, but
#12 shuts up tight and begins to doodle furiously.

250. MEDIUM SHOT   #'S 4, 5, 6, 7

>   #5
>   (Looking at window)
>   Look at how dark it's getting. We're
>   gonna have a storm.

There is a pause.

>   #5
>   Boy it's hot.

He yanks open his tie and fans himself with some papers. Then
idly, he turns to #4. #4 still sits there in tie and jacket,
seemingly not bothered by the heat at all. #5 looks at him.

>   #5
>   (Grinning)
>   Don't you sweat?

>   #4
>   (Coldly)
>   No, I don't.

#5, surprised at #4's coldness, turns away. There is a pause. #6
looks around a bit nervously.

                              #6
                  Uh, listen, I was wondering if maybe we
                  shouldn't take another vote.

                              #7
                  Great idea. Maybe we can follow this one
                  up with dancing and refreshments.

        #6 gives #7 a look, and then turns to the Foreman.

                              #6
                  Mr. Foreman?

251. MEDIUM SHOT   #'S 10, 11, 12, FOREMAN

                         FOREMAN
                  It's all right with me. Anyone doesn't
                  want to vote?

        He looks around the table. There is no answer. #12 doodles away,
        still annoyed with himself.

                              #3
                  I think we ought to have an open ballot.
                  Call out our votes, y'know? Let's see
                  who stands where.

                         FOREMAN
                  That sounds fair. Anyone object?

        There is no answer.

                         FOREMAN
                  All right. I'll call off your jury
                  numbers.

        He takes a pencil and paper and draws a line down the middle of
        the paper.

                         FOREMAN
                  I vote guilty.

        He makes a check on one side of the line.

                         FOREMAN
                  Number two?

252. CLOSE UP   #2

He has a hard decision to make. He thinks for a long moment.

                    #2
          Not guilty.

                         FOREMAN
                    (Off)
          Number 3?

Camera pans down to #3. He is staring at #2.

                    #3
                    (Sharply)
          Guilty.

Camera pans to #4. He sits back, relaxed, at ease.

                         FOREMAN
                    (Off)
          Number 4?

                    #4
          Guilty.

                         FOREMAN
                    (Off)
          Number 5?

                    #5
          Not guilty.

                         FOREMAN
                    (Off)
          Number 6?

Camera pans down to #6. He stares down at the table, picking at a
piece of cuticle on his thumb. His decision is difficult too.

                    #6
                    (Low)
          Not guilty.

As soon as he speaks he puts his sore thumb in his mouth, sucks on
the cuticle. Camera pans to #7. He is looking disgustedly at #6.

                         FOREMAN
                    (Off)
          Number 7?

#7

Guilty.

253. CLOSE UP   #8

> FOREMAN
> (Off)
> Number 8?

#8

Not guilty.

Camera pans to #9. He is in the process of taking a pill out of a bottle.

> FOREMAN
> (Off)
> Number 9?

#9

Not guilty.

Camera pans to #10. He is touching his tender nose appraisingly.

> FOREMAN
> (Off)
> Number 10?

#10

> (Loud)
> Guilty!

Camera pans to #11. He watches #10 with some distaste.

> FOREMAN
> (Off)
> Number 11?

#11

Not guilty.

Camera pans to #12. He doodles concentric circles on a pad.

> FOREMAN
> (Off)
> Number 12?

#12's pencil stops. He stares down at the table, thinking. There is a pause.

FOREMAN
(Impatiently)

Number 12?

#12

Guilty.

Camera pans to Foreman. He tallies his marks quickly.

FOREMAN

Six to six.

254. MEDIUM CLOSE UP   #7

He repeats his Clem McCarthy take-off.

#7

<u>And</u> we go into extra innings here!

He gets up and heads for the water fountain, camera panning with him. As he passes #10, #10 starts to rise, annoyed. Camera holds on #10.

#10

Six to six! I'm telling you, some of you people in here are out of your minds. A kid like that.

#9
(Mildly to #10)

I don't think the kind of boy he is has anything to do with it. The facts are supposed to determine the case.

#10
(Down to #9)

Ah, don't give me any of that! I'm sick and tired of facts. You can twist 'em any way you like. Know what I mean?

He walks away. Camera holds on #9. He half rises, angrily, and calls after #10.

#9
(Indicating #8)

That's exactly the point this gentleman has been making. I mean

> #9 (cont.)
> you keep shouting at the top of
> your lungs. . . .

#8 puts his hand on #9's shoulder. #9 looks at him. #8's ex-
pression says, "he isn't worth over-exciting yourself." #9 sits
down, quite agitated. He takes out a handkerchief and mops his
brow with it. We hear ad lib conversation at the water cooler.

> #9
> I'd like to be a little younger.
> That man. . . .

He stops, unable to go on. Then, trying to calm himself:

> #9
> It's very hot in here.

#8 nods sympathetically.

> #8
> D'you want some water?

> #9
> No thanks.

#9 continues to mop his brow. #8 rises and camera holds on medium
close-up of him as he walks to the window. He stands there, looking out. It has grown considerably darker now, oppressively
still. The room is silent save for a murmur of voices at the
fountain. #8 runs his hand over his face wearily. Then he opens
his tie.

255. MEDIUM SHOT   #'S 7, 10, 3 AT THE WATER FOUNTAIN

#3 is drinking. #7 holds a cup under the faucet. #10 waits his
turn. #7 turns to the window. His cup overflows. He turns to
it, steps away from the fountain and begins to drink, staring at
the window. #2 walks into shot to wait his turn at the fountain.

> #2
> It's going to rain.

> #7
> (Sarcastically)
> No!

#2 meekly turns away and gets a paper cup. #7 turns to him.

#7
How come you switched?

#2
Well, it just seemed to me. . . .

#7
(Interrupting)
I mean you haven't got a leg to
stand on. You know that, don'tcha?

#2
Well I don't feel that way. There're
a lot of details that never came out. . . .

#10
(Interrupting)
Details! You're just letting yourself
get bulldozed by a bunch'a what d'ya
callem . . . intellectuals.

#2
(Mildly)
Now that's not so.

#10
Ah come on. You're like everybody
else. You think too much, you get
mixed up.
(To #3)
Know what I mean?

#2
(Annoyed)
Now listen, I don't think you have
any right to. . . .

But #10 has crumpled his cup, flipped it on the floor and walked
away, leaving #2 in the middle of a sentence.

#2
(Softly)
Loudmouth!

#2 turns to #7, opens his mouth as if to speak, then, decides not
to. He walks over to the other window, camera dollying with him.
He puts his head against the glass and stares out. It is darker
now than before.

255A.CLOSE UP   #8

Still at window staring out. We see a portion of the skyline behind him, outside window. There is absolute silence in the room.

255B.LONG SHOT   ENTIRE ROOM FROM OVERHEAD

There is no movement in the room. Everyone waits for the storm
now. And suddenly it comes. We hear only the sound of the rain,
pouring down into the silence. No lightning. No thunder. Heads
turn toward the windows. There is no talk. The rain pours down
as if this were a tropical storm.

255C.MEDIUM SHOT   #8

He steps back from the window as the rain splashes in. Then he
reaches forward and closes the window. We hear the sound of the
other window being closed by #2. #8 stares out the window.

255D.LONG SHOT   ENTIRE JURY

From Foreman's end of table. They all stare at the windows silently. The room is quite dark now. The rain pours down.

255E.)
255F.) MEDIUM SHOTS   GROUPS OF JURORS
255G.)

Their faces in shadows for the first time, staring at the depress-
ing spectacle of the rain.

255H.MEDIUM SHOT   THE FOREMAN

Seated at table. Finally he gets up and camera follows him as he
walks over to the door. Next to it is a light switch. He flips
it on.

255I.LONG SHOT   THE ENTIRE JURY

There is a flickering of light, and then the overhead fluorescent
lamps come on full, throwing harsh white light on to the jurors.
At the same moment we hear the first crack of thunder. (Throughout the remainder of the play the rain continues, and now and then
there are flashes of lightning and the rumble of thunder.) The
foreman walks over to the windows now, and looks out. Camera
moves in on him. He stands next to #8.

FOREMAN
(Low)

Wow!

He speaks almost to himself.

FOREMAN
Look at that, will ya!

#8 nods and continues to look out.

FOREMAN
Think it'll cool things off?

#8
(Looking at him)
Yeah, I guess so.

FOREMAN
(Whistles)

Boy! Look at it go! Reminds me of the
storm we had last . . . November something.
What a storm! Right in the middle of
the game. We're behind 7-6, but we're
just startin' to move the ball, off
tackle, y'know! Boom! Boom! Boom!
Boy I'll never forget that. We had this
kid Slattery. A real ox. Wish I had
another one like him.

He looks up to find #8 looking at him.

FOREMAN

Oh. I probably forgot to tell you I'm
assistant head coach at the Andrew J.
McCorkle High School. That's in Queens.

#8 nods, smiles briefly and looks out the window.

FOREMAN

So anyway we're movin' real nice.
Their line is comin' apart. I'm tellin'
ya, this Slattery! Boy!
(He chuckles)
And all of a sudden it starts to come down
cats and dogs. It was murder. I swear I
almost bawled. We couldn't go nowhere!

#7
(Off)
Hey, let's get this fan goin' in here.
What d'ya say?

The Foreman turns to the sound of the voice. He looks at #8 for a
moment. Then he walks across the room, camera moving with him.
#7 stands under a wall fan looking up at it. Foreman walks over
next to him and looks up. Then he gets a chair, pulls it over to
the fan and stands up on the chair. He reaches up and turns on
the fan. It starts to turn slowly. He watches it for a moment.
Then he climbs down and turns around as if waiting for applause.
No one speaks. His smile fades, and camera follows him as he
slowly walks to his seat and sits down.

255J. MEDIUM SHOT   #7

He is back in his seat now. He looks up at the fan. Then he
takes a page from his scrap pad, crumples it up and flips it up at
the fan. He tears off another page and repeats this business.
And another.

255K. CLOSE UP   THE FAN

A wad of paper hits it, and is flung off by the blades.

255L. MEDIUM SHOT   #'S 3, 4

Standing near the water fountain. The wad of paper strikes #3 in
the shoulder. He turns around angrily.

#7
(Off, calling)
Sorry.

#3 turns back to #4.

#3
(Low)
What a stupid thing to do.

#4 bends to get a drink of water. #3 waits till he straightens
up.

#3
Some rain, huh?

#4, drinking, nods.

                        #3
           Well, what d'ya think of this thing?
           It's even-steven.

#4 nods as he drinks.

                        #3
           Kind of surprising, isn't it?

                        #4
           Yes.

                        #3
           Listen, that business before, you know
           where what's-his-name, that tall guy over
           there was baiting me, I mean that doesn't
           prove anything. Listen, I'm a very exci-
           table person, y'know. So where does he get
           off to call me a public avenger, and a
           sadist and everything? Anybody in
           his right mind'd blow his stack,
           wouldn't he? He was just trying to
           bait me.

                        #4
                    (Wryly)
           He did an excellent job.

We hear jumbled ad lib conversation in background.

                        #3
                    (Missing this)
           Now I'm being sincere about this.
           I'm no small potatoes like some of
           these people. I run a messenger
           service that employs over sixty-
           five workers. Well maybe that
           doesn't mean anything to you, but
           I consider myself a respectable
           citizen, and I'm trying to do my
           duty in here very sincerely. He has
           no call to act like that. I mean
           I could really've belted him one!

                        #10
                    (Off)
           Listen, I'll tell you what I think.

#'s 3 and 4 turn in the direction of his voice.

256. MEDIUM SHOT   #10, STANDING AT HIS SEAT

> #10
> We're goin' nowhere here. I'm
> ready to walk into court right now
> and declare a hung jury。 There's
> no point in this thing goin' on
> any more.

257. LONG SHOT   THE ENTIRE JURY

Most of them are seated now. #'s 3 and 4 walk back to their
seats。

> #7
> I go for that too. Let's take it
> into the judge and let the kid take
> his chances with twelve other guys.

> #8
> I don't think the court will accept
> a hung jury. We haven't been in
> here very long。

> #7
> (Standing up)
> Well let's find out!

> #11
> I am not in favor of this。

> #7
> (To #11)
> Listen, this kid wouldn't stand a
> chance with another jury and you
> know it.
> (Turning to the others)
> C'mon, we're hung. Nobody's gonna
> change his opinion. Let's take it
> inside。

258. MEDIUM SHOT   #'S 5, 6, 7

> #5
> You still don't think there's any
> room for a reasonable doubt?

#7
No I don't!

259. CLOSE UP   #11

#11
Pardon. Maybe you don't fully
understand the term reasonable
doubt. . . .

260. MEDIUM SHOT   #'S 4, 5, 6, 7 SHOOTING PAST #11'S PROFILE

#7 reacts strongly to this. He walks around the table until he
is standing behind #4, speaking angrily to #11 as he goes.

#7
What d'ya mean I don't understand
it? Who d'ya think you are to talk
to me like that?
(To all)
How d'ya like this guy? I'm tellin'
ya they're all alike. He comes over
to this country running for his life
and before he can even take a big
breath he's telling us how to run
the show! The arrogance of the guy!

#5
(To #7)
Wait a second! Nobody around here's
asking where you came from!

#7
I was born right here!

#5
Or where your father came from!

#7 doesn't answer, but stares at #5, amazed at this unexpected
outburst.

#5
Where does it hurt us to take a few
tips from people who come running
here for their lives? Maybe they
learned something we don't know.
We're not so perfect!

                    #11
                 (Mildly)
          Please. It doesn't matter. . . .

                    #7
                 (To #5 on top of #11's
                 lines)
          Okay homely philosopher . . . but lemme
          tell you something. Nobody around
          here's gonna tell me what words I
          understand and what words I don't.
          Hear?
                 (Pointing at #11)
          Especially him!

#7 stalks back to his seat, camera panning with him. He sits
down. During the Foreman's next lines #7, indignantly looks
around, feeling that he has won his skirmish, until finally his
eyes meet #8's. #8 looks at him long and hard, and finally #7
breaks and turns away.

                 FOREMAN
                 (Off)
          All right. Let's stop the arguing
          for two minutes in here. Who's got
          something constructive to say?

Camera holds on #'s 7 and 8. There is a silence. Then #8 turns
toward the others.

                    #8
          I'd like to go over something, if you
          gentlemen don't mind.

On the word gentlemen he looks pointedly at #7.

                    #8
          An important point for the prosecution
          was the fact that the boy, after he
          claimed he was at the movies during
          the hours the killing took place,
          couldn't name the pictures he saw or
          the stars who appeared in them.
                 (Pointing across at #4)
          This gentleman has repeated that point
          in here several times.

261. MEDIUM SHOT CENTERED ON #4

#4

That's correct. It was the only
alibi the boy offered, and he himself
couldn't back it up with any details
at all.

262. MEDIUM SHOT CENTERED ON #8, SHOOTING OVER #4'S SHOULDER

#8

Putting yourself in the boy's place,
if you can, do you think you'd be
able to remember details after an up-
setting experience such as being
struck in the face by your father?

263. MEDIUM SHOT CENTERED ON #4, SHOOTING OVER #8'S SHOULDER

#4

I think so, if there were any special
details to remember. He couldn't remember the movies at the theatre he
named because he wasn't there that
night.

264. MEDIUM SHOT CENTERED ON #8, SHOOTING OVER #4'S SHOULDER

#8

According to police testimony in court
he was questioned by the police in the
kitchen of his apartment while the
body of his father was lying on the
floor in the bedroom. Do you think
you could remember details under those
circumstances?

#4

I do.

#8

Under great emotional stress?

#4

Under great emotional stress.

#8

He remembered the movies in court.
He named them correctly and he
named the stars who played in them.

265. MEDIUM SHOT   CENTERED ON #4, SHOOTING OVER #8'S SHOULDER

                        #4
              Yes, his lawyer took great pains to
              bring that out. He had three months
              from the night of the murder to the
              day of the trial in which to memorize
              them. It's not hard for a lawyer to
              find out what played at a particular
              theatre on a particular night. I'll
              take the testimony of the policeman
              who interrogated him right after the
              murder, when he couldn't remember a
              thing about the movies, great emotional
              stress or not.

266. MEDIUM SHOT   CENTERED ON #8

   #8 stands up and walks slowly to a position behind #6, camera
   panning with him. When he reaches his position, shot will include #'s 4, 5, 6, 8.

                        #8
              I'd like to ask you a personal question.

                        #4
              Go ahead.

                        #8
              Where were you last night?

                        #4
                   (Puzzled)
              I was home.

                        #8
              What about the night before last?

                        #10
                   (Off)
              Come on, what is this?

                        #4
                   (In #10's direction)
              It's perfectly all right.
                   (To #8)
              I was at my office till 8:30. I went
              straight home and to bed.

#8
And the night before that?

#4
(Beginning to strain)
That was . . . Tuesday. The night be-
fore that? I . . . was . . . oh yes. That
was the night of the bridge tournament.
I played bridge.

#8
And Monday night?

#7
(Off)
When you get him down to New Year's
Eve, 1952, lemme know.

#10 lets out a loud laugh, which degenerates into a phlegmy cough.

#4
(Trying to remember)
Monday.

There is a pause.

#4
Monday night.
(Remembering)
Monday night my wife and I went to
the movies.

#8
(Fast)
What did you see?

#4
(Faster)
"The Scarlet Circle".
(He smiles)
It's a very clever who-done-it.

#8
What was the second feature?

#4
(Straining)
The . . . I'll tell you in a minute.

> #4 (cont.)
> The . . . Remarkable Mrs. Something.
> Mrs. . . . uh . . . Bainbridge. "The
> Remarkable Mrs. Bainbridge".

There is a pause.

267. CLOSE UP   #2

> #2
> I saw that. It's called "The <u>Amazing</u>
> Mrs. Bainbridge."

268. MEDIUM SHOT   SAME AS 266

> #4
> (Embarrassed)
> The . . . Amazing Mrs. Bainbridge. Yes.
> I think that's right.

> #8
> Who was in "The Amazing Mrs. Bainbridge"?

There is a long pause as #4 strains for the names.

> #4
> Barbara . . . Long, I think. She's a
> dark, very pretty girl. Barbara . . . Lang . . .
> Lane . . . something like that.

> #8
> Who else?

268A.CLOSE UP   THE SIDE OF #4'S NECK

A single drop of sweat glistens there, and then rolls down into
his collar. He moves uncomfortably.

268B.MEDIUM SHOT   SAME AS 266

> #4
> Well, I'd never heard of them before.
> It was a very inexpensive second feature,
> with unknown . . .

> #8
> (Interrupting)
> And you weren't under an emotional

                              #8   (cont.)
                    strain, were you!

#4 doesn't answer for a long moment.

                              #4
                         (Quietly)
                    No, I wasn't.

269. MEDIUM SHOT   #'S 9, 10

                              #9
                    I think the point is made.

There is a silence. #10 blows his nose.

                              #10
                    Big point!

                              #9
                    I think it is a big point.

                              #10
           What?   Just because he
                    (Indicating #4)
           can't remember the name of some two-bit
           movie star? I suppose that <u>proves</u> the kid
           was at the movies.

                              #9
                         (Quietly)
           No. But it indicates that no one can
           prove he wasn't. He might have been at
           the movies and forgotten what he saw.
           It's possible. If it's perfectly normal
           for this gentleman
                    (Indicating #4)
           to forget a few details, then it's also
           perfectly normal for the boy. Being
           accused of murder isn't necessarily
           supposed to give him an infallible memory.

                              #10
                         (To #9)
           You can talk till your tongue is
           draggin' on the floor. The boy is
           guilty. Period. Know what I mean,
           my friend?

They look at each other for a moment, and then #9 turns away.

                    #10
          Who's got those cough drops.

270. MEDIUM SHOT   FOREMAN #2

                    #2
            (Staring hard at #10)
          They're all gone, my friend.

He flips the empty box across the table. The Foreman watches it
slide, and then looks up.

                  FOREMAN
          Y'know there's something we're for-
          getting here that I was just thinking
          about. Well that's the whole business
          that dragged out forever, y'know with
          the psychiatrist, where he got all
          involved. . . .

271. MEDIUM SHOT   FOREMAN, #'S 10, 11, 12

                    #10
          Now don't start with all that phoney
          psycho-whatever-you-call it stuff.
          What a racket that is! Filling
          people's heads with all that junk.
          Listen I've got three psychiatrists
          keeping their cars in one of my
          garages. The whole three of 'em are
          crazy!

                  FOREMAN
          Listen, there's a point I'm tryin' to
          make here. Do you mind?

                    #10
          I wouldn't give you a nickel for a
          psychiatrist's testimony.

272. CLOSE UP   #8

                    #8
            (Meaning #10)
          Why don't you let the man talk. You
          can take five minutes on the useless-

#8 (cont.)
ness of psychiatry when he's finished.

273. CLOSE UP   #10

He glares angrily at #8 for a moment, then turns away, and blows his nose hard.

274. MEDIUM SHOT   CENTERED ON FOREMAN

                    FOREMAN
              (Looking peculiarly at #8)
Thanks.
              (To all)
What I was gonna say was, the psy-
chiatrist definitely stated that the
boy had strong homicidal tendencies.
I mean that he felt like killing
somebody half the time. Well, not
felt like, that he was, what d'ya
call it, capable. He described all
those tests, inkblots and all that
stuff, and he said the kid is definitely a killer-type. Am I right?

                    #12
Check. I think he said something
about paranoid tendencies if I'm not
mistaken.

                    FOREMAN
Right. Whatever that is, he said it.
              (To all)
Let's not forget, we're talking about
a boy who's always had murder on his
mind.

                    #12
              (Proudly)
His <u>unconscious</u> mind.

                    FOREMAN
              (Stolidly)
Nobody else's.

                    #11
I beg pardon, in discussing. . . .

#10
(Interrupting. Mimicking)
I beg pardon. . . . What are you so polite
about?

#11
(Looking straight at #10)
For the same reason you are not.
It's the way I was brought up.

They stare at each other for a moment. Then #11 turns to the
others.

#11
In discussing such a thing as the
murder potential we should remember
that many of us are capable of
committing murder. But few of us do.
We impose controls upon ourselves to
prevent it. The most these psychiatric
tests can accomplish along these lines
is this. They can tell us that some
day a particular person may commit a
murder. That's all. They prove
nothing.

275. MEDIUM SHOT   CENTERED ON #4

#4
Then how come they're admitted in
evidence?

276. MEDIUM SHOT   #'S 10, 11, 12

#11
They have many uses, of course. In
this case they added to the general
impression the prosecution was trying
to create. Perhaps we would find that
if we twelve men took the same tests,
one or two of us might be discovered
to have unconscious desires to kill,
and the potentiality of carrying them
out. Yet none of us has. To say
that a man is capable of murder does
not mean that he has committed murder.

                              #10
                          (Angry)
                  But it can mean it. Listen, if they
                  said the kid is capable of killing,
                  he could've killed, couldn't he?

277. MEDIUM SHOT   #'S 7, 8

   #7 is looking at his watch and up at the wall clock disgustedly.
   #8 leans down to #10.

                              #8
                  You're the one who said, and I quote,
                  "I wouldn't give you a nickel for a
                  psychiatrist's testimony!"

278. MEDIUM CLOSE UP   #10

   He knows he's been trapped, and he's angry about it. He speaks
   through gritted teeth.

                              #10
                          (To #8)
                  Boy, I'm telling you, I'd like to. . . .

   He stops and slams his fist on the table. Then he gets up and
   walks around the table trying to control himself. Camera pans
   with him. When he reaches #8 he stands over him for a minute.
   #8 doesn't look up at him. He stands there staring at #8 blackly.

                          FOREMAN
                      (Off, nervously)
                  Listen, just let's take it easy here.

   #10 finally walks away from behind #8. Camera holds on #8 for a
   moment, across table we can see #'s 5, 6, 7. #8 still looks
   calmly straight ahead. Then he reaches out to the middle of the
   table and pulls the switch-knife out of the table. He closes it.
   Then he flicks it open. Then he closes it. While this is happening we hear the following.

                              #6
                  What time is it?

                              #5
                  There's a clock on the wall right
                  behind you.

#7
(As #6 turns)
It's five of six.
(A pause)
Man, look at that rain!

#10 has walked over to side of room. We see him in background as
he angrily sits in a chair against the wall, where he will stay
through the entire next sequence until after the vote. #8 still
toys with the knife.

279. MEDIUM SHOT   CENTERED ON #2

He looks down at #8

#2
Say could I see that a second?

280. LONG SHOT   ENTIRE JURY FROM BEHIND FOREMAN

#8 closes the knife and slides it across table toward #2. While
this goes on we hear the Foreman's lines.

FOREMAN
Well we're still tied up six to six.
Who's got a suggestion?

#12
Let's get some dinner.

#2 open the knife and examines it.

#5
Why don't we wait till seven? Give it
another hour.

#12
Okay with me.

Camera now begins to move in on #2 as he speaks.

#2
Um . . . there's something I'd like to say.
I mean it's been bothering me a little,
and as long as we're stuck. . . . Well, there
was this whole business about the stab
wound and how it was made, the downward
angle of it, you know?

At conclusion of these lines, camera is on medium shot of #'s 2, 3, 4, shooting over Foreman's shoulder.

> #3
> Don't tell me we're gonna start with
> that. They went over it and over it.

> #2
> I know they did, but I don't go along
> with it. The boy is 5 feet 7 inches
> tall. His father was six two. That's
> a difference of seven inches. It's a
> very awkward thing to stab <u>down</u> into
> the chest of someone who's more than
> a half a foot taller than you are.

#3 stands up. He points to the knife.

> #3
> Give me that.

#2 does so.

> #3
> Look, you're not gonna be satisfied
> till you see it again. I'm gonna give
> you a demonstration.

#3 walks to a position behind and to the left of Foreman, camera dollying back with him. He looks at table. Camera covers right side of table in background.

> #3
> Somebody get up.

There is a pause. No one moves for a moment. Then #8 stands up. He walks along the table towards #3. Finally he reaches him. They stand looking at each other for a moment. There is absolute silence in the room.

281. CLOSE UP   #3

> #3
> Okay.
> (Over shoulder to #2)
> Now watch this. I don't want to have
> to do it again.

He turns back to #8 and looks squarely at him, measuring him.

282. CLOSE UP   #8

Waiting.

283. CLOSE UP   #3

> #3
> I'm six or seven inches shorter than
> you. Right?

> #2
> (Off)
> That's about right. Maybe a little
> more.

> #3
> Okay. Let it be more.

284. MEDIUM SHOT   #'S 3, 8 WITH MOST OF JURY IN BACKGROUND

#3 flicks open the knife, changes its position in his hand and
holds it aloft, ready to stab downward. He looks steadily at #8
and #8 at him. Then suddenly he stabs downward hard.

> #2
> (Shouting)
> Look out!

The blade stops about an inch from #8's chest. #8 doesn't move.
#3 smiles.

285. CLOSE UP   #8

He closes his eyes for a second and opens them as we hear following two lines over several ad lib remonstrations. Several of the
jurors run over to #'s 3 and 8.

> #6
> (Angry)
> That's not funny!

> #5
> (Yelling)
> What's the matter with you!

286. CLOSE UP   #3

> #3
> Now just calm down. Nobody's hurt.
> Right?

287. CLOSE UP   #8

> #8
> (Quietly)
> No. Nobody's hurt.

288. MEDIUM SHOT   #'S 3, 8 AND REST OF JURY IN BACKGROUND

#3 looks at the rest of the jury challengingly. No one says any-
thing. Then, still holding the knife at #8's chest, pointing
down and in, he speaks over his shoulder to #2.

> #3
> All right. There's your angle. Take
> a look at it. Down and in. That's
> how I'd stab a taller man in the chest
> and that's how it was done. Now go
> ahead and tell me I'm wrong.

289. MEDIUM CLOSE UP   #2

He looks at it for a moment and then, after looking up at #3 as
though to say something, turns away and walks to his seat.

290. MEDIUM SHOT   CENTERED ON #8

He still stands there as #3 turns, flips the knife into the table
and walks away. Several other jurors stand around him, including
the Foreman and #12. #12 walks over to him and, using his closed
hand, simulated stabbing #8 in the chest.

> #12
> Down and in. I guess there's no
> argument.

He moves to his seat as do some of the other jurors. Several
jurors walk to the water cooler, and #7 goes to his jacket on the
coat rack for more cigarettes. #8 turns and walks to the table.
He takes the knife out of the table and closes it. Camera moves
in on him as he flicks the knife open, takes it by the blade with
his left hand changes its position in his right hand and makes a
downward stab with it. Then quickly he closes it and turns to
the table. He stands between the Foreman's seat and #2's seat.

291. MEDIUM SHOT   FOREMAN, #'S 8, 2, 3, SHOOTING OVER #10'S EMPTY
     CHAIR

                                #8
                    Has anyone in here ever stabbed a
                    man?

He is greeted with a few laughs. He looks at #3 as the jurors at
the water cooler move to their seats.

                                #8
                    Have you?

                                #3
                    All right, let's not be silly.

                                #8
                    Have you or haven't you.

                                #3
                         (Loud)
                    I haven't!

                                #8
                    Well where do you get all your in-
                    formation about how it's done? Have
                    you ever seen a knifing?

                                #3
                    How do I know!

                                #8
                    Don't you think seeing a man knifed
                    would make a pretty vivid impression
                    on you?

#3 doesn't answer.

                                #8
                    Well have you ever seen a knifing?

                                #3
                         (Loud)
                    No!

                                #8
                    All right. I want to ask you something
                    now. The boy was pretty experienced

                        #8   (cont.)
              with one of these things. He was even
              sent to reform school for knifing some
              one, isn't that so?

                           #2
              That's right.

                           #8
              All right, take a look at this.

292. CLOSE UP   #8

     He takes the knife, holds it in front of him, and releases the
     blade. It springs out. Then he takes the blade with his left
     hand while he changes the position of the knife in his right hand
     preparatory to stabbing in an overhanded motion. Then he stabs.

                           #8
              Doesn't that seem like an awkward way
              to handle a knife?

293. CLOSE UP   #3

                           #3
                        (Annoyed)
              It's the way I'd use a knife if I felt
              like using a knife.

294. MEDIUM SHOT   CENTERED ON #8

     He closes the knife. Holds it underhanded in front of his belly,
     and releases the blade.

295. MEDIUM SHOT   CENTERED ON #5

     He stands up swiftly.

                           #5
                        (Loud)
              Wait a minute.

     Then he looks around the table, as though remembering something
     he had never wanted to think of again. He turns toward #8.

                           #5
              Give me that.

He reaches out for it. #8 walks into the shot, gives him the
knife. He takes it, closes it, holds it in his hand gingerly.
He looks down at it.

> #5
> (Low)
> I hate these things.

> #8
> Have you ever seen a knife fight?

> #5
> Yes.

> #8
> Where?

> #5
> On my stoop. In my backyard. In the
> lot across the street. Switch-knives
> came with the neighborhood where I
> lived. Funny, I wasn't thinking of
> it. I guess you try to forget those
> things.

> #8
> How do you use a switch-knife?

> #5
> Underhanded.

He flicks it open, and, holding it underhanded, slashes swiftly
forward and upward.

> #5
> Like that. Anyone who's ever used a
> switch-knife'd never handle it any
> other way.

> #8
> Are you sure?

> #5
> I'm sure.

He closes the blade, and flicks it open again.

> #5
> That's why they're made like this.

             #8
        (Looking at #7)
    The boy is pretty handy with a knife,
    isn't he?

296. CLOSE UP   #7

#7 looks back at #8 sourly.

297. MEDIUM SHOT   #'S 3, 4, 5, 8

             #8
        (To #5)
    Do you think he could have made the
    kind of wound that killed his father?

             #5
    Not with the experience he'd had all
    his life with these things.
        (Holding up the knife)
    No, I don't think he could. He'd
    go for him underhanded. . . .

             #3
        (Interrupting)
    How do you know? What, were you
    standing right in the room when the
    father was killed?

             #5
    No. And neither was anyone else.

             #3
        (Standing, to #8)
    You're giving us a lot of mumbo-jumbo
    here! I don't believe it.

             #4
        (Calmly)
    I don't think you can determine what
    type of wound this boy might or might
    not have made simply because he knows
    how to handle a knife.

             #3
    That's right. That's absolutely right.

#8 walks around toward the Foreman's end of the table, camera
panning with him. He reaches Foreman's chair. Shot now includes

#'s 2, 8, Foreman and 12. #8 looks at #12.

> #8
>
> What do you think?

298. CLOSE UP   #12

He is confused, trying to be honest. He hesitates for a moment.

> #12
>
> Well . . . I don't know.

> #3
>
> (Off)
>
> What d'ya mean you don't know?

#12 looks at him silently.

299. MEDIUM SHOT   #8 AND JURORS ON FOREMAN'S RIGHT, SHOOTING FROM BEHIND FOREMAN

#8 begins to walk down towards #7. Camera moves in as he does. #7 is looking up at the wall clock, and comparing it with his watch. #8 looks at him.

> #8
>
> What about you?

#7 looks from the clock to #8. Camera is in close on him now. Then he looks around the table.

299A. MEDIUM SHOT   CENTERED ON #4

> #4
>
> Just a minute. According to the
> woman across the street. . . .

299B. MEDIUM CLOSE UP   #7

> #7
>
> (Interrupting)
>
> Listen, I'll tell you something.
> I'm a little sick of this whole thing
> already. All this yakkin's gettin' us
> nowhere, so let's break it up here.
> I'm changing my vote to not guilty.

300. CLOSE UP   #3

#3

You're what?

301. MEDIUM SHOT   CENTERED ON #7

He gets up nervously, and starts to walk down past #'s 8, 9, 10, 11, 12.

#7

You heard me. I've had enough.

302. MEDIUM SHOT   #'S 7, 9, 11 IN FOREGROUND, SHOOTING ACROSS TABLE AT #3

#7 is walking towards #11. #3 stands up furiously and leans across table toward #7.

#3

What d'you mean you've had enough?
That's no answer!

#7 stops walking. He is behind #10's empty seat. He looks across at #3.

#7

Hey listen you! Just worry about
yourself, willya?

#11 turns and looks at #7.

#11

He's right. That is not an answer.

#11 stands up and faces #7, full in camera.

#11
(Strongly)

What kind of a man are you? You have
sat here and voted guilty with everyone
else because there are some baseball
tickets burning a hole in your pocket.
Now you have changed your vote because
you say you're sick of all the talking
here.

#7

Listen buddy. . . .

#11
(Overriding him)
Who tells you you have the right
to play like this with a man's
life? This is an ugly and terrible
thing to do! Don't you care. . . .

#7
(Loud)
Now wait a minute! You can't talk
like that to me!

#11
(Passionately)
I can talk like that to you! If you
want to vote not guilty then do it
because you're convinced the man is
not guilty . . . not because you've had
enough! And if you think he's guilty . . .
then vote that way!

#11 reaches the peak of his rage now. #7 blinks at the power of
him.

#11
Or don't you have the . . . the guts to
do what you think is right. . . .

#7
Now listen. . . .

#11
(Hard)
Guilty or not guilty?

#7
(Hesitantly)
I told you. Not guilty.

#11
Why?

#7
I don't have to. . . .

#11
You do have to! Say it! Why?

They stare each other in the eyes for a long moment. Then #7
looks down.

                        #7
                      (Low)
          I . . . don't think he's guilty.

#11 looks at him disgustedly, then sits down. #7 stands there
defeated.

303. CLOSE UP   #8

                        #8
          I want another vote.

There is a silence in the room.

304. CLOSE UP   FOREMAN

                      FOREMAN

          Okay, there's another vote called
          for. I guess the quickest way is
          a show of hands. Anybody object?

He looks around the table questioningly. There is no answer.

                      FOREMAN
          All those voting not guilty raise
          your hands.

305. LONG SHOT   THE ENTIRE JURY, SHOOTING FROM BEHIND #7'S SEAT

#7 is still standing. #10 still sits in chair at side of room.
#'s 2, 5, 6, 7, 8, 9, 11 put up their hands immediately. The
Foreman starts to count the upraised hands. Camera moves in
slowly, as he counts, on #'s 11, 12 and Foreman himself.

                      FOREMAN
          One. Two. Three. Four. Five.
          Six. Seven.

The seventh number is #11. #12's hand is down, but his face is a
mask of indecision. As the Foreman's counting finger moves past
him, he suddenly raises his hand.

                      FOREMAN
          Eight.

The Foreman stops counting and looks around the table. Slowly
now, almost embarrassedly, he raises his own hand.

> FOREMAN
>
> Nine.

He lowers his hand.

> FOREMAN
> All those voting guilty.

306. MEDIUM SHOT   #'S 3, 4, 5, AND IN BACKGROUND AGAINST WALL, #10

#10 jumps to his feet, angrily raising his hand. #'s 3 and 4
raise their hands.

> FOREMAN
>   (Off)
> Three.

They lower their hands.

> FOREMAN
>   (Off)
> The vote is nine to three in favor
> of acquittal.

#10 is standing angrily now behind #4.

> #10
> I don't understand you people! I mean
> all these picky little points you keep
> bringing up. They don't mean nothing!

He starts a walk around table. Camera pans with him till he
reaches his seat. He stands behind it. He continues to talk during his walk. Everyone is seated at table now but #10.

> #10
> You saw this kid just like I did.
> You're not gonna tell me you believe
> that phoney story about losing the
> knife, and that business about being
> at the movies. Look, you know how
> these people lie! It's born in them!

He whips out a handkerchief and blows his nose.

                              #10
          I mean what the heck, I don't have to
          tell you. They don't know what the
          truth is! And lemme tell you, they
          don't need any real big reason to kill
          someone either! No sir!

307. MEDIUM SHOT   CENTERED ON #5

As #10 talks, #5 gets up from his seat and walks over to the coat
rack. He stands with his back to #10.

                              #10
          You know, they get drunk . . . oh
          they're very big drinkers, all of
          'em, and bang, someone's lying in
          the gutter. Oh, nobody's blaming
          them for it. That's how they are!
          By nature! You know what I mean?
                    (Shouting it violently)
          Violent!

308. MEDIUM SHOT   CENTERED ON #10

#9 gets up from the table and walks to the window, stands with his
back to #10 as #10 talks.

                              #10
          Human life don't mean as much to
          them as it does to us!

#11 gets up and walks to the other window as he goes, #10 whirls
to him.

                              #10
          Hey, where are you going?

#11 pays no attention, stands with his back to the window. #10
turns back to the table. He begins to sound slightly desperate.

                              #10
          Look, these people're lushing it up
          and fighting all the time, and if
          somebody gets killed, so somebody
          gets killed! They don't care. Oh
          sure, there are some good things
          about 'em too. Look, I'm the first
          one to say that.

309. LONG SHOT   THE ENTIRE JURY

    #8 gets up and walks to the nearest wall, and stands with his face
    to it.

                            #10
                    I've known a couple who were okay,
                    but that's the exception, you know
                    what I mean?

    #2 gets up, and a moment later so does #6. They each walk to po-
    sitions along the wall, and stand with their backs to #10.

                            #10
                    Most of 'em, it's like they have no
                    feelings. They can do anything.
                    What's going on here?

310. CLOSE UP   #10

                            #10
                        (Louder)
                    I'm tryin' to tell you you're making
                    a big mistake, you people. This kid
                    is a liar! I know it. I know all
                    about them! I mean what's happening
                    in here? I'm speaking my piece, and
                    you. . . .

311. MEDIUM SHOT   THE RIGHT SIDE OF JURY, FROM BEHIND FOREMAN

    The Foreman gets up and walks to the water cooler. #12 follows
    him. They stand with their backs toward #10.

                            #10
                    Listen to me! They're no good!
                    There's not a one of 'em who's any
                    good.

    #7 gets up and walks to the window, stands with his back to #10.

                            #10
                        (Looking around wildly)
                    Boy, are you smart! Well I'm telling
                    you we better watch out! This kid
                    on trial here, his type. . . . Well don't
                    you know about them?

312. MEDIUM SHOT   CENTERED ON #3

> He gets up and, standing at his seat, turns his back on #10. #4
> gets up and starts the long walk around the table toward #10.

> > > #10
> > (Hysterical)
> > What are you doing? Listen to me!
> > I'm trying to tell you something!

313. MEDIUM CLOSE UP   #10

> He gesticulates wildly.

> > > #10
> > There's a danger here! These people
> > are wild! Don't you know about it?
> > > (Roaring)
> > Listen to me!

> He turns furiously, and finds himself face to face with #4.

> > > #10
> > > (Softer)
> > Listen to me!

> #4 stares at him as he trails off into silence. There is a long
> pause.

> > > #4
> > > (Quietly)
> > If you open your mouth again I'm
> > going to split your skull!

> #4 stares contemptuously at #10. There is no sound, no move.
> Then #10 looks down at the table.

> > > #10
> > > (Very softly)
> > I'm only tryin' to tell you. . . .

> There is a long pause. Then #4 turns and walks away from him.

314. LONG SHOT FROM ABOVE   THE ENTIRE JURY

> The only movement and sound in the room are #4's footsteps. He
> walks slowly back to his seat. We see the entire room. The
> other ten jurors stand in various attitudes and postures around

the walls of the room, their backs to #10. #4 reaches his chair.
He pulls it out and sits down. Then, slowly, the jurors begin to
return to their seats. #10 stands, head down, without moving,
until the last of the jurors have silently taken their seats.
Then he begins a walk which takes him to a chair at the far end
of the room against a wall. He sags into it, beaten. He lowers
his head into his hands and sits there.

315. MEDIUM CLOSE UP   #8

As is everyone else, #8 is embarrassed. He looks around the
table. Then he clears his throat.

> #8
> (Slowly)
> It's very hard to keep personal
> prejudice out of a thing like this.
> And no matter where you run into
> it, prejudice obscures the truth.

He pauses. There is silence.

316. MEDIUM SHOT   CENTERED ON #4.

#4 looks at #8 steadily.

> #8
> (Softly)
> Well I don't think any real damage
> has been done here. Because I
> don't really know what the truth is.
> No one ever will, I suppose. Nine
> of us now seem to feel that the de-
> fendant is innocent, but we're just
> gambling on probabilities. We may
> be wrong.

317A.MEDIUM CLOSE UP   #8

> #8
> (Looking at #4)
> We may be trying to return a guilty
> man to the community. No one can
> really know. But we have a reason-
> able doubt, and this is a safeguard
> which has enormous value to our system.
> No jury can declare a man guilty un-
> less it's sure.

317B.CLOSE UP   #4

    Listening.

                        #8
               We nine can't understand how you
               three are still so sure.

318. CLOSE UP   #8

    He pauses for a moment.

                        #8
               Maybe you can tell us.

319. MEDIUM SHOT   CENTERED ON #4

    He looks strongly at #8.

                        #4
               I'll try.

    He looks at #3, and then back to #8.

                        #4
               You've made some excellent points.
               The last one, in which you "proved"
               that the boy couldn't have made the
               kind of overhand stab wound that
               killed his father was very con-
               vincing.

    He stands up and stretches, and then continues to stand.

                        #4
               But I still believe the boy is guilty
               of murder. I have two reasons. One:
               The evidence given by the woman across
               the street who actually <u>saw</u> the murder
               committed.

                        #3
               And how, brother! As far as I'm con-
               cerned that's the most important testimony.

#4 looks down at #3 with some coldness.

                              #4
              And two. The fact that this woman
              described the stabbing by saying she
              saw the boy raise his arm over his
              head and plunge the knife <u>down</u> into
              the father's chest. She saw him do
              it . . . the wrong way.

                              #3
                          (Excitedly)
              That's right! That's absolutely
              right!

320. MEDIUM SHOT   CENTERED ON #8

He listens carefully as #4 goes on, and we can see that he has no
real answer to this.

                              #4
              Now let's talk about this woman for
              a minute. She said that she went to
              bed at about 11 o'clock that night.
              Her bed was next to the window and
              she could look out while lying down
              and see directly into the boy's
              window across the street.

321. LONG SHOT   THE ENTIRE JURY

                              #4
              She tossed and turned for over an
              hour, unable to fall asleep. Finally,
              she turned toward the window at about
              ten minutes after twelve and, as she
              looked out, she saw the killing through
              the windows of the passing el train.

322A.MEDIUM SHOT   CENTERED ON #4

                              #4
              She says that the lights went out
              immediately after the killing but
              that she got a good look at the boy
              in the act of stabbing his father.
                          (He simulates an overhand
                          stabbing movement with
                          his arm to accent this
                          statement)

> #4 (cont.)
> As far as I can see, this is unshake-
> able testimony.

> #3
> That's what I mean! That's the whole
> case!

> #4
> (Leaning over to #8, and
> mimicking him)
> What do you think?

322B. CLOSE UP #8

#8 hesitates for a moment, then doesn't answer.

323. MEDIUM SHOT CENTERED ON #4

He looks in the direction of #12.

> #4
> How about you?

324. MEDIUM SHOT #12

He has never been sold on voting not guilty, and is now swayed in
the opposite direction, yet he is apprehensive about how he will
look in the eyes of the other jurors if he shifts his vote again.

> #12
> Well . . . I don't know. There's so
> much evidence to sift.

He pauses, and chews at a fingernail.

> #12
> This is a pretty complicated business.

He looks around indecisively.

> #4
> (Off)
> Frankly, I don't see how you can
> vote for acquittal.

> #12
> Well, it's not so easy to arrange

                    #12 (cont.)
          the evidence in order. . . .

                       #3
             (Off)
          You can throw out all the other
          evidence. The woman saw him do it.
          What else do you want?

                       #12
             (Torn)
          Well maybe . . .

                       #3
             (Off)
          Let's vote on it.

                          FOREMAN
             (Off)
          Okay. There's another vote called
          for. Anybody object?

                       #12
             (Suddenly)
          I'm changing my vote. I think he's
          guilty

He looks down at the table, ashamed.

325. MEDIUM CLOSE UP   #8

     Turning his head toward #12, angry, upset, but helpless.

326. MEDIUM CLOSE UP   #3

     Smiling slightly.

                       #3
          Anybody else?

     He looks around the table challengingly.

                       #3
          The vote is eight to four.

     There is a pause.

327. MEDIUM SHOT   #'S 11, 12

#12, tormented, gets up and walks to the window.

                    #11
                 (To #3)
            Why is this such a personal triumph
            for you, this one vote?

328. MEDIUM SHOT   #'S 2, 3, 4

                    #3
                 (Grinning)
            I'm the competitive type!
                 (To all)
            Okay, now here's what I think. I think
            we're a hung jury. Let's take it inside
            to the judge.

There is no answer to this.

                    #3
            Well I want to hear an argument. I
            say we're hung.

He turns toward #8.

329. MEDIUM SHOT   #'S 7, 8, 9, SHOOTING OVER #3'S SHOULDER

                    #3
            Come on. You're the leader of the
            cause. What about it?

                    #8
                 (Quietly)
            Let's go over it again.

                    #3
                 (Annoyed)
            We went over it again!
                 (Indicating #12 with a
                 wave of his hand)
            Batton, Barton, Durstine and Osborn up
            there is bouncin' backwards and forwards
            like a tennis ball. . . .

330. CLOSE UP   #12

Standing at the window. He turns around.

#12
(Hurt)
Say, listen . . . what d'ya think you're
saying here. You have no right to. . . .

331. MEDIUM SHOT   CENTERED ON #3, SHOOTING BETWEEN #8 AND #9

#4 has his eyeglasses off and is polishing them.

#3
(To #12)
I apologize on my knees.
(To #8)
Come on! Let's get out from under this
thing. I'm sicka arguing with you already.

#4
(To #3)
There's no point in getting nasty
about it. You keep trying to make
this into a contest.

#3
(Grudgingly)
Okay.

#4
Maybe we can talk about setting some
kind of a time limit.

#7
(Off)
Once around to the dealer.

#4 looks witheringly in his direction. Still polishing his
glasses he turns around to the wall clock and peers up at it.

#4
It's um . . .

He squints and then puts on his glasses.

#4
. . . quarter after six.

He turns back to the table, takes off his glasses and lays them
down on the table. He looks tired now. He closes his eyes and
clasps his fingers over the marks left by his eyeglasses at the

sides of his nose. He rubs these areas as he speaks.

> #4
> Someone before mentioned seven o'clock.
> I think that's a point at which we
> might begin to discuss the question of
> whether we're a hung jury or not.

331A.CLOSE UP #9

He is looking closely at #4, and obviously as thought of something tremendously exciting.

> #9
> (Leaning forward)
> Don't you feel well?

331B.CLOSE UP #4

He looks up at #9, annoyed.

> #4
> I feel perfectly well. . . . Thank you.
> (To all)
> I was saying that seven o'clock
> would be a reasonable time to . . .

331C.MEDIUM SHOT   CENTERED ON #9 OVER #4'S SHOULDER

> #9
> (Excited)
> The reason I asked about that
> was because you were rubbing your
> nose like . . .

#9 notes #4 glaring at him.

> #9
> I'm sorry for interrupting. But you
> made a gesture that reminded me . . .

> #4
> (Interrupting)
> I'm trying to settle something here.
> Do you mind?

> #9
> I think this is important.

#4 looks at him, for a moment, then shrugs and leans back, relinquishing the floor.

> #9
>   Thank you.

He looks around the table for a moment, then back at #4.

> #9
>   I'm sure you'll pardon me for this,
>   but I was wondering why you were
>   rubbing your nose like that.

331D.MEDIUM SHOT   #'S 3, 4

331E.MEDIUM SHOT   CENTERED ON #9

> #3
>   (Annoyed)
>   Ah come on now, will ya please!

> #9
>   (Sharply to #3)
>   At this point I happen to be talking
>   to the gentleman sitting next to you.

331F.MEDIUM SHOT   #'S 3, 4, SHOOTING PAST #9'S PROFILE

#3 looks annoyed. During these next lines he sighs deeply, gets up from the table and strolls to the water cooler.

> #9
>   (To #4)
>   Now, why were you rubbing your
>   nose?

> #4
>   Well, if it's any of your business
>   I was rubbing it because it bothers
>   me a little.

> #9
>   I'm sorry. Is it because of your
>   eyeglasses?

> #4
>   It is. Now could we get on to
>   something else?

                    #9
          Your eyeglasses make those deep
          impressions on the sides of your
          nose. I hadn't noticed that before.
          They must be annoying.

                    #4
                (Angrily)
          They are annoying.

331G.MEDIUM SHOT   #'S 7, 8, 9

                    #9
          I wouldn't know about that. I've
          never worn eyeglasses.

     He points to his eyes and smiles slightly.

                    #9
          Twenty-twenty.

                    #7
          Listen, will you come on already
          with the optometrist bit!

                    #9
                (Firmly to #7)
          You have excellent recuperative
          powers!

     #7 looks disgustedly at him. Now #9 turns to #4. Camera moves in
     on #9's face for close-up.

                    #9
                (Quietly)
          The woman who testified that she
          saw the killing had those same
          marks on the sides of her nose.

331H.CLOSE UP   #4

     Digesting this.

331I.LONG SHOT   ENTIRE JURY

     There is a silence in the room for a moment. Then we hear a slow
     babble of ad lib conversation. #9 stands up, very excited.

#9
                    Please!

The conversation continues.

#9
                    Please!

It quiets down.

331J.MEDIUM SHOT   CENTERED ON #9

                         #9
            Just a minute, and then I'll be
            finished. I don't know if anyone
            else noticed that about her. I
            didn't think about it then but I've
            been going over her face in my mind.
            She had those marks. She kept
            rubbing them in court.

He demonstrates.

                         #5
                    (Off)
            He's right! She did do that a lot.

                         #7
            So what if she did?

                         #9
            This woman was about forty-five years
            old. She was making a tremendous
            effort to look thirty-five for her first
            public appearance. Heavy make-up.
            Dyed hair. Brand-new clothes that
            should have been worn by a younger woman.
            No eyeglasses. Women do that. See if
            you can get a mental picture of her.

331K.MEDIUM SHOT   #3

At water cooler, glaring at #9. He begins to stride toward the
table, camera dollying with him. He ends up standing behind #5,
shouting across at #9.

                         #3
                    (Loud)
            What d'ya mean, no glasses? You

               #3 (cont.)
don't know if she wore glasses.
Just because she was rubbing her
nose. . . .

               #5
She had those marks. I saw 'em.

               #3
So what! What d'ya think that
means?

               #6
          (Standing up to #3)
Listen, I'm getting so sick of your
yelling in here. . . .

               #5
          (Jumping up, to #6)
Come on. Cut it out.

He looks at #5 and then turns away from #3.

331L. CLOSE UP   FOREMAN

              FOREMAN
Listen, I saw 'em too. He's right.
I was the closest one to her. She
had those deep things, what d'ya
callem, uh . . . you know . . .

He massages the spot on his nose where they would be.

331M. MEDIUM SHOT   #'S 4, 5, 6, and 3, SHOOTING PAST #9'S PROFILE

#3 standing behind #5.

               #3
            (Shouting)
Well, what point are you making here?
She had dyed hair and marks on her nose.
I'm asking ya what does that mean?

               #9
            (Quietly)
Could those marks be made by anything
other than eyeglasses?

                        #4
                   (After a pause)
          No. They couldn't.

                        #3
                    (To #4)
          Listen, what are you saying here?
          I didn't see any marks.

                        #4
          I did. Strange, but I didn't think
          about it before . . .

                        #6
          Now that we're talking about it, I
          saw them. I mean it never occurred
          to me . . .

#3 steps back, thinking. #9 leans back and opens his bottle of
pills. He slips one tiny pill under his tongue. He suddenly
looks very old and very tired.

331N.MEDIUM SHOT   #8, #9

#8 looks warmly at #9. #9 drops the stopper of his bottle. #8
picks it up for him, smiles at him, hands it to him.

331O.MEDIUM SHOT   #'S 3, 4, 5, SHOOTING PAST #'S 8 AND 9

                        #3
                   Well what about the lawyer? Why
                   didn't he say something?

                        #8
                   There are twelve people in here
                   concentrating on this case. Eleven of
                   us didn't think of it either.

                        #3
                   Okay, Clarence Darrow. Then what about
                   the District Attorney? You think he'd
                   try to pull a trick like that, have her
                   testify without glasses?

                        #8
                   Did you ever see a woman who had to
                   wear glasses, and didn't want to because
                   she thinks they spoil her looks?

331P.CLOSE UP   #6

                        #6
            My wife. Listen, I'm telling ya,
            as soon as we walk outa the house . . .

                        #8
                    (Off, interrupting)
            Maybe the District Attorney didn't
            know either.

                        #6
            Yeah, that's what I was just gonna
            say.

331Q.MEDIUM SHOT   CENTERED ON #3

    He is stopped by this momentarily. He stares around the room.

                        #3
            Okay. She had marks on her nose.
            I'm givin' ya this. From glasses.
            Right? She never wore 'em out of
            the house so people'd think she
            was gorgeous. But when she saw
            this kid kill his father she was
            in the house. Alone. That's
            all.

331R.CLOSE UP   #8

                        #8
                    (Across to #4)
            Do you wear your glasses when you
            go to bed?

331S.MEDIUM SHOT   #'S 3, 4

                        #4
            No, I don't. No one wears eyeglasses
            to bed.

331T.LONG SHOT   ENTIRE JURY

    There is silence, save for the sound of the rain. No one moves.

                        #8
            It's logical to say that she wasn't

#8 (cont.)
wearing them while she was in bed,
tossing and turning, trying to fall
asleep.

#3
(Angry)
How do you know?

#8
I don't <u>know</u>. I <u>guessed</u>. I'm also
<u>guessing</u> that she probably didn't
put on her glasses when she turned
and looked casually out of the
window. And she herself said that
the murder took place just as she
looked out, and the lights went
off a split second later. She
couldn't have had time to put
glasses on then.

#3
Wait a second . . .

#8
(Strong)
And here's another guess. Maybe
she honestly thought she saw the
boy kill his father. I say that
she saw only a blur.

#3 walks furiously over to #8. Camera dollies in on them.

#3
How do you know what she saw?

He turns to the others.

#3
(Loud)
How does he know all these things?

He turns back to #8.

#3
You don't know what kind of glasses
she wore! Maybe she was farsighted.
Maybe they were sun glasses! What

                                #3 (cont.)
                        do you know about it?

                                #8
                        I only know that the woman's
                        eyesight is in question now.

331U.CLOSE UP   #11

                                #11
                        She had to be able to identify a
                        person 60 feet away, at night,
                        without glasses.

331V.CLOSE UP   #2

                                #2
                        You can't send someone off to
                        die on evidence like that.

331W.MEDIUM SHOT   #3 STANDING BEHIND #8

                                #3
                        Don't give me that!

                                #8
                        Don't you think that the woman
                        might have made a mistake?

                                #3
                            (Shouting)
                        No!

                                #8
                        It's not possible?

                                #3
                        No! It's not possible.

#8 turns away and walks down toward #12, camera panning with him.
He speaks to #12's back.

                                #8
                        Is it possible?

                                #12
                            (Quietly)
                        Yes.

#8 walks around the room, camera panning with him, to #10 who still sits slumped in the chair. He stands over #10.

> #8
> (Softly)
> Do you think he's guilty?

#10 shakes his head tiredly, giving in completely. #8 turns to the table.

332 THROUGH 341 INCL. -- ELIMINATED

342. MEDIUM SHOT   #8 IN FOREGROUND, #'S 6, 7, 9, AND #3 IN BACKGROUND

#3 stands behind #9.

> #3
> I think he's guilty!

#8 walks toward the table, camera panning with him. #4 is now in shot.

> #8
> Does anyone else?

> #4
> (Quietly)
> No. I'm convinced.

> #3
> (Angrily to #4)
> What's the matter with you!

> #4
> I have a reasonable doubt now.

> #9
> It's eleven to one.

343. CLOSE UP   #3

He glares angrily at all of them.

> #3
> (Loud)
> Well what about all the other evi-
> dence? What about all that stuff . . .
> the knife . . . the whole business.

344. CLOSE UP   #2

> #2
> You said we could throw out all the
> other evidence.

345. CLOSE UP   #3

Glaring at #2, speechless. Now camera dollies back slowly, holding on #3. He stalks down towards the Foreman's end of the
table, not able now to sit down with the others. He stands with
his back towards them. There is a long pause. He is full in
camera at left of frame. The others, in background, all watch
him and wait. #3 doesn't move.

> #7
> (Very subdued)
> Well what d'we do now?

There is another long pause.

> #5
> (To #3)
> You're alone.

#3 whirls around furiously.

346. LONG SHOT   THE ENTIRE JURY, SHOOTING FROM BEHIND #7

#3 is far in background.

> #3
> (Loud)
> I don't care whether I'm alone or
> not. It's my right!

#8, who still stands behind #4, speaks softly but firmly.

> #8
> It's your right.

They all wait.

347. CLOSE UP   #3

Watching them as if at bay.

348. CLOSE UP   #8

Watching.

348A.MEDIUM SHOT   THE FACES OF #'S 2, 4, 5, 6, 7

Watching.

348B.MEDIUM SHOT   THE FACES OF #'S 9, 11, 12, FOREMAN

Watching.

349. CLOSE UP   #3

Staring at them.

> #3
> Well what d'ya want! I say he's
> guilty.

350. CLOSE UP   #8

> #8
> We want your arguments.

351. CLOSE UP   #3

> #3
> I gave you my arguments!

352. CLOSE UP   #8

> #8
> We're not convinced. We want to
> hear them again. We have as much
> time as it takes.

353. LONG SHOT   ENTIRE JURY, SHOOTING FROM BEHIND #7

#3 is far in background. He stands there, frustrated, for a
moment. Then he begins. Slowly the camera moves in on him.

> #3
> Everything . . . every single thing that
> came out in that courtroom, but I mean
> everything . . . says he's guilty. Do
> you think I'm an idiot or something?
> Why dontcha take that stuff about the
> old man . . . the old man who lived there . . .

#3 (cont.)
and heard everything, or take the
knife, what, just because he . . . found
one exactly like it? That old man saw
him. Right there on the stairs. What's
the difference how many seconds it was?
What's the difference? Every single
thing. The knife falling through a
hole in his pocket . . . you can't prove
that he didn't get to the door. Sure,
you can hobble around the room and
take all the time you want, but you
can't prove it! And that stuff with
the el! And the movies! Now there's
a phoney deal if I ever saw one. I
betcha five thousand dollars I'd remember the movies I saw the night I
killed my father . . . as if I ever would!
I'm telling you, every single thing
that went on has been twisted and
turned in here. That business with
the glasses, how do you know she
didn't have them on? The woman testi-
fied in court . . . and that whole thing
about hearing the boy yell. . . . Listen,
I've got all the facts here! You
guys. . . .

He pauses and looks around.

#3
(Shouting)
Well what d'ya want? That's it!

354. CLOSE UP   #8

Waiting.

355. CLOSE UP   #3

Looking furiously around.

356. LONG SHOT   THE ENTIRE JURY, FROM BEHIND #3.

#3
That's the whole case!

No one answers.

                              #3
                    Somebody say something.

No one does.

                              #3
                    You lousy bunch of bleeding hearts!

No one moves. Everyone watches.

                              #3
                    You're not gonna intimidate me!

There is no answer.

                              #3
                    I'm entitled to my opinion!

There is no answer. And suddenly he strides swiftly to #8,
stands in front of him staring at him with utter hatred. Camera
moves in on them. #3 clenches his fists and stares at #8. #8
stares impassively back. It seems as though #3 must inevitably
hit #8. #8 waits for it, hands down. #3 half-raises both fists,
stands there tensely, his face contorted in silent rage. Then
suddenly he turns to the table and bangs both fists down on it.
Camera moves in close on his face.

                              #3
                         (Thundering)
                    All right!
                         (Softly now)
                    Not guilty.

Camera holds on his face close, as he suffers silently, while we
begin to hear the quiet noise of chairs being moved and footsteps
shuffling about the room. We hear a knock on the door and the
door being opened.

357. LONG SHOT   THE ENTIRE JURY, SHOOTING DOWN FROM BEHIND FOREMAN'S
      PLACE

Everyone is up. The guard stands in the doorway. Silently the
jurors get their belongings and begin to walk toward the door.
Camera moves in close on door, catching the face of each juror as
he exits.

358. LONG SHOT   THE JURY ROOM

Only #'s 3 and 8 are left now. #8 walks to the door. He stands in the doorway and looks back at #3. Then he steps out of the room. #3 still stands at the table, head down. The guard looks at him.

> GUARD
> (Politely)
> Let's go, mister.

#3 looks up. Then slowly he goes for his coat. He gets it, puts it on, and slowly walks toward the door. The guard steps outside. As #3 passes the table he stops, then walks over to it. The knife is sticking in it. He reaches over, pulls it out. He holds it up in front of him and looks at the doorway. Then, with a last burst of anger he flips it into the table. It quivers there. He turns and walks out, slamming the door. The knife quivers in the table in the empty room. Camera moves in for eye-level shot of the knife. Behind it we see the window. Rain beats against it.

DISSOLVE TO:

359. MEDIUM SHOT   A REVOLVING DOOR

The door to the courthouse building, shooting from outside. Rain beats against it. It begins to turn now, and the jurors start to emerge. One by one they walk into the rain, each reacting with his own maneuvers. One turns up his collar. One pulls down his hat. One holds a newspaper over his head. They begin to move down the steps in groups and singly now. #8 is alone. He walks into close-up, rain beading his face. He raises his collar, looks around, and then walks off. The others begin to spread out now. Some turning left, some right, some going straight ahead. Camera moves back and up, ending with a long shot, through the pelting rain, of the steps and the jurors spreading out silently in all directions, never to see each other again. And finally they are gone, and the rain beats down on the empty steps.

FADE OUT

the Defiant Ones

1958—A Stanley Kramer Presentation;
released by United Artists
Director Stanley Kramer
Script Nathan E. Douglas and Harold Jacob Smith
Source Based upon story, "The Long Road,"
by Douglas and Smith
Stars Tony Curtis, Sidney Poitier, Lon Chaney,
Theodore Bikel

Producer-director Stanley Kramer began his movie career as a film editor and script writer in 1933. In 1942 he became a producer and has produced such films as *The Moon and Sixpence, Home of the Brave, Champion, The Men, High Noon, Death of a Salesman, Member of the Wedding,* and *The Caine Mutiny.* As a director his credits include, in addition to this picture, such films as *Not as a Stranger* (1955), *The Pride and the Passion* (1957), *On the Beach* (1959), *Inherit the Wind* (1960), *Judgment at Nuremberg* (1961), *It's a Mad, Mad, Mad World* (1963), and *Ship of Fools* (1964).

The Defiant Ones, both in its subject and treatment, stands out oddly in this record.

Reaction by the critics was favorable, but mixed. *Newsweek* called it "Hollywood's most distinguished picture of the year" and added that it was a "triumph of motion picture dramaturgy." In the first of two favorable notices for the New York *Times* Bosley Crowther called it a "remarkably apt and dramatic visualization of a social idea—the idea of different men brought together in the face of misfortune in a bond of brotherhood." The *New Yorker* and *Time* praised the original screenplay especially, and so did Stanley Kauffmann when he wrote of Douglas and Smith in *The New Republic:* "They have abjured the rhapsody of uplift and so have made an extremely moving social drama." *Commonweal,* on the other hand, in a mixed review criticized it as a picture that "aims at universality, but doesn't make the grade."

The New York Film Critics' Poll honored *The Defiant Ones* as "Best

Picture of 1958"; Kramer received the director's award, and the screen-writers were also honored for their efforts. Douglas and Smith were further honored with the Academy Award for the best original screenplay of the year. It is currently listed with four stars in *Movies on T.V.* and described as "fine, mature fare."

Still, all has not been roses. Pauline Kael, never an enthusiast for the works and ways of Stanley Kramer, gives the picture a good going-over in "The Intentions of Stanley Kramer" (*Kiss Kiss Bang Bang* [New York, 1968]). She acknowledges that it is probably Kramer's best picture, then takes it to pieces on several counts. "The joker in *The Defiant Ones*," she writes, "was that although white liberals were pleased at the demonstration of solidarity, Negroes in theaters could be heard jeering at Poitier for sacri-ficing himself for his white 'brother.' Moviegoers with good memories amused themselves by pointing out that *The Defiant Ones* was *The Thirty-Nine Steps* in drag, and by noting that the episode about the farm woman was badly lifted from *La Grande Illusion*—with the convenient substitution of Negro for Jew (a familiar device in Kramer productions)."

It should prove interesting to the student to compare and contrast the treatment of the black man's character here and in the script from ten years later—*In the Heat of the Night.*

The Script Of the text it should be noted that the master scenes are not numbered. There has been a good deal of minor revision of the script, all occurring after its original date of January 20, 1968. Perhaps the most important single revision is the running motif of the transistor radio which was added in revisions made on the script.

Credits Producer, Stanley Kramer; Director, Stanley Kramer; Screen-play, Nathan E. Douglas and Harold Jacob Smith; Art Director, Fernando Carrere; Music, Ernest Gold and W. C. Handy; Photography, Sam Leavitt; Editor, Frederic Knudtson.

Cast	John "Joker" Jackson:	Tony Curtis
	Noah Cullen:	Sidney Poitier
	Sheriff Max Muller:	Theodore Bikel
	Captain Frank Gibbons:	Charles McGraw
	Big Sam:	Lon Chaney
	Solly:	King Donovan
	Mac:	Claude Atkins
	Editor:	Lawrence Dobkin
	Lou Gans:	Whit Bissell
	Angus:	Carl Switzer
	The Kid:	Kevin Coughlin
	The Woman:	Cara Williams

Awards   Received Academy Awards (1958) for "Best Script" and "Best Black and White Photography." Received New York Film Critics' Awards for "Best Film," "Best Direction," "Best Screenplay."

OVER THE TITLES and THROUGHOUT PART OF THE OPENING SCENE, WE HEAR a
voice singing. The song is not really a sad one -- but the untrained
quality of the voice -- and the repetitive nature of the lyric, gives
it a haunting, almost dirge-like feeling.

FADE IN: MALE VOICE (sings)

EXT. ROAD -- LONG SHOT -- HIGH   (The repetition of the
ANGLE -- NIGHT   rich timbre of the voice
                                            gives it an oddly mourn-
                                            ful quality)

The road barely seen in the grey down-
pour, winds through wooded hills. The   Long gone,
rain clouds hang like dirty tattered
curtains in the sky, and put a snake-
like sheen on the old-fashioned hump-   Ain't he lucky.
back, two-lane asphalt. A truck, its
headlights crawling the length of the
road like an insect, can be seen in   Long gone,
the far distance.

SUPERIMPOSE TITLES --   To Kentucky --

LONG SHOT -- TRUCK
                                          Long gone --
As it curves around the back road
and along the edges of a dismal and
forbidding swamp somewhere between   What I mean,
Florida and the Mason Dixon Line.

MED. LONG SHOT -- TRUCK   Long gone Sam

As it skids on the slick turtle-back
asphalt. It's a two and a half ton   On the bowling green;
box-bodied truck.

DISSOLVE TO: Bowling green,

INT. TRUCK CAB -- CLOSE TWO
SHOT -- JENNINGS & BAKER   Sewing machine,

JENNINGS is a leather-faced man
of indeterminate middle years. He   Little kitten sitting
squints through the windshield as he   on a sewing machine,
drives, swinging the wheel in order
to keep the vehicle in the center of
the road. It has a tendency to slip   Sewing machine,
over the side of the raised center, as
though trying to hurl itself into the

ditch. BAKER is a younger man,
pink-cheeked, with hard blue eyes.

OVER THE SCENE the same song
continues to be heard, but muffled
now and sometimes covered by the
sounds of the wet tires and the motor.

Baker squirms nervously.

> JENNINGS
> What are you scrounging
> around for?

> BAKER
> My jeans bind.

> JENNINGS
> I told you a million times,
> corduroys or whipcords --
> that's what you need for a
> long trip like this.

> BAKER
> Only thing good for a trip
> like this is a submarine.
> (indicates singing from
> back of truck with a jerk
> of his head)
> Listen to him. All the way
> from Walkerville.

> JENNINGS
> (begins to be irritated)
> Leave him be. He's got
> enough trouble now.

> BAKER
> (refers to singing)
> It's beginning to get on
> my nerves.

REVERSE ANGLE -- SHOOTING
THRU WINDSHIELD

The lights of an oncoming car are

Sewing machine,

Sew so fast --

Sewed eleven stitches

In the little cat's tail . . .

That cat is long gone,

Ain't he lucky,

Long gone --

To Kentucky . . .

Long gone,

Ain't he lucky,

Long gone,

To Kentucky --

Long gone --

What I mean,

Long gone Sam

On the bowling green;

Bowling green,

Sewing machine,

seen in the distance.

        BAKER
Watch this guy!

        JENNINGS
Let me drive, will you?

Jennings swings the truck over
to the side of the road.

EXT. ROAD -- MED. SHOT

As the vehicles pass, the truck
sways dangerously close to the
ditch.

INT. CAB -- CLOSE TWO SHOT

Jennings wrestles the truck back
onto the road. Baker is pale and
perspiring. There's a short pause.

        JENNINGS
These windshield wipers stink.
You can hardly see anything.

        BAKER
You're going awful fast for a
man that can't hardly see
anything.

        JENNINGS
    (kiddingly)
* * * <u>Nervous eh?</u>

        BAKER
What do you mean, nervous?
* * * <u>These moron truckers drive</u>

Little kitten sitting
  on a sewing machine,

Sewing machine,

Sewing machine,

Sew so fast --

Sewed eleven stitches

In the little cat's tail . . .

That cat is long gone,

Ain't he lucky,

Long gone --

To Kentucky . . .

Long gone,

Ain't he lucky,

Long gone,

To Kentucky --

P. 343
    [What's the matter, kid . . . you nervous?]

    [Them crazy contract truckers trying to
    get those Florida melons to Baltimore]

    [Them fellas only trying to make a living.]

BAKER (Cont'd)
like speed was going out of
style tomorrow . . .

Long gone --

JENNINGS
  You can't help it if you
drive contract. You want to
make the payments . . . you got to
go fast.

What I mean,

Long gone Sam

BAKER
You ain't got no truck to pay for.

On the bowling green;

JENNINGS
  (placatingly)
Okay . . . okay . . . I'll slow
down.

Sewing machine,

Little kitten sitting
on a sewing machine,

BAKER
  (pause)
Rain sure brings out that
swamp stink . . .

Sewing machine,

Sewing machine,

JENNINGS
What time is it? My back's
beginning to ache.

Sew so fast --

Sewed eleven stitches

BAKER
About nine o'clock.

In the little cat's tail . . .

JENNINGS
We're an hour and a half late
already . . .

That cat is long gone,

Ain't he lucky,

* * *

Long gone --

BAKER
Listen to him. We oughta
make him ride up here --
see how much singin' he'd
do.

To Kentucky . . .

Long gone,

Ain't he lucky,

Long gone,

To Kentucky --

Long gone --

The rest of his sentence is drowned
out by the roar of another truck as
it looms up out of the dark and is
gone. Baker has stiffened in his
seat at the sight of the approaching
headlights.

            BAKER
* * * They're coming.

            JENNINGS
What the * * * hell are you so
jumpy about?
            * * *
            JENNINGS
         (voice rising)
Will ya stop yelling?
            * * *
            BAKER
No, I don't care! And don't
try to tell me to keep quiet.

He twists toward the source of the
singing and yells.

          BAKER (cont'd)
Shut up, * * * dammit!

INT. VAN OF TRUCK -- CLOSE
SHOT -- BAKER

His face appears through the small
barred window.

What I mean,

Long gone Sam

On the bowling green;

Bowling green,

Sewing machine,

Little kitten sitting
  on a sewing machine,

Sewing machine,

Sewing machine,

Sew so fast --

Sewed eleven stitches

That cat is long gone,

Ain't he lucky,

P. 345

    [Slow down, willya!]

    [heck]

    [What do you mean, jumpy? What do
I care if some fat slob in Baltimore
don't get to eat melon for breakfast
tomorrow . . .]

    [All right! So you don't care! Will
ya stop yelling! [beefing!]]

    [goddamit!]

CAMERA PULLS BACK slowly across
faces of men, who sit on the wooden
benches that line the sides
of the dim-lit truck.

CAMERA APPROACHES the source
of the singing. The men are chained
in pairs. They are tired, hard-bitten
faces. CAMERA HOLDS on the singer.
He is a rock-faced powerfully
muscled Negro. The man he is
chained to is equally powerful,
equally rock-faced -- white. The
white man is sitting as far away from
the Negro as the four-foot chain will
comfortably allow. All the men are
completely self preoccupied, and no
one responds to the command to shut up.

> BAKER'S VOICE (O.S.)
> * * * I SAID SHUT UP!!

The white man, JACKSON, looks
toward Baker's voice, then turns
to CULLEN, the Negro.

> JACKSON
> (mockingly)
> You heard what the captain said,
> nigger. . . . Why don't you shut
> up . . .

Long gone --

To Kentucky . . .

Long gone,

Ain't he lucky,

Long gone --

To Kentucky --

Long gone --

What I mean

Long gone Sam

On the bowling green;

Bowling green,

Jackson has really been mocking Baker, but the Negro stops singing. He
turns slowly to look at Jackson. He rises slowly to his feet, his body
balancing against the truck sway and, with an almost terrifying strength,
he pulls Jackson up by the chain. The men stand face to face for a
long moment.

> CULLEN
> (quietly and simply)
> You call me a nigger again, Joker,
> and I'll kill you.

A slow smile crosses Jackson's face and his body tenses.

P. 346
   [GODDAMIT!]

                              JACKSON
                          (equally quiet)
                     Make your move, boy. . . .

As Cullen lunges toward Jackson, a flood of headlights from an
approaching truck stabs into the truck interior. There is a shriek of
brakes and a sharp sway and everything crashes into darkness.

The sudden silence is shocking, intensified by the now audible
sound of the rain over which comes the hiss of escaping steam.
A broken wheel upended, barely visible in the grey night, turns
slowly.

FADE IN: * * * Same_wheel -- still. Change_lighting on_wheel.

EXT. ROAD -- FULL SHOT -- PRE-DAWN

* * * Straight_cut_to headlights_-- ambulance comes in, pulls to_
a full_stop.

Ambulances and Sheriff's cars cluster around the wreckage like
hungry insects. Flood lights from the cars light the scene.
Men mill about. The most seriously injured are already taken
away. The others are waiting their turn, lying on stretchers.

CAMERA MOVES IN TO CLOSE SHOT OF SHERIFF, MAX MULLER. He is
leaning over one of the injured persons. He's a medium-sized
man. He seems strangely gentle to be a Sheriff. Although he
hesitates before speaking, it's a result of thinking rather
than indecision.

                               * * *

                              MULLER
                     Just a minute.
                          (to prisoner)
                     Hurt bad?

                              PRISONER
                     I can stand it . . .

[ATTENDANT
                          (to Sheriff)
                     Ready for this one, sir?]

                         MULLER
                  (to man on stretcher)
            Did you notice the driver turn
            his head -- maybe to look back
            into the cab?

                         PRISONER
            I don't know what happened.
            We were watching those two guys
            about to tangle and the next thing
            we're in the ditch. That's all
            I remember.

                         MULLER
                  (sighs -- to attendant)
            All right, you can take him.

He rises and stares after him thoughtfully. A uniformed STATE
TROOPER approaches Muller.

                         TROOPER
            Excuse me, Sheriff. The governor's
            on the phone.

                         MULLER
            Thanks.

CAMERA PULLS BACK as Muller goes to police car. In the b.g. can be
seen the rescue operations.

CLOSE SHOT

At the police car. Muller speaks into radio-phone.

                         MULLER
            Muller speaking.
                  (he listens; then in
                  a tired voice)
            No, governor, nobody dead. . . .
            Side-swiped -- Yes . . . only two
            escaped. . . . -- Yes, governor . . .
            I know what my first obligation is . . .
            we're still waiting for the dogs. . . .
            Yes, governor, any minute now --
            I got a call in to Warden Comisky. . . .
            Yes, governor . . . I'm quite sure you
            will.

He hangs up and stares at the phone distastefully. He turns away,
CAMERA PANNING; a sandy-haired comfortable looking man is revealed
standing near him.

> EDITOR
> Hello, Max. Am I first?

> MULLER
> Hello, Dave. You're the only
> one I called.

> EDITOR
> Anything new?

> MULLER
> Nothing I haven't already told
> you. The drivers are still
> unconscious. The men don't
> know anything, or won't say.

> EDITOR
> Who was that on the phone?

> MULLER
> The governor.

> EDITOR
> Anything I can print?

> MULLER
> (drily)
> Sure. He says he's going to
> get to the bottom of this.

> EDITOR
> (smiles)
> That's nice of him.

> MULLER
> It's an election year.
> (to a passing State Trooper)
> Try Warden Comisky again. We
> need that laundry for the dogs.

> STATE TROOPER
> Yes, sir.

He starts to go.

                    MULLER
          And call Marysville again.
          See if they've located that
          dog-boy yet.

The Trooper exits as another approaches Muller with a thermos and
some paper cups.

                    2nd TROOPER
          Here you are, Sheriff.   Some
          hot coffee.

                    MULLER
          Thanks.

                    2nd TROOPER
               (hands Editor a cup)
          It's hot.

                    MULLER
               (looks O.S.)
          Now, what the devil?

MED. SHOT -- REVERSE ANGLE -- STATION WAGON

As it bumps across ditch. Eight men pile out. They're civilians,
dressed in hunting clothes, carrying a variety of arms, rifles,
shotguns, etc. An amiable, beefy man acts as spokesman for the
group. His name is LOU GANS.
                         * * * Put in boy with
                                 radio

                    LOU
          Here we are, Max.

                    MULLER
          Who sent for you?

Frank Gibbons, Captain of the State Police, approaches Max. The Captain
is in his forties, an efficient and thoroughly professional policeman.

                    CAPTAIN
          I sent for them Sheriff.

                    MULLER
          What am I gonna do with them?

                    CAPTAIN
          Deputize them. You can't work
          short-handed.

Muller looks at him. The Captain explains:

                    CAPTAIN
          I only have twelve men. If the
          road-blocks don't pick them up,
          we may have to fine-comb a lot
          of ground before we flush them.

Muller turns to the men.

                    MULLER
                (shakes his head)
          Well -- watch how you play with
          those guns.

                    LOU
          You're kidding, Max. After all
          the times we been hunting together --
          Just like running rabbits . . .

                    MULLER
                (coldly)
          These are men.

                    LOU
                (cheerfully)
          Same thing.

                    MULLER
          No, easier. They're going to run
          until they can't run anymore.
          They'll walk until they fall down.
          They'll pick themselves up and
          stumble until they fall again.
          They'll hear the dogs coming
          closer. When they can't stand on
          their feet, they'll crawl. We'll
          get them.

                    LOU
          We just want to give you a hand,
          Max, help out.

                         MULLER
               You want to be helpful, Lou?

                          LOU
                    Sure, Max.

Muller hands him empty paper cup.

                         MULLER
               Good. Get rid of this.

He goes to the patrol car. Lou stares after Muller and
crumples the cup.

TWO SHOT -- EDITOR AND MULLER

Near patrol car, including Patrolman at radio-phone.

                         EDITOR
               They'll come in handy.

                         MULLER
                    I guess so.

                         EDITOR
               What about those two that escaped?

                      STATE TROOPER
                       (at radio-phone)
                    Warden Comisky on the phone,
                    Sheriff.

                         MULLER
                       (to the Editor)
                    Tell the Captain to give you the
                    transfer records. You can get
                    everything you want from them.
                       (into phone)
                    Hello, Warden? . . . Max Muller here . . .

CLOSE SHOT -- WOUNDED PRISONER -- HIGH ANGLE

On stretcher. A patrolman is unlocking the irons from his wrists
so he can be put into ambulance. CAMERA PANS up with irons as
patrolman rises and TRUCKS with him as he goes to patrol car and
drops the irons into it on the top of a heap of others.
CAMERA CONTINUES TO TRUCK to CLOSE SHOT of Editor who has papers
in his hand.

                         EDITOR
                    (reads from records)
               Noah Cullen -- Negro . . . man-
               slaughter . . . 10 to 20. Parole
               refused . . . Solitary . . . work camp. . . .
               John Jackson . . . Caucasian . . . armed
               robbery . . . 5 to 10 . . . attacked
               guard . . . additional five . . . parole
               refused. . . .

The Sheriff comes into SHOT.

                         EDITOR
                    (to Sheriff Muller)
               How come he chained a white
               man to a black?

                         MULLER
               The warden's got a sense of humor.

                         EDITOR
               What did he say?

                         MULLER
               He said not to worry about catching
               them. They'll probably kill each
               other before they go five miles.

                                        * * *
                                   CUT TO: NIGHT OR
                                   DAY FOR LIGHT

* * *

EXT. COUNTRY -- FULL SHOT -- HIGH ANGLE -- PRE-DAWN

Joker Jackson and Noah Cullen running through the wild country.
As they plow through the scrub brush, the four feet of chain that
binds them jerks them off stride, erratically. They come to a
stream that edges a swamp and fall on their faces to drink.

CLOSE TWO SHOT

At edge of stream. The men lift their faces out of the water and

---

[FADE OUT]

[FADE IN]

lean back against a boulder. They are breathing hard and they
show the signs of the all night trek. They are scratched,
bruised, dirty, near exhaustion . . . all of which we see through
an overlay of the exhilarated tension of escape.

> JACKSON
> Daybreak pretty soon.

> CULLEN
> Pretty soon now. . . .
> Wish it'd hurry.

A sudden recollection sweeps the expectancy momentarily from
his face.

> JACKSON
> Lucky we were standing up when
> it hit. . . .

> CULLEN
> (sardonically))
> Yeah . . . lucky we was standing . . .

> JACKSON
> (laughs softly)
> Man, they're gonna be short-handed
> on that road gang today. . . .
> (pause)
> Wish daybreak'd hurry up. . . .
> (pause)
> How far you think we come?

> CULLEN
> Eight miles . . . maybe ten.
> We're at swamp-edge, now.

> JACKSON
> Where's swamp-edge?

> CULLEN
> Forty-fifty miles north of Colby. . . .

> JACKSON
> You sound like you know this
> country.

> CULLEN
> (shortly)
> Used to haul turpentine up

CULLEN (Cont'd)
above a ways.

He reaches into his pocket for a cigarette, strikes a match to light it. It is his last cigarette. He crumples the pack and throws it away.

JACKSON
Watch that light!

CULLEN
(laconically)
If they close enough to see us . . .
they close enough to catch us. . . .

Jackson, mulling this over, begins to realize the fact of his escape. A slow smile crosses his face, then broadens into a grin as an inspiration occurs to him. He reaches into his own pocket for a pack of matches and lights one.

CULLEN
What're you doing?

JACKSON
Daybreak . . . I'm making some daybreak. . . .

CULLEN
You crazy?

JACKSON
What do you mean crazy? . . . I been buried in a rock for seven years . . . and time's on my back.

The match burns down to his fingers and he drops it. As he stamps it out, he notices his prison shoes . . . looks at them for a long, wondering moment.

JACKSON
Look at them . . . look at those shoes . . .
dead street shoes!

A sudden idea strikes him and his free hand paws the ground feverishly, searching for a rock. Cullen is forced to accommodate to the pull of the chain.

CULLEN
What's the matter with you?

Jackson finds the rock he wants, stares at it as he hefts it.

>   JACKSON
> How far did you say we come?

>   CULLEN
> 'Bout ten miles . . .

>   JACKSON
>   (totally self-preoccupied as
>   he stares at the rock)
> Ten miles . . . ten miles off dead street. . . .
> I been walking down dead street
> seven long years . . . and I turned the
> corner ten miles back!

An almost frenzied burst of energy seizes him. He pulls the
chain taut across the boulder . . . using it as an anvil. He gives
the rock a final heft.

>   JACKSON
> No more dead street shoes!

The rock crashes down on the chain.

>   JACKSON
>   (hefting rock)
> No more dead street!
>   (the excitement
>   mounts in him)
> I'm gonna buy me a pair of white
> buck shoes!

The rock crashes down.

>   JACKSON (cont'd.)
> A new white suit and a striped
> silk shirt! I'm going to be
> Charlie Potatoes . . . Charlie Potatoes,
> coming down the street . . .

The rock crashes down. . . .

>   JACKSON (cont'd.)
> With a panama hat and a good-
> looking gal. . . .

The rock crashes down. He looks suddenly up at Cullen.

                          JACKSON
                    (holding rock out to
                    Cullen)
               Here, boy, here . . . your right hand's
               free. Hit her! Hit her hard! . . .
               Smash her! . . . Come on, boy!

Cullen reacts to the term "boy". He takes the rock, hefts it
slowly as he muses aloud.

                          CULLEN
                    (sardonically)
               "Boy", hah? . . . Yassuh, boss . . .
               yassuh, boss . . .

He pounds a mighty blow against the chain.

                          CULLEN (cont'd.)
               . . . No more yassuh, boss!

                          JACKSON
                    (as Cullen hefts the rock)
               I'll dance down the street
               and the bands'll be playing!

The rock crashes down.

                          CULLEN
               . . . No more yassuh, boss!

As Cullen hefts rock:

                          JACKSON
               I'll grab a boat to Rio and
               I'll never be found! . . .

Crash of the rock.

                          CULLEN
               No more yassuh, boss!

As Cullen hefts the rock:

                          JACKSON
               I'll never be found!

                          CULLEN
               NO MORE YASSUH, BOSS!!

Cullen smashes the rock against the chain. The stone shatters
against the chain. There is a moment's stunned silence.

> CULLEN
> (softly, almost
> wonderingly)
> It won't break . . . it won't break. . . .

Jackson rises slowly to his feet. The look of fantasy has been
replaced by a look of grim swift purpose. Cullen is still
kneeling, staring at the remnants of the broken rock.

> JACKSON
> (sharply)
> Let's go.

The chain snaps taut as Cullen, roused from his preoccupation
looks up at Jackson.

> CULLEN
> Go where?

> JACKSON
> (urgently)
> Pineville . . . we head for Pineville.

> CULLEN
> Pineville's south. I don't go south. . . .

> JACKSON
> I used to know a girl in Pineville.
> If she's still there we get these broke.

> CULLEN
> Then what? I'm a strange colored
> man in a white south town. . . . How long
> you think before they pick me up?

> JACKSON
> Get off my back. You ain't married
> to me. What do I care. . . .

> CULLEN
> (softly)
> You married to me all right, Joker.
> (indicates chain)
> Here's the ring.
> (pause, then flatly)

                    CULLEN (Cont'd)
And we ain't going south on no
honeymoon, Joker. We going north!

                    JACKSON
                  (scornfully)
Through the swamp!?

                    CULLEN
I used to work a turpentine camp
about sixty miles north of here.
There's a train come to pick up the
turpentine every day. It comes out
of the west end of the swamp moving
slow and it goes across the line to
the paint makers up north in Ohio.
                  (pause)
We try for the train. . . .

                    JACKSON
How long you been in jail?

                    CULLEN
Eight years. . . .

                    JACKSON
How do you know that train's still
running?

                    CULLEN
                  (stubbornly)
I don't know. . . .

                    JACKSON
                  (triumphantly)
You don't know. You're asking me to
go sixty miles and you don't even
know! Whatta you inviting me on? . . .
A long walk off a short pier and all
I come up with's a wet head? . . .
Nothing doing! Come on!

He pulls violently on the chain. Cullen, refuses to get to his
feet. Cullen starts to laugh and this infuriates Jackson. He
drags Cullen along the ground, Cullen's full, taunting laughter
ringing in his head. He stops and glares down at Cullen,
breathing hard with anger and the effort. Cullen is kneeling.

                    CULLEN
              (looks up at Jackson:
               softly)
          Charlie Potatoes . . . hah?

                    JACKSON
          Yeah. . . .

                    CULLEN
          You gonna dance down that street
          with a gal on one arm . . .

                    JACKSON
          Yeah. . . .

                    CULLEN
              (indicates chain)
          . . . and this on the other?

                    JACKSON
              (tautly)
          Shut up!

                    CULLEN
          You're gonna grab a boat to Rio -- ?

                    JACKSON
          Yeah!

                    CULLEN
          Carrying your own anchor?

                    JACKSON
          We can break it!

Cullen rises slowly. The men stand face to face.

                    CULLEN
              (softly taunting)
          Gonna bite it through with your
          teeth?

                    JACKSON
              (furiously)
          Maybe your head's hard enough!

His free hand swings in a long arcing punch at Cullen.
Cullen catches his wrist and for a long moment they stand
in tense, unmoving struggle.

                    CULLEN
    The time's gona come, Joker . . .
    the time's gonna come . . . and if you
    want it to be right here . . . right
    now . . . it's okay with me. . . .

                    JACKSON
                (tauntingly)
    You kinda got the advantage of me,
    boy . . . you kinda hard to see in
    the dark.

                    CULLEN
    But you can hear me, Joker . . . and you
    better listen to what I got to
    say. . . . There's only one way I can
    walk out of this free, Joker. We
    go north together . . . or together we
    gonna go them ten miles right
    back onto dead street!

The full meaning of Cullen's threat grows slowly in Joker's
mind. He stares at Cullen and, slowly, his arm relaxes.
Cullen lets it fall.

                    JACKSON
    You're right, boy . . . you're sure
    right . . . that time's gonna come . . .
    it's sure gonna come.

                    CULLEN
                (flatly)
    North's up that way. . . .

Jackson's slow contemptuous smile fails to conceal the anger
in his eyes as he slowly turns toward the north and begins
to move. . . .

EXT. ROAD -- CLOSE SHOT -- DOGS -- DAY

Two cages on back of truck fill SHOT in CLOSEUP. One cage
contains four bloodhounds, the second, two vicious airedales.
All of them set up a terrific clamor. CAMERA PULLS BACK,
revealing Muller and Captain, lunches in hand, staring at
the dogs. On the door panel is printed "Richard's Orthopedic
Fit-Rite Shoes." A fussy little man, SOLLY, in elaborate
hunting boots, pops out from behind the wheel and approaches
them. He's followed by his assistant, WILSON, a leather-faced
taciturn man of indeterminate age. In b.g. are wreckers,

clearing away the overturned trucks. In addition to Sheriff's
and Trooper's cars is a sheriff's jeep and a station wagon,
rigged up as a commisary, around which are grouped troopers
and deputies, eating and drinking coffee. There's an almost
festive air about the scene.

> SOLLY
>(dog-boy, shrilly)
>Don't aggravate the dogs!

> MULLER
>What?

> SOLLY
>You're eating right in front of
>them. Don't you think they have
>feelings?

> CAPTAIN
>Calm down, Solly. Nobody meant
>to hurt their feelings. This is
>Sheriff Muller.

> SOLLY
>Oh, hello Sheriff.
>(apologetically)
>I didn't mean to holler, Sheriff,
>they're very high strung. This is
>my assistant, Wilson.

Sheriff starts to give him his sandwich.

> SOLLY (cont'd.)
>No, no, no! They only get fed
>once a day.

> CAPTAIN
>He's mighty fussy about his dogs.
>Got reason to be, too.

> SOLLY
>(to Sheriff)
>You'd never guess what goes into
>training these dogs. I'm at it
>every spare minute.

He gazes fondly at his dogs.

> CAPTAIN
> When he's not selling shoes.
> That's a pretty sharp pair of
> boots you got there, Solly.

> SOLLY
> (matter of factly)
> Built-in-arches, cushioned sole.
> Retails for $14.95. I can get it
> for you wholesale. You too, Sheriff.

CLOSE SHOT -- AIREDALES

They lunge viciously at the Sheriff, frighteningly brutal.

BACK TO SCENE:

Muller draws back from the cage.

> MULLER
> What are those?

> SOLLY
> The airedales?
> (laughs)
> I can tell you don't have much
> experience with dogs.

> MULLER
> (drily)
> Not that kind.

> SOLLY
> (blithely)
> Bloodhounds won't bite a hamburger.
> These'll bring the men down when we
> catch up with them.

> MULLER
> We won't be needing them.

> CAPTAIN
> We're dealing with two pretty
> * * * dangerous criminals, Sheriff. You
> can't tell what we're liable to
> run into.

[tough]

> MULLER
> How * * * <u>dangerous</u> can they be, chained
> together?

> CAPTAIN
> (brusquely)
> Excuse me a minute, Solly.

He takes Sheriff by the arm and turns him away.

> CAPTAIN (cont'd.)
> Look, Sheriff, it's your show,
> but if your views are humanitarian,
> you better start thinking about the
> farmers hereabouts as well as your
> own deputies. For my part, the
> dogs come with us. I have my own
> men to think about.

> MULLER
> (after a moment)
> All right -- but kept in leash.
> (to Solly)
> You hear? Keep those dogs leashed,
> and don't let them go unless <u>I</u> tell
> you.

He exits SCENE.

> CAPTAIN
> Get busy, Solly. You'll find the
> old clothes in the back of the
> squad car.

> SOLLY
> I'll have to make a wide circle,
> -- your men have been milling around
> pretty good.

> CAPTAIN
> (to Trooper)
> Get everybody together.

As the men gather. Solly in b.g. goes to squad car. CAMERA
PANS with Captain as he joins Sheriff at jeep. Muller is

looking at map spread on hood of jeep.

TWO SHOT -- SHERIFF, CAPTAIN

Muller looks up.

> MULLER
> Nothing to the East.

> CAPTAIN
> We would have heard from the
> road blocks by now.

> MULLER
> Only two directions they can go
> in. Either North across the swamps
> toward Cumberland. . . .

> CAPTAIN
> (points)
> There's a State Trooper's barracks
> at Cumberland. Why don't we get
> them moving down toward us, and we
> can pick them up in a pincers move-
> ment.

> MULLER
> (looks at Captain;
> startled)
> A pincers movement!

Lou enters b.g.

> MULLER (cont'd.)
> (rises)
> They'll probably head South toward
> Colby anyhow. The swamp's a pretty
> unhealthy place.

He turns to Lou who is hovering in the b.g.

> MULLER (cont'd.)
> What is it, Lou?

> LOU
> Here, Max. Your wife said to give
> you this.

He hands Muller a sweater.   The men are gathering around to
the summons of the trooper.   The Captain turns to Max.

                    CAPTAIN
          Do you want to brief them, Sheriff?

The Sheriff pulls his head through the sweater and cocks a
humorous eye at the Captain.

                    MULLER
          Go head.

Muller looks around to see what Solly is doing while the
Captain mounts the hood of the jeep and addresses the men.

                    CAPTAIN
          * * * All right, turn off that radio.
               (crisply military)
          All right men, we're ready to
          move out.   Sheriff Muller is in
          charge -- I'm second in command.
          You'll take your orders from us.

CLOSE SHOT -- SOLLY

At squad car.   He lifts out paper carton and reaches in.   He
pulls out tattered dirty undershirt and sniffs it automatically.
CAMERA PANS with Solly who has dropped the shirt back into the
box and carries the whole thing over to his own pick-up.   Wilson
has gotten the dogs on leashes.   Solly scatters the clothes,
blankets, on the ground and urges the dogs to smell.

                    CAPTAIN'S VOICE
          At the command to proceed, you
          will deploy into two groups in
          skirmish line formation -- pivoting
          on the headquarters group which
          will consist of Sheriff Muller
          and myself. . . .

CLOSE LOW ANGLE SHOT -- CAPTAIN

In his smart uniform, he's the picture of army efficiency.

                    CAPTAIN
          The state troopers will constitute
          group one, and will assume the right
          flank.

CAMERA PANS DOWN to Sheriff who looks up at the Captain with
a look of puzzled, but tolerant amusement. Editor is also
in SHOT. He catches the Sheriff's eye. The Sheriff shrugs
and both men smile. The barking of the dogs, a new note,
makes the Sheriff look O.S.

HIGH ANGLE SHOT -- SOLLY AND DOGS -- SHOOTING PAST CAPTAIN IN F.G.

The dogs are excited and the dog-men have to cling to the
leashes of the excited beasts. They mill around sniffing as
Solly and Wilson walk them to the periphery of the group
attending the address by the Captain.

> CAPTAIN
> You will stay in sight of each
> other -- no more than twenty five
> yards apart at any time. Our
> pace will be gauged by the speed
> of the dogs.

CLOSE SHOT -- MULLER AND EDITOR

Both men are closely watching the action of the dogs and not
paying attention to the Captain's speech.

> CAPTAIN'S VOICE (o.s.)
> So far as we know, the men we're
> after are not armed. Two shots
> will mean you have found them.
> The dogs and first aid will be with
> headquarters group. . . .

A new bugling from the dogs focusses Muller's attention.

CLOSE SHOT -- SOLLY AND DOGS -- SHOOTING TOWARD GROUP IN B.G.

The dogs are yelping joyfully, anxious to be off on the trail.

> SOLLY
> (equally excited -- shouts)
> Sheriff! . . . Captain! . . we got it!
> Old Ginger picked it up right away!
> (to Ginger)
> Good girl . . . good girl . . .

LOW ANGLE SHOT -- CAPTAIN -- SHOOTING PAST SHERIFF IN F.G.

                    CAPTAIN
            One more thing. . . .

Muller looks up at the Captain impatiently.

                    CAPTAIN (cont'd.)
            This may take a couple of days -- maybe
            longer. So you'd better check your gear.
            Rations, ponchos -- your new deputies can
            check with the troopers. Don't forget,
            keep your lines dressed and don't fall behind.
                (looks down to Sheriff)
            Just a minute.

He jumps down from the hood of the jeep.

                    CAPTAIN
                (smartly)
            Anything you want to add, Sheriff?

                    MAX
                (reassuringly)
            No. . . . You did fine.

Max smiles benignly as he closes a button on the Captain's blouse.

                    MAX (cont'd.)
            Deploy.

The Captain doesn't quite know how to take the Sheriff, but is
definitely annoyed.

FULL SHOT * * * Boy turns radio on again.

As the men straggle into a ragged line fanning out from Solly,
Wilson and the dogs, followed by the Sheriff, Editor and the Captain.

                                                        CUT TO:

EXT. RIVER -- DAY -- CLOSE SHOT -- HIGH ANGLE -- THE WATER

The surge of the river, swollen with spring rains, is a mound
of carved green glass, before it shatters against a rock,
shiny black and half-drowned in the raging torrent.

CAMERA PANS UP to CLOSE LOW ANGLE SHOT -- CULLEN AND JACKSON

They are staring at the rushing water with a stoicism of men for whom retreat is a greater threat than dangers before them. Jackson rouses himself. He looks up and down the river and then shrugs.

> JACKSON
> (speaks over the muted
> roar of the waters)
> Come on --

He steps to the edge of the river, but feels the restraint of the chain. Cullen still stares bemused at the river, his face wooden.

> CULLEN
> How deep do you think it is?

Jackson looks at him coldly.

> JACKSON
> What's the difference?

Cullen remains unmoving. Jackson looks back at him.

> JACKSON (cont'd.)
> You wanted to go north, didn't
> you?

Cullen moves as though in the grip of a nightmare. Jackson turns to face the water. Cullen follows him, CAMERA PANNING. The full sweep of the river is revealed; rapid, churning angrily, shredding itself into white ribbons against the rocks, interspersed with areas of deceptively smooth slicks of oily black water, hiding the boiling currents beneath.

CLOSE TWO SHOT -- THE MEN

They slide, hip deep into the water. The chill water makes them gasp. They have to struggle to keep their footing. As they proceed, the uneven bottom and weight of surge, makes them lurch awkwardly, pulling against the chain that binds them together, sometimes knocking one or the other off balance. CAMERA PULLS BACK with them as they struggle for footholds. They climb out of the backwash to shallower water. The currents here are stronger, but there are rocks on which to step, albeit wet and slippery. Cullen, by comparison, is clumsy and uncertain.

TWO SHOT DIFFERENT ANGLE

The men are a quarter way across, and their painful progress becomes slower as they lose strength. Cullen steps on a boulder,

slips, tries to catch his balance, and falls with bruising force
into the rocky shallows, pulling Jackson after him.

MED. SHOT   SHOOTING UP STREAM

Both men are at the mercy of the rushing water, tumbling TOWARD
CAMERA. They try to get their feet under themselves, but can't.
They are smashed against rocks to which they try to cling, but
either the current or the weight of the other man tears them loose.
They roll over and over, sometimes one on top of the other. . . .

CLOSE TWO SHOT   REVERSE ANGLE

They flounder INTO SHOT. Jackson smashes into a half-submerged
rock and clings to it desperately. He has to hold not only his
own weight, but the insistent pull of Cullen who lies helplessly
spread-eagle, downstream, smothered in the swift rapid, strung
out by chain and arm, like a grotesque fish brought to surface.
Jackson bares his teeth with the effort -- his head falls back as
his fingers are slowly torn from the rock. They both slip into
the current.

CLOSE SHOT   BOULDER

as the two men enter SHOT. Jackson breaks the shock with his
hands. Cullen, half-drowned, crashes head first into the
boulder. His body goes limp. Jackson pauses for a moment to
catch his breath. There's a moment's respite during which he holds
Cullen's head above the water.

TIGHT TWO SHOT   THE TWO MEN

Jackson looks around toward shore and back to Cullen who is
still knocked out. Jackson stares at him panicked. He struggles
and gains a footing. He half lifts Cullen and starts stumbling
toward a quiet backwash, revealed, as CAMERA PANS.

MED. SHOT   BACKWASH

The water deepens as they progress. Cullen slips and disappears
under the water. Jackson half walks, half swims, dragging the inert
body of Cullen after him. He lands him in the shoals like a huge fish.

CLOSE TWO SHOT   BANK OF RIVER

Jackson frantically rolls him and slaps his face.

                        JACKSON
        Cullen! . . . Cullen! Snap out
        of it!

Cullen coughs and strangles, wards off the stinging blows. Jackson
sinks down by him gasping with the effort of the ordeal. Cullen pulls
himself up in sitting position after a moment and shakes his head.

                        CULLEN
        Thanks.

                        JACKSON
        For what?

                        CULLEN
        For pulling me out. . . .

Jackson stares at him.

                        JACKSON
                (after a beat; coldly)
        Hell, I didn't pull you out. I
        just kept you from dragging me in.

He rises and stares down coldly at Cullen. He waits until Cullen
rises painfully. Cullen stumbles up the bank after Jackson.

                                            CUT TO:

    EXT. EDGE OF SWAMP -- NEAR STREAM -- DAY * * * Run through ahead
    (SAME AS ABOVE IN "DECISION SCENE")   of this
    CLOSE SHOT -- REVOLVER

Two shots are fired. CAMERA PULLS BACK REVEALING the Captain of
the state troopers who holsters his gun. He bends and picks up
a cigarette stub. He examines it with satisfaction. The men in
the b.g., including Sheriff, Editor, come running in from the
line. Solly is busy calling his dogs together and leashing them.
Wilson holds back the wildly barking airedales on leash -- they
were disturbed by the shots.

                        SHERIFF
                (as he approaches)
        What is it?

                        CAPTAIN
                (triumphantly)
        You didn't approve of dogs!

                         SHERIFF
                    (sees butt Captain holds)
               What are you talking about? I got
               nothing against dogs. They're man's
               best friend, aren't they?

The Captain inspects the butt closely.

                         SHERIFF (cont'd.)
                    (mildly)
               What are you looking for --
               lipstick?
                    (to Solly who has
                     approached)
               All right, Solly. Get going.

                         SOLLY
               Wait a minute, Sheriff. I can't
               run my dogs anymore today. They
               need a rest.

                         CAPTAIN
               We have another good hour of light
               yet.

Muller looks at him and starts to ease off his pack.

                         MULLER
               Never mind, our men need a rest too.

                         SOLLY
                    (to Sheriff)
               Okay?

                         MULLER
               Okay, Solly.

The Captain is building up steam.

                         SOLLY
                    (to dogs)
               Come on kids.

Solly leads his dogs off.

                         CAPTAIN
               They got a pretty good head
               start, Sheriff.

Muller squats on the ground with a grunt of satisfaction. He
starts to pull off his boots.

> MULLER
> They have to rest too.

He looks up at the Captain who is staring angrily at him.

                                                    CUT TO:

EXT. SWAMP EDGE -- ALMOST NIGHTFALL -- INSERT:CLOSEUP -- HUGE BULLFROG
It opens its grinning mouth and croaks with startling force. It's
hard to discern swamp from the spongy ground; the undergrowth, the
trees, Spanish moss impinge on and overrun the low lying ground.
The two men are stalking something unseen along the edge of the
swamp. The dim closeness of the jungle is thickened by the over-
powering croaking of frogs. The men move into CLOSE LOW ANGLE TWO
SHOT, their faces harsh and angular in the cold rays of the setting
sun. The Negro holds up his hand for quiet and poises his stick.

FULL SHOT -- SWAMP EDGE

Cullen makes a sudden lunge.

INSERT: FROG

It leaps forward TOWARD CAMERA and o.s.

BACK TO SCENE:

> JACKSON
> Did you get him?

Cullen stabs frenziedly at the ground. Jackson joins him, beating at
the undergrowth. Cullen loses his balance and falls pulling Jackson
to the ground with him. Jackson winces with the pain of his wrist.

CLOSE TWO SHOT -- HIGH ANGLE

Both men search in the grass frantically. Jackson comes up
triumphantly, holding the giant bullfrog by the leg.

> JACKSON
> Got him.

                                                DISSOLVE TO:

EXT. SWAMP EDGE -- JACKSON & CULLEN -- NIGHT -- CLOSE SHOT -- FIRE

A row of wet cigarettes are lined up to dry beside the fire. CAMERA PULLS BACK: The men are seated close to a small fire, ignoring one another, as far apart from each other as the chain length will permit. Cullen's eyes are focussed on the spitted frog which Jackson keeps turning over the little blaze. It is now night and the myriad swamp noises form a sharp and intrusive backdrop for the scene. Occasionally an odd noise breaks the pattern and, to these odd noises, Jackson reacts with nervous irritability.

> JACKSON
> Listen to them. . . . What are they?

> CULLEN
> Night birds mostly . . . bugs. . . .

> JACKSON
> Wish they'd shut up!

CLOSE TWO SHOT -- THE TWO MEN

Jackson lifts the cooked frog's legs from the fire, and hands one to Cullen.

> CULLEN
> (almost automatically)
> Thanks. . . .

Jackson does not reply. He is totally concentrated on his food. There is a sudden and close scream of a night bird. Jackson reacts as sharply as if he had been bee-stung.

> JACKSON
> (defensively)
> I keep listening for the dogs.

> CULLEN
> Too soon.

> JACKSON
> They must've started by now. . . .
> How fast you think they can go. . . ?

> CULLEN
> (flatly)
> No road in here. They gotta come
> by foot . . . same as us.

The men lapse into silence again. Again Jackson is examining the night noises.

                    JACKSON
               (over-casually --
               indicating the swamp)
          Animals in there?

                    CULLEN
          Some.

                    JACKSON
          What kind?

                    CULLEN
          All kinds. . . .

                    JACKSON
          Dangerous ones?

                    CULLEN
          Some. . . .

                    JACKSON
          Like what? . . .

                    CULLEN
          Gators . . . black bear . . . wild pig. . . .

                    JACKSON
          How come they don't make noise?

                    CULLEN
          They animals. They either hunting
          or being hunted. Either way . . .
          you don't make noise.

                    JACKSON
               (digesting this)
          I go with that.

Jackson has finished eating. He throws the bones into the fire, licks
his fingers. He squats near the fire and selects a dry cigarette
which he puts in his mouth, the rest he carefully puts in his pocket.
He lights up. The lull after the talk seems to intensify the night
noises.

                    JACKSON
          Listen to them . . . millions of them

                         JACKSON (Cont'd)
              talking . . . and none of them under-
              stands what the other one's saying.

                         CULLEN
                       (shrugs)
              They just bugs . . .

                         JACKSON
                       (scornfully)
              * * * Bugs are people. Nobody understands
              nobody. Them animals are smarter. You
              keep quiet . . . and hunt for yourself.
              I go with that.

A sudden and incredibly sharp scream of animal agony slices
through the night like a razor. Both men are startled, then
Cullen, recognizing what it is, relaxes.

                         JACKSON
                       (concerned)
              What's that?

                         CULLEN
              Weasel scream. Hoot owl musta
              got him.

                         JACKSON
              Thought you said they didn't make
              noise?

                         CULLEN
                       (quietly)
              Only when they dying. . . .

There is a pause while Jackson mulls this over, and when he
speaks, it is half to himself.

                         JACKSON
              That's a great way to live . . .
              you keep quiet all your life
              and the only time you open your
              mouth is when you're dying. . . .

They look at each other for a moment as though the common

---

realization had produced a moment of understanding, but their
mutual angers are too near the surface still, and they avert
their gazes. Jackson hands Cullen his half-smoked cigarette.

                    CULLEN
        Thanks. . . .

                    JACKSON
              (irritably)
        Why don't you cut it out?

                    CULLEN
        Huh?

                    JACKSON
        You keep saying thanks. . . .
        I hate that word "thanks".

                    CULLEN
              (shrugs)
        Don't mean nothing.

                    JACKSON
              (short, bitter laugh)
        No, hah? You try making your living
        with that word . . . you find out.
        Lemme tell you something. I used to
        park cars for tips down in Natchez . . .
        a big fancy hotel. Fella'd give me his
        car I had to say "thank you, sir". Here
        I was doing something for him, but I
        had to say "thank you, sir." * * *
              (coldly serious)
        It learned me how you gotta live.
        Those folks that live at that fancy
        hotel down in Natchez . . . they know
        how to live all right. You gotta be
        Charlie Potatoes . . . the man with
        the money . . . then you don't hafta
        bow down to nobody!
              (pause, then quietly)

P. 377   [And when I brought the car back . . . I had to
                  say "thanks" again! The louder I said it,
                  the bigger the tip. You think I was saying
                  thanks to him? I was saying it to the tips.
                  I was thanking the tips they were gonna give
                  me! . . .]

                    JACKSON (Cont'd)
        You know something . . . even when they'd
        give me no tip . . . I still had to say
        thanks. That word got so it was like
        sticking a needle in me every time I
        heard it. That can happen with a word. . . .
        You know what I mean, boy?

Cullen looks up sharply at the word "boy".

                    CULLEN
                 (coldly)
        Yeah! I know what you mean! And I
        got the needle sticking in me right now.
                 (measures his words)
        Don't call me boy!

The men stare at each other. Jackson smiles slowly as he reads
the cold anger in Cullen's eyes and realizes he has found a way
to ride him.

                    JACKSON
                 (over-emphasizing the word)
        Why, you're just too sensitive, maaan.

                    CULLEN
                 (angrily)
        I'm too nothing.

                    JACKSON
                 (blandly)
        You're too nothing all right, but I'm
        gonna give you a piece of advice . . .
        because I like you, maaan. You oughtta
        learn to take things the way they are, * * *
        . . . and don't keep fighting them . . .
        less you just wanna keep unhappy.
        I can see you gotta learn how to
        live, maaan!

                    CULLEN
                 (coldly; contemptuously)
        Like you . . . in that fancy hotel, hah?

[maaan . . . the way they are]

                    JACKSON
                (blandly)
    Yeah . . . just like me in that fancy
    hotel. . . .

                    CULLEN
                (angrily, mocking)
    They going to let me in that hotel,
    too, huh?

                    JACKSON
                (the coup de grace)
    Sure. Through the back door . . . if
    you're carrying a bucket and a mop.

                    CULLEN
    And you through the front . . . just
    long enough to collect your tip!

                    JACKSON
                (beginning to be nettled)
    What's eating you . . . what I called
    you in the truck?

                    CULLEN
    That's part of it.

                    JACKSON
                (taunting)
    It's what you are -- like calling
    a spade a spade. I'm a hunky. I
    don't try to argue out of it. You
    can call me a bohunk, I don't mind.

                    CULLEN
    * * * Ever hear tell of a bohunk in the
    woodpile? Ever catch a bohunk by
    the toe?

                    JACKSON
                (sets his trap)
    It depends on how you mean it.

                    CULLEN
                (challenges angrily)
    How did <u>you</u> mean it?

P. 379   [Ever hear tell of a dirty black bohunk?]

                    JACKSON
Like I said it! * * * Do̱n'̱t̲ c̲ro̱w̲d̲ me̱.̲
I don't make up no names.

                         CULLEN
              (overrides him)
* * * N̲o̱ -- You breathe it in when you're
born and * * * it comes out every time you
open your mouth.

                    * * *

                    JACKSON
Th̲a̱t̲ n̲a̱me̲ su̱r̲e̲ bu̱g̲s̲ yo̱u̲,̲ do̱n'̱t̲ i̱t̲?

                         CULLEN
Yeah!

                    JACKSON
* * * That's the way you were born -- and
it's your tough luck. I didn't make
the rules.

                         CULLEN
* * * Yo̲u̲ su̱r̲e̲ li̱v̲e̲ by̲ 'e̲m̲.̱

                    JACKSON
              (nettled)
Everybody lives by them. Everybody's
stuck with what he is. . . . Even them
swamp animals!

P. 380

[Don't come crying to me.]

[You don't have to!] [from then on]

                    [JACKSON
              (taunts)
That name sure bugs you, don't it?
You keep rubbing it like a sore muscle. . . .

                    CULLEN
Sure. Guys like you don't give it a
chance to heal.]

[(coldly) I'm not the guy that dealt you low card.]

[No. But you sure live by them—don't you?]

                        CULLEN
            Even that weasel . . . !

                        JACKSON
            You calling me a weasel!?

                        CULLEN
                (slow, cold contempt)
            No. I'm calling you a white man.

Cullen spits into the fire and stretches out. Jackson stares at him
angrily, filled with his own impotent rage.

                                        CUT TO:

EXT. EDGE OF RIVER -- DAY -- CLOSE SHOT DOGS * * * <u>RUNNING</u> <u>SHOT</u> <u>OF</u> <u>DOGS</u>

They're yelping and make essays at but don't dare the raging flood.
They splash around the edge hysterically.

CAMERA PULLS BACK to include Solly who is trying to get the dogs
together, Muller, Captain and the Editor . . . others in b.g.

                        SOLLY
                (as excited as the dogs)
            Hyah! . . . Hyah! . . . Come back here!

He gets his dogs together and leashed as the others approach.

                        SHERIFF
            How does it look, Solly?

                        SOLLY
            They're across the river, all right.

Muller gauges the swift run of the water, turns and crosses to the
<u>jeep that bounces across the ground toward them</u>. The other men follow.

GROUP SHOT AT JEEP

                        SHERIFF
                (to driver)
            Get my office.

                        CAPTAIN
                (needling him)
            Thought you said they'd head south?

                        SHERIFF
                    (blandly)
            Tnat's why I never bet on horses.

                        DRIVER
                    (holds phone to Muller)
            Here you are, sir.

                        MULLER
            Thanks.
                    (curtly to Captain)
            Check your map. See if you can find
            us a crossing.
                    (into phone)
            Muller speaking. You can kill the road-
            blocks. They've headed north. . . . No,
            there's no chance of them circling back . . . they're
            already across the MacHenry.
                    (pause)
            Well, the trail is still pretty fresh --
            we should have them in a day or two. . . .
            No, no strain, everything's going fine.
                    (pause)
            The jeep can't go any further -- We'll
            have to pack in our own rations.
            Thanks. . . . We'll make it alright. Call
            my wife, will you? Tell her everything's
            okay. . . . Right.

He hands the phone back to the driver and turns to the Captain and
the Editor who are studying the map.

                        MULLER (Cont'd.)
            Got anything?

                        CAPTAIN
                    (pointing to map)
            We can ford * * * here. * * * Turn_off_
            that_radio.

* * * It_goes off.

                        MULLER
            Fine.

[it] [and pick up the trail on the other side
                    of the river.]

He starts to turn away.

                    CAPTAIN
          That detour is going to cost us a
          couple of hours.

                    MULLER
          It can't be helped.

                    CAPTAIN
          * * * I th_ink it can.

Muller looks at him quizzically.

                    CAPTAIN (Cont'd.)
          * * * Call Cumberland while the jeep's
          still here.

                    MULLER
          Oh, that again.

                    CAPTAIN
                 (earnestly)
          Those men had a twelve hour start,
          and we're about to lose two more. . . .

                    MULLER
                 (impatiently)
          Why don't you stop trying to turn
          this into a three ring circus?

                    CAPTAIN
                 (stubbornly)
          It's no circus to me, Sheriff.
          Catching men is my business.

                    MULLER
                 (loses his temper)
          And making the decisions is mine!

Lou, completely unaware of the tensions in the group approaches
Max, his face creased with preoccupied concern.

P. 383   [Yes]

                [Listen, Sheriff, why don't you]

                         LOU
                Say, Max. . . .

The Sheriff whirls on him.

                         MULLER
                      (sharply)
                What is it?

                         LOU
                   (plaintively)
                I don't know. I got something
                the matter with me.

                         MULLER
                What are you talking about?

                         LOU
                Look.
                      (he bares his arm)
                I'm all swole up. And here. . . .

He pulls open his collar.

                         EDITOR
                That's poison ivy.

Max finds a release for his anger.

                         MULLER
                      (laughs)
                Oh, for Pete's sake!

                         LOU
                      (hurt)
                What are you laughing about. It's
                driving me nuts.

                         MULLER
                In a war you got to expect casualties.
                      (still chuckling)
                What do you think we ought to do,
                Captain -- cite him for a purple heart?
                      (gestures to jeep -- to Lou)
                Get in. You can go back with the jeep.

He turns back to the Captain. The interlude with Lou has dissipated
the anger and he is again in full control.

                    MULLER
          Look, Frank, why don't you relax?
          We're after a couple of poor slobs
          who right now are probably looking
          for absolution and a square meal.
          And if they don't find it -- and they
          won't -- that twelve hour lead today
          will be down to two hours tomorrow . . .
          and then one hour . . . and then nothing.

                    CAPTAIN
                 (coldly)
          You make it sound awfully easy.

                    MULLER
                 (grins)
          It is. . . . Just like running rabbits.
                 (turns to Lou)
          Isn't that right, Lou?

                    LOU
                 (through swollen lips)
                 (without rancor)
          Go to hell.

Max laughs and turns to the men.

                    MULLER
                 (raises his voice)
          All right, men, let's go to work!

FULL SHOT -- HIGH ANGLE * * * Turns on radio again. Captain reads.

The jeep cuts back along the line of march. The men follow
the lead of the Sheriff as they follow the river bank south. . . .

                                             CUT TO:

EXT. SWAMP -- CLOSE TWO SHOT -- DAY

Jackson lies huddled against Cullen's back. The sun shines in
his eyes. He opens his eyes without moving. For a moment he
doesn't know where he is. He turns his head and sees that he
is lying against the Negro. A spasm distorts his face. He rolls
over and sits up. The chain jerks Cullen's arm. He sits up
abruptly, blinking in the sunlight.

> CULLEN
> (startled)
> What's the matter?

> JACKSON
> (coldly)
> We better get going.

He gets up. Cullen sits for a moment rubbing his temples.
He too gets up.

> JACKSON
> (coldly)
> Come on.

They start out.

DISSOLVE TO:

EXT. PINEY WOODS -- FULL SHOT -- DAY -- RAIN

The pine stand runs down to the edge of the swamp. The morning sun
barely penetrates the gloomy scene. The two men trudge wearily
across the marsh grass into the park-like stand of trees, CAMERA
PANNING. Their footsteps are muffled in the heavy carpet of pine
needles, that leave the ground bare of growth. Cullen halts suddenly.

MED. CLOSE TWO SHOT -- DIFFERENT ANGLE -- RAIN

Cutting through the heavily wooded country is a wagon trail. The
two men are standing at the edge of the road, staring.

> CULLEN
> Wagon road. Never came down so far.

> JACKSON
> Sure we're going right?

> CULLEN
> That's north alright.

> JACKSON
> Looks good to my feet.

ROAD -- DIFFERENT ANGLE

The men advance to the center of the road.

                    JACKSON
Like walking barefoot on a rug.
Let's go.

                    CULLEN
We better stick to the brush 'til
it's dark.

                    JACKSON
We lose too much time.

                    CULLEN
Where there's a road, there's people.

                    JACKSON
Out here?

                    CULLEN
That road's going someplace.

                    JACKSON
              (stubbornly)
We walk close together, nobody
see the chain.

                    CULLEN
              (laughs shortly)
We make a pretty sight, you and me.
Man see us, he say, where you two
fellas going? Us? Me and my buddy
here, we just out for a stroll!

Sound of horse and wagon.

                    VOICE (o.s.)
Git up! . . . Tch, tch . . .
Come on there. . . .

The two men are frozen for a moment, and then they dive over the
embankment of the other side of the road, CAMERA PANNING to clay pit.

EXT. PIT -- MED. SHOT -- LOW ANGLE SHOOTING UP FROM BOTTOM

as the two men hurtle down . . . and land with a splash on muddy
bottom.

CLOSE TWO SHOT -- JACKSON AND CULLEN

The wagon drives by overhead.

>   JACKSON
>   (anxiously)
>   Do you think he. . . . ?

>   CULLEN
>   Shhh. . . !

The sounds of the wagon fade.

>   JACKSON
>   (looks around)
>   What is this?

Cullen shrugs.

>   CULLEN
>   Looks like an old clay pit. There's
>   the shovel.

Jackson follows Cullen's gaze up and o.s.

LOW ANGLE SHOT -- RUSTY OLD SHOVEL

tipped at a crazy angle outlined against the sky, resting on
edge of pit.

BACK TO SCENE

>   JACKSON
>   We better get out of here.

They take a turn of chain around their hands to ease their cut
wrists where the iron bites into their flesh, and start climbing.
They grasp small bushes to help them up, dig their shoes into the
clay, but the bushes rip out, they lose their footing. The white
man starts slipping first and slowly drags Cullen after him. They
claw at the mud but inexorably slide to the bottom. They remain
panting for a moment.

>   CULLEN
>   (coldly)
>   Let loose on your chain.

They drop the chain freeing their other hand.

                    JACKSON
          All right, let's try it.

                    CULLEN
          Back here. We get a running start.

They back up and rush at the clay bank, dig their feet in and
hook their fingers into the red ooze. The white man is getting
better traction. Cullen's feet start slipping and he freezes.

                    JACKSON
          Climb.

                    CULLEN
          I can't.

                    JACKSON
          Climb, damn you!

                    CULLEN
          I'm slipping.

He slides and drags the white man after him. They rest. Jackson
glares venomously at Cullen.

                    JACKSON
          Maybe somebody climb on somebody's
          shoulders.

Cullen, without a word, kneels against clay bank. Jackson climbs
on his shoulders. Cullen slowly straightens up, lifting Jackson.

                    JACKSON
          All right?

                    CULLEN
          Go ahead.

Jackson carefully digs his heels in and climbs.

                    JACKSON
          Give me some slack.

Cullen holds his manacled hand higher in the air. Jackson takes
another careful step.

                    CULLEN
          That's all the slack. I got to move.

He takes a step and holds.

                    JACKSON

        You okay?

                    CULLEN
        Okay. Go ahead.

                    JACKSON
                   (grunts)
        Almost to the top.

                    CULLEN
        I'll come up one more notch.
Jackson reaches over the top, grabs for a bush with his manacled
hand, doesn't have enough chain and misses; he starts to slide.

                    JACKSON
        Damn you!

                    CULLEN
        Don't be in a hurry.

                    JACKSON
        Give me more chain.

                    CULLEN
        I got to lift myself up, don't I?

Jackson loses his balance.

                    JACKSON
        Look out!

They both come tumbling down the bank. In a fit of fury, Jackson
scrambles to his feet and throws himself at the bank. His action
slams Cullen, who wasn't expecting this, face down in the mud.
They lie panting, their faces flat against the mud bank, inches
apart. They are entirely covered by the red clay so that only
their eyes are discernible. They glare at each other with all of
the fury of their misplaced anger and frustration.

                    CULLEN
                   (after a pause)
        Maybe we get us some wood.

Jackson agrees without words. They push themselves away from the

slope and gather armfuls of the rotten roots, branches and broken
planks that lie at the bottom of the pit. They trudge laboriously
back to the bank and start imbedding the pieces of wood into the
mud wall, so that a crude but close-packed reinforcement is built
up from the bottom to a height of about four feet. Without waiting
for a consultation, Jackson crouches face against the bank.

> JACKSON

>Come on.

Cullen mounts his shoulders.

> JACKSON (Cont'd)

>Don't start till I tell you.

His neck cords with the effort as he slowly stands and, carefully
placing his feet, climbs the reinforced four-foot buttress with
Cullen crouched on his shoulders.

> JACKSON (Cont'd)
> (gasps)

>Now.

Cullen, very slowly, puts his weight on Jackson's shoulders and
pushes up until his waist is even with the top of the bank, grabs
the head of the old crane and rolls over the top carefully.

> CULLEN

>Okay. I'm over. Take a wrap around
>the chain.

Jackson obeys. He can't look up for fear of losing his balance.
Cullen puts a slow strain on the chain. He almost loses his footing
but recovers and in a moment Jackson is scrambling over the edge.
They collapse simultaneously and breathe hard for a moment. Jackson
takes out a cigarette and lights it. Cullen looks at him. He sees
that Jackson is favoring his wrist and the laceration has become red
and infected. He reaches for Jackson's hand.

> JACKSON
> (jerks his hand away)

>What are you doing?

> CULLEN

>Let me see that.

> JACKSON

>What for?

                         CULLEN
           It looks infected.

                         JACKSON
           What are you going to do?

                         CULLEN
           It needs fixing.

                         JACKSON
           Don't do me no favors.

Their eyes meet and hold.

                         CULLEN
                       (quietly)
           I ain't doing you no favor.

Jackson slowly extends his arm. Cullen takes Jackson's hand and
looks at the wrist critically. He unties the bandana from his
neck and pushes Jackson's iron cuff up; he gently swabs the wound.
He shakes his head and bends again to scoop up a handful of clay.
He carefully plasters the wrist and ties the bandana around it.

                         JACKSON
           What's that for?

                         CULLEN
           Poultice.

The white man sits there, staring blankly for a moment.

                         JACKSON
           Feels good. . . . Nice and cool. . . .

Cullen doesn't respond. Pause

                         JACKSON (Cont'd)
           What do you want me to do -- say
           thanks?
               (no response)
           Thanks. . . !
               (pause)
           Thanks, thanks, THANKS!
               (no response from Cullen)
           Ahhh. . . !

He draws angrily on his cigarette.

                    CULLEN
                  (quietly)
          That word sure bugs you, don't it?

Jackson looks at Cullen uncertainly. He's not sure this is a taunt.

                    CULLEN
                  (pause)
          Maybe you got something there. . . .
          I been saying it all my life. When
          I was a kid and my pa took me to church.
          I didn't have shoes, and I hollered
          "Thank you Lord" as loud as the rest
          of the kids. . . . They didn't have
          no shoes either.

                    JACKSON
          Hell, I didn't get my first pair of
          shoes 'til I was damned near twelve --
          store bought, especially, I mean.

He hands Cullen the butt of his cigarette. After a moment,
Jackson rises.

                    JACKSON (Cont'd)
          Let's go.

Cullen rises and grinds out cigarette.

                    CULLEN
                  (casually)
          We walk in step, it'll be easier
          on our wrists.

                    JACKSON
                  (looks at Cullen
                   thoughtfully)
          Sure.

As they start out -- * * * walking in step

                                            CUT TO:

EXT. ROUGH TERRAIN -- DAY -- (RAIN OPTIONAL) -- OVERCAST

FULL SHOT -- POSSE * * * Boy with radio open

as they slog through rugged country. They're beginning to show signs of fatigue.

LOW ANGLE SHOT -- POSSE * * * Editor_here

CAMERA PANNING as the men approach and can be seen in
perspective down the line. One of the men is limping badly.
Another pauses to reset the straps of his pack.

CLOSE FOLLOW SHOT -- MULLER * * * Boy with radio

the strain is beginning to tell on him. He glances down the line
worriedly.

CLOSE FOLLOW SHOT -- CAPTAIN

he glances up and sees the Sheriff looking worried. He smiles grimly.

CLOSE FOLLOW SHOT -- MULLER

he catches the look of the Captain, sighs and plods on.

FULL SHOT

as the posse, spearheaded by Solly and the dogs, APPROACH CAMERA.
CAMERA PANS with them as they advance, until only the farthermost
man in the line who can be seen, finally disappears.

                                        CUT TO:

EXT. EDGE OF SETTLEMENT -- FULL SHOT -- ALMOST NIGHTFALL -- RAIN

As Cullen and Jackson rise into shot, they edge carefully over a
fallen tree trunk and look down over the town. The "town" is a
cluster of shacks hovering on either side of the road. One building
on the opposite side of the road has a store-front window. It is near
a barn-like shed that has a braced arm under the peaked eave, with
block and tackle to lift the barrels of turpentine into the wagons.

Cullen and Jackson are facing a row of debris, outhouses and flapping
laundry. Lights are on in the houses. They speak in guarded tones.

                       JACKSON
              I don't see nobody.

                       CULLEN
           Suppertime.

                    JACKSON
          Don't look like much.

                    CULLEN
          They don't do nothing but
          collect turpentine. There's
          the storage shed.

He points to the barn-like structure.

                    JACKSON
          That the company store?

                    CULLEN
          Yeah.

                    JACKSON
          It's right in the middle of
          everything.

TWO SHOT -- REVERSE ANGLE

                    CULLEN
          There's food in there -- tools
          too. Waiting for us.

                    JACKSON
          Maybe that ain't all that's waiting
          for us. See them?

He points O.S.

LONG SHOT -- SETTLEMENT -- THEIR POV -- CAMERA PANS ALONG

Telegraph wires, which can be seen leading to the store.

BACK TO SCENE:

                    JACKSON
                  (worried)
          They sure must have heard by now.

                    CULLEN
          It's pretty quiet. . . .

                    JACKSON
          They ain't going to be waiting for
          us with no brass band.

The both men study the town, worried.

>   JACKSON
>   Maybe we ought to pass -- find a
>   better set-up tomorrow.
>
>   CULLEN
>   What tomorrow? As long as we're
>   wearing these . . .
>   (he rattles the chains)
>   . . . we're a billboard telling
>   who and what we are.

A pause as they frown at the lights below. A dog barks in the
distance. Another answers close by.

>   JACKSON
>   How do you figure the odds?
>
>   CULLEN
>   Them dogs got me worried.

Jackson takes a deep breath.

>   JACKSON
>   If we lucky we get our arms free
>   and our bellies full in one quick
>   shuffle.

Jackson and Cullen slide down. Jackson takes out a cigarette.

They settle down behind the log barrier, watching the lights
below intently.

They rarely look at each other as they speak, but look out over
the town. Their words are compulsive, nervous intimacies, shaped
in the atmosphere of a zero hour.

>   JACKSON
>   All them guys out there sitting
>   around the table. . . .
>   (he takes a drag)
>   With the woman putting out the
>   steaming platters.

Cullen grunts. Jackson shivers and pulls his collar closer.

                    JACKSON (Cont'd)
                 (pause)
        I can smell that cooking all the
        way out here.

                    CULLEN
        Wind's blowing in the other direction.

                    JACKSON
        Maybe it is. But it's blowing in
        my mind, too. . . .

                                        CUT TO:

EXT. EDGE OF CLAY PIT -- NIGHT -- LOW ANGLE SHOT -- CRANE SHOVEL

It is lit by the flickering light of a small camp fire. CAMERA
PANS DOWN arm of abandoned, rusty shovel, to CLOSE SHOT camp fire
on which steams a pot of coffee, located in the lea of the canted
crane cab. CAMERA PULLS BACK as the Editor reaches into SHOT and
takes coffee pot off fire, revealing Max who paces up and down.
A fine drizzle saturates everything and puts sheen on their ponchos.
Max is beginning to look harrassed as he pauses to watch the Editor
pour two cups. * * * Radio going.

                    MULLER
        I don't understand it. By all the
        odds they shouldn't have gottn
        this far.

                    EDITOR
                 (holds out cup of coffee)
        Here, Max. . . .

Max takes the coffee, and squats beside the Editor, hunched over
the meager flames.

                    MULLER
        I figured we'd grab them some time
        today. . . .

He stops and looks up as someone approaches.

LOW ANGLE SHOT -- CAPTAIN

He stops and looks up as someone approaches.

GROUP SHOT

                         EDITOR
               Sit down. How about a cup of hot
               coffee?

The Captain remains standing.

                         CAPTAIN
                    (to Max)
               I thought you might want the
               casualty report.

                         MULLER
                    (after a pause)
               Sure. Go ahead.

                         CAPTAIN
               Three men.

                         MULLER
               How bad?

                         CAPTAIN
               Two sets of foot blisters and
               a sprained ankle.

                         MULLER
               Send them back.

                         CAPTAIN
               Sombody'll have to go with them.

                         MAX
                    (pause)
               Pick somebody out.

                         CAPTAIN
               That's one for each man. Six men
               altogether out of the line.

                         MULLER
               What about it?

                         CAPTAIN
               Solly says the trail isn't getting
               any hotter.

                         MULLER
               So?

                        CAPTAIN
            So I'd like it to be a matter of record
            that I requested help -- and you refused.
            It's your responsibility.

                        MULLER
                    (nods wearily)
            It's my responsibility. Anything else
            you'd like to remind me of?

                        CAPTAIN
                    (coldly pointed)
            Just this. I'm civil service. I don't
            have to worry about my job.

Muller returns the other's cold look without expression. The
Captain turns and leaves. CAMERA MOVES IN on Editor and Max. The
Editor looks at Max quizzically.

                        EDITOR
            He's got a point.

                        MULLER
                    (irritably)
            * * * If I listened to him I'd be
            calling out the marines. * * *

                        EDITOR
            He won't have to if those men get away
            because you refused to call in * * * help.
                    (Muller looks at him)
            I'd have to print it, Max. It wouldn't
            look so good in print.

                        * * *

Muller throws away the dregs of his coffee with an annoyed
gesture.

                        MULLER
            Let me tell you something, Dave.

P. 399   [The only thing pointed about him is his
                head.]

                [What is he trying to do, make a fool of me?]

                [outside]

> MULLER (Cont'd)
> I've got a wife, two kids and a
> mortgage. My job as Sheriff pays
> me sixty eight hundred a year. It
> comes in steady, and I don't have
> to work too hard. It's a good
> set-up and I like it. But don't
> frighten me about losing it. I
> can always go back to practicing law.

> EDITOR
> (smiles and shakes his head)
> Max -- no offense -- we've been
> friends a long time. Stop kidding
> yourself. It's been years since
> you practiced law.

CLOSE SHOT -- MAX

The dancing firelight nimbly shapes and reshapes Max's facial
planes; his eyes remain a staring, brooding entity. There is a
long pause. . . .

* * *

CUT TO:

EXT. TOWN -- NIGHT

LONG SHOT -- SHOOTING PAST CULLEN AND JACKSON IN F.G.

There are fewer lights. A woman sloshes a dish pan of slop into
a pig pen. The noise of the animals comes OVER SCENE.

> CULLEN
> Slopping the hogs. That means
> supper's over.

P. 400

> [MAX
> So it wouldn't look good.

> EDITOR
> It'll look worse on the election
> returns.]

> [MULLER
> (almost to himself)
> You know, I never thought it was
> possible to hate someone you'd never
> seen. . . . But I'm beginning to hate
> those two men. . . .]

                    JACKSON
                  (pause)
        I used to feed the hogs at the
        prison farm sometimes. . . .
                  (reminiscently)
        That was a nice farm.

                    CULLEN
        Yeah. . . . Nice farm . . . all
        that machinery.

                    JACKSON
        Fella'd get himself a farm -- he'd
        have a pretty sweet set-up.

                    CULLEN
        Sure. As long as the fella don't
        have to scratch it out with hand
        tools and a mule --

                    JACKSON
        Leastways you always got enough
        to eat.

                    CULLEN
        I worked thirty-six acres by hand.
        My wife helped me work it too --
        and sometime's even my little kid.
        And even then we didn't always have
        enough to eat.

Jackson looks at him.

                    JACKSON
        I didn't know you were married.

Cullen doesn't answer.

                    JACKSON (Cont'd)
        What's the matter, you been Jodied?

Cullen looks at him, puzzled.

                    JACKSON (Cont'd)
        Jody get her?

                    CULLEN
        Who's Jody?

> JACKSON
> Jody. You don't know Jody with the
> big green Cadillac? He gets all
> them women, their men's in jail.
> Jail gates close, house door opens --
> in comes Jody. Man comes out of
> jail, no more wife. That man's
> been Jodied.

Cullen looks out across the town. Jackson watches him for a
second. He feels the strange impulse of compassion that comes
from witnessing the inner suffering of a grown man and would
like to offer help -- but both impulses are so foreign to him,
he doesn't know how. He kneels beside Cullen and he too over-
concentrates on watching the town. One of the lights below
goes out.

EXT. TOWN -- LONG SHOT -- NIGHT

There are only a half dozen lights left remaining in the town.

TWO SHOTS -- CULLEN AND JACKSON

Watching intently.

> JACKSON
> One down, five to go.

> CULLEN
> Yeah.

> JACKSON
> (after a pause)
> What about your kid?

> CULLEN
> He was just five years old when I
> left. He don't even remember me
> by now.

> JACKSON
> Kids don't forget so easy.

> CULLEN
> What's he got to remember -- a
> one page letter once a week?
> (pause)
> And I can't even write good.

Jackson glances at Cullen a moment then turns his head toward the town again. He is uncomfortable with Cullen's self-revealment and doesn't know how to cope with it in his usual off-hand defensive pattern. He struggles for the words and then blurts with disproportionate violence:

> JACKSON
> * * * Everybody winds up alone. Not
> just you -- everybody! That's the
> way it is.

Pause. Jackson hands Cullen the butt. Cullen drags deeply on the cigarette.

> CULLEN
> You got * * * people?

> JACKSON
> I got an old man around someplace --
> (laughs wryly)
> The last time I seen him since I was
> fourteen was the night I got out of
> the army and we spent half my bonus
> check getting lushed up together.
> (pause)
> It feels funny getting drunk with
> your old man.
> (pause)
> Ahhh! I got nothing against him.

> CULLEN
> (laughs shortly)
> My paw was * * * a bible-thumper.
> All the time tryin' to teach us.

> JACKSON (Cont'd)
> (turns to Cullen)
> I used to work in automobiles. . . .

> CULLEN
> You a mechanic?

P. 403   [Nobody's got . . . I mean]

              [a family?]

              [all the time trying to teach us things out of
              the bible.]

                    JACKSON
          Best transmission man in the
          state. . . . Hydramatic, dynaflow. . . .
          You name it.

                    CULLEN
          I used to be a body and fender man --
          paint too.

                    JACKSON
          Thought you were a farmer.

                    CULLEN
          That's how I saved up to buy my farm.

                    JACKSON
                 (impatiently)
          Okay. Good enough. To you it
          meant a farm. You know what it
          meant to me? A buck eighty an
          hour. Forty hours a week. Week
          in and week out -- Ripping your
          fingers to pieces. And for what?
          For some * * * dude to be able
          to drive his Cadillac without
          even having to shift.

                    CULLEN
          One eighty an hour. That's pretty
          good pay.

                    JACKSON
                 (getting excited)
          To you. You know what it meant to
          me? Saturday night in a gin mill
          being Charlie Potatoes with a red
          head -- or a blond. . . . Anything
          you want and Monday morning you're
          back in the pit with grease in
          your eyeballs. . . .

                    CULLEN
          Somebody got to fix them cars.

                    JACKSON
Let some other sucker fix them.
All I want to do is drive them.

                    CULLEN
                 (drily)
You got to buy them first.

                    JACKSON
                 (scornfully)
On a buck eighty an hour? That's
just a stop-over for a second-hand
Chevvy -- Not for me, brother --
I got smart.

                    CULLEN
* * * Sure -- that's_how_come you
wound up_in jail.

                    JACKSON
* * * Ah -- I was a sucker for so
long I didn't know how to be a big
enough taker -- I was only a
stealer. . . . You got to be a big
crook. You a big enough crook
you can get away with anything.

He stares into the darkness moodily.

                    CULLEN
                 (after a pause)
Just a few more lights. Them men
down there smoking their pipe --
The women doing the dishes. . . .

                    JACKSON
How do you know? You can't see.

                    CULLEN
                 (softly)
I can see.

P. 405   [You so smart, how come you wind up in jail?]

                     [Because]

                    JACKSON
               (after a pause)
          What did they get you for?

                    CULLEN
               (coldly)
          Manslaughter.

                    JACKSON
          * * * <u>Great</u>. . . .

                    CULLEN
          Man come on my land because I
          didn't pay the note. He talked
          mean. When I give him an argu-
          ment, he pulled a gun. I took
          it away from him.

                    JACKSON
          Did you mean to kill him?

                    CULLEN
               (simply)
          I killed him.

                    JACKSON
               (mulls it over)
          Didn't do you much good.

                    CULLEN
          No.

                    JACKSON
               (shakes his head)
          * * * You got to learn to roll
          with the punches.

                    CULLEN
               (with sudden anger)
          Everytime I rolled with a punch
          I found myself rolling in mud!

                    JACKSON
          What are you getting so mad about?

[(impressed) What happened?]

          [That's what's wrong with you.]

                    CULLEN
I ain't getting mad -- I been
mad since I was born. . . .

                    JACKSON
I'm just telling you the facts of
life. If you don't want to listen --

                    CULLEN
No! I don't want to listen. I been
listening to that stuff all my life.
From my wife. Even in the letters she
sent me, she'd say "Be nice." They
throwed me in solitary, she said, "Be
nice." Before they put me in jail,
man'd short weight me when I turned in
my crop, I'd give him an argument, she
say, "Be nice or you get into trouble."
I'd listen to her teach my kid the same
thing and I'd try to explain to her --
but I never could make her understand.
All she understand is being afraid.
          (pause)
That's what Jodied me. Not no playboy
in a green Cadillac. I couldn't make
her see how I felt. All of a sudden
there was nothing left to say. And I
stopped writing . . .
          (pause)
    . . . and after awhile I stopped hearing.

After a moment, he stirs nervously and looks over the barricade.

                    CULLEN (Cont'd)
Ain't they never going to sleep?

Jackson joins him, looking down.

LONG SHOT -- SETTLEMENT -- SHOOTING PAST THE MEN IN F.G.

More lights go out. Only one light remains, directly before
them. A man comes out of one of the houses almost directly
below them, and goes to the outhouses.

                    CULLEN
          (muses)
Sometimes I used to think if I could
ever get her away someplace . . . where

                    CULLEN (Cont'd)
            folks wasn't so afraid -- maybe she'd
            stop being so afraid.

REVERSE ANGLE -- TWO SHOT

They're leaning over the log, elbow to elbow, watching the
settlement below.

                    JACKSON
            What are you going to do once we
            get loose from this jackpot?

                    CULLEN
            Keep going. New York, Chicago --
            Detroit.
                (shrugs)
            Get a job in a garage. . . .

                    JACKSON
            Hah! You ain't going to catch
            Charlie Potatoes working for some-
            body else. I'm going into business
            for myself -- open my own garage.
                (blandly)
            You could even come in with me.

Cullen looks at him quizzically.

                    JACKSON (Cont'd)
            Sure. Why not?
                (frowns)
            There's only one problem. . . .

                    CULLEN
                (stiffens)
            What's that?

                    JACKSON
                (dead pan)
            Who's going to handle the cash?

Cullen relaxes, a slow smile breaks over his face. A sound from
o.s. brings them sharply alert. Cullen stares into the darkness.

                    CULLEN
                (tensely)
            There he goes.

LONG SHOT -- THEIR POV -- BACK YARDS

The man has come out of the outhouse, buckling his pants as he heads toward the shack.

TWO SHOT -- REVERSE ANGLE

> JACKSON
> (grins nervously)
> That just about buttons it up
> for the night.

> CULLEN
> Let's go.

They crawl over the log and crouch there for a moment.

> JACKSON (Cont'd)
> (whispers)
> Head for the chicken house.

> CULLEN
> Make it the well. I need a drink bad.

> JACKSON
> Okay.

Still crouched over, they run for the well. CAMERA PANNING with them.

TWO SHOT -- AT WELL

The two men slide behind the protection of the wall. Their hard breathing seems unnaturally loud in quiet. A dog barks in the distance. The sleepy clucking of the hens in their coops hangs on the air. The two men rest and listen, crouched in the mud at the edge of the well. Cullen studies Jackson's face. The scene is conducted in whispers.

> JACKSON
> (uncomfortably)
> What are you looking at?

> CULLEN
> Your white face. It shine out like
> a full moon.
> (grins)
> Don't take it wrong.

> JACKSON
> What am I supposed to do about it?

> CULLEN
> I don't know anything you can do
> about it now, except, maybe --

He digs into the wet ground and holds out a handful of mud.
Jackson stares at him for a moment and then digs into the mud
and smears his face and hands.

> JACKSON
> That better?

> CULLEN
> Yeah.   Here.   You missed a spot.

He patches Jackson's makeup.

> CULLEN (Cont'd)
> Now only the meanness shine through.

> JACKSON
> Then we sure look alike.

> CULLEN
> (grins)
> Check.   How about that drink?

They rise cautiously.   The bucket is on the edge of the well,
still half full.

> JACKSON
> Somebody mighty thoughtful, didn't
> empty the bucket.

Jackson lifts the bucket and drinks deeply.   Cullen reaches eagerly
for the bucket.   The chain snags on a projection just as he's about
to tip it to his mouth.   It slips from his hands and bounces on the
edge.   Jackson lunges for it, but it falls down the well, raking the
sides with a hollow booming.   The handle screeches wildly as the rope
unwinds.   Cullen throws himself at the handle and stops it.

> CULLEN
> Oh, Lord! . . .

They stand frozen as the rear door of the shack opens and casts

a bar of light that just falls short of the well. A man in
underwear appears in the door.

> MAN
> (shouts)
> Who's there?

> JACKSON
> (moans)
> Wake up the whole town! . . . The
> whole town gonna be down on us! . . .

The man turns back into the doorway.

> MAN
> (calls into house)
> Get me my flashlight! . . . And my gun. . . .

> JACKSON
> Let's get out of here.
> (breathlessly)
> The chicken coop!

They bend over and run.

MED. SHOT -- MAN IN DOORWAY

He hears a fluttering and cackling from the henhouse. He listens
hard. A woman in a nightgown appears in the doorway in back of him
with a gun and flashlight. An eight-year old kid hangs onto her.

> WOMAN
> What is it, Betts?

> MAN
> Give me those and get back into
> the house!

CAMERA PANS with him as he goes cautiously to the well.

MED. SHOT -- AT WELL

The man studies the well, looks down it.

> MAN
> (mutters)
> Damn kid never learn to empty
> the bucket and tie it up. . . .

CAMERA PANS with him as he goes to chicken coop.

CLOSE TWO SHOT -- JACKSON AND CULLEN

They huddle against the back of the chicken coop. They listen
tensely as the footsteps approach. The steps halt close by.
They hold their breaths.

FULL SHOT -- CHICKEN HOUSE

The man plays the flashlight on it.

CLOSE TWO SHOT

Cullen and Jackson watch the beam with fascination. It comes
closer and Jackson pushes Cullen's head down and ducks his own.
The flashlight plays on them -- passes over them. The footsteps
crunch in the gravel and then move off.

They still don't move. Presently there is a rhythmic squeak of
the bucket being raised. The men lift their heads cautiously.

FULL SHOT -- YARD

The man ties up the bucket and goes to the shack where the
woman waits.

                    WOMAN
          What was it, Betts?

                    MAN
          Your son. He didn't tie up the
          bucket again. Now go to bed

The door shuts and the lights go out.

TWO SHOT -- AT CHICKEN COOP

They're still huddled against the back wall.

                    JACKSON
                (softly)
          Lucky, lucky. . . .
                (turns to Cullen)
          How about it?

                    CULLEN
          Might as well. . . .

They rise and circle henhouse cautiously, CAMERA PANNING, and cut between two shacks.

MED. SHOT -- DIFFERENT ANGLE

As they emerge from between the shacks and pause at the edge of the road. The town is dark.

They cross the street and tiptoe up to the store.

TWO SHOT -- AT STORE FRONT

They climb the creaking two steps with painful care. Cullen pauses and tries the door. It doesn't budge.

>   JACKSON
>   The window. . . .

They go over to the window. Jackson puts his weight gradually on the sash. He strains but it won't budge. Cullen nudges him and they start around toward the back.

MED SHOT -- ALLEYWAY

They stop at a side window.

>   JACKSON
>   (whispers)
>   Wait a minute. . . .

Cullen nudges Jackson out of the way and leans on the window, trying to raise it. He strains silently, but no use.

>   JACKSON
>   Must be nailed shut. . . .

They continue to the back of the store.

MED. SHOT -- BACK DOOR

They pause at the door. It's padlocked. They look at each other.

>   JACKSON
>   Bust it open!

>   CULLEN
>   Make enough noise to wake up
>   the dead. . . .

                        JACKSON
              It ain't the dead I'm worried
              about. . . .

He suddenly gets an inspiration, nudges Cullen and points to the
roof. They look around for a way to get on the roof . . . see a
barrel. Between them they get the barrel under the eave.
Jackson climbs up.

HIGH ANGLE SHOT -- ROOF

A tin smoke-vent is in the f.g. Jackson's head appears over the
edge of the roof. He looks around.

LOW ANGLE SHOT -- CULLEN AND JACKSON

Cullen waits impatiently for Jackson to report.

                        CULLEN
              See anything?

                        JACKSON
              Nothing but an old tin chimney.

Cullen climbs up on the barrel too and looks.

HIGH ANGLE SHOT -- ROOF

The heads of the two men are visible over the edge of the roof.

                        CULLEN
              Maybe we pull it out and make
              the hole big enough.

CLOSE TWO SHOT

                        JACKSON
              You're crazy as a one-eyed cat.

But he hitches himself over the edge of the roof, and rolls over
to make room for Cullen.

HIGH ANGLE SHOT -- ROOF

Tin smoke-vent in f.g. Jackson crabs over the roof as Cullen joins
him. They approach the air vent on hands and knees. Jackson
reaches for the vent, but Cullen taps his arm and points to the
guy wires. They unscrew the screw-eyes and the wires fall slack.

Cullen goes to the vent and moves it gently back and forth, loosening it. There is a protesting rasp of metal and both men freeze at the sound. No repercussions . . . Cullen goes back to work.

Every time the metal squawks, Cullen freezes and the two men stare at each other. Sweat shines on Cullen's face. Jackson moves close and tries to muffle the noise by pressing his body close to the metal tube. He rocks back and forth with Cullen's movements. There is a scraping and the vent suddenly comes loose someplace down below. . . . They sink back on their haunches and catch their breaths.

Jackson leans forward on his knees after a moment and painstakingly lifts the long metal tube out of the hole. It sticks. He's about to heave on it.

> CULLEN
> Hold it!

> JACKSON
> It's stuck.

> CULLEN
> It's a joint in the pipe, caught
> on this here apron. . . .

Cullen digs his finger under the tin skirt nailed to the roof through which the pipe goes and puts a slow strain on it. The inch-and-a-half long galvanized nails give reluctantly. It suddenly breaks loose and there's a clattering below. Cullen loses his balance and sits back abruptly. A dog starts to bark somewhere in the neighborhood. It stops as suddenly as it began. There's something ominous in the sound. They listen intently. All remains quiet.

They lift the sectional pipe carefully out of the hole and lay it gingerly on the roof. Cullen kneels at the hole and carefully starts ripping off shingles. . . . Jackson joins him. . . . They stack the shingles neatly.

DISSOLVE TO:

EXT. ROOF -- CLOSE TWO SHOT -- NIGHT

They have opened a hole large enough for a man to enter, between two beams that support the roof. Cullen peers down the hole.

> CULLEN
> Can't see a thing.

He starts to lower his legs down the hole but Jackson pushes him aside. He lowers his legs down the hole, grasps the edge of the beam and skins from sight, hanging from his hands.

>   JACKSON'S VOICE (O.S.)
>   (gasps)
>   I'm gonna have to drop.

>   CULLEN
>   You make too much noise. Grab
>   aholt the chain.

>   JACKSON'S VOICE (O.S.)
>   I'm slipping! . . .

>   CULLEN
>   Grab the chain! . . .

Cullen gathers in the slack and braces himself. Jackson's fingers slide off the beam.

INT. STORE -- FULL SHOT -- LOW ANGLE -- JACKSON

He slips off the roof beam, hangs for a moment by one hand, slips, and jerks in mid-air as the chain breaks his fall. Jackson utters a strangulated scream. He struggles for a moment to reach the iron that cuts into his wrist -- and then goes suddenly limp.

EXT. ROOF -- CLOSE SHOT -- CULLEN

He is bent over the hole in the roof, holding Jackson's weight on the chain.

>   CULLEN
>   (worriedly)
>   Hey! . . . You, Joker, you all
>   right? . . .

He crimps the chain over the beam-edge and squats, dropping his legs into the hole. He eases the chain until he's almost doubled over before he feels slack.

INT. STORE -- FULL SHOT -- LOW ANGLE -- JACKSON

His limp body is lowered to the surface of a counter. Cullen grabs the edge of the beam and swings down through the hole into the room. He hangs full length by one hand, his legs thrashing, trying to find footing. He lets go.

CAMERA PANS as he hits counter and bounces off Jackson to the floor.
There is a prolonged clatter of canned goods. He lies there,
stunned -- and he finally looks up to see Jackson's lacerated wrist
dangling over his face. He gets to his feet and bends over the
unconscious man. The back door rattles unexpectedly. Cullen's
head jerks -- he nearly panics. He shakes Jackson.

> CULLEN
> Come on, wake up . . . this ain't no
> time . . . wake up, hear? . . .

> VOICE (O.S.)
> Who's in there?

A light cuts across the room. Cullen's eyes slew around. Someone
is shining the light through the side window. Cullen ducks before
it hits him.

> ANOTHER VOICE (O.S.)
> What's going on?

> FIRST VOICE (O.S.)
> Somebody's in there. I heard them. . . .

> THIRD VOICE (O.S.)
> How'd they get in?

> FIRST VOICE (O.S.)
> Beats me. Everything's locked up.
> Think we should break in?

> SECOND VOICE (O.S.)
> I'll get Claude and fetch the keys.

Jackson comes to and stares around stupidly. He struggles to get
up on his elbows, but Cullen claps his hand over his mouth and pushes
him back to the counter just before the searching light hits him.

> THIRD VOICE (O.S.)
> Can you see anything?

> FIRST VOICE (O.S.)
> No, but I know they're in there. . . .

The light passes over them. Cullen pulls Jackson to the floor
beside him behind the counter. They listen. There is the sound
of voices. Dogs start barking -- an epidemic of staccato yelps
that spreads from house to house.

                         JACKSON
              What we gonna do?

                         CULLEN
              Hang onto me the best you can, baby.
              We getting out of here.

EXT. STORE -- FULL SHOT -- ROAD

Lights are coming on in the houses. A few men and dogs are
turning out. Flashlights cut a pattern across the road.

INT. STORE -- CLOSE TWO SHOT -- JACKSON AND CULLEN

Crouched behind the counter. CAMERA PANS with them as they get to
front of store. They pause as they see the activity in the street
through the plate glass. A more ominous sound in the back of the
store makes them stiffen -- the rattle of the padlock as someone
unlocks it.

                         CULLEN
              Now! . . .

Acting as a shield, with Jackson close behind him, Cullen jumps
through the plate glass window.

EXT. STORE -- MED. SHOT

As the two men stumble into the road. Someone sees them and
shouts. CAMERA PANS with them as they run down the road.

EXT. ROAD -- MED. SHOT -- REVERSE ANGLE

As Cullen and Jackson run up toward CAMERA. The crack of a rifle
and then the whine of a bullet is heard.

                         CULLEN
                       (pants)
              Got to get off this road.

He pulls Jackson after him and runs through an alley between two
shacks.

EXT. REAR OF SHACKS -- MED. SHOT

The two men emerge. Cullen starts back toward the center of the
settlement. Jackson pulls him up.

                         JACKSON
          What's the matter with you?

                         CULLEN
          Back track -- We never be able to
          outrun them. . . .

CAMERA PANS with them as they stumble through the back yards. A
small dog appears, it seems out of nowhere, and yaps at their heels.

MED. TWO SHOT

Cullen and Jackson stop in an agony of frustration. Jackson
kicks at the feisty dog. Cullen throws a stick at it. The
sounds of the men on the road approach.

                    CHILD'S VOICE (O.S.)
          Here, Tige! . . . Here, Tige! . . .

The dog persists. Jackson looks around wildly -- sees an opening
under one of the shacks, calls Cullen's attention to it.

                         CULLEN
                       (to dog)
          Get away! . . . Get away! . . .

Both men dive for the opening as the sounds of the pursuit gets
closer.

MED. SHOT -- UNDER SHACK

As the two men wriggle on their bellies over the dank earth. They
turn and try to placate the crazily barking dog, cajoling in
intense guarded tones.

                         CULLEN
          Go 'way, dog . . . please go'way. . . .

                         JACKSON
          Call him to you! . . . Call him to you! . . .

                         CULLEN
          Here, doggie! . . . Nice doggie. . . .

                         JACKSON
          Nice Rover . . . come on, Rover. . . .

                    CHILD'S VOICE (O.S.)
          Here, Tige! . . .

                    CULLEN
          Tige! . . .

                    JACKSON
          Here, Tige . . . come on, Tige, that's
          a good boy. . . .

                    CULLEN
          Come on, doggie. . . . Nice Tige. . . .

The excited animal dances just out of their reach.

                    WOMAN'S VOICE (O.S.)
                    (stridently)
          Tommy! . . . Tommy, you come back here!

                    MAN'S VOICE (O.S.)
          Sounds like it's coming from back here.

                    CHILD'S VOICE (O.S.)
          Here, Tige! . . .

                    JACKSON
                    (pleads)
          Please, doggie. . . . No. . . .
                    (holds out his fist)
          I got something for you. . . . Come on,
          Tige, see what I got for you! . . .

As the dog ventures close, still yapping; Jackson continues:

                    JACKSON (cont'd)
                    (eagerly)
          Come on . . . come on . . .

Jackson makes a quick lunge for the dog.

EXT. REAR OF SHACK -- MED. SHOT

As child wanders INTO SCENE.

                    CHILD
          Here, Tige. . . .

There is a sharp yelp and the barking ceases abruptly.

                              CHILD (cont'd)
              Tige? . . .

A woman in nightgown comes INTO SCENE, sees the boy and yanks
angrily at his arm.

Man with flashlight and shotgun ENTERS SCENE from alley. He plays
the light on the woman. She makes no attempt to cover herself.

                              MAN
              Any trouble back here, Miz Collins?

                              WOMAN
              No trouble, excepting as how you
              men folk rile up the whole place.

                              MAN
              We're protecting you, ma'am.

TWO SHOT -- CULLEN AND JACKSON

Jackson holds the dog tightly, one hand clamped over its muzzle.
They can see the legs of the people who are talking. They pet
the dog frantically.

                              WOMAN'S VOICE (O.S.)
              What's the trouble?

                              MAN'S VOICE (O.S.)
              Couple of guys bust into the company
              store. Joe King seen them when they was
              running away. Got in through a hole in
              the roof, they did.

                              WOMAN'S VOICE (O.S.)
              I hope they busted in good!

                              MAN'S VOICE (O.S.)
              Now that ain't nice, ma'am.

                              WOMAN'S VOICE (O.S.)
              And it ain't no excuse for you men folk
              to run off in the night and leave us all
              alone. We could be killed in our beds.

MED. SHOT -- BACK YARD

                    MAN
        That would be a pity, ma'am . . . seein'
        as how pretty you look.

                    WOMAN
        All right, Seth, you can put away your
        flashlight now. You seen all you're
        going to see for one night.

                    MAN
                 (smiles)
        Yes, ma'am.

She takes child by the hand, turns and strides back towards her house.

                    CHILD
        Ma. . . .

                    WOMAN
        You keep quiet. You as bad as
        your father.

The child breaks away.

                    CHILD
                 (shrilly)
        Here, Tige! Here, Tige! Here, Tige!

The woman catches him again.

                    WOMAN
        I swear, child, anymore fussing out of
        you and I'm gonna lock you in the shed
        for a week!
                 (to the man)
        I can see fine, Seth Jones, thank you
        very kindly.

                    MAN
                 (snaps off light and sighs)
        Yes, ma'am. . . .
                 (as he moves away)
        I ever find them two, I'm gonna
        say thank you before I shoot them.

CLOSE TWO SHOT -- CULLEN AND JACKSON

They're still frantically petting dog. Jackson still holds it.
In whispers:

                    JACKSON
     Quiet, baby . . . quiet. . . .

                    CULLEN
     Ease up on him. . . . You choke
     him to death.

                    JACKSON
     I got him all right.

                    CULLEN
     We better get out of here while
     we can.

                    JACKSON
     What about the mutt?

                    CULLEN
     Let him go. He's all right.

                    JACKSON
     Let him go?

                    CULLEN
     That's right, Joker, let him go. . . .

Jackson reluctantly puts the dog down but still holds it. It
licks his face.

                    JACKSON
     It likes me.

He looks at Cullen and releases the dog. It scampers around,
enjoying its freedom, panting happily. Cullen starts to crawl
out. Jackson follows.

EXT. SHACK'S REAR -- MED. SHOT

As the men emerge, cautiously look around and cut across the yard at
right angles to the road. The dog has disappeared. After a moment,
the little dog streaks after them from the b.g. in back of CAMERA.

                                        DISSOLVE TO:

EXT. FOREST -- MED. SHOT -- CULLEN AND JACKSON -- NIGHT

As they follow a path over a hill. The dog is still following
them. They try to shoo it back home, but the dog thinks it's a
game and gambols around them happily.

                         JACKSON
         Shoo! . . . go on home, dog! . . .

They stop.

                         CULLEN
         Go on, dog . . . scram!

Jackson squats down. Cullen reaches down and throws a stick at it.
It circles and jumps into Jackson's arms. Jackson looks at the dog
in his arms. He puts it on the ground where it waits patiently,
its tail going violently. Cullen just looks at it.

                         JACKSON
                       (angrily)
         Go on home, you damfool dog! . . .
         You got a home to go to . . . go on!

The dog looks up at him. Jackson suddenly slaps the dog. It
yelps and circles away.

                         JACKSON
                   (his voice breaks)
         Go on! . . .

He picks up stones and throws them at the dog. It runs back, but
presently sits down, out of range, and looks at them dolefully.
The men stare at the small animal.

                         JACKSON
         Damn mutt! . . .

He turns and stumbles up trail, Cullen following. They look
back. The dog still sits watching them.

MED. CLOSE SHOT -- WOODS

As they turn to continue, a man breaks out of the woods (JOE) and
comes face to face with them. They are all immobilized with surprise
for a moment. They grapple with the man before he has a chance
to use his gun. There is a wild struggle.

                         JOE
         Help!

An arm is raised and the chain comes down over the man's head.
The man falls heavily. They try to run for it. A sapling catches
the chain and they are thrown to the ground.

CLOSE TWO SHOT -- CULLEN AND JACKSON

They struggle to their feet and are about to run again, but suddenly
stop. . . . Needle-like beams fix them to the spot. CAMERA PULLS BACK
and reveals the men from town who now surround them. Cullen and
Jackson are focused in the light of flashlights, the chain swinging
between them reflecting back the light. A heavy set man appears to
be the leader (MAC).

> MAC
> All right -- don't move!

The others surround the two men, their rifle barrels glinting in the
light. Mac moves to the body of the fallen man and bends over him.
Other men with flashlights keep joining the circle, until Cullen and
Jackson are the brilliant hub of more than a dozen radiating beams.

> ONE OF THE MEN
> (approaching)
> Did you get them?

> ANOTHER MAN
> (to Mac)
> Who is it?

> MAC
> Joe. They hurt Joe.

Mac rises and goes over to the two chained men.

> A MAN
> Is he bad?

> MAC
> He's bleeding like a stuck pig.

The men close the circle around Jackson and Cullen more tightly.

> MAC (Cont'd)
> One of you get the doc. Frank,
> and a couple of you, carry Joe
> down. Rafe -- get Big Sam.

They carry Joe down. Mac approaches Cullen and Jackson, his
light inches away from their faces.

> MAC
> Looks like you two boys are in

MAC (Cont'd)
for trouble. . . .
    (he peers more closely
      at Jackson)
Say! . . . this one's white! . . .

CUT TO:

EXT. TOWN -- CLOSE SHOT -- BONFIRE IN ROAD -- NIGHT

CAMERA PULLS BACK and reveals men and some women warming themselves
at the fire.

FULL SHOT -- STREET

Cullen and Jackson are led down the street. The crowd makes way for
the two men. Their guards push them roughly against the wall of
the shed.

CLOSER SHOT -- CULLEN AND JACKSON

Quarantined in an open area, surrounded by armed men, stand
Cullen and Jackson -- their backs to the wall of the storage shed.
They lean against the wall, dull with nervous strain and fatigue.

FULL SHOT -- REVERSE ANGLE

The men who ring the two prisoners carry their guns negligently
at ready. A submerged feeling of tension manifests itself in an
unnatural silence -- when they talk, it's in subdued tones -- although
there is an air about it of a nocturnal picnic. Several of the
men have mugs of coffee in their hands. Women are pouring and
serving. There is a stir among them, and all eyes turn to a
house in which the lights are shining. BIG SAM comes out and
elbows his way through the crowd. He's a giant of a man in his
late forties. His movements and tone of voice are gentle, but
suggest controlled power. He's obviously looked upon as a leader.

The people make way for him as he comes down into the clearing
that surrounds the prisoners, CAMERA PANNING with him into a
CLOSE GROUP SHOT with Jackson and Cullen. He stares at them for
a long moment as though studying them. The two prisoners stare
back at him dully.

BIG SAM
    (finally)
You the two been running away from
the road gang?

                        JACKSON
            Yes, sir.

                        BIG SAM
            You sure run into trouble now.

He turns away from them, Mac detaches himself from the periphery
of men and grabs Big Sam's arm.

                        MAC
            How is he, Sam?

                        BIG SAM
            Doc is sewing him up now.

                        MAC
                    (insists)
            How is he?

                        SAM
                    (frowns)
            I don't know. He hasn't come to yet.

                        MAC
                    (turns)
            Get rid of the women, Rafe.

FULL SHOT

FEATURING Rafe in f.g., as several of the men circulate in the crowd.

                        RAFE
                    (to woman -- quietly)
            Come on, ladies, time for you all
            to be in bed. . . .

                        A WOMAN
                    (disturbed)
            What are you men fixing to do?

                        RAFE
            Old-fashioned prayer meeting, ma'am.
            Men only. . . . Come on -- hurry it up.

                        MAC
            Prayer meeting. That's pretty
            good. Hey, Rafe, you got the rope?

CLOSE GROUP SHOT -- WOMEN -- CHILDREN

The women are frightened. They gather their things together.

> WOMAN
> (to child -- sharply)
> Get in the house -- quick now!

Other women hastily gather up their children and herd them indoors.

FULL SHOT -- DIFFERENT ANGLE -- MAC -- BIG SAM IN F.G.

Mac turns to the men watching the prisoners -- and then looks negligently at the prisoners themselves.

The guards tense up and close the circle around the prisoners threateningly.

A heavy coiled rope sails through the air and lands almost at the feet of the two prisoners from O.S. Mac goes over and picks it up. Mac starts bending the rope. The two prisoners stare at it with rigid fascination.

> JACKSON
> (blurts -- hoarsely)
> Give us a break, buddy!

Mac turns to him.

> MAC
> I ain't your buddy. You got
> your buddy.

He saunters over to the two prisoners, the rope in his hand.

> MAC (Cont'd)
> (to Jackson)
> Which one of you did it?

Jackson doesn't answer. Mac turns to Cullen.

> MAC (Cont'd)
> Did you do it?
> (silence)
> Why'd you do it?

A man snickers in the b.g. Mac turns to Jackson. He's enjoying himself.

                    MAC (Cont'd)
               (indicating Cullen)
          Why'd he do it?
               (no answer)
          You protecting your buddy?

A rope is thrown over the arm extending from the peak of the
storage shed.

Jackson doesn't answer.

                    MAC (Cont'd)
          Don't matter. You're both gonna
          hang.

                    JACKSON
               (blusters)
          Look mister, you can't do anything
          to us. We're escaped cons. . . .

                    MAC
          So?

                    JACKSON
          So they're out looking for us now.
          What do you think will happen when
          they find us?

                    MAC
          You're going to be crow meat when they
          find you, that's what's going to happen.

                    JACKSON
          You won't get away with it!

                    MAC
          Nobody's going to know who pulled
          the rope.

He turns and grins at the men behind him. The second rope is
thrown over the overhead arm.

                    JACKSON
               (desperately)
          Don't you know there's a big reward
          out for escaped cons?

                    MAC
                (coldly)
        Rewards always say, dead or alive.

                    JACKSON
                (almost hysterical)
        You don't understand! . . . You can't
        lynch me -- I'm a white man!

CLOSE-UP CULLEN

He stiffens -- turns and looks at Jackson with a strained expression
on his face.

BACK TO SCENE:

                    MAC
        You are? I'll tell you the kind of
        white man you are.
                (turns to Cullen)
        Spit on him.

                    BIG SAM
                (protests disgustedly)
        For God's sake, Mac. . . .

                    MAC
                (insistently)
        Go on! Spit on him.

                    BIG SAM
        Mac --

Mac whirls viciously on Sam.

                    MAC
        Let me alone, Sam!

The mob presses in.

                    OTHERS
        Sure -- let him alone. . . .

                    MAC
                (grins suddenly)
        We're just having a little fun.

He turns back to Cullen.

```
               MAC (Cont'd)
              (harshly)
    Come on!  Come on!  You heard me! . . .
```

Cullen doesn't move. Mac slaps Cullen across the face. Cullen
stares with cold anger at him for a second. He spits at Mac.
There is a moment of shock. Mac recovers and drives a fist
into Cullen's face. Cullen staggers back.

Several men exclaim angrily and move in on Cullen. Before he can
recover from the blow, Cullen is struck with a rifle butt. Mac
pushes past the angry men to get at Cullen and sinks a blow into
his stomach. Cullen drops to the ground, pulling Jackson down to
his knees by the chain. Big Sam wades in after Mac and pulls him off.

```
                    BIG SAM
                   (roars)
         Wait a minute! . . . Wait a minute!
```

The crowd holds back momentarily.

```
                    MAC
                   (dangerously)
         Get out of my way, Sam, or you're
         going to have trouble too.
```

Big Sam has hold of Mac's shirt.

```
                    BIG SAM
         I told you, Joe's going to be all right.
```

```
                    MAC
         You told me.  Fine.
```

He knocks Big Sam's hand down and turns back to the two prisoners.
Sam swings him around.

```
                    BIG SAM
         You don't give a damn, do you?
```

```
                    MAC
         There are more important things
         right now.
```

Big Sam steps in front of the two prisoners, intercepting Mac.
He turns to the others.

                    BIG SAM
              (challenges angrily)
          How about the rest of you --
          you want to lynch them?

He picks up the rope.

                    BIG SAM (Cont'd)
          Here! You, Glover! . . .
              (offers rope to
              one of the men)
          You're so anxious, go ahead, tie it
          around their necks. . . . Go ahead! . . .

He turns to another.

                    BIG SAM (Cont'd)
          All right, Packer -- You want
          blood. . . .

He picks up an axe lying near the fire. Throws it to him.

                    BIG SAM (Cont'd)
          Cut them up! . . .
              (to the others)
          You want to burn them?

He picks up a burning brand from the fire.

                    BIG SAM (Cont'd)
          Here! . . . Gouge out their eyes!

The men stand indecisively. Mac suddenly grabs the burning brand
out of Big Sam's hand and runs to the cringing prisoners. Big Sam
catches him and smashes his ham of a fist to his jaw. Mac falls
like a stone.

                    BIG SAM (Cont'd)
              (breathing heavily)
          Any more big men?

The doc comes out of the house in the b.g. He's not really a doctor,
but a scrawny worker who served as a first aid helper in the last war.

                    DOC
              (calls cheerfully)
          He's all right. He's okay.

He comes down to them.

> DOC (Cont'd)
> Scalp wound. Had to take six
> stitches, but he's okay.
> (sees Mac on ground)
> What's the matter with him?

His words fall into the silence and are absorbed. He looks at
the silent men quizzically.

> BIG SAM
> (wearily)
> Lock them up. I'll send them back
> with the wagons in the morning.

He walks OUT OF SHOT.

DISSOLVE TO:

EXT. TOWN -- FULL SHOT -- PRE-DAWN

The streets are empty and the houses dark.

CUT TO:

INT. SHACK -- FULL SHOT

Cullen and Jackson are bound together, back to back in the
cramped tool shed. Jackson is sullen and nervous. Cullen's face
shows signs of the beating. Jackson faces a small window.

> JACKSON
> It'll be light pretty soon.
> (pause)
> Why'd you have to go and do a crazy
> thing like that? They might've beat
> us to death -- they still might. . . .

> CULLEN
> (drily)
> What have you got to live for anyway --
> breaking your back on a road gang the
> next ten years?

> JACKSON
> It's better than being dead.

> CULLEN
> (quietly; after a pause)
> You ever been on a lynch?

> JACKSON
> (aggressively)
> Why?

> CULLEN
> Nobody ever as scared as you
> without they seen a lynching.

> JACKSON
> (snarls)
> Yeah, I seen a lynch. I seen what
> they do to a guy -- drag him out of
> jail in the middle of the night!
> A mob as crazy as that one out there.
> Maybe they start drinking -- and
> thinking. Maybe Big Sam falls
> asleep. Then maybe they come for
> us! Then what?

> CULLEN
> (softly)
> That's easy. . . . Just tell them
> you're a white man.

Jackson is about to reply angrily, but his attention is caught by
something he sees through the window. He stiffens.

> JACKSON
> They're coming for us! . . .
> I told you!

The SOUND of footsteps approach -- the protesting screech of
metal on metal as the door is jimmied open. Big Sam ENTERS SHOT.

> JACKSON
> (terrified)
> What do you want? I didn't hear
> any wagons being hitched up.

Sam looks at them for a long moment, draws out his hunting knife.

> JACKSON
> What're you gonna do? Please,
> mister! . . .

Sam looks at him with distaste. He goes to them and slashes
their bonds. They shake off the ropes and massage their limbs.

                    BIG SAM
          Get out.

                    JACKSON
          Where -- what do you mean?

                    BIG SAM
          I'm letting you go.

                    JACKSON
               (worried)
          What for?
               (to Cullen)
          Don't go. . . . They must be
          waiting for us.

One of the ropes is still knotted around Jackson's handcuffed wrist.
He's having trouble getting it off. Big Sam reaches over with his
knife to help. Jackson looks down and suddenly seizes the man's wrist.

CLOSEUP -- WRISTS

Jackson's and Big Sam's, side by side. Big Sam's wrist shows livid
scars where a manacle had bitten in deeply sometime in the past.

BACK TO SCENE:

Big Sam looks at Jackson coldly.

                    BIG SAM
               (quietly)
          Let go.

Jackson drops his hand. Cullen has also seen the tell-tale scars.
Big Sam moves to the door and holds it open. Cullen pauses.

                    CULLEN
          How about letting us have that crow bar?

                    BIG SAM
          Don't push your luck, boy.

                    CULLEN
               (stubbornly)
          A cigarette?

Big Sam silently hands him his pack.

Cullen and Jackson move to the door.

> BIG SAM
> Just a minute.

The two men pause.

> BIG SAM (Cont'd)
> In case you get caught. Nobody
> let you out of here, understand?
> You broke out by yourselves.

> JACKSON
> Thanks.

> BIG SAM
> (coldly)
> Run, chicken run.

The two men run to the shelter of the nearby woods. CAMERA HOLDS
on Big Sam in the F.G. He watches as they disappear. . . .

EXT. SAVANNAH -- LONG SHOT -- HIGH ANGLE -- DAY

The two men are running with a shuffling gait.

> DISSOLVE TO:

EXT. DIFFERENT PART OF SAVANNAH -- MED. CLOSE TRUCKING SHOT -- DAY

Both men are near exhaustion as they stagger along.

> CUT TO:

EXT. SETTLEMENT -- LATE AFTERNOON -- CLOSE SHOT -- BIG SAM

He's looking o.s.   The snarling of dogs comes over. He grimaces
almost as though in pain.

MED. SHOT -- DIFFERENT ANGLE -- BIG SAM IN F.G.

Max is talking to the man with the bandaged head. Workers, their
wives and members of the posse are clustered around. Solly and
his assistant hold the dogs.

                    BIG SAM
            Get away from the dogs before
            somebody gets hurt!

CLOSE SHOT -- MAX

He turns sharply.

                    MAX
                (echoes irritably)
            Solly, get those dogs out of
            here before somebody gets hurt!

He turns back to the man with the bandaged head.

                    MAX (Cont'd)
            All right -- they hit you. Then
            what happened? What did you do
            to them?

                    MAN
            I don't know. . . . The next thing
            I know, Doc was fixing me up.

Max clamps his lips together with impatience. He turns to Mac
who is standing nearby, CAMERA TRUCKING.

                    MAX
            Do you know what happened?

Mac stares at him stonily.

                    MAX
                (to a woman)
            You!

No response. CAMERA TRUCKS with him down the line. The faces
are closed. He stops before another woman.

                    MAX
            Were you blind and deaf last
            night too?

                    WOMAN
                (coldly)
            They send us women away.

                        MAX
        Why?

                        WOMAN
        * * * <u>Ask</u> <u>them.</u>

Max confronts Big Sam.

                        MAX
        What did you do with them, Sam?

                        BIG SAM
                (blandly)
        Like I told you, Sheriff. We
        locked them up. They broke out.
        Got away.

                        MAX
        Those jimmy marks are on the
        outside of the door. They didn't
        break out. Somebody came and got
        them.

                        SAM
        I wouldn't know about that, Sheriff.
        I run a turpentine camp, not a jail.

                        MAX
        Who came for them, Sam? Who came
        and got them?

Sam shrugs.

                        MAX
        Sam, if you took them out and lynched
        them . . . you'd better tell me about
        it now because the dogs'll find them
        anyway.

                        SAM
        Why should we kill them, Sheriff?
                (he looks o.s. at the
                 snarling dogs)

P. 438   [Menfolk don't like women messing in their
                  dirty business.]

POV SHOT   DOGS

> SAM'S VOICE
> You're much better equipped for it.

BACK TO SCENE:

The sheriff stares hard at Big Sam. Max turns away from Big Sam abruptly.

> MULLER
> (loud and sharp -- to Solly)
> Solly! Get going!

> SOLLY
> We've been going since daybreak . . .
> my dogs are bushed. . . .

> SHERIFF
> (almost violently)
> Get going or I'll commandeer them
> and run them myself!

The deputies look dismayed at this announcement.

> A DEPUTY
> Wait a minute, Max, how about
> us? We're dead on our feet.

The others chime in:

> DEPUTIES
> Have a heart, Max. . . . It's going
> to be dark pretty soon anyway. . . .
> What's the matter with tomorrow? . . .

Max whirls on them.

> MULLER
> (shouts)
> What do you think this is, a
> picnic? You wanted to be deputies,
> didn't you? Well you are and
> you're under orders! Pick up your
> gear and get ready to move out.

He turns to the Captain.

                    MULLER (Cont'd)
                  (almost viciously)
          Call Cumberland. Tell them I want
          every man they can spare. I want
          them to sweep south along the west
          edge of the swamp. . . .

                    CAPTAIN
          They'll have to be field equipped.
          It'll be dark before they start.

                    MULLER
                  (violently)
          I don't care when they start, just
          get them moving!

                    CAPTAIN
                  (with a hint of a smile)
          Yes sir!

He turns and goes. The Editor comes up beside the Sheriff and looks
at him curiously. CAMERA MOVES IN on them. The Sheriff is staring
off after the Captain. The tempest has subsided.

                  * * * EDITOR
                  (with thoughtful bitterness)
          You know, that's the first time
          I've seen him smile. . . .

                                            CUT TO:

EXT. CANE BRAKE -- MED. SHOT -- CULLEN AND JACKSON -- LATE AFTERNOON

as they ENTER SHOT. Jackson stumbles and falls.

                    JACKSON
          Wait . . . wait. I got to rest.

They stop and drop to the ground, both panting.

                    JACKSON (Cont'd)
          We must have run a million miles --
          How far you think we run?

Cullen doesn't answer. Jackson reacts. He'd meant this as an

overture -- an attempt to bury the hostility between them which
grew in the lynching and previous scenes. He steals glances at
Cullen who doesn't look at him. Cullen lights his cigarette;
Jackson's hostility, frustration and guilt grows.

> JACKSON (Cont'd)
> (attempted levity)
> You sure can run. * * * Kill us
> both if I didn't make you stop.

No answer.

> JACKSON (Cont'd)
> (irritably)
> Why don't you say something? What
> have you got to squawk about -- we
> got away -- didn't we?
> (silence)
> You got nothing to say, hah? You
> ought to be down on your hands and
> knees thanking me. You didn't put
> up any fight -- I had to do all the
> talking. . . .

Looks for a cigarette of his own and doesn't have one. Cullen
looks at him contemptuously -- throws his cigarette to the ground.

> JACKSON (Cont'd)
> Don't give me that look. . . . You
> should have got what was coming to
> you, spitting in that guy's face --

He has picked up the cigarette, and almost as a reflex he tears off
the end of the butt and raises it to his lips -- Cullen whirls and
slaps the cigarette out of his mouth.

Jackson leaps to his feet, and Cullen is up with him. . . . The men
face each other, seething. The corrosive anger, hatred, shame --
and the bottled up, accumulated rage, boils over, their raw nerves
aching for the too long postponed conflict.

> CULLEN
> (icy)
> What's the matter -- afraid of
> catching my color?

[like hell]

                    JACKSON
      You picking up a hand to me?

                    CULLEN
               (with cold contempt)
      To you! * * * <u>The big shot and</u>
      <u>the taker</u> -- You're nothing. . . .
      You're just a talker!

                    * * *

* * * <u>Jackson</u> strikes Cullen who barely defends himself.

                    CULLEN
      Go on -- tell me the big talk about
      Charlie Potatoes when the chain's off
      and nobody's chasing you.

* * *

                    CULLEN (Cont'd)
      Go on, tell me. . . .

                    * * *

He slugs Cullen with his free arm. Their blows and counter-
blows continue and form rhythmic hammer beats against the
background of the impassioned jumble of words.

                    CULLEN
      You can't huh? . . . You can't and you
      never will because you're nothing! You're
      not even a man -- You're a monkey on a
      stick -- that's what you are -- * * * The
      mob pulled the string and you jumped! . . .

P. 442   [The maker and the taker—]
                        [JACKSON
            Shut up!]

[He]

[Cullen smashes his arm into Jackson.]

                        [JACKSON
            Shut up!]

            [a monkey on a stick!]

* * *

                    CULLEN
        * * * You said one day we're going to
        tangle -- the time was going to come. . . .
        That time is <u>now</u>! !

Jackson is goaded into a bitter frenzy. He lashes out at Cullen.
Cullen blocks the blow and crashes his fist into Jackson's face.
Jackson falls and pulls Cullen down with him. They're both weak,
and the blows are ineffectual. They're both crying with angry
frustration as they try to gouge, kick, scratch, bite as they
roll in the cane brake. . . .

CLOSE TWO SHOT

Jackson has gotten the chain around Cullen's neck and pulls
desperately.

                    JACKSON
            I'll kill you!

                    CULLEN
                (straining against
                the chain)
            That's right, white man . . . you kill
            me . . . solve all your problems . . .
            make you a big man . . .

Cullen slowly forces Jackson's arm back.

                    CULLEN (Cont'd)
                (as they struggle)
            . . . all your problems. . . . Only it
            ain't so easy to kill me -- is it?

Cullen breaks the grip and they roll over to the edge of the
trampled area. . . .

There is a movement in the grass over their heads.

                    VOICE (O.S.)
            Put up your hands.

P. 443   [JACKSON
            I said shut up! . . .]

        [Make me—go on, make me.]

They raise their heads and stare O.S.

CLOSE LOW ANGLE SHOT -- BOY

He holds a twenty-two on them. He is a rugged 11-year old kid.
He's not fooling.

CLOSE SHOT -- GROUP

The tableau is held for a moment.

Jackson leaps at the kid murderously. Cullen pulls him up short
on the chain but not before the kid has dropped the gun and
stumbled backwards. He trips, hits his head and lies still.
Jackson is still in the grip of panic -- he moves toward the
fallen youngster. . . .

> CULLEN
> What are you going to do?

> JACKSON
> (dazed)
> I don't know. Let's get out of here.

> CULLEN
> Wait a minute * * *

> JACKSON
> No! Let's go! There might be
> people around!

Cullen bends over the kid.

CLOSE SHOT

As Cullen leans over the boy, takes him in his arms. He tenderly
brushes the boy's hair back off his forehead. He feels the back
of the kid's head.

> CULLEN
> Just a bump.

The kid opens his eyes.

CLOSEUP -- CULLEN -- LOW ANGLE -- BOY'S POV

[The Kid might be hurt.]

Cullen looming over him.   To the child, he looks frightening and
grotesque.

CLOSE GROUP SHOT

The kid stiffens in Cullen's arms.

>   KID
>   (screams)
>   Let me go!

He scrambles to his feet and runs behind Jackson, clings to his legs.

>   KID (Cont'd)
>   Keep him away from me.   Don't
>   let him hurt me!

Cullen, still on his knees, looks up from the child to Jackson.

CLOSEUP -- JACKSON

He can't hold Cullen's gaze.

CLOSEUP -- CULLEN

He smiles sardonically.   He turns back to the child.

CLOSE GROUP SHOT

>   CULLEN
>   Where * * * do you live, * * * kid?

The kid looks up at Jackson.

>   JACKSON
>   (subdued)
>   Go on.   Answer him.

>   KID
>   Over the hill.

>   CULLEN
>   That way?

>   JACKSON
>   Answer him.

[sonny?]

                    KID
      Yes.

                    CULLEN
      What * * * <u>are</u> you doing here?

                    KID
      Hunting.

                    CULLEN
      How come your * * * <u>pa</u> lets you
      out hunting alone?

                    KID
      * * * <u>He ain't here no more</u>.

                    CULLEN
      Who * * * <u>do</u> you live with?

                    KID
      * * * my mom.

The two men exchange looks.

                    JACKSON
      Just the two of you?

                    KID
      Yes, sir. How come you chained
      together like that? You taking
      him to jail?

                    JACKSON
               (exchanges glances
                with Cullen
      Something like that. You must have
      a lot of friends, a bright * * * kid
      like you. Neighbors.

                    KID
      Uh, uh. Just Mom and me. We
      work the farm. Sometimes on

P. 446   [daddy]

               [Ain't got no daddy.]

               [Just]

               [little]

Sunday we go over to Cumberland
to see my Uncle George.

Jackson looks up at Cullen.

                    JACKSON
          We better take you home, * * * kid.

Cullen picks up the twenty-two and rises. The kid looks
fearfully at Cullen.

                    * * *

They start out.

                              DISSOLVE TO:

EXT. CABIN -- FULL SHOT -- FIELD -- SUNDOWN -- * * * Open_on woman
                              coming_into light

Adjoining cabin. The two men and the child come around the spring
house. They walk into CLOSE GROUP SHOT and pause.

                    KID
                 (shouts)
          Hey, mom!

                    JACKSON
          No need to holler, kid.

CAMERA PANS with them as they approach cabin door. The place is
typical of the backwoods farms, weathered grey, bare of paint,
but fairly well constructed. The one step to the door needs repairing.
Jackson is about to push the door in when it opens. She stares at
Jackson -- her eyes run down to the chain on his wrist and to Cullen
who stands in back of him holding the gun. Her eyes widen -- She
sees dried blood on the child's forehead.

                    WOMAN
                 (stridently)
          What did they do to you?

                    KID
                 (he runs to her)
          Nothing, mom, I fell down.

P. 447   [kid]

                    [CULLEN
          Okay. Let's go.]

She presses him against her thighs. She's a well-built young
woman, plain, with tired lines around her mouth and eyes. The
white man sways with fatigue.

> WOMAN
> What do you want?

> JACKSON
> Don't get excited, lady. We
> just want something to eat.

She looks at Jackson and stands aside. Jackson pushes past her.

INT. CABIN -- FULL SHOT

As they enter. It's a utility room, containing beds, as well as
tables and chairs. A lean-to attached is the kitchen. It is
clean, and apparent in the touches of color, are the woman's
efforts to fight off the dirt and warm up the barren wood.

Jackson almost falls rather than sits at the table. Cullen kicks
out a chair and sits down beside him.

> JACKSON
> (to woman)
> Where are you going?

> WOMAN
> You said you wanted something
> to eat.

> JACKSON
> Okay.

As the kid starts to go with his mother --

> JACKSON (Cont'd)
> Kid. You stay here.

She moves to the kitchen. Comes back a moment later with a dish
of mush. She puts it in front of Jackson. Jackson lifts the
spoon. He pauses. The woman is still standing by the table.

> JACKSON
> Where's his?
> (no answer)
> Get him some mush!

                    WOMAN
                 (to boy)
            Get him some mush.

The kid obeys. The woman watches Jackson.

                    JACKSON
                 (through a mouthful)
            Hey, kid. Got a sledge and a
            chisel?

                    KID
            In the shed.

                    JACKSON
            Go get it.

The woman starts out too.

                    JACKSON (Cont'd)
            You stay here.

The woman subsides.

                    KID
            Okay, ma?

                    WOMAN
            Go ahead.

* * * The boy leaves.

                    * * *

P. 449   [JACKSON
                  You got any coffee?

                         WOMAN
                    (she starts up)
                  I'll have to heat it.

                        JACKSON
                  Never mind, we'll wait till
                  the kid gets back. . . .

                         WOMAN
                  Where you from?

Jackson looks up at her and doesn't answer. Cullen
continues to eat.]

> JACKSON
> You got any coffee?

> WOMAN
> It's on the stove.

> JACKSON
> Never mind -- we'll wait till
> the kid gets back.

Their eyes lock for a moment, then the woman's eyes drop the
iron cuff and chain on Jackson's wrist. It is almost as if she had
really seen it for the first time. Jackson's eyes follow hers
down to the chain. Automatically, he drops his hand out of sight
beneath the table, then swiftly he looks back up at her. Their
eyes meet again. Unconsciously he runs his hand through his
hair in a small involuntary grooming gesture.

> WOMAN
> (quietly)
> I'll get your coffee --

She turns and walks slowly o.s. Jackson, a look of puzzled
wonder reacting to just the hint of warm sympathy follows her
across the room with eyes -- turns, catches Cullen watching him --
avoids his eyes -- looks around room. Woman returns and puts a
coffee pot and things on table. She goes to cupboard and
places a pan of cornbread on the table too.

> WOMAN
> I got some cornbread . . . it's cold,
> but I made it this morning.

> JACKSON
> Thanks. . . .

> WOMAN
> (simply)
> You're welcome. . . .

An embarrassed silence

> WOMAN
> Where you from?

No answer from Jackson.

                    WOMAN (Cont'd)
          You can talk to me. . . . You don't
          have to be afraid to talk to me.
          It gets lonesome here.

                    * * *

He looks at the woman, catching Cullen watching him; avoids his
eyes and looks around the room.

                    JACKSON
                  (awkwardly)
          That's a nice picture.

                    WOMAN
                  (flattered)
          I made it myself.

                    JACKSON
                  (surprised)
          Yeah?

                    WOMAN
          It ain't so much. You buy them in
          the store with the paint. It's got
          numbers on it -- I just fill it in.
          They got all kinds with pictures
          on the boxes how it should look.

                    JACKSON
          It's pretty.

                    WOMAN
          I like pretty things.

P. 451   [WOMAN (cont'd)
            You can talk to me. You don't have
            to be afraid to talk to me. . . .
                    (pause)
            I got some corn bread— It's cold,
            but I made it this morning.
                    JACKSON
            Thanks.
                    WOMAN
            It gets lonesome here.]

                    JACKSON
          That other one -- did you paint
          that too?

                    WOMAN
          This?
               (laughs embarrassedly)
          No -- I cut it out of a magazine.

                    JACKSON
          What is it?

She goes to the picture and reads the caption:

                    WOMAN
               (falteringly)
          It says, "A scene of gay revel-ery
          at the . . . Mardi Gras, in Old New
          Orleans."

                    JACKSON
          Yeah? I been to the Mardi Gras.

                    WOMAN
          Is it really like says?

                    JACKSON
          I seen better things.

                    WOMAN
          You mean it's not like it says?

                    JACKSON
          Oh . . . it's okay. Music and
          dancing . . . pretty gals.

                    WOMAN
          I must look awful -- I been doing
          the washing.

Their eyes meet for a moment. They both look away. A moment of
embarrassed silence. She picks up the pot and fills up both
plates. Cullen looks up at her, but her eyes are on Jackson.

                    WOMAN (Cont'd)
          You going to be staying long?

                         JACKSON
          No.

                         WOMAN
          They coming after you?

Jackson bends down over his plate. Cullen continues to eat
methodically.

                         WOMAN (Cont'd)
                      (hesitates)
          There's a train. . . .

Jackson looks at her sharply. Cullen's spoon pauses.

                         WOMAN (Cont'd)
          It hits the ridge one o'clock in the
          afternoon. That's a good place to
          catch it. It goes slow up the ridge.

                         JACKSON
          You know a lot about that train.

                         WOMAN
                      (softly)
          My husband used to work for the line.

Kid enters.

                         KID
          Here's the sledge -- and here's
          the chisel.

Both men have stopped eating and are staring at the hammer and
chisel.

                         WOMAN
          You want your coffee?

With one accord the men push back their chairs and grab up the
hammer and chisel.

                         CULLEN
                      (feverishly)
          Over here.

He indicates the hearth stone. They squat down. Cullen lays
down the gun.

                        JACKSON
            Got enough room to swing it?

                        CULLEN
            You just hold that chisel!

Jackson lays his wrist on the stone and holds the chisel over the
cuff. Three ringing blows and the iron falls off his wrist.

                        CULLEN
                Now me.

They exchange instruments. Jackson aims carefully. One smash
and the iron separates. Jackson looks at Cullen and grins sickly.
Cullen reaches for the gun. Both men measure each other.

                        CULLEN
                    (licks his lips)
            We cut loose now.

Jackson's grin fades. His eyes hood. Without warning, he drops the
hammer, staggers. Cullen catches him and carries him to the bed.

                        WOMAN
            What's the matter with him?

                        CULLEN
            He's sick. Got poison in his system.

She goes over to him and cringes at the sight of the wounded wrist.

                        WOMAN
            Johnny, get water in the big pot
            and put it on the stove.

                        CULLEN
                    (without conviction)
            You stay here, kid.

                        WOMAN
                    (blazes)
            Do like I told you!

                        KID
                Okay, ma.

Cullen sits wearily at the table with the rifle under his arms.
He nurses his sore wrist. He cradles his head on the rifle stock.

> CULLEN
> Oh, Lordy, I'm tired.

The woman stands there. The rhythmic breathing of Cullen indicates he's fallen asleep. She looks at Cullen and then at Jackson. Her eyes are brooding.

> WOMAN
> (hoarsely)
> Hurry up with that water!

DISSOLVE TO:

INT. CABIN -- MED. CLOSE SHOT -- JACKSON AND WOMAN -- NIGHT

The woman is putting cold compresses on Jackson's forehead. Her hunger for a man is clear in the way she looks at him. Her hand hovers over his chest and comes to rest on his bicep. Cullen O.S. stirs restlessly. She looks around, withdraws her hand guiltily.

INT. CABIN -- CLOSEUP -- CULLEN -- NIGHT

sleeping on table. Woman's hand reaches INTO SHOT and grasps barrel of gun cautiously. CAMERA PULLS BACK. She slowly eases it out from under the sleeping Cullen without awakening him. She turns and goes quickly back to the bed.

CLOSE TWO SHOT -- WOMAN AND JACKSON

She puts down the rifle near the bed and leans over the sleeping man. He tosses fitfully. She wets the cloth from a bucket on the floor and gently wipes Jackson's perspired face. His wrist is neatly bandaged. She puts her hand on his forehead to see if he's feverish -- and glances down at his bare torso. Her fingers touch his bearded face as she draws her hand away. The man suddenly starts awake. He rises on his elbows. He stares around wildly.

> JACKSON
> Where did he -- ?

> WOMAN
> Shhhh!

Recognition comes into the man's eyes. He looks up at her face. The whole scene is played in whispers.

                    JACKSON
              (whispers hoarsely)
          Where's Cullen?

                    WOMAN
              (indicates with a nod)
          Him?

Jackson looks over and sees Cullen is asleep.

                    JACKSON
              (raises on his elbow)
          How long I been asleep?

                    WOMAN
          Couple of hours.

                    JACKSON
              (after a pause -- sharply)
          Where's the kid?

                    WOMAN
          Over there.
              (nods to alcove)

                    JACKSON
          I better wake Cullen.

She puts her hand to his forehead.

                    WOMAN
          You're feverish. You need more rest.
          You've got plenty of time.

                    JACKSON
          What time is it?

                    WOMAN
          Two o'clock.

He sinks back on the bed.

                    JACKSON
              (pause)
          You been sitting here all night?

                    WOMAN
          Yes.

                    JACKSON
          Why didn't you go to sleep?

                    WOMAN
          I better put a new dressing on.

She keeps her eyes lowered. Jackson watches her -- lost in his
own musings.

                    JACKSON
          Hm. . . .

                    WOMAN
               (looks up at him)
          What is it?

                    JACKSON
          I was just thinking of the last time
          somebody sat up all night taking care
          of me.

                    WOMAN
               (tentatively)
          Your wife? . . .

                    JACKSON
               (humorously)
          Nah. It was a skinny old guy with a
          mustache in the prison hospital. He
          was an orderly. Had red eyes and a
          dirty T shirt -- and I had a sun-stroke
          from working on the road gang. . . .
               (looks at her)
          I'm not married.

                    WOMAN
               (after a pause)
          What's it like?

                    JACKSON
          What's what like?

                    WOMAN
          You know -- prison.

                    JACKSON
               (shrugs)
          How are you going to explain it? . . .

                    WOMAN
          Is it lonesome?

                    JACKSON
               (pause)
          What happened to your old man?

                    WOMAN
          He run out. Eight months ago.
          I been stuck here.

                    JACKSON
          Yeah. It must get pretty lonesome
          for you.

                    WOMAN
          It's like that in jail, isn't it?

                    JACKSON
               (slowly)
          Yeah. It's like that.

                    WOMAN
               (intensely)
          Does it ever get real bad?

                    JACKSON
          Sure.

                    WOMAN
          No. I mean so bad you feel like you're all
          empty inside like a -- an empty pitcher --
          and you want to fill it up with tears. . . ?

                    JACKSON
          You got it wrong. You fill it up
          with tears, you're a goner.

                    WOMAN
               (desperately)
          What can you do?

                    JACKSON
               (pause)
          Dreams! Fill it up with dreams.

                    WOMAN
               (agitated)
          But you got to know about something

                    WOMAN (Cont'd)
before you can really dream about it. . . .

                    JACKSON
Why?

                    WOMAN (Cont'd)
I was born twenty miles from here.
I don't know anything else.

                    JACKSON
You don't have to <u>know</u>. All you have
to do is <u>want</u>. Then you make up the
pictures in your head.

                    WOMAN
What kind? What kind of pictures?

                    JACKSON
Different things. Different people --
different places. . . . Sometimes there's
music and lights and paper streamers --
and you're dancing in the streets. . . .

                    WOMAN
Like the Mardi-Gras?

                    JACKSON
Like the Mardi-Gras. . . . And sometimes
you're on a boat on a green ocean -- and
you're sailing somewhere . . . someplace
you've never even been before -- you don't
even know the name . . . with a white beach
and a hot sun and tall buildings made of
glass. . . . And there's always somebody
waiting for you. Somebody clean and warm.
And -- nice. . . .

There is a poignancy, a dream-like quality in his pained remembrance
of long deprivations.

                    WOMAN
Is she -- is she beautiful?

                    JACKSON
I . . . I better wake Cullen.

He starts to get up, but she places her hands on his chest.

                              WOMAN
                    No -- no! . . . Not yet. Don't go yet. . . .

He sinks back on the bed slowly. Her hands remain on his bare
chest. He looks down at her hands and then up into her eyes.
Her eyes don't waver from his.

                              WOMAN (Cont'd)
                            (softly)
                    Is she prettier than me? . . .

                              JACKSON
                    It's been so long . . . I get the dreams
                    mixed up with the real thing. . . .

                              WOMAN
                    It's real.

She takes her hands away.

                              JACKSON
                    Don't go away.

                              WOMAN
                    I'm not going away.

She pulls the pins restraining her long hair, bends over him and
shakes her head so that it cascades down, a fresh-smelling curtain
shielding their faces in intimate privacy. Jackson rolls his
face in the loose strands.

                              JACKSON
                            (murmurs)
                    Don't go away.

                              WOMAN
                    I'm right here . . . I'm right here. . . .

                                          * * * DISSOLVE:

INT. CABIN -- CLOSEUP -- JACKSON -- DAY

A shaft of sunlight falls on his sleeping face. He squints
involuntarily and sits up abruptly. He's obviously much refreshed.

                              [FADE IN
                              EXT.—VERY LONG SHOT—SUNRISE
                              over the hills]

He twists in his bed and takes in Cullen, who is still sleeping, and the kid. The woman quickly comes to his side and holds her finger to her lips.

> JACKSON
> (whispers)
> What time is it?

> WOMAN
> (whispers)
> Five.

> JACKSON
> I better wash.

He swings his feet off the edge of the bed.

> WOMAN
> Outside. Here's some soap.

As he takes the soap their hands touch.

> WOMAN (Cont'd)
> How do you feel?

> JACKSON
> (gently)
> Fine.

> WOMAN
> I'll get you a towel.

CAMERA PANS as he tiptoes out of door. He stops -- sees rifle. He picks it up and exits.

CLOSE SHOT -- WOMAN

She turns and gets a towel. Pauses thoughtfully and then goes to bureau and she sees something in the drawer -- takes it out. A man's shirt. She considers it for a moment and then takes it and the towel and exits, carefully closing the door after her.

EXT. CABIN -- NEAR WELL -- DAY

Jackson, stripped to the waist, is splashing water on himself exuberantly. Woman ENTERS SHOT and stares at his white skin and moving muscles of his shoulders. Jackson shakes his head and hands -- the drops of water glisten in the early morning sun.

                              JACKSON
                    Whooie!

He sees the woman. She holds out the towel to him. He pauses as
he sees the somber warmth in her eyes. He takes the towel and
rubs himself vigorously.

                              JACKSON (Cont'd)
                    That feels good.

                              WOMAN
                    I made you some breakfast.

She hands him the shirt.

                              JACKSON
                         (curiously)
                    Your old man's?

                              WOMAN
                    You're just about the same size.

He looks around the place and breathes deeply.

                              JACKSON
                    You're a good looking woman. He
                    must have been crazy to leave all this.

                              WOMAN
                    This place is no good. It needs a man.

                              JACKSON
                    He'll be back one of these days.

                              WOMAN
                    I won't be here if he does.

                              JACKSON
                    Where do you figure on going?

                              WOMAN
                         (challenges)
                    Where do you?

She moves close to him. Jackson stops short and stares at her.

                              JACKSON
                    I'm long gone, lady. Bound for Rio.

He turns to enter the house. She grabs his arm.

                      WOMAN
            Wait a minute.

                     JACKSON
            Ain't got time.

                      WOMAN
            Don't you like me?

                     JACKSON
               (suddenly serious)
            Yeah. I like you. I like you a lot.

                      WOMAN
            Take me with you.

                     JACKSON
            On my back? You going to ride
            that freight with me?

                      WOMAN
            We don't have to! I've got a car. . . .

Jackson's attitude changes. He's alerted.

                     JACKSON
               A car!

                      WOMAN
            In the shed. . . . In the back.
            But it's busted -- it won't start. . . .

Jackson is gone before she can finish.

FULL SHOT -- SHED

In the shed is a pre-war Plymouth that looks its age. Jackson
ENTERS SHOT -- he moves with nervous energy. His touch is sure.
He opens the hood of the car. The woman approaches.

                     JACKSON
               (from under the hood)
            Get in! . . . Get in, and try it!

                     WOMAN
            What?

                              JACKSON
                           (impatiently)
                    Try it. Try to start it.

She gets into the driver's seat excitedly, presses the starter.
No result. She looks stricken.

                         JACKSON (cont'd)
                 How long's it been sitting like this?

                              WOMAN
                    Three weeks.

                              JACKSON
                 The battery. Got a crank?

He doesn't wait for her to answer, but goes to the trunk of the car.
He throws things out of the trunk in a paroxism of impatience -- finds
the crank. He goes to the front of the car and cranks feverishly,
takes another turn. It kicks back, but doesn't turn over. He winces
with the pain, grasps the crank again and spins it feverishly . . .
the car starts. As Jackson comes around the car, the woman gets out
and stands face to face with him.

                              JACKSON
                        (grins triumphantly)
                 The distributor cap was loose.

                              WOMAN
                       (urgently and over the
                         sound of the car)
                    Let's go. Now.

                              JACKSON
                    Take it easy --

                              WOMAN
                 You said you didn't have time.

                              JACKSON
                    I'll wake up Cullen.

                              WOMAN
                    No!

Jackson stops.

                         WOMAN (cont'd)
                 We can't take him!

                    JACKSON
    Why not?

                    WOMAN
    They'll recognize you in a minute!

                    JACKSON
    They'll spot us anyhow.

                    WOMAN
    They'll be looking for <u>two</u> <u>men</u>.
    We'll travel as man and wife.

                    JACKSON
                (confused)
    What about Cullen?

                    WOMAN
    What's the difference if they're
    following one or two of you?
    You're not hurting his chances any!

                    JACKSON
                (it's going too fast for him)
    The kid -- what about the kid?

                    WOMAN
    We can drop him off at my brother's
    in Cumberland. Double back and go
    south.

                    JACKSON
    I got to think.

She puts her arms around his waist and clings to him.

                    WOMAN
                (passionately)
    Nothing to think about except you
    and me -- together. . . . Please! . . .
    . . . Please! . . .

He grabs her violently and kisses her.

MED. SHOT -- SHED -- DIFFERENT ANGLE -- CULLEN IN F.G.

He's grinning crookedly. CAMERA PANS with him as he walks toward
them. They break apart guiltily. Jackson reaches over and shuts
off the motor.

                    CULLEN
              (into the sudden silence)
         Nice shirt.
              (he looks at them curiously)

                    JACKSON
         We're going south.

Cullen looks at him and then at the woman. Understanding dawns.

                    CULLEN
         We?

                    JACKSON
         Me and her.

                    CULLEN
         In that?

                    JACKSON
         It runs.

                    CULLEN
         They'll be watching the roads.

                    JACKSON
              (nettled)
         They'll be watching where the dogs
         are going.

                    CULLEN
         That makes me the bait.

                    JACKSON
         You said it yourself -- as long as
         we're together we're a billboard
         that says come and get us.

The woman doesn't understand why Jackson appears to be justifying
his action to Cullen, but speaks to bolster Jackson's decision.

                    WOMAN
         He's too weak to travel on foot anyway.

                    JACKSON
              (defensively)
         You got the same chance alone --
         maybe better.

Cullen stares at them.

>   CULLEN
>   You got it all figured out.
>   There's nothing more to say.

>   WOMAN
>   I'll get you something to eat.

She hurries O.S. Cullen starts to cut toward the front of the
house, without looking at Jackson. Jackson follows him.

FULL SHOT AT WELL

Cullen goes to the well and starts to wash from the bucket.
Jackson approaches him.

>   JACKSON
>   Say, Cullen. . . .

Cullen turns and stares at him.

>   * * *

Cullen shakes the water off himself.

>   WOMAN
>   (to child)
>   Get washed.

The kid goes to the well. Cullen moves toward the house, CAMERA
PANNING. Jackson and the woman follow.

P. 467

>   [JACKSON (cont'd)
>   (awkwardly)
>   Take care, hear?

>   CULLEN
>   Sure. Yeah.

The woman comes out with a bag of sandwiches and a
mug of coffee. The child follows her out.

>   WOMAN
>   I got some sandwiches.

>   CULLEN
>   (curtly)
>   Thanks.]

                    CULLEN
          How far to the railroad from here?

                    WOMAN
          Twelve miles -- if you want to go
          through the hills. . . .

                    CULLEN
          What do you mean if I want to go
          through the hills. Is there another
          way?

The woman doesn't answer immediately.

CLOSE SHOT -- WOMAN

                    WOMAN
                 (casually)
          Yes. You can short-cut through
          the swamp down below here.

BACK TO SCENE:

                    CULLEN
          The swamp don't sound too good to me.

He takes the coffee and sandwiches from her.

                    WOMAN
          There's a path. Save you a couple
          of hours -- and make it harder for
          the dogs. You can follow it easy
          in the daylight.

                    CULLEN
          How do I find it?

                    WOMAN
                 (points)
          Take this path straight down to the
          swamp. About an hour's walk it stops.
          The water isn't over a foot deep. You'll
          see a big cypress on your left about a
          half a mile. It stands way out over
          everything. Head for it.

                    CULLEN
          Then what?

                              WOMAN
              Once you get there, you got nothing to
              worry about. Head west until you get
              to the railroad. You can't miss it.

Cullen hands her back the empty mug.

                              CULLEN
              Thanks for the grub.

He turns abruptly and starts down the hill.

                              JACKSON
                    Cullen!

                              CULLEN
                         (pauses)
                    Yeah?

                              JACKSON
                    So long.

                              CULLEN
              Sure. So long . . . Joker.

He turns and goes on. Jackson watches him until he disappears.

                              WOMAN
                    Come on.

He picks up the gun and follows her into the house.

INT. CABIN -- FULL SHOT

The woman is hastily packing. Jackson enters and goes over to
the fireplace. He puts the gun down and pauses as he sees
Cullen's bandana on the floor. He bends and picks it up -- studies
it. The woman comes over and takes the bandana out of his hand.

                              WOMAN
                    I'll burn that.
                         (hands him a bundle)
                    Here. Take this to the car.

He suddenly grabs her. His hunger for her arises out of his inner
turmoil, his sense of guilt, his need for reassurance.

                         WOMAN
             Not now. . . . Please. . . . The
             boy might come in.
                  (she pushes him away)
             Don't be mad, honey, there's plenty
             of time. . . .

The boy comes in and sees them. The woman breaks away quickly.

                         WOMAN
                  (to the boy)
             We're going away on a trip, honey.
             To Cumberland.

                         KID
             Now?

                         WOMAN
             Now. Go outside and get the clothes
             off the line like a good boy. Hurry.

                         KID
             Cumberland! . . . With him?

                         WOMAN
             Yes. You like him, don't you?

                         KID
             Sure. He's all right.

                         JACKSON
                  (to the woman)
             You better talk to him.

                         WOMAN
             On the way. He's a smart kid.
                  (to the boy)
             Go on.

The boy goes. Jackson picks up the chain.

                         JACKSON
                  (uneasily)
             What'll happen if they catch him?

                         WOMAN
             Don't worry -- they won't.

                    JACKSON
        What makes you so sure. . . ?

                    WOMAN
        Stop worrying -- He'll never tell
        anybody where you are -- He'll
        never be able to. . . .

                    JACKSON
        What're you talking about?

                    WOMAN
        He'll never get out of that swamp. . . .
        * * *

                    JACKSON
        Didn't you tell him right?

                    WOMAN
        There is no right way. It's all
        bogs and quick-sand.

                    JACKSON
                (shocked)
        Why'd you do it?

She stops her hectic preparations and looks at him.

                    WOMAN
        Suppose they caught him -- what
        if he told them?

                    JACKSON
                (furious)
        What if he told them what?

He slams the chains on the table.

        What could he tell them?

                    WOMAN
                (frightened and perplexed)
        So they wouldn't come looking. So
        we could have time. . . .

                        JACKSON
              Time for what!?

                        WOMAN
                   (confused; she's losing him)
              Time for us to get away -- get to a city-
              a big city -- big enough so they'll
              never find you. . . .

She reaches out to him. He turns away from her.

                        WOMAN (Cont'd)
                   (desperately)
              I got four hundred dollars insurance
              money saved up. . . . We could live good!
              Eat in restaurants every day -- go to
              shows. . . . You can start a new life --
              We can sell the farm later if we need
              more money. . . .

The kid comes in. He picks up the chains.

                        KID
              What should I do with these?

                        JACKSON
                   (bitterly)
              You're a smart kid, like your mother.
              You think of everything.

                        WOMAN
                   (quickly)
              Drop them down the well.

                        JACKSON
              Sure. Like you dropped Cullen into
              the swamp.

The woman turns on him.

                        WOMAN
              I did it for you!

                        JACKSON
              You did nothing for me!

                        WOMAN
              For us! . . . For the two of us!

Full stop.

> JACKSON
> You don't even know my name.

> WOMAN
> (confused by the
> sudden switch)
> I don't care what they call you.

> JACKSON
> (flatly)
> Johnny. My name's Johnny. Call
> me Johnny.

> WOMAN
> Johnny! . . . Johnny! . . . I love
> you, Johnny.

> JACKSON
> (harshly)
> You don't love me. You don't even
> know me.

> WOMAN
> Johnny! Please! . . . We don't have
> time. You said so yourself they were
> coming after you.

> JACKSON
> You don't know anything about me.

* * *

P. 473

> [WOMAN
> What are you getting so excited
> about that nigger for—?

He whirls on her furiously.

> JACKSON
> (barely controlled)
> Shut up!

She backs away from the look on his face.

> WOMAN
> What's the matter—what did I say
> wrong?

He kicks back the chair. She grabs his arm.]

> WOMAN
> Where are you going?

> JACKSON
> Get away from me.

She clings to him. The kid watches, wide-eyed.

> WOMAN
> Johnny . . . Johnny listen . . . don't
> leave me. . . . All my life I've been
> waiting to get away from here. From
> the mud gumbo -- from the loneliness.
> I'd see my husband two days a week.
> He didn't come back. I don't blame him.
> I don't want to stay here either. . . .
> I want to go with you. . . . I want get
> away, you can understand that, can't you?

> JACKSON
> Let go!

They struggle as Jackson tries to get loose from her. The kid runs
to get the gun. Jackson throws the woman down. The boy fires the
gun at Jackson. Jackson staggers but continues out of the door. The
boy goes to his sobbing mother who lies on the floor. . . .

* * * She knocks gun away.

> DISSOLVE:

EXT. LONG SHOT -- CABIN IN F.G.

Led by the yapping dogs, the posse emerges from the trees into the
clearing.

> DISSOLVE TO:

EXT. CABIN -- FULL SHOT -- SPRING HOUSE IN F.G. -- DAY

Woman and son are by front door. The yard is swarming with the men.
Solly has his dogs in leash. In f.g. a man comes out of spring house.
CAMERA MOVES in with him as he goes to Sheriff and the Captain, who
are talking to woman. Muller seems to have aged. His eyes are red-
rimmed and he's sunken into himself. The Captain by contrast is still
natty and clean-shaven. He carries the ball for the Sheriff and looks
to him from time to time for approval.

                        CAPTAIN
                    (crisply)
            Did they pick up any weapons --
            guns, knives?

                        WOMAN
            No.

                        CAPTAIN
            Well, didn't they say anything?
            About where they were heading?

                        WOMAN
            I didn't hear.

                        MAN
            They're not around here.
            Everything's clear.

                        CAPTAIN
                    (to kid)
            You must have heard something
            sonny. What'd they talk about?

Johnny looks up at his mother and keeps his mouth shut.

                        MULLER
            They ate, and then what did they do?
            They must have taken something with them.

                        WOMAN
            Nothing you could put them in jail for.

The Captain looks at the Sheriff seeking a commission of annoyance.
The Sheriff remains stony-faced. The Captain returns to the attack:

                        CAPTAIN
            You sound like you're not cooperating.

                        SOLLY (O.S.)
            I got the trail. . . !

                        MULLER
                    (dully)
            Let's not waste any more time here.
            Thanks, ma'am.

The Captain leaves the interrogation reluctantly. They follow

Solly down the hill. CAMERA MOVES IN on the bitter face of the
woman. She presses the child close to her side.

DISSOLVE:

EXT. SWAMP -- LONG SHOT -- JACKSON -- DAY

He's running recklessly through the swamp, careening off trees,
charging into lacerating bushes. He pauses frequently to catch
his breath and yell.

> JACKSON
> (voice splits with fatigue)
> Cullen! . . . Cullen! . . . Cullen! . . .

He plunges on again.

CLOSE SHOT -- JACKSON

He pauses again. The blood is soaking through his shirt. He
staggers and almost falls.

> JACKSON
> Culle-e-n! . . .
> (listens -- to himself
> raggedly)
> Damn you, Cullen! . . .

CAMERA PANS with him as he runs, half-falling, headlong down the path.

CLOSE SHOT -- CULLEN -- DIFFERENT PART OF THE SWAMP.

Cullen is hidden behind foliage, listening apprehensively.

> JACKSON'S VOICE (O.S.)
> (from middle distance)
> Cullen! . . . Cullen! . . .
> (pause -- almost a scream)
> Cullen! . . .

Cullen breaks off a stick to defend himself. He wipes the perspiration
from his eyes. He doesn't know what to do -- hesitates to expose
himself. The SOUNDS of Jackson's approach come closer.

FULL SHOT -- JACKSON -- staggering through swamp. He trips and falls, picks himself up and weaves. * * *

CLOSE SHOT -- CULLEN -- hiding. The perspiration drips off his face.
CAMERA PANS to Jackson who blunders weakly INTO SHOT.

>   JACKSON
>   Damn you, Cullen -- where are you?

Cullen steps out directly in front of Jackson, INTO SHOT.

>   CULLEN
>   What do you want?

>   JACKSON
>   (with relief)
>   Cullen! . . . Where you been hiding,
>   Cullen? . . . I been running.

He sinks to the ground.

>   CULLEN
>   You alone?
>   (Jackson nods)
>   They catch up?
>   (Jackson shakes his head)
>   How come you here? What do you
>   want with me?

>   JACKSON
>   She told you wrong. You're going
>   the wrong way.

>   CULLEN
>   Why should she do that?

>   JACKSON
>   In case you squeal if you get caught.

>   CULLEN
>   What's the matter with your arm?

>   JACKSON
>   The kid winged me. * * *

Cullen bends and exposes wound. Looks at it critically.

P. 477   [blundering in water waist deep]

                        CULLEN
              * * * If we hit high ground, we
              can make good time.

                        JACKSON
              I can't make it.

                        * * *

Cullen tears off piece of shirt and binds the wound.

                        CULLEN
              Sure.

Cullen helps Jackson to his feet. They cut across swamp to
higher ground, CAMERA PANNING.

                                            CUT TO:

EXT. SAVANNAH -- DAY -- FULL SHOT

The posse led by dogs as they slog through swamp terrain.

DIFFERENT ANGLE -- the posse comes to a halt while Solly runs the
hounds around the edge of the swamp. Muller and the Captain in f.g.
The dogs bay.

CLOSE SHOT -- SOLLY AND BLOODHOUNDS. The dogs have picked up the trail.

                        SOLLY (calls)
              Here's where they cut off!

TWO SHOT -- MULLER AND CAPTAIN * * * RADIO

                        CAPTAIN
                   (to Muller over the din
                    of the dogs)
              From the sound of them, it's a fresh
              trail, Max.

P. 478   [Go on—cut across to high ground—you
                haven't got much time.
                        CULLEN
                Go to hell.]
                        [JACKSON
                No sense both of us getting caught. Get
                out of here. Just about make it as it is.]

                    CAPTAIN (Cont'd)
                  (shouts)
         Solly -- bring up the airedales!

                    SOLLY
                  (shouts)
         Wilson! . . .

The Sheriff turns to look at the airedales that Wilson is bringing up.

POV SHOT -- DOGS -- The threat is in their silent submissiveness as
Wilson brings them up.

GROUP SHOT -- FEATURING EDITOR AND SHERIFF -- The Editor looks from
the dogs to the Sheriff. The Sheriff feels the other one's eyes on
him. It takes an effort for him to meet the Editor's. His eyes
travel slowly back to the killer dogs.

POV SHOT -- (CLOSER) -- DOGS -- Wilson holds them on a short leash.

BACK TO GROUP SHOT -- The Sheriff tears his eyes away from the
dogs with an effort. He's like a man emerging from a dream.

                    MULLER
         Wait a minute.

                    CAPTAIN
         What's the matter?

                    MULLER
         Those dogs. . . .

                    CAPTAIN
         What about the dogs?

                    MULLER
         No dogs.

                    CAPTAIN
                  (exasperated)
         Let's not go over that again, Max. ▾. . .

                    MULLER
         No dogs!

There is a pause. The Captain's face hardens.

CAPTAIN

We passed the County line early this
morning, Max. I didn't want to have
to bring it up. It's out of your
jurisdiction.

The Captain motions Wilson up who is holding the airedales. Solly
approaches to unmuzzle them.

MULLER
(sharply to Solly)
Wait a minute, Solly!

Solly pauses.

CAPTAIN
(impatiently)
We're wasting time, Max.

MULLER
(angrily)
We're supposed to find them --
not execute them!

CAPTAIN

They're dangerous criminals, and
they escaped. They cost the state
enough money already.

SOLLY

I'm certainly not going to turn my
trackers loose without the other dogs. . . .

CAPTAIN

When I want your opinion, Solly,
I'll ask for it. Max, we've been
on this chase for four days and
we're less than ten miles from the
state border. If they can get across
before the dogs bring them down,
somebody else will have to do the job
for us. ⋅ What are you trying to do,
make us look like a bunch of fools?

The Sheriff smiles grimly and exchanges a look with the Editor.
It's an echo of something he'd said himself.

                    SHERIFF
                  (quietly)
          No killer dogs, Frank.

                    CAPTAIN
                  (blows)
          It's standard procedure, Max!
          Standard Procedure! I don't care
          whether they live or die. They
          knew what they were getting into
          when they ran away. I'm giving the
          orders. Go ahead, Solly.

CLOSE SHOT -- SOLLY AND DOGS

Solly has the muzzles off the dogs. Unmuzzled, the dogs sense
the promise of action. The slaver in their excitement. He bends
to unleash them.

CLOSE SHOT -- MULLER

looking at the dogs. A look of disgust twists his face. He
deliberately raises his gun and aims it at the dogs.

                    MULLER
          If you make one move, Solly, I'm
          going to shoot them.

FULL SHOT -- CAPTAIN AND MULLER

                    CAPTAIN
          For God's sake, Max!

                    MULLER
                  (tightly)
          Are you going to listen to me?

                    CAPTAIN
                  (after a pause,
                   exasperated)
          Hold everything, Solly.

                    MULLER
          I'll go on ahead. Give me a
          couple of bloodhounds. If
          anything happens, you can let
          the other dogs loose.

                    CAPTAIN
                  (brusquely)
              Too much of a risk.

                    * * *

EXT. ROUGH COUNTRY -- CLOSE TWO SHOT -- TRUCKING WITH CULLEN
AND JACKSON -- DAY -- SWAMP

Cullen half carries Jackson. They're both close to exhaustion.

                    JACKSON
              Can't make it . . . can't make it. . . .

                    CULLEN
              Sure we can.

                    JACKSON
              How much further?

                    CULLEN
              Pretty soon now. . . .

                    JACKSON
              Why did she do like that?

P. 482   [MULLER
                    (still holding gun)
              We look at these things different, Frank.
                    (pause)
              Well?

                    CAPTAIN
                    (indecisively)
              They're not like human beings, I keep
              telling you! They're like animals.

                    SOLLY
                    (querulously)
              What am I supposed to do?

                    CAPTAIN
              I don't like it.

                    MULLER
              I didn't ask you to like it.

                    CAPTAIN
                    (finally)
              I'll hold off until we spot them.
              That's all I promise.]

                        CULLEN
            She was just trying to help you. . . .

                        JACKSON
            She sure helped.

                        CULLEN
            Can't blame a body for what they
            don't know.

                        JACKSON
            I blame her.

They pause for breath. The distant sound of locomotive whistles
is HEARD.

LONG SHOT -- TRAIN

as it climbs up slope.

CLOSE TWO SHOT * * * COME_OUT_OF_BRUSH_TO_TRESTLE_

They both look at each other and start to run.

MED. SHOT TRAIN

Picking up speed.

CLOSE TRUCKING TWO SHOT

The men are running headlong.

MED. SHOT -- MEN RUNNING

Cullen trips and falls. Jackson grabs his arm and they continue.

CLOSE TRAVELING SHOT -- TRAIN

Including cab and engine.

MED. CLOSE PANNING SHOT -- MEN

Running. Jackson is lagging behind.

CLOSE -- (LOW ANGLE) -- SHOT -- TRAIN

As it roars past.

MED. SHOT -- HIGH ANGLE

As the men emerge on the right-of-way. The train is almost on
them. They still have to scramble up a high embankment. As they
start up, the engine comes abreast and then passes them.

MED. CLOSE SHOT

SHOOTING DOWN on men as they scramble up embankment. Cullen
has to reach down and haul Jackson up.

CLOSE TWO SHOT -- REVERSE ANGLE

The cars are clattering past. Cullen urges Jackson to follow him.

CLOSE FOLLOW SHOT -- TOWARD FRONT OF TRAIN

The two men running. Cullen glances back.

CLOSE FOLLOW SHOT -- SHOOTING TOWARD REAR OF TRAIN

Men running. The caboose at the end of the train is overtaking
them. There is a look of desperation on Cullen's face. The train
is going too fast for them. Jackson can't make it. He leans out,
reaches back and catches Jackson's outstretched hand. Jackson is
running so fast he's half falling forward. Cullen makes a jump
for the rungs of a handhold -- clings by one hand. He glances back.

CLOSEUP -- CULLEN

His face is twisted with the strain. His hand is slowly losing
its grip.

MED. SHOT -- TRAIN

The men being swept along with it. Jackson loses his footing and
is being dragged.

CLOSE SHOT -- CULLEN

He loses his grip.

MED. SHOT

Both men shoot away from the train; they hurtle down the embankment.

CAMERA HOLDS on retreating train -- a profound silence falls.

CLOSE HIGH ANGLE SHOT -- CULLEN

He's cut and bruised. He lifts himself to his elbow painfully
and looks around. He crawls to Jackson who lies sprawled, not far
from him, CAMERA PANNING. Jackson is barely conscious.

>   CULLEN
>   How you doing, Joker?

>   JACKSON
>   (whispers)
>   Okay.

>   CULLEN
>   Hurt bad?

>   JACKSON
>   I feel * * * gre_at_. . . .

>   CULLEN
>   Sure you do. . . .

Cullen drags him over into the shade.

>   JACKSON
>   You sure make somebody a fine
>   old lady some day.

>   CULLEN
>   Ain't it the truth?

SOUND of dogs in the distance. Jackson looks up at Cullen.

>   * * *

>   CULLEN
>   Rest easy. . . .

>   JACKSON
>   Cullen. . . .

>   CULLEN
>   Yeah. . . .

P. 485   [fine]

>   [JACKSON
>   Them the dogs?]

                          JACKSON
          We gave them a hell of a run for it. . . .
          * * * (pause)

                          CULLEN
                    (softly)
          * * * We sure did.

A small sound of pain escapes Jackson. Cullen shifts over,
takes Jackson's head on his lap. . . .

                          * * *

Pause. The sound of the dogs grows louder.

                          JACKSON
          Cullen. . . .

                          CULLEN
          Yeah. . . .

                          JACKSON
                    (weakly)
          Remember that song you were singing
          in the truck?

                          CULLEN
          * * * Yeah. . . .

                          JACKSON
          That sure seems a long time ago.
                    (laughs weakly)
          Charlie Potatoes. I'm mashed potatoes
          now.

P. 486   [damn near made it.]

                [We made it, alright, John. We made it.]

                          [CULLEN
                Here. . . . That better?]

                [The one about long gone?]

                          [JACKSON
                Go on—sing it.

                          CULLEN
                Sure.]

                        CULLEN
                You doing all right.
                        * * *
                    (starts to sing)
                Long gone, ain't he lucky. . . .

Jackson groans. Cullen puts his arm around the white man's
shoulders without interrupting his singing.

After a moment, when the sound of the dogs are close, Cullen looks
up without stopping his song. . . .

MED. SHOT -- REVERSE ANGLE -- CULLEN'S POV

The Sheriff -- alone -- approaches. His footsteps slow and stop.
Even the dogs are quieted.

FULL SHOT -- HIGH ANGLE

The troopers, the deputies, the dogs in leash -- the Sheriff, alone
between his men and the prisoners. . . .

Cullen cradles the white man in his arms -- He continues to sing.

                        CULLEN
                    (sings)
                . . . Long gone, what I mean,
                Long gone Sam on the Bowling Green --
                I mean he's long gone . . .

                                        FADE OUT:

Appendix

Something of the complexity of modern filmmaking, of the hard and carefully coordinated labor that goes into any production, is suggested by the following two documents.

The first is the initial and closing pages of the final shooting schedule for *The Best Man* (1963). The usual shooting schedule, unless the production is very elaborate, is based on thirty working days. Note that the film is not shot in order of the sequence of scenes. The large number of extras and minor cast numbers needed and the specific days when a location is available and accessible to film equipment are a few factors that help to determine the production sequence as actually drawn up. The problem of the production manager is to arrange the shooting in such a way as to keep costs down efficiently, yet at the same time to permit the director, the principals, and the crew to create the best possible work.

The second item supplements the first. It is a sample from the daily call sheets for Samuel Goldwyn, Jr.'s production of *The Young Lovers* (1963), a low-budget picture with a small cast and limited crew. Note that for the ten numbered scenes only two actors, Peter Fonda and Sharon Hugueny, are involved and only two exterior settings, both on location at the U.C.L.A. campus, which is in Westwood, not far from Hollywood. Yet, including stand-ins, a technical crew of 45 is required, together with 15 vehicles, and a catered lunch for 77. In case of inclement weather, or some other necessity, a cover set—"Schwartz' Classroom"—is indicated. Note that this same studio interior is listed on the advance schedule as the set for the next two working days, September 9 and 10; also given for those two days are the scenes to be shot and their order.

PROD. NO. ___914-83___ TITLE ___THE BEST MAN(MILLAR/TURMAN PROD)___

DIRECTOR ___F SCHAFFNER___ PRODUCER ___MILLAR/TURMAN___ ART DIR. ___L WHEELER___

PROD BREAKDOWN ASST. ___D.MODER___ SCRIPT DATED ___8-30-63___

DAYS ___30 PLUS___ START DATE___9-16-63___ FINISH DATE ___10-25-63___ TYPED ___9-3-63___
9 DAYS REHEARSAL

FINAL   SHOOTING SCHEDULE

DATE	SET	PAGES	SEQ	SC'NS	CAST
1st DAY 9-16	STAGE #8 INT. RUSSELL SUITE(D) SCS: 11,12 Meet Alice-Jensen enters. Hockstader appears	5			Russell #1,Alice #7,Jensen #2 Hockstader #3
	TOTAL PAGES	5			
2nd DAY 9-17	LOCATION: AMBASSADOR HOTEL INT. CANTWELL HQTRS(D) SC: 16 Cantwell on TV. He & Don exit. Pickup TV for Sc 15A	3			Cantwell #8, Announcer,Don Cantwell #9, bit photographer, Spastic,announcer #2, 60 extras (attendants,re-porters,photog-raphers, men, women, tv crew, guards, 10 Cantwell girls) tv cameras,news-reel camera, tv boom,big sign "Go with Joe" Books,coffee
	INT. KITCHEN(D) SC: 17 Cantwell & Don meet cleaning woman	1 2/8			Cantwell #8,Don #9,cleaning wo-man bit,3 police etc,4 Russell girls,5 kitchen help

PROD. NO. ___914-83___ TITLE ___THE BEST MAN___

DATE	SET	PAGES	SEQ	SC'NS	CAST
2nd DAY CONT'D	INT. HOTEL LOBBY(D) SC: 43 After lunch 2 ladies thru lobby to elevator	1			Mrs. Gamadge #5, Mabel #10, Senator bit,boys(men 2)bits,5ad libs, extras from int (men,women, elev operator, desk clerk,bell hops) posters, pictures
	TOTAL PAGES	5 2/8			
3rd DAY 9-18	LOCATION: AMBASSADOR HOTEL INT. BAROQUE ROOM(D) SC: 42 Ladies luncheon.Alice & Mabel do best to knife each other	6 2/8			Alice #7,Mabel #10,Mrs.Gamadge #5,Janet #6,Mrs. Claypoole bit #19, Reporters #1 & #3(35),Mrs. Anderson #77, Mrs.Merwin #20, 32 extras(4 busboys,photographers,20 women,8 men)drinks
	TOTAL PAGES	6 2/8			
4th & 5th DAYS 9-19 & 9-20	LOCATION: AMBASSADOR HOTEL INT. BALLROOM(N) SCS: 22,23,24,25,26,27,28,28A 28B,29,29A,29B,29C,29D,30,30A 31,31A Dinner party.Hockstader introduces candidates & wives. Celebrity sings.	9 1/8			Russel #1,Jensen #2,Hockstader #3,Tom #4,Mrs. Gamadge #5,Alice #7,Cantwell #8, Don #9,Mabel #10 Claypoole #11, John Merwin #12 Celebrity #1 & #2,Oscar Anderson #13,Mrs.Claypool #19,Mrs.Merwin #20,Chairman #17 Reporter #51, waiter bit, wives at table dignitaries,men,

PROD. NO. __914-83__ TITLE __THE BEST MAN__

DATE	SET	PAGES	SEQ	SC'NS	CAST
4th & 5th DAYS CONT'D					women, 3 waiters orchestra,news-men,photograph-ers
	TOTAL PAGES	9 1/8			
6th & 7th DAYS 9-23 & 9-24	STAGE #8 INT. RUSSELL SUITE(D) SCS: 13,14 Hockstader talks politics with Bill & tells him of his cancer condition. Mrs. Gamadge enters, passes advice to Alice. Bill exits.	9 4/8			Russell #1,Mrs. Russell #7, Hockstader sc 12 #3,Jensen,#2 Mrs. Gamadge sc 14 #5,Janet reporters in hall,man Luggage clothes,bar set-up
	TOTAL PAGES	9 4/8			
8th & 9th DAYS 9-25 & 9-26	STAGE #8 INT. RUSSELL SUITE(D) SCS: 44,44A Russell bathes as Claypoole pledges support. Hockstader enters. Jensen brings in Bascomb who tells about Cantwell's past in army.	8			Russell #1, Claypoole #11, Jensen #2, Hockstader #3, Bascomb #15,aide (sb)1 valet,1 room service
	INT. CANTWELL HOME(FOR TV SET SC) SC: 18C Mother Cantwell interviewed.	2/8			Interviewer,Mrs. Cantwell, T.V. announcer
	INT. SENATE RM(D)(FOR TV SET SC) SC: 18B Cantwell questions Mafia man	4/8			Cantwell,Mafia man,voice over, Extras?
	TOTAL PAGES	8 6/8			
10th DAY 9-27	STAGE #8 INT. RUSSELL SUITE SC: 47 Bascomb finishes story. Jensen says he has arranged meeting.	6			Russell #1, Hockstader #3, Jensen #2, Bascomb #15, Alice #7

PROD. NO. **914-83** TITLE **THE BEST MAN**

DATE	SET	PAGES	SEQ	SC'NS	CAST
10th DAY CONT'D	As Russell leaves Hockstader has attack,asks for doctor				
	TOTAL PAGES	6			
11th DAY 9-30	LOCATION: BASEMENT BOMB SHELTER INT. BOMB SHELTER(D) SC: 51 Cantwell reads document,greets Marcus & explains his innocence. Marcus rushes out door into newsmen	5 5/8			Russell #1, Cantwell #8, Bascomb #15, 6 newsmen & photographers
	TOTAL PAGES	5 5/8			
12th DAY 10-1	LOCATION: BASEMENT BOMB SHELTER INT. CORRIDOR OUTSIDE BOMB SC: 52 SHELTER(D) Cantwell poses w/Marcus for photographers	7/8			Cantwell #8,Don #9,Bascomb #15 Jensen #2,photographer bit, reporter bit,6 reporters & newsmen
27th DAY 10-22	INT. LIMO(PROCESS)(D) SC: 64 Russell 7 Alice riding to arena	1 4/8			Russell #1,Alice #7,driver?, mockup limo,process plates to cover
	INT. LINEN CLOSET(D) sc; 49 Russell & Cantwell meet. Big discussion as Cantwell asks Russell to withdraw from race. 2 exit to hall	4 4/8			Russell #1, Jensen #2, Cantwell #8,Don #9
	TOTAL PAGES	6 6/8			
28th DAY 10-23	LOCATION: AMBASSADOR HOTEL INT. PALM COURT(D) SCS: 1,2 Russell talks to press	5 1/8			Russell #1, Jensen #2, reporters #1,#2, #3,#4,#5,fan,35 extras(reporters men,women,1

PROD. NO. _914-83_ TITLE _____ THE BEST MAN

DATE	SET	PAGES	SEQ	SC'NS	CAST
28th DAY CONT'D					bartender,1 guard,2 waiters) no tv camera
	EXT. PALM COURT(D) SC: 3 Russell tries to call wife on phone. No luck	6/8			Russell #1, Jensen #2,5 reporters,fan, from sc 1, reporters,man Indian,men, women,elderly lady(SB)6yr old boy(SB)3 Russell girl w.worker, banners,bass drum,mixed buttons
	TOTAL PAGES	5 7/8			
29th DAY 10-24	LOCATION: AMBASSADOR HOTEL EXT. POOL AREA(D) SCS: 4,5,6,7 Two at pool meet Mrs. Gamadge. They talk, she exits	4 5/8			Russell #1, Jensen #2,Mrs. Gamadge #5,girl bit sc 7,tv interviewer sc 7 100 extras (husky woman golfer(SB)men bathers,women bathers,men, women,waiters, tv crew, photogs newsmen,5 Cantwell girls) tv camera transistor radios, private cameras
	INT. HOTEL LOBBY(D) SC: 8 Continuation of pool seq 2 men to elevator	6/8			Mrs. Gamadge, Russell,Jensen, men,women,2 bellhops,from 100 in scs 4-7
	TOTAL PAGES	5 3/8			

PROD. NO. 914-83   TITLE   THE BEST MAN

DATE	SET	PAGES	SEQ	SC'NS	CAST
30th DAY	LOCATION: AMBASSADOR HOTEL <u>EXT.</u> AMBASSADOR(D) SC: 40 Jensen entering,meets Lazarus	6/8			Jensen,Lazarus, 45 extras(15 picket line (some colored)5 Cantwell girls, man on stilts,2 attendants,men, women,photogs, newsmen,doorman) cars,Jensen's car,Lazarus car
	EXT. AMBASSADOR HELIPORT(D) SC: 58A Cantwell & Aide board copter	1/8			Cantwell #8, Aide bit,men, women,pilot, copter
	EXT. AMBASSADOR SWIM POOL(N) SC: 35 Hockstader asks Claypoole to be VP. Supporter talks to him	7/8			Hockstader #3, Tom #4,Claypoole #11,supporter bit,40 extras (men,women, servers,see colored help)
	TOTAL PAGES	1 6/8			
POST LAST PRODUCTION	INT. COPTER(D) SC: 58B Cantwell on walkie-talkie	3/8			Cantwell,Aide, Pilot,shoot in flight,copter
	TOTAL SCRIPT PAGES	134 7/8			

****

TIGERTAIL PROD., INC.

4th day of shooting   CALL SHEET   Prod. No. 5000

PICTURE: "THE YOUNG LOVERS"   DIRECTOR: SAMUEL GOLDWYN, JR.

SHOOTING CALL: 8:00 A.M.   DATE: FRIDAY, SEPT.6, 1963

SET AND SCENE NO.

     EXT. CAMPUS PARKING ENT. (D) U.C.L.A.
         Scs. 189, 190

     EXT. SMALL PARKING LOT (D) U.C.L.A.
         Scs. 214, 215, 216, 217, 218, 219, 220, 221

                 COVER SET: INT. SCHWARTZ' CLASSROOM

- -

CAST & BITS	CHARACTER & WARDROBE	HAIRDRESSING	MAKEUP	ON SET
PETER FONDA	EDDIE		7:15	8:00
SHARON HUGUENY	PAM	6:00		8:00

STANDINS: THRU GATE

T. CONNERS   MR. FONDA w/car   7:00
1 WOMAN   MISS HUGUENY w/car 7:00

- -

                 ADVANCE SCHEDULE

MON. 9/9   INT. SCHWARTZ' CLASSROOM (D) Scs. 68, 69, 70, 71,
&   72, 73, 74, 75, 76,
TUES.   77, 78, 79, 80.   STAGE 4

           INT. SCHWARTZ' CLASSROOM (D) Scs. 262, 263, 264,
                                   265, 266, 267, 268,
                                   269, 270, 271, 272,
                                   273.   STAGE 4

           INT. SCHWARTZ' CLASSROOM (D) Scs. 103, 104, 105
                                   188C   STAGE 4

           INT. CLASSROOM   Sc. 188D   STAGE 4

CAMERA	TIME:		PROPERTY	TIME:
1 Camera	6:30		1 Property Master	6:30
1 Cameraman	6:42		2 Asst Prop Man	6:30
1 Operator	6:42		Tarragoo's car	6:30
2 Assistants	6:30		Eddie's Motorcycle	6:30
			Pam's Car	7:00

TECHNICAL

			RESTAURANT	
1 Key & 2nd Grip	6:30			
4 Co Grips	6:30		77 Lunches	11:30
1 Greensman	6:30		1 Gals Coffee Box donuts	7:00
1 Laborer	6:30			

ELECTRICAL

HOSPITAL

			1 1st Aid Man	6:30
1 Gaffer & Best Boy	6:30			
8 Lamp Opers	6:30		TRANSPORTATION	
1 Generator	6:30			
1 Gen Operator	6:30		1 Standby Car	6:42
1 Booster Lights	6:30		1 Car	7:00
			1 Car	7:30
WARDROBE			1 Bus (41)	6:30

1 Ward Man	6:30		1 Grip Trk	ON LOC
1 Ward Girl	6:30		1 Prop Trk	ON LOC
			1 Ward Trk	ON LOC
MAKEUP			1 Sound Jeep	ON LOC
			1 Elec Trk	ON LOC
1 Makeup Man	6:00		1 Generator Trk	ON LOC
1 Hairstylist	6:00		P.U. trk	ON LOC

SOUND			1 LU Driver	6:30
1 Mixer	6:42			
1 Recorder	6:30			
1 Mikeman	6:30			
1 Cableman	6:30			

STILL

1 Still Man	7:00

Glossary

Above the line expenses (cost)   cost of staff, talent, and story in preparation and production of a motion picture.

Absolute film (also **abstract film**)   a nonrepresentative film whose parts are composed of moving visual patterns.

Abstract music   musical accompaniment to a scene or scenes which aims at more than **crutch music;** based upon correspondence or juxtaposition with the structure and rhythm of the images on the screen.

Abstract set   a nonrepresentational setting without a definite period or locale.

Academy players directory (casting bible)   several volumes listing professional actors available for American film productions; includes photographs.

Accelerated motion (also **fast motion** and **speedup motion**)   by slowing down the camera mechanism during shooting, the resulting projection of action at standard rate (24 frames per second) will appear to be taking place at greater speed; often used for farce or comic effect, also to emphasize mechanistic order; opposite of **slow motion.**

Accent light   a small spotlight focused on a specific detail of a subject; usually placed to one side of the subject or used as backlighting.

Action   anything recorded by the camera in a shot; the command, "Action!" beginning a shot, may be given only by the director.

Action director (also **second unit director**)   a supplementary director for action scenes and scenes without dialogue which do not require the presence of the director.

Action still   a still photograph taken of a scene as it appears in the film, distinguished from other types of still photographs taken during production, such as **art stills, production stills, publicity stills.** See also **Unit still photographer.**

Ad lib   extemporaneous dialogue and action not in a prepared script; or working without a script.

Adapt   to translate and to change a story, novel, play, or other property for the purpose of making a film.

Aerial shot   photograph taken from helicopter, airplane, balloon.

Against the grain (opposite of **on the nose**)   any artistic technique in any aspect of the filmmaking process in which one element is used unconventionally, in contrast to audience experience and expectation, to create a sense of conflict, "mixed feelings," and to comment upon the convention violated.

Allusion   as in literature, an explicit or implicit referenee to another film or films achieved by dialogue, impersonation, music, visual style of shots.

Angle   see **Camera angle.**

Animation   process by which drawings or objects are photographed so that when shown there will be the illusion of movement.

Answer print (also **first-trial print**)   first combined print received from the laboratory and approved as representing the standard for all subsequent prints.

Arc (also **brute**)   a large, high-powered carbon light used to illuminate a set for filming.

Arrange   to adapt the music created by the *composer* for various voices and instruments.

Art director   designs and supervises all sets, exterior and interior, in studio and on location. See also **Production designer.**

Art film   used to describe any film, foreign or domestic, ostensibly not intended for large-scale commercial release and distribution.

Art house (or **theater**)   a theater specializing in the presentation of art films.

Art still   a photograph made of a film actor, not taken from the context of actual filming.

Assemble   to begin the editing process by collecting separate shots and arranging them in order.

Assistant cameraman   member of camera crew, charged with loading the camera with raw stock and with focusing of lenses.

Assistant director   doubles as an assistant to the director and to the unit production manager; generally serves as foreman of the set; specifically charged with handling all bit players and extras, with presence of all players for their shots, notification of all players of their calls, also transportation and set discipline.

Associate producer   an immediate assistant to the producer; when the producer is involved in the making of more than one film, he may be charged with the making of one film.

Atmosphere   details of setting, costumes, extras, properties which establish verisimilitude; or aspects of lighting, photography, direction, editing which contribute to convey an emotional mood.

Attitude   the use of **objective** and **subjective** shots by the filmmaker to reveal a meaning or to make a point or statement.

Audience participation shots   any shots in a film in which actors seem to speak to, act, and react to the theater audience or the camera *as camera;* or any scenes or shots in which the audience is explicitly introduced to the process of making the film being seen.

Auteur (French for author)   the filmmaker, in particular, the director, viewed as analogous to the author of a book in the sense that he has authority and control over the creation of the film and responsibility for the finished work, and each work becomes part of his canon; assumes that the director is a responsible artist with a recognizable cinematic manner and style and an artist's concern for specific subjects and areas of experience.

Avant garde   used loosely to describe any films in which form or content or both are experimental.

Back lighting   light directed into the subject and towards the camera from a point behind the subject.

Back projection (also **rear projection**)   projection of a film of an action or setting through a transparent screen, in front of which another action or scene may be filmed. See also **Process shot.**

Background (**bg**)   that portion of the setting or frame farthest, in real or apparent distance, from the camera.

Background light   light placed on the background to create a visual separation of the subject of a shot from the background.

Background music   music composed and arranged to accompany particular action or dialogue in a film; sometimes prerecorded.

Background players (**crowd**)   see **Extra.**

Backing   a flat background, which can be a photograph or painting, against which actors are filmed.

Backup schedule   an alternate to the scenes to be shot in regular shooting schedule in the event that, for any reason, the regular schedule cannot be followed.

Balance   when the process of **dubbing** has been completed and the film is a single unit with a single sound track, the editor balances it, equalizing, insofar as possible, the footage in each reel, prior to any preview showing.

Barndoor   a black flap used to block light from shining into the camera lens.

Below the line expenses (**cost**)   all production expenses involved in filmmaking, including technical facilities, staging and studio costs.

Big closeup   see **Closeup.**

Bit (**player**)   an actor with a small speaking part.

Bits (of business)   miscellaneous movements, actions, gestures created by the director and actors for dramatic purposes and for characterization.

Blocking (also to **block in**)   rehearsal preparation by the director, assistants, actors, and crew in arranging the composition of a scene, with special emphasis on positions, movements, and gesture of the actors; may involve the use of diagrams or sketches or marking the set with chalk lines or tape; also the initial arrangement of lights. See also **Rough in.**

Blowup   an enlargement of a photograph or a particular part of a photograph, or an enlargement of any printed material.

Body makeup woman   a woman charged with all makeup used for female members of the cast, except those specifically reserved for the makeup artist under union regulations.

Bold   a take which has not been printed, has been put aside, and held in reserve for possible use.

Boom   a mobile suspended microphone, held near actors but out of camera range, to record dialogue. See also **Camera boom.**

Breakdown   an estimated budget for the making of a film, derived from analysis of the script, and subdivided according to estimates of necessary shooting time required, cast and crew, technical resources, and materials.

Bridge music   music designed to accompany and support visual transitions in the film.

Bridging shot   any shot inserted during editing to cover a break in continuity. See also **Insert.**

Broad (also **broadside**)   a reflector light containing two powerful bulbs, creating an even flood covering an angle of roughly sixty degrees.

Brute   see **Arc.**

Budget   the overall estimated and allocated expense for the making of a film, or for any particular aspect of the process; also a daily sheet, issued to cast and crew, indicating which scenes are to be shot on the following day and which people will be required. See also **Call sheet.**

Burnt up   scenes in which set or actors are overlighted.

Busy   anything in action or setting which distracts from the intended focus of interest.

Butterfly lighting   light is placed in front of the subject and shadow reduced to a delicate minimum; used chiefly in closeups, for glamor.

Call sheet   a mimeographed list, prepared by the assistant director and the unit production manager, indicating the requirements and calls for the next day's shooting; includes cast, crew, and equipment required.

Calls   estimated time for various members of cast and crew to report for work.

Cameo part   a bit part in a picture for which a star is cast.

Camera motion picture camera designed to take photographic images on cinematographic film; conventionally a 35 MM camera for commercial filming, but 16 MM cameras, and, occasionally, 8 MM cameras, are also used; capable of using a wide variety of lenses.

Camera angle the position or standpoint of the camera in terms of the scene and the subject being filmed; unless otherwise specified, is usually assumed to be eye level. See also **High angle shot** and **Low angle shot.**

Camera boom (also **crane**) a mobile crane with a platform for the camera which can be used for either fixed or moving shots, and allows for movement horizontally and vertically, backward and forward.

Camera operator second man of the camera crew; operates the camera physically, responsible for frame and focus.

Cameraman (also **cinematographer** and **director of photography**) senior member of the camera crew; supervises all operations of the camera and the lighting of sets and actors; with director creates the composition of the shots.

Cant (**frame** or **shot**; also **oblique angle, slant frame**) a shot made with the camera slightly tilted, to create a special effect or to exaggerate normal angles.

Cast the actors participating in a film, including **stars, featured players, bit players,** and **extras.**

Casting director responsible for keeping records of actors suitable for parts and available for work on a film.

Cheat shot a shot in which a portion of a subject or part of an action is excluded from view to create an illusion or suggest a special effect.

Cinéaste (French for filmmaker) the ordering mind of the director.

Cinema of ideas as in theater of ideas, filmmaking for ideological or social purpose, or films which probe and question intellectual concepts in the context of fiction as well as in the documentary.

Cinéma vérité (also **direct cinema**) deriving from technique of newsreels and documentary filming; deliberate imitation of style and manner of a happening; a conscious attempt to represent an unplanned, accidental filming.

Cinematography the art of recording motion photographically and reproducing it for audiences.

Cinemobile Mark IV a single, 35-foot, bus-like vehicle, created and designed by Fouad Said, containing all necessary equipment, bathrooms, dressing rooms, and space for a staff and crew of fifty, which is rapidly replacing the huge caravans of trucks and vehicles necessary for filming on location; a self-contained unit, this vehicle has been widely and successfully used in filming recent American pictures at a variety of locations.

Clapper (also **number board** and **slate**) a pair of hinged boards which are clapped together at the beginning of each numbered take so that sound and picture can be synchronized in editing; a slate on which the scene number and take number are written and photographed.

Clip   a short section or sequence from a film.

Close medium shot (also **close middle shot, MCS**)   a shot of indefinite distance between a medium shot and a close shot; a close medium shot of a human subject is usually a bust shot.

Closeup (**CU,** also **close shot, CS, tight shot**)   shot in which the camera, actually or apparently, is close to the subject; in terms of an actor, it usually includes area from shoulders to top of head or face only; variations are the large closeup or big closeup, focused on one part of an object or part of the face or anatomy of an actor.

Combined continuity   a complete verbal and numerical record of the finished film, including action, dialogue, sounds, camera angles, footage, and frames, prepared by the **script supervisor.**

Commentary (also **voice over narration**)   descriptive or narrative talk in accompaniment with the film.

Composer   creates music for a film.

Composite print (British: **combined print**)   an edited, completed, positive print of the film, or strip of film, containing all sound tracks.

Composition   the arrangement and real or apparent movement of subjects in frame, shot, scene, or sequence, together with qualities of perspective, lighting, photography. The composition of a single shot is often analyzed analogously to the composition of a painting.

Comprehensive shot   a complete shot of a large area or large-scale action. See also **Establishing shot.**

Continuity   the editorial organization of shots and sequences, with transitions between them, in a film.

Continuity editing   editing which is tied to establishing definite story points; distinguished from **dynamic editing.**

Contrast   the relationship of the elements of brightness in a picture.

Costume designer   designs and creates wardrobe for a film.

Costumers   maintain clothing and wardrobe during production, assist players in dressing, and stand by on set.

Cover   the number of **setups** and **takes** used in filming a scene.

Cover set   a set in readiness for filming in the event that, for any reason, the regular filming schedule cannot be followed.

Coverage   the amount of film, the number of takes and footage, from various angles, allotted by the director in the filming of a scene or sequence.

Crab dolly   a small wheeled platform mount for the camera, which may be moved on level ground by hand; is moved by **grips;** used for easy movement over level ground or on studio sound stage floors; may be moved in any direction (crabbed). See also **Dolly.**

Crane shot (also **boom shot**)   a shot taken by a camera from a camera boom.

Credits (also **screen credits**)   the names of members of staff, cast, and crew who are officially credited, that is, recognized according to custom, contracts, and union regulations, in the film.

Cross-cut (also **parallel editing**)   juxtaposition of two or more separate shots or scenes with parts of each presented alternately so that separate actions are represented as simultaneous.

Crutch music   mood pieces supporting scenes; principal problem is timing to end simultaneously with the scene.

Cut   (1) an individual strip of film; (2) a transition between two separate shots joined together so that the first shot is instantaneously replaced by the second; (3) as a verb, to trim and join shots together, to edit a film; (4) a shot; (5) an instruction to terminate a shot, given only by the director.

Cutaway   a shot apparently taking place at the same time as the main action of a scene; most commonly a **reaction shot.**

Cut-in (also **insert shot**)   a shot of some detail of the main action other than the faces of actors involved.

Cut-in scene   a scene taken separately and inserted into a film.

Cutout   parts of film discarded by the film editor.

Cutter   the **film editor;** also refers to his assistants.

Cutting bench   a special, vinyl-surfaced table used by film editors.

Cutting on movement   a method associated with the **match cut;** when cutting between shots of the same subject in an apparently continuous time sequence, the cut is made on the motion of the subject to reduce audience awareness of the cut.

Cutting piece   an illusory blending of widely separated locations or sets into an apparent whole.

Cutting room   room or space assigned to the editor and his assistants for editing the film.

Dailies (also **rushes**)   film photographed on the previous working day, developed, printed, **rough cut,** and screened on the following day for the benefit of the director and his staff; also daily progress reports on the production.

Day for night   shooting night scenes in daylight, using filters and other technical devices to simulate darkness.

Deep focus   sharp focus for a **long shot** or **far shot.**

Deep focus lens   a lens permitting simultaneous focus for a closeup and a long shot background in the same shot.

Depth of field   the distance to and from the camera in which an actor can move or an object can be moved without becoming out of focus.

Depth of focus   the extent to which a lens can focus on near and distant objects at the same time.

Dialing control of the sound during filming by the **mixer;** unwanted sounds can be dialed out.

Dialogue (also **lines, words**) all spoken words in a film.

Dialogue director (also **coach**) assigned to rehearsal of lines and prompting of players.

Differential focus photographing an object in sharp focus with rest of the shot out of focus.

Diffusion screens screens used to control light and shadow on a set. See also **Reflectors.**

Diffusor material which is used to soften a beam of light.

Direct cut a cut, but stipulated direct cut in script directions to emphasize this particular form of transition rather than to leave it optional; often used at a place where, conventionally, the editor might use another transition.

Directional movement real or apparent movement of the subjects of a shot or scene as blocked and arranged by the director as a part of his composition and **structured rhythm;** movement, within a frame, may be left (**l**) or right (**r**), towards the background (**bg**) or foreground (**fg**) of the shot; also applied to arrangements of static objects on a set which may be photographed in such a way, by moving the camera, by lens adjustment, or by changing the angle, as to make objects seem to move, as, for example, when the camera imitates the **point of view** of a moving character; also applied to the relationship of movements and motion in separate shots and scenes linked together in editing.

Director responsible for all aspects of filmmaking from the beginning of production to release.

Dissolve (also **lap dissolve** and **mix**) the merging of one shot into the next, produced by superimposition of the two shots and a fade out of the first and a fade in of the second; usually a laboratory process, but can be done in the camera while shooting.

Documentary film a nonfiction film on subjects of general interest.

Dolly a wheeled platform serving as a camera mount which can be man-handled in any direction; sometimes called **trolley** when mounted on tracks.

Dolly in (also **track in**) moving the camera towards the subject, decreasing the distance of the shot.

Dolly out (also **track out**) moving the camera backwards, away from the subject, increasing the distance of the shot.

Dolly shot (also **travelling shot, tracking shot**) a moving shot, usually made of a moving subject. See also **Following shot, Running shot, Trucking shot.**

Domestic release commercial release of a film to be shown in theaters in the U.S. and Canada.

Double see **Stunt double.**

Dress extra an **extra** reporting for work in his own tuxedo or full dress, her own evening gown.

Dubbing (also **mixing** and **rerecording**) process of combining all sound tracks, including music, sound effects, and dialogue, into one synchronized sound track for the film; also the process of synchronizing foreign language dialogue for foreign language versions of a completed film.

Dupe negative a negative made from a positive print.

Dynamic editing a style of editing suitable to action scenes and characteristic of documentary filmmaking where the film is "made" in editing; its quality is rapid pace and maximum visual impact in combinations of shots.

Dynamic frame any device or technique which serves to make the screen itself appear either to enlarge or decrease in size.

Editor (also **cutter**) responsible to the director for entire process of editing and assembling the film, from first takes to final **work print**, including all technical aspects, optical and sound.

Establishing shot a shot which serves to locate the action for the scene to follow.

Expressionism in cinema refers to a filmmaking movement in post-World War I Germany; characterized by deliberate artifice in lighting, costumes, and sets, by symbolic or mime-like acting, by fantasy or strong elements of the fantastic.

Exterior (EXT.) shooting done outdoors, on location, or on the lot of the studio.

Extra (also **screen extra**) a member of the cast used for background purposes and authenticity; if the extra acts or reacts in a scene, a silent bit, he receives additional pay. See also **Stand-in.**

Eye level (also **horizontal**) the standard camera angle, assumed unless otherwise specified by the director or the script.

Eyepiece viewing lens attachment to camera permitting the operator to see exactly what the camera lens will record. See also **Viewer.**

Fade the screen is blank (dark) with no image projected; a fade, in context of a film, usually serves as a distinct break in continuity, clearly setting off one sequence of shots from another; a slow fade calls for a very gradual diminishment of light and the image until the screen is blank.

Fade in the gradual appearance of a picture on the screen.

Fade out the gradual disappearance (fading) of picture and images from the screen, ending with a blank screen.

Far shot (also **very long shot, extreme long shot, distance shot**) a shot which includes not only the entire setting, but also the details of a distant background.

Fast motion (effect) see **Accelerated motion.**

Fast tempo the overall sense of timing, of "fast and slow" scenes and sequences in a film, is determined not by the speed of photography or by the physical speed or movement of subjects filmed, but by narrative and visual context and, chiefly, by the editorial craft in cutting. The effect of fast tempo might be achieved through cross-cutting or by dynamic editing.

Favoring (also **featuring** and **centering on**)   in any two shot or group shot, this direction calls for photography which will stress the significance of one or more of the characters involved.

Featured player   an actor with a major part who receives screen credit (billing), but who is ranked below the stars.

Feeler print   a print made from the edited negative of the work print with all effects inserted, but before final mixing.

Fill light   light placed so as to control the shadows cast by the **key light.**

Film grain   the size of the particles composing the light-sensitive layer of a film; a shot or print is said to be grainy when these particles are clearly visible in projection.

Filters   transparent glass or gelatin placed in front of or behind the camera lens or, in color filming, the tone relationships; among the standard filters used are *neutral density filters*, a gray filter uniformly cutting down on the light hitting the lens; *polarizing filters*, used especially to decrease sunlight and reflections on glass and water; *diffusion filters*, which serve to soften hard lines and are used for facial closeups; *fog filters*, which create a foggy effect; for black-and-white films, a *color filter*, which lightens its own color and darkens its compliment; and *color-compensating filters*, used to control illumination and give good color rendition.

Final negative   the edited negative from which the composite print is made.

Fine grains   duplicate negatives of the film ordered from the laboratory for technical and editorial use.

Fixed (also **static**) **camera**   shooting from any angle or distance when the camera remains in a fixed position throughout the shot; distinguished from **mobile** or **moving camera.**

Fixed frame   a shot in which the camera is fixed (static) and in which there is no background movement.

Flash forward   shot, scene, or sequence interrupting the ongoing time sequence of a film by introducing action or events to come; it may refer forward to scenes which will be viewed or may imply future time and events outside the chronology of the film.

Flash shot   a shot of very few frames and short duration, therefore almost subliminal in effect; often used as an insert within the context of an ongoing shot or scene to represent a fragment of subjective memory or an intimation or intuition of future time.

Flashback   a shot, scene, or sequence, introduced into the chronological sequence of a film and breaking that sequence by referring to time past; it may refer back to action already seen or may introduce narrative elements or subjective memory of the past into the imagined present of the film.

Flip (also **flipover wipe** and **flip frame**)   a transitional device in which the frame of one shot revolves 360 degrees, and flips over, ending its revolution with the frame of the next shot.

Floor   any part of a studio where shooting is in progress; the ground level of any set, exterior or interior.

Focus   to adjust the lens of a camera (or projector) in order to keep a sharply defined image.

Following shot   a shot in which the camera moves or seems to move to follow a moving actor or object. See also **Running shot.**

Footage   a length of film measured in feet; often used loosely to refer to a shot, scene, or sequence of a film.

Foreground (fg)   that part of the scene immediately in front of the camera.

Foreshadowing   cinematic or narrative (or both) means of preparing the audience to accept as probable some future action or event.

Form cutting   the framing in a following shot of a subject or compositional arrangement which has a shape or contour in some way similar to an image in the shot preceding it; the relationship and juxtaposition of the two can serve as a simple comparison (as in a simile in poetry), or, by association, within the context of the film, or by allusion, can be raised to the higher power of metaphor and symbol.

Frame (sometimes **still**)   a single photograph in the series printed on a length of cinematographic film; in photographing a scene or shot the frame of the shot, seen through the eyepiece of the camera, or the **viewer,** determines the staging areas (background and foreground, left and right) and the composition of the shot or scene; anything which can be seen is said to be *in frame;* anything in the scene or shot which cannot be seen is *out-of-frame* or *off-frame* (of); see also **Off-camera** and **On-camera;** the average ninety-minute feature film is made up of 129,000 separate frames or 8,100 feet of film.

Frame line   the dividing line separating each single frame from the next.

Frame slant   a shot in which the camera is slightly tilted on its axis so that the image appears on the screen off center, in a tilted position. See also **Cant.**

Freeze shot   the repetition of a single frame for an extended time, done either in camera while photographing or by editing, so that, when seen in projection, the shot appears to freeze, to be a still photograph. See also **Zoom freeze.**

Front lighting (also **pancake lighting**)   the light source is from approximately the same position and angle as the camera; serves to flatten out planes and angles.

Full shot   a shot of indeterminate distance, from any angle, but fully including the subject of the shot; when applied to actors, the shot calls for the full body to be in frame.

Gaffer   the electrical foreman of the set; also may be used, loosely, to designate any foreman of any production department or crew.

General shot   any shot from any angle in which a complete action or a large part of the set is visible.

Glass shot   a shot in which part of the background or setting is painted or photographed on glass or other transparent material, which is placed between the camera and the subject so that it will merge with the full-size set being photographed.

Gobo (also **nigger**)   a black screen, mounted adjustably, used to control light falling on the camera.

Greensman (also **nurseryman**)   charged with all trees, plants, shrubbery, and flowers not in vases on exterior or interior sets; responsible for required seasonal changes.

Grip   a skilled set laborer, general, all-purpose set assistant; the foreman is known as the **key grip** or **head grip.**

Group shot   a shot of unspecified distance and angle, concentrating upon three or more characters.

Hand-held camera (HH)   use of a camera—a 16 MM camera whose film will subsequently be blown up to 35 MM—without any conventional fixed or mobile mounting; characteristic of documentary and direct cinema filming; *effect* of hand-held camera can be imitated with conventional camera mounting; though held by hand, the camera can be firmly controlled by means of body braces, shoulder rests.

Hatchet lighting   light source placed ninety degrees from the camera to create a half-shadow effect on the subject.

Head-on shot   a shot in which the action appears to come directly towards the camera; most often used in relation to **trucking shot.**

Heavy   a movie villain.

Hi hat   a small, low mount for the camera for very **low angle** shooting, or for shooting a few inches off the floor.

High angle shot (also **high shot**)   a shot taken by any means from an elevated angle in terms of the subject; sometimes referred to as **shooting down** or **looking down.**

Implicit music   music for film which, in addition to supporting the physical sense of action (see also **Kinetic music**), also serves to fit with visual image and dialogue to convey a parallel or corresponding mood, and likewise to accentuate visual techniques and transitions.

In sequence   shooting on a schedule which follows the sequence and order of the shooting script; this is very seldom done, for reasons of economy and efficiency.

Incidental music music apparently coming from a real sound source in the scene, as for example, radio, jukebox, musical instrument.

Inkie an intensely bright incandescent lamp.

Insert (1) a shot, usually a closeup, used to reveal a **title** or any subject in detail; (2) any material cut into a scene, though not shot in the making of the scene, by the editor; (3) also a camera car used for mobile photography.

Intercut a short cut used within a larger sequence. See also **Cross-cut.**

Interior (INT.) any set which represents an indoor situation; distinguished from **exterior.**

Interpolated shots see **Insert.**

Intertitles (also **titles,** distinguished from the **main title** or **titles and credits**) any shot of any written or printed material inserted in any scene or sequence of a film.

Invisible cutting (also **invisible editing**) unobtrusive cutting by means of **match cuts** or by **motivation,** intended to distract audience attention from awareness of editing.

Iris in to open up the photographed image from a pinpoint or small portion of the frame until the whole frame is filled with the picture.

Iris out to close down the photographed image to a pinpoint or small portion of the frame.

Irising a gradual opening up or closing down of the photographed image from or to a pinpoint; can be done in camera by means of an *iris diaphragm* or by **masking;** can be accomplished in laboratory by optical or chemical means; a transitional device for linking one scene to another.

Juicer any electrician working on the set.

Jump cut (distinguished from a **match cut**) in perjorative sense, refers to any poorly made match cut; used as a deliberate artistic device, it represents the cutting out of footage which would give the sequence a conventional continuity; also a cut in which the camera angle changes slightly on the cut, giving an impression of a jump in action.

Key light the main source of light illuminating the subject of a shot.

Kinesthetic involvement the result of artistic techniques designed to involve the audience in sharing physical and psychological feelings of the film.

Kinetic music music designed to accompany and express the actions shown in a scene or sequence.

l left; stage left or frame left.

Lap dissolve see **Dissolve.** See also **Overlap shot.**

Lay behind musical term; music to be subdued and unobtrusive in accompaniment to a scene.

Lens turret a rotating device on the camera which carries two or more lenses which may be turned swiftly into position during shooting.

Library shot   any shot taken from a film library for use in a film; a shot not taken for a particular film, but used in it. See also **Stock shot.**

Lighting the set   with very few exceptions all sets, exterior and interior, in studio and on location, must be **lit**, that is, illuminated by lights and controlled by reflectors, diffusion screens.

Location   any place outside a studio and its lot where exterior or interior shooting takes place; such shooting is said to be *on location; local* location is within easy driving distance of the studio; any other location is classified as *distant.*

Long lens   a lens with a focal length greater than normal, therefore including a narrow angle of a scene; incorrectly called a **telephoto lens.**

Long shot (ls)   shot taken at a distance from the action or subject, conventionally not less than fifty yards and often at a greater distance; a long shot need *not* be a **full shot** including a complete setting or action.

Loop film (also **cyclic film**)   a short film with its ends joined together which can be run through a projector without interruption in continuous repetition.

Looping   process by which actors replace lines made on the original sound track, for purposes of clarity and inflection, in a studio sound recording room; a loop film is prepared and projected and the actor repeats his lines, timing (**synchronizing**) his words with his filmed lip movements; frequently used, wrongly, for **dubbing.**

Lot   any land owned by a studio and situated near sound stages where shooting may take place; also a term for the entire studio; something is located as happening *on the lot* or *off the lot.*

Low angle shot (also **camera looking up**)   the camera is situated below the subject of the shot, shooting upward.

Low key   (1) when only a few highlights are used to illuminate the subject and a large portion of the set is shadowy, the lighting is called *low key;* (2) similarly the subject may be shot in low key by stopping down the lens opening of the camera; (3) finally, a dark print, in color or black and white, is low key.

Low truck shot   a moving shot taken from a low angle.

Main title (also **title and credits**)   the title of the film; usually shown in combination with the screen credits.

Makeup artist   responsible for all makeup; except, when making up female players, union regulations confine the makeup artist's activities to area from top of head to apex of breastbone, from fingertips to elbows; also responsible for creation of all character effects, as, for example, wounds, scars, aging; and responsible for mustaches, beards, and male wigs.

Map location   convention, established by earliest filmmakers and followed ever since, in which the frame is viewed as analogous to a map; thus right-to-left movement indicates movement east to west and vice versa, and the top of the frame may suggest north, the bottom, south; from this beginning developed more sophisticated means of directional cutting, using a rhythm of lines of movement within a shot, scene, and sequence.

Married print   see **Combined print.**

Mask   a shield or shape placed in front of the camera lens to eliminate (that is, mask out) some part of the shot.

Mask shot   shot made with lens covered to limit what can be filmed; most often used (analogous to insert shot) to simulate a shot seen through an object, as, for example, a keyhole or crack, telescope, gun sight, binoculars, or camera.

Master film   the final edited negative from which all theatrical prints are made.

Master scene   the overall scene, as indicated in the shooting script and by the director, considered as a unit, without regard to the breakdown of the scene into separate shots and takes or the cutting within the scene by the editor.

Master shot   a single shooting or take of an entire piece of dramatic action.

Match cut   a carefully unobtrusive cut designed to blend the action of two shots so closely together that the effect of cutting is minimized.

Matte shot   a special effects process whereby two separately shot sequences are combined harmoniously into one print, giving the effect of being done at one time and in one location; related to **process shot.**

Meal penalty   a union regulation requiring that on all location shooting the entire film company must be fed at precisely specified hours and with high quality food; failure to meet this regulation requires that the producer must pay a penalty to all workers.

Medium (or **middle**) **close shot** (**MCS**) or **closeup** (**MCU**)   a shot of indeterminate distance between a medium shot and a close shot; basically a close shot in which a larger part of the subject than usual is visible.

Medium long shot (**MLS**)   shot of indefinite distance between medium and long, tending towards the long shot but retaining the medium shot's characteristics of clear identity of persons and at least part of the immediate setting.

Medium shot   by convention a shot made from between five and fifteen yards' apparent distance and including a subject or group in entirety.

Metteur en scène (French; also *réalisateur*)   director, filmmaker.

Middle shot (**mid-shot;** also **American shot**)   a medium shot which focuses on the subject from the knees up.

Mise en scène (French)   scenery, setting, and staging; involves, for the director, direction of actors in delivery of lines and in blocking (planning) their movements; also includes planning individual camera shots.

Mixer   on the set, a member of the sound crew who operates a sound console in conjunction with the camera; charged with obtaining clear and distinct sound recording during shooting; during dubbing, any one of several sound men who dial in and dial out sounds from the various tracks, creating the sound track for the film.

Mobile (also **motion**) **camera**   the capacity of the camera to be changed in distance and angle between shots, or to move or seem to move during a single shot.

Model shot   any shot in which a model or an object or objects is photographed.

Montage   (1) term used by Sergei Eisenstein to describe rhetorical arrangement of shots (sometimes single frames) in juxtaposition with each other in order to produce or imply another unit independent of the separate elements forming it; defined by Ernest Lindgren in *The Art of the Film* as "the combination in art of representative fragments of nature to form an imaginative whole which has no counterpart in nature"; (2) French term for the editing process; (3) American term for an assembly of short shots used to indicate a passage of time and events within that time span.

MOS (also **wild picture**)   any shots, scenes, or sequences taken without sound; when used in script directions it calls for a silent unit.

Motivation   establishing probability or causality for anything in the film whether in narrative of script, action, and characterization of actors, or in the editing cuts and transitions.

Moving shot (also **running shot**)   any shot in which the camera, by any means, follows with actors or objects moving in that scene.

Moviola   originally a trade name, now used for all brands of the special projection machine used by film editors; machine allows the editor to run the film at various speeds, backwards and forwards, to stop on any single frame, and to view the film closely through a magnifying device.

Muddy scene   a scene which is inadequately or badly lighted.

Multiple exposure (double exposure)   two or more exposures made on the same series of frames.

Multiple images   special effects method which produces any number of images of the same shot or subject in a frame, or a variety of separate images in the same frame and shot.

Music editor (also **music cutter**)   assigned as technical aid and assistant to the composer.

Mute negative   negative of sound film not including the sound track.

Mute print   positive print of sound motion picture not including the sound track.

Narrative editing   see **Continuity editing**.

Negative cost   the total expense of making a film.

Negative cutter   a specialist at the photographic laboratory, responsible for matching the original negative, frame by frame, with the final work print created by the film editor, to create the master film.

Negative cutting the editorial work done at the photographic laboratory to match the original negative with the final work print.

Neorealism (Italian: *réalismo*) post-World War II movement in Italian cinema, lasting into the 1950s; characterized by a direct and simple style of filmmaking, and use of natural settings and unprofessional actors.

New Wave (French: *nouvelle vague*) a contemporary movement in French filmmaking, based upon the concept of the director as *auteur;* developed by critics writing for *Cahiers du Cinéma,* some of whom have since proved theory in practice, directing distinguished films.

Newsreels filmed shorts of recent news events widely shown in theaters prior to the development of television and TV news programs; significant in the development of the documentary film.

Nonsynchronous sound (distinguished from **synchronous sound** in which a sound effect is precisely matched to the visual image apparently producing the sound) the use of the sound without the visual image, the sound substituting for and implying the visual image; also applied to unrealistic sound in which the sound does not derive directly from the visual image but comments on it, as, for example, a scene showing the stockmarket with stockbrokers shouting, but the sound is of barking dogs and roaring beasts.

Objective camera by careful application of various techniques, the director seeks to divert audience attention away from any sense of filmmaking and to present the subject in a seemingly objective manner, as if the camera were merely recording events.

Off-camera (also **off-frame, of,** and **off-screen, os**) any action or dialogue or sound taking place out of view in a particular shot, scene, or sequence.

On-camera (also **on-screen**) action, dialogue, or sound happening in frame, directly experienced by the spectator in a particular shot, scene, or sequence.

On the nose any aspect of a film, visual, auditory, or narrative, presented in an explicit and conventional fashion; perjoratively, a cinematic cliché.

Optical effects any effects carried out or created in the optical department of a film-processing laboratory; in addition to a variety of laboratory effects, many effects usually created by camera or editing can be created in the laboratory by complex processes.

Optical printer a device which makes it possible for images from one film to be photographed on another film.

Optical zoom a simulated **zoom shot** created in the laboratory.

Out-take any take that is not used in the completed film.

Overlap in sound or dialogue; a sound or words from one shot or scene intruding upon another, either carried over from a previous scene or anticipating the next.

Overlap shots a series of shots of the same action from different angles with the effect of extending the time and distance covered by the action.

Overlay one sound track superimposed on another in dubbing.

Overshooting the practice by most film directors of shooting and printing far more film of a given scene than can be used in the finished film, for the purpose of allowing maximum flexibility and creativity during editing; an average feature film, 8,100 feet, is reduced by editing from 200,000 feet of printed takes.

Over-shoulder shot shot, sharing the viewpoint of a character, but including a portion of the character's back and shoulders in the foreground.

Package subject of film to be made, together with basic staff, cast, and crew available and interested to work on it; and frequently including a draft of the screenplay, along with a breakdown.

Paint in to add objects, by various means, to a photographed scene as a special effect.

Pan (also **panoramic shot**) to rotate the camera head on its pivot or axis in a horizontal plane in order either to keep a moving subject in view or to move across a stationary scene. See also **Swish-pan.**

Pan down/pan up (British) to move the camera in a vertical plane, down or up, towards the subject. See also **Tilt shot.**

Parallel editing (also **parallel action**) an editing technique of presenting separately shot sequences of action happening in different locations as related to each other by shifting the audience viewpoint back and forth between the separate sequences. See also **Cross-cut.**

Peep show (also **kinetoscope**) one of the earliest forms of motion picture involving the use of a vertically moving, sprocketed film strip, seen by a single viewer through a slit or eyehole.

Photofloods small, bright lights used for general illumination.

Photoplay in early days (1914), a euphemism for movies, result of a contest for an appropriate term; a film version of a stage play, with minimal adaptation for cinema.

Pickups shots filmed after the completion of the regular shooting schedule and during the editing phase of production; refers to minor material, not involving extensive reshooting, but merely shots needed for transitions, continuity.

Playback use of a recorded sound track during shooting or in looping in order to synchronize action, sound, lip movements, and dialogue.

Point of view (**POV**) an aspect of **subjective camera**; calls for the camera to simulate, by position, angle, and distance, the view of a subject in the scene of action taking place in that scene; unlike the over-shoulder shot, a point of view shot does not usually include the observing subject or subjects in its frame.

Polecats single ceiling-to-floor poles used as mounts for light fixtures.

Position camera position is defined as static (fixed) or moving.

Prescoring any music **scored** before production of a film.

Print a positive copy of negative film; a **take** indicated to be sent to the laboratory for processing and reproduction.

Process shot (also **back projection, rear projection**) a scene shot against the background of a moving picture, which is projected through a transparent screen behind the actions being filmed; thus the process shot joins together the two separate units of film in one unit; a conventional example is the shot of two actors in an automobile with a shot of moving traffic projected behind them for verisimilitude.

Producer financier, and responsible overall for the making of a film, from idea through theatrical release, domestic and foreign.

Production designer an art director with exceptional responsibility and control, including costumes, props, makeup, decorations, and style, as well as sets.

Production manager see **Unit production manager.**

Production still any still photograph taken of any aspect of a film in production.

Prop any object seen or used on any set except painted scenery and costumes.

Prop box wheeled, portable, piano-size boxes containing all materials necessary for props and their maintenance; also applied to any portable vehicle, including moving van, used by the prop man.

Prop man (also **property master**) responsible for all objects used in the action of a film, excluding scenery and costumes.

Property the story of subject matter of a film to be produced; or a finished film.

Post-synchronize (British; **looping** [U.S.]) recording dialogue with projected film.

Publicity still any still photograph taken before, during, or after the shooting of a film for the purposes of publicity and advertising, including display photographs often used at the entrance of theaters.

Pull back (PB) a camera direction indicating that the camera moves, or seems to move, back away from the subject.

Put in (a special effect) to create an effect by augmenting or increasing something actually photographed; for example, flames of a fire may be *put in* a scene.

Quartz light (also **halogen**) specially designed incandescent light capable of extremely high intensity and heat; thus a powerful source of illumination.

Quick cutting editing of film in short shots for an effect of rapidity.

Raw stock film that has not yet been used, exposed, or processed.

Reaction shot a shot featuring the response or reaction of one or more characters to an action already seen or about to be seen.

Reduction (opposite of enlargement and **blowup**) process by which a film made in one width is produced in a smaller width; for example, 35 MM is *reduced* to 16 MM or 8 MM prints.

Reel a strip of film on a spool; standard reel is 2,000 feet for American 35 MM projectors.

Reflector light a light with a built-in reflector; may be either a spotlight for concentrated light beam or floodlight with evenly diffused illumination.

Reflectors reflecting boards used to control, boost, and direct sunlight or lighting.

Relational editing editing of separate shots to link them together associatively and intellectually.

Release print a film for general theatrical showing.

Release script (British) script version of the finished film. See also **Combined continuity.**

Remake another filmed version of a previously produced property.

Rembrandt lighting dramatic and shadowed lighting; term is attributed to Cecil B. De Mille upon receipt of a telegram complaining that sender "couldn't even see the characters' faces half the time" in a De Mille film. "Tell him it's Rembrandt light," De Mille replied.

Retakes takes made again of unsatisfactory material already shot and viewed in rough form.

Reverse angle shot a shot made in opposite direction, that is, *reversed*, from the preceding shot.

Reverse motion camera photographing with film running backward so that when projected the actions or movements appear in reverse sequence; important for special effects.

Riffle book (also **flip book** and **kineograph**) an early (1868) patented precursor of the motion picture in which a succession of parts of a movement are depicted on pages of a book so that by swiftly thumbing the pages, the viewer enjoys the illusion of a moving image.

"Roll it" (also **"roll 'em"**) a director's cue for the start of filming or projection of a film.

Rough cut print a first assembly of the total film in rough form and without music and dubbed sound effects.

Rough in arrangement and blocking of lighting on the set prior to shooting.

Running lines rehearsing dialogue.

Running shot a shot in which the camera moves or seems to move keeping up with a moving actor or object.

Running time the length of time a film will take to be projected at standard projection speed.

Rushes see **Dailies.**

Scenario (also **production script**) see **Script.**

Scene   a series of **shots** taken at same setting or location from any number of camera angles and positions.

Scoring call   assignment of musicians and conductor for purpose of recording the music track for a film.

Scoring stage   special sound stage designed for scoring the music track of a film during projection of the sequences to be scored.

Screenplay   preproduction, written version of film including settings, scenes, characters, dialogue, and usually some indicated camera directions.

Scrim   framed netting used in order to soften, diffuse, or eliminate light on the set.

Script (shooting script)   a version of the screenplay as revised and prepared for production.

Script supervisor (also **script clerk**)   keeps track of everything happening during shooting, that is, logs the shooting in terms of the shooting script; serves as reminder and prompter; prepares combined continuity when filming and editing are complete.

Second unit   a self-contained production unit for the filming of scenes and sequences not requiring the director or principals of the cast.

Seconds   assistants to the assistant director.

Sequence   a number of scenes linked together by time, location, or narrative structure to form a unit of a motion picture.

Serials   brief one- or two-reel films involving the same central characters, and presented on a continuing basis; traditionally each unit ending with an unresolved problem or situation (a cliffhanger) which is resolved at the outset of the next episode.

Series   short films involving the same chief characters, and each film a complete episode in itself.

Set   any place, exterior or interior, on location or in a studio, designated and prepared for shooting in the production of a film.

Set decorator   furnishes and decorates the set.

Set dresser   responsible for details of settings and locations during production.

Set painter   responsible for painting, maintaining, aging all painted parts of the set, also for eliminating reflections.

Setup   relationship between the location of the camera, the area of the set or scene, and the actors; a single camera position.

Shadowmakers   devices in many sizes and shapes used by cameramen to create shadows and to filter light.

Sharpness   the extent or relative degree in which details in a shot are presented with photographic clarity and definition; when details are clear and distinct, easily identified and perceived, they are said to be *sharp.*

Shoot   to film a shot, scene, sequence, or entire motion picture.

Shoot up/down   to shoot from a low angle or a high angle on the subject.

Shooting ratio   the ratio of film shot to the final footage of the completed film.

Shooting schedule   an advance schedule of work assignments, together with sets, cast, costumes, and equipment required.

Short   any standard film of less than 3,000 feet in length.

Shot   (1) a single continuous unit of film taken at one set and from one camera setup; (2) a single photograph or frame; (3) a notation of camera angle, distance, movement involved in one setup; (4) a printed **take;** editorially, any consecutive strip of frames; (5) **cut** is sometimes used for any shot or part of a take in editing.

Shotgun microphone   a special microphone designed to pick up and isolate particular sounds against a noisy background.

Skip framing   a laboratory simulation of accelerated motion; printing only a portion of the original negative frames gives effect of speeded-up action; opposite of **double framing,** which slows down action.

Slow motion   effect of slowing down natural action or rhythms; either by filming actions at faster rate than usual, then projecting at standard rate, or by optical effects in the laboratory.

Sneak preview   an unannounced trial showing of a new film before a regular theater audience.

Soft focus   effect derived from shooting slightly out of focus.

Sound   an integral part of all but silent films consisting of dialogue, music, and sound effects.

Sound boom   a boom for placing the recording microphone close to the actors in a scene.

Sound crew   all technicians on the set charged with the recording of dialogue and sounds and the dialing out of unwanted noise during shooting; a separate unit from the camera crew, but working in close coordination with them.

Sound effects editor   responsible for overseeing the preparation of separate tracks and for the final dubbing of the sound track.

Sound montage   use of dialogue, music, or sound effects to relate separate settings or sequences.

Special effects   technical tricks in photography or processing designed to create illusions; anything added to the film after shooting, in the laboratory or in editing.

Special effects expert   handles the design, mechanics, and engineering of any required special effects which cannot be created in camera or by laboratory.

Splicing   joining together separate pieces of processed film.

Split screen (also **half-wipe**)   frame in which two or more images are simultaneously seen.

Spotlight   any light which projects an intense and narrow beam.

Stand-in   an extra who takes the place of an actor during times of light arrangement and camera adjustment.

Star   a principal member of the cast with a leading dramatic role in the film; a major box-office attraction, not necessarily an actor or actress.

Static position   a setup in which the camera is in a fixed position and does not move or seem to move; for example, though actors move about within the frame or move out of the frame, the camera does not move with them or follow, but continues throughout the shot to shoot from an established angle, recording the same fixed frame.

Steal a shot   to photograph subjects who are not aware of being filmed.

Step outline (also **synopsis**)   a brief story outline indicating the dramatic structure of a screenplay yet to be written.

Stock shot (**stock footage**)   use of film not specifically photographed for the motion picture being produced.

Stop camera (also **stop photography**)   two separate camera operations film the same shot, the two shots becoming one shot in viewing.

Stop printing   the repetition of a single frame or image, created in laboratory, to **freeze** or stop action.

Story   preproduction, it is the narrative line of the script augmented by the storyboard; in filming and after, the story is the organization of shots and sequences into continuity.

Story analyst   a professional reader, preparing synopses and analyses of published material and recommending likely film properties.

Storyboard (also **continuity sketches**)   a preliminary, cartoon-strip form version, in sketches, prepared from the shooting script, breaking down action into a controlled sequence of possible shots.

Straight cut (also **direct cut**)   a cut called for where, by convention, another kind of editorial linking or transition might be expected.

Stretch out   a bus-type limousine for transportation to and from locations.

Structured rhythm (also **structural rhythm**)   generally applied to the overall sense of harmonious order of a film, deriving from the director's artistry and control; in film the elements are multiple, including and combining the basic narrative structure of the story, the patterns and arrangements of sound, music, and dialogue, the composition of light and shadow, the angles and movement of the camera, the editorial devices for separating and joining shots, scenes, and sequences; more specifically, structural rhythm in film refers to the purely visual aspects of the director's art, ranging from the composition of individual frames and shots to the relationships, established by likeness and contrast, of sequences, and their significance within the complete aesthetic experience of the film.

Studio driver   all-purpose professional vehicle driver; also drives cranes, fork-lifts, trucks, tractors.

Studio stock wardrobe, props, and other materials in possession of a studio.

Stunt any piece of action requiring the use of a professional stuntman.

Stunt coordinator experienced stuntman who acts as foreman of any group of stuntmen.

Stunt double a stuntman who bears a close photographic resemblance to a particular actor.

Stuntman a professional performer of all potentially dangerous action—leaps, falls, horse falls, fights, fainting—in a film.

Subjective camera (also **subjective shots**) shots created so that the audience views them as if from the literal or subjective point of view of a character; shots indicative of the filmmaker's feelings and attitudes towards characters, objects, events, when the process of filmmaking has been established, explicitly or implicitly, as part of the cinematic experience.

Subtitles (1) in silent films, the insertion of printed dialogue, comment, and description into filmed scenes or between scenes on subtitle cards; (2) in foreign language films not dubbed into English, the use of white letters on some dark part of the frame to give a translation of dialogue; (3) any title other than the main title.

Sun gun small, battery-powered unit used chiefly in documentary filming for night shooting, following a subject from exterior to interior, and as a fill light in sunlight.

Superimposition two or more shots within the same frame, an effect achieved either by camera or in laboratory; may apply also to sounds on tracks.

Survey search for and establishment of the locations for various shots to be used in a film.

Swish-pan (also **whip shot**) a rapid panning movement of the camera from one viewpoint or position of the set to another with the effect of blurring intermediate details in movement.

Synchronous sound sound timed and simultaneous with visual images.

Take each separate recording made of a shot while filming; a shot may consist of any number of takes; when any take is converted into a positive print from the negative, it becomes a **print**; also, in acting, a strong reaction.

Telephoto lens (also **true telephoto lens**) a lens with an exceptionally long focal length, able to focus on a very narrow angle of a scene.

Tests preliminary examinations, often by shooting film, prior to actual production, designed to check costumes (*wardrobe tests*), makeup, and talent (*screen tests*).

Theme a musical sequence, analogous to *leitmotif*, associated in a film with a character, an action, a place; in film overall, the basic idea or subject of the film.

Thin   (1) in sound, a sound too weak or vague for its purpose; (2) in acting, a two-dimensional role; (3) in writing, a part of the narrative which is not strongly created or a character not sufficiently developed.

Tilt shot (**tilt up/tilt down**)   shot made by moving camera on its pivot or axis in a vertical plane.

Title   any written or printed material used in the context of a film, as distinguished from the **main title** announcing the title of the film itself.

Tracking shots (also **trucking, travelling**; sometimes **dollying**)   shots in which a mobile camera, mounted on tracks, a truck or other vehicle, or a dolly, moves with the subject or moves towards or away from the subject of a shot.

Trailer (also **theatrical trailer**)   a short sequence of film used to advertise a feature film, and often derived from it, for theatrical showing.

Treatment   intermediate stage in development of script, basically narrative in form, between step outline and screenplay.

Trim   to cut or shorten in editing.

Trim can (also **out-take**)   a film can where marked and numbered frames, cut out of a sequence in editing, are kept.

Trims and outs   all frames of unused film left over at any stage of editing; these are stored in studio vaults for any possible future use.

Trucking shot   loosely, any moving shot with camera on mobile mounting; strictly, a moving shot with camera mounted on a truck or van.

Two-shot   shot of two characters, the camera usually as close as possible while keeping both in the shot.

Typage acting   use of stock photographs from a film library of faces which, when cut into a dramatic sequence, seem to be reacting to the filmed situation and events.

Undershooting   filming sequences with too little footage to permit adequate editorial coverage.

Unit production manager   executive officer for the producer; from beginning is charged with execution of all the producer's plans, with budgeting, personnel, scheduling, picking locations, serving as manager and foreman for all crews and departments.

Unit still photographer   member of production staff responsible for taking all action, production, publicity, and art still photographs.

Utility man   lowest ranking titled member of a production crew; charged with running errands and general janitorial duties on the set.

Viewer   a small hand-held lens device with frame lines precisely fitting the subject to be shot, permitting the director and the cameraman to examine possible shots without having to move the camera; the camera operator also has a similar instrument attached to his camera.

Voice over (**VO**)   dialogue, comment, or narration coming from off-screen.

Wardrobe   department charged with all aspects of costumes and clothing.

Whip shot (also **zip pan**)   see **Swish pan.**

White telephone film   a type of film popular in the thirties, characterized by great luxury, opulent settings; often a musical film.

Wide angle lens   a lens of shorter focal length than is standard; creates an exaggerated perspective, increasing the apparent distance between the foreground and background of a shot.

Wigwag   an automatic red warning light which flashes outside the door of studio sound stages whenever sound is being recorded on the set.

Wild lines   dialogue not recorded on camera.

Wild sound (also **wild track**)   any sound not recorded to synchronize precisely with the picture taken; may be recorded during shooting or separately.

Wipe   a link between two shots, both sharing the screen briefly before the second image replaces the first; there are a wide variety of possible wipes in terms of direction; a *half-wipe* is a split-screen effect; a *soft wipe* has a slightly blurred edge between the two cuts.

Work print (also **copy print, cutting copy**)   any initial version of the uncompleted film used for editing, dubbing, preliminary screenings.

Wrangler   a handler for horses used in a film.

Zoom (shot)   a shot made by using a lens of varying focal lengths, permitting the change from wide angle to long lens or vice versa during an uninterrupted shot; camera can *zoom in* or *zoom out;* not as dimensional as an equivalent dolly shot with fixed lens but moving camera; *zoom in* effect can be simulated in laboratory with **optical zoom** in which an area of a frame can be progressively enlarged.

Zoom freeze   a zoom shot ending with a **freeze**, or apparent still photograph.

Bibliography

Film Art, History

Altshuler, Thelma C. *Responses to Drama: An Introduction to Plays and Movies*. Boston: Houghton Mifflin, 1967.

Amelio, Robert, with Anita Owen and Susan Schaefer. *Willowbrook Cinema Study Project*. Dayton: Pflaum, 1970.

Anderson, Joseph L., and Donald Richie. *Japanese Film: Art and Industry*. New York: Grove, 1960.

Armes, Roy. *The Cinema of Alain Resnais*. New York: Barnes, 1968.

————. *French Film*. New York: Dutton, 1970.

————. *Screen Series: French Cinema*. New York, Barnes, 1970.

Arnheim, Rudolf. *Film as Art*. Berkeley: University of California, 1957.

————. *Visual Thinking*. Berkeley: University of California, 1969.

Baker, Fred. *Events: The Complete Scenario of the Film*. New York: Grove, 1970.

Balazs, Béla. *Theory of the Film*. New York: Roy, 1953.

Balcon, Michael. *Twenty Years of British Films, 1925–1945*. Falcon, 1947.

Ball, Robert Hamilton. *Shakespeare on Silent Film*. New York: Theatre Arts, 1968.

Balshoffer, Fred J., and Arthur C. Miller. *One Reel a Week*. Berkeley: University of California, 1968.

Barbour, Alan G., with Alvin H. Marrill and James Robert Parish. *Karloff*. Kew Gardens, N.Y.: Cinefax, 1969.

Bardeche, Maurice, and Robert Brasillach. *History of Motion Pictures*. New York: Norton, 1938.

Barnouw, Erik, and S. Krishnaswamy. *Indian Film*. New York: Columbia University, 1963.

Barr, Charles. *Laurel and Hardy*. Berkeley: University of California, 1968.

Barry, Iris. *D. W. Griffith: American Film Master.* New York: Museum of Modern Art, 1965.

Battcock, Gregory. *The New American Cinema.* New York: Dutton, 1967.

Baxter, John. *Hollywood in the Thirties: A Complete Critical Survey of Hollywood Films from 1930–1940.* Paperback Library, 1970.

——. *Science Fiction in the Cinema.* New York: Barnes, 1970.

——. *Science Fiction in the Cinema: A Complete Critical Review of SF Films from A TRIP TO THE MOON (1902) to 2001: A SPACE ODYSSEY.* New York: Paperback Library, 1970.

Bazin, André (tr. by Hugh Gray). *What is Cinema?* Berkeley: University of California, 1967.

Behimer, Rudy, with Terry-Thomas and Cliff McCarty. *The Films of Errol Flynn.* New York: Citadel, 1969.

Bellone, Julius (ed.). *Renaissance of the Film.* New York: Macmillan, 1970.

Bennett, Joan, and Lois Kibbee. *The Bennett Playbill.* New York: Holt, Rinehart and Winston, 1970.

Benoit-Lévy, Jean. *The Art of the Motion Picture.* New York: Coward-McCann, 1946.

Bluestone, George. *Novels into Film.* Berkeley: University of California, 1966.

Blum, Daniel, and John Kobal. *A New Pictorial History of the Talkies.* New York: Grosset & Dunlap, 1970.

Bobker, Lee. *Elements of Film.* New York: Harcourt, Brace & World, 1969.

Bogdanovich, Peter. *The Cinema of Alfred Hitchcock.* New York: Museum of Modern Art, 1963.

——. *The Cinema of Howard Hawks.* New York: Museum of Modern Art, 1962.

——. *The Cinema of Orson Welles.* New York: Museum of Modern Art, 1961.

——. *John Ford.* Berkeley: University of California, 1970.

Bowser, Eileen. *Film Notes.* New York: Museum of Modern Art, 1969.

Brownlow, Kevin. *How It Happened Here.* New York: Doubleday, 1968.

——. *The Parade's Gone By.* New York: Alfred Knopf, 1968.

Butler, Ivan. *Religion in the Cinema.* New York: Barnes, 1969.

Calder-Marshall, Arthur. *The Innocent Eye: The Life of Robert J. Flaherty.* New York: Harcourt, Brace & World, 1963.

Cameron, Ian (ed.). *The Films of Jean-Luc Goddard.* New York: Praeger, 1970.

——. *The Films of Robert Bresson.* New York: Praeger, 1970.

——. *Second Wave.* New York: Praeger, 1970.

——, and Elizabeth Cameron. *Dames.* New York: Praeger, 1969.

——, and Robin Wood. *Antonioni.* New York: Praeger, 1969.

Carey, Gary. *Lost Films.* New York: Museum of Modern Art, 1970.

Carmen, Ira H. *Movies, Censorship, and the Law.* Ann Arbor: University of Michigan, 1966.

Casty, Alan Howard. *The Dramatic Art of Film.* New York: Harper & Row, 1970.

————. *The Films of Robert Rossen.* New York: Museum of Modern Art, 1969.

Ceram, C. W. *Archaeology of the Cinema.* New York: Harcourt, Brace & World, 1965.

Clarens, Carlos. *Horror Movies.* Berkeley: University of California, 1968.

————. *An Illustrated History of the Horror Film.* New York: Putnam, 1967.

Cocteau, Jean. *Cocteau on the Film.* New York: Roy, 1954.

Conway, Michael, and Mark Ricci. *The Films of Marilyn Monroe.* New York: Citadel, 1964.

————, Dion McGregor, and Mark Ricci. *The Films of Greta Garbo.* Introduced by Parker Tyler. New York: Citadel, 1963.

Cowie, Peter. *The Cinema of Orson Welles.* New York: Barnes, 1965.

————. *International Film Guide, 1964.* New York: Barnes, 1965.

————. *International Film Guide, 1965.* New York: Barnes, 1966.

————. *Screen Series: Sweden.* New York: Barnes, 1970.

————. *Seventy Years of Cinema.* New York: Barnes, 1969.

————. *Three Monographs: Antonioni, Bergman, Resnais.* New York: Barnes, 1963.

Crowther, Bosley. *The Lion's Share.* New York: Dutton, 1957.

————. *Movies and Censorship.* New York: Public Affairs Committee, 1962.

Deming, Barbara. *Running Away From Myself: A Dream Portrait of America Drawn from the Films of the Forties.* New York: Grossman, 1969.

Deschner, Donald. *The Films of Spencer Tracy.* New York: Citadel, 1969.

Dickens, Homer. *The Films of Gary Cooper.* New York: Citadel, 1970.

————. *The Films of Marlene Dietrich.* New York: Citadel, 1969.

Dickinson, Thorold, and Catherine De la Roche. *Soviet Cinema.* London: Falcon, 1948.

Dimmitt, Richard B. *Actor's Guide to the Talkies.* 2 vols. Metuchen, N.J.: Scarecrow, 1967.

————. *Title Guide to the Talkies.* 2 vols. Metuchen, N.J.: Scarecrow, 1965.

Donner, Jorn. *The Personal Vision of Ingmar Bergman.* Bloomington: Indiana University, 1964.

Douglass, Drake. *Horror.* New York: Collier Books, 1969.

Dunne, John Gregory. *The Studio: A Cinéma Vérité Study of Hollywood at Work.* New York: Farrar, Straus & Giroux, 1968.

Durgnat, Raymond. *The Crazy Mirror: Hollywood Comedy and the American Image.* New York: Horizon, 1969.

————. *Eros in the Cinema.* New York: Fernhill, 1966.

————. *Films and Feelings.* Cambridge, Mass.: M.I.T., 1967.

————. *Luis Buñuel.* Berkeley: University of California, 1970.

————. *Nouvelle Vague: The First Decade.* Loughton (Essex), Eng.: Motion Publications, 1966.

————, and John Kobal. *Greta Garbo.* New York: Dutton Pictureback, 1965.

Eisenstein, Sergei M. *Film Form.* New York: Harcourt, Brace, 1949. Paperback by Meridian, New York, 1957.

————. *The Film Sense.* New York: Harcourt, Brace, 1942. Paperback by Meridian, New York, 1957.

———— (ed. by Jay Leyda). *Film Essays and a Lecture.* New York: Praeger, 1970.

Eisner, Lotte H. (tr. by Roger Greaves). *The Haunted Screen: Expressionism in the German Cinema and the Influence of Max Reinhart.* Berkeley: University of California, 1969.

Enser, G. S. *Filmed Books and Plays, 1928–1967.* New York: British Book Centre, 1969.

Essoe, Gabe. *The Films of Clark Gable.* New York: Citadel, 1969.

————. *Tarzan of the Movies: A Pictorial History of More Than Fifty Years of Edgar Rice Burroughs' Legendary Hero.* New York: Citadel, 1968.

An Evaluative Guide to Films on Jobs, Training and the Ghetto. New York: American Foundations on Automation and Employment, 1970.

Everson, William K. *The American Movie.* New York: Atheneum, 1963.

————. *The Bad Guys: A Pictorial History of the Movie Villain.* New York: Citadel, 1964.

————. *The Films of Laurel and Hardy.* New York: Citadel, 1969.

————. *A Pictorial History of the Western Film.* New York: Citadel, 1969.

Feldman, Joseph, and Harry Feldman. *Dynamics of the Film.* New York: Hermitage, 1952.

Fenin, George N., and William K. Everson. *The Western.* New York: Orion, 1962.

Feyen, Sharon. *Screen Experience: An Approach to Film.* Dayton: Pflaum, 1970.

Films 1968: A Comprehensive Review of the Year. New York: Catholic Office for Motion Pictures, 1968.

Finkler, Joel. *Stroheim.* Berkeley: University of California, 1970.

Fischer, Edward. *The Screen Arts.* New York: Sheed and Ward, 1960.

Five Catalogues of the Public Auction of the Countless Treasures Acquired From Metro-Goldwyn-Mayer. 5 vols. Los Angeles: David Weisz, 1970.

Ford, Charles. *Histoire du Western.* Paris: Pierre Horay, 1964.

Franklin, Joe. *Classics of the Silent Screen: A Pictorial Treasury.* New York: Bramhall House, 1959.

Fulton, A. R. *Motion Pictures: The Development of an Art Form From Silent Films to the Age of Television.* Norman: University of Oklahoma, 1960.

Gessner, Robert. *The Moving Image: A Guide to Cinematic Literacy*. New York: Dutton, 1970.

Gibson, Arthur. *The Silence of God: Creative Response to the Films of Ingmar Bergman*. New York: Harper & Row, 1969.

Gifford, Denis. *British Cinema—An Illustrated Guide*. New York: Barnes, 1968.

Gilson, Rene. *Jean Cocteau*. New York: Crown, 1969.

Gish, Lillian (with Ann Pinchot). *The Movies, Mr. Griffith and Me*. Englewood Cliffs: Prentice-Hall, 1969.

Goodman, Ezra. *The Fifty Year Decline and Fall of Hollywood*. New York: Simon and Schuster, 1961.

Gow, Gordon. *Suspense in the Cinema*. New York: Barnes, 1968.

Graham, Peter. *A Dictionary of the Cinema*. New York: Barnes, 1964.

———. *New Wave: Critical Landmark*. New York: Doubleday, 1968.

Graham, Sheilah. *Confessions of a Hollywood Columnist*. New York: Morrow, 1969.

———. *The Garden of Allah*. New York: Crown, 1970.

Grierson, John. *Grierson on Documentary*. Berkeley: University of California, 1970.

Griffith, Richard. *The Cinema of Gene Kelly*. New York: Museum of Modern Art, 1962.

———. *Fred Zinneman*. New York: Museum of Modern Art, 1958.

———. *Marlene Dietrich: Image and Legend*. New York: Museum of Modern Art, 1959.

———. *The Movie Stars*. New York: Doubleday, 1970.

———. *Samuel Goldwyn: The Producer and His Films*. New York: Museum of Modern Art, 1956.

———. *The World of Robert Flaherty*. London: Gollancz, 1953.

———, and Arthur Mayer. *The Movies*. New York: Simon and Schuster, 1957.

———, and Paul Rotha. *The Film Till Now*. New York: Funk and Wagnalls, 1949.

Guarner, Jose Luis. *Rossellini*. New York: Praeger, 1970.

Guback, Thomas H. *The International Film Industry: Western Europe and America Since 1945*. Bloomington: Indiana University, 1970.

Guiles, Fred Lawrence. *Norma Jean: The Life of Marilyn Monroe*. New York: McGraw-Hill, 1969.

Hampton, Benjamin B. *A History of the Movies*. New York: Covici, Friede, 1931.

Henri, Jim. *The World's Most Sensual Films*. Chicago: Merit Books, 1965.

Henderson, Robert M. *D. W. Griffith: The Years at Biograph*. New York: Farrar, Straus & Giroux, 1970.

Heyer, Robert, and Anthony Meyer. *Discovery in Film*. Paramus, N.J.: Paulist, 1969.

Hibbin, Nina. *Screen Series: Eastern Europe.* New York: Barnes, 1970.

Higham, Charles. *Hollywood in the Forties.* New York: Barnes, 1968.

————, and Joel Greenberg. *Hollywood In The Forties: A Complete Critical Survey of Hollywood Films 1940–1950.* New York: Paperback Library, 1970.

Hofmann, Charles. *Sounds for Silents.* New York: D. B. S. Publications, 1970.

Houston, Penelope. *The Contemporary Cinema.* Baltimore: Penguin, 1963.

Huaco, George. *The Sociology of Film Art.* New York: Basic Books, 1965.

Huettig, Mae D. *Economic Control of the Motion Picture Industry.* Philadelphia: University of Pennsylvania, 1944.

Hughes, Robert (ed.). *Film Book 1.* New York: Grove, 1959.

Hull, David Stewart. *Films in the Third Reich.* Berkeley: University of California, 1969.

Hunnings, Neville. *Film Censors and the Law.* New York: Hillary, 1967.

Huss, Roy, and Norman Silverstein. *The Film Experience: Elements of Motion Picture Art.* New York: Harper & Row, 1968.

Isaksson, Folke, and Leif Furhammar. *Politics and Film.* London: November Books, 1970.

Ivens, Joris. *The Camera and I.* New York: International Publishers, 1969.

Jacobs, Lewis. *The Rise of the American Film.* New York: Teachers College, Columbia University, 1967.

———— (ed.). *The Emergence of Film Art.* New York: Hopkinson and Blake, 1969.

————. *Introduction to the Art of the Movies.* New York: Noonday, 1960.

———— (ed.). *The Movies As Medium.* New York: Farrar, Straus & Giroux, 1970.

Jarratt, Vernon. *The Italian Cinema.* New York: Macmillan, 1951.

Jarvie, I. C. *Movies and Society.* New York: Basic Books, 1970.

Jensen, Paul. *The Cinema of Fritz Lang.* New York: Barnes, 1969.

————, and Arthur Lennig. *Karloff and Lugosi: Titans of Terror.* New York: Atheneum, 1971.

Kitses, Jim. *Horizons West: Anthony Mann, Budd Boetticher, Sam Peckinpah: Studies of Authorship Within the Western.* Bloomington: Indiana University, 1970.

Knight, Arthur. *The Liveliest Art: A Panoramic History of the Movies.* New York: Macmillan, 1957.

Kracauer, Siegfried. *From Caligari to Hitler.* New York: Noonday, 1959.

————. *Theory of Film.* New York: Oxford University, 1960. Paperback by Galaxy, New York, 1965.

Kuhns, William. *Themes: Short Films for Discussion.* Dayton: Pflaum, 1970.

————, and Thomas F. Giardino. *Behind the Camera.* Dayton: Pflaum, 1970.

————, and Robert Stanley. *Teaching Program: Exploring the Film.* Dayton: Pflaum, 1970.

————, and Robert Stanley. *Exploring the Film.* Dayton: Pflaum, 1970.

Kyrou, Ado (tr. by Adrienne Foulke). *Luis Buñuel.* New York: Simon and Schuster, 1963.

Lahue, Kalton C. *Collecting Classic Films.* New York: Amphoto, 1970.

————. *Continued Next Week.* Norman: University of Oklahoma, 1964.

————. *A World of Laughter: The Motion Picture Comedy Short, 1910–1930.* Norman: University of Oklahoma, 1966.

Larsen, Otto N. *Violence and the Mass Media.* New York: Harper & Row, 1970.

Lauritzen, Einar. *Swedish Films.* New York: Museum of Modern Art, 1962.

Lawson, John Howard. *Film: The Creative Process.* New York: Hill and Wang, 1964.

Lebel, J. P. (tr. by P. D. Stovin). *Buster Keaton.* New York: Barnes, 1967.

Levin, Martin (ed.). *Hollywood and the Great Fan Magazines.* New York: Arbor House, 1970.

Limbacher, James I. *Using Films: A Handbook for the Program Planner.* New York: Educational Film, 1967.

Linden, George. *Reflections on the Screen.* Belmont, Calif.: Wadsworth, 1970.

Lindgren, Ernest. *The Art of the Film.* New York: Macmillan, 1948. 3rd ed. 1968.

Lindsay, Vachel. *The Art of the Moving Picture.* Introduction by Stanley Kauffmann. New York: Liveright, 1970.

Low, Rachel. *The History of the British Film (1896–1906, 1906–14, 1914–18).* London: Allen & Unwin, 1948–50.

MacCann, Richard Dyer. *Film and Society.* New York: Scribner's, 1964.

————. *Hollywood in Transition.* Boston: Houghton Mifflin, 1962.

———— (ed.). *Film: A Montage of Theories.* New York: Dutton, 1966.

Madsen, Axel. *Billy Wilder.* Bloomington: Indiana University, 1969.

Manoogian, Haig P. *The Film-Maker's Art.* New York: Basic Books, 1966.

Manvell, Roger. *The Film and the Public.* Baltimore: Penguin, 1955.

————. *Films.* Harmondsworth (Middlesex), Eng.: Penguin, 1950.

————. *New Cinema in Europe.* New York: Dutton, 1965.

————. *New Cinema in the USA: The Feature Film Since 1946.* New York: Dutton Picturebacks, 1968.

————, and John Huntley. *Technique of Film Music.* New York: Hastings House, 1957.

McBride, Joseph (ed.). *Persistence of Vision.* Madison: Wisconsin Film Society, 1968.

McGuire, Jerimiah. *Cinema and Value Philosophy.* New York: Philosophical Library, 1968.

McVay, J. Douglas. *The Musical Film.* New York: Barnes, 1968.

Michael, Paul. *The Academy Awards: A Pictorial History.* New York: Bonanza Books, 1964.

————. *The American Movies Reference Book: The Sound Era.* New York: Prentice-Hall, 1969.

————. *Humphrey Bogart: The Man and His Films.* Indianapolis: Bobbs-Merrill, 1965.

Milne, Tom (ed.). *Losey On Losey.* New York: Doubleday, 1968.

————. *Rouben Mamoulian.* Bloomington: Indiana University, 1969.

Montagu, Ivor. *Film World: A Guide to Cinema.* Baltimore: Penguin, 1965.

————. *With Eisenstein in Hollywood.* New York: International Publishers, 1969.

Morella, Joe, and Edward Epstein. *Judy.* Introduction by Judith Crist. New York: Citadel, 1969.

Moussinac, Leon (tr. by D. Sandy Petrey). *Sergei Eisenstein.* New York: Crown, 1970.

Murphy, George (with Victor Lasky). *Say . . . Didn't You Used to Be George Murphy?* New York: Bartholomew House, 1970.

Museum of Modern Art Film Library. *Film Notes, Part 1, The Silent Film.* New York: Museum of Modern Art, 1949.

Mussman, Toby (ed.). *Jean-Luc Goddard.* New York: Dutton, 1968.

Negri, Pola. *Memoirs Of A Star.* New York: Doubleday, 1970.

Nemcek, Paul. *The Films Of Nancy Carrol.* New York: Lyle Stuart, 1970.

Nemeskurty, Istvan. *Word and Image.* Budapest: Corvina, 1969.

Nicoll, Allardyce. *Film and Theatre.* New York: Crowell, 1936.

Nilsen, Vladimir. *Cinema as Graphic Art.* New York: Hill and Wang, 1959.

Nitsch, Hermann. *Orgies Mysteries Theatre.* Darmstadt: Marz Verlag, 1969.

Nizhny, Vladimir. *Lessons With Eisenstein.* New York: Hill and Wang, 1963.

Nowell-Smith, Geoffrey. *Luchino Visconti.* New York: Doubleday, 1968.

O'Leary, Liam. *The Silent Cinema.* New York: Dutton, 1965.

Osborne, Robert. *Academy Awards.* New York: Schwords, 1969.

Pechter, William S. *Twenty-four Times a Second.* New York: Harper & Row, 1970.

Perry, George. *The Films of Alfred Hitchcock.* New York: Dutton Picturebacks, 1965.

Powdermaker, Hortense. *Hollywood, the Dream Factory.* Boston: Little, Brown, 1950.

Quirk, Lawrence. *The Films of Joan Crawford.* New York: Citadel, 1969.

Ramsaye, Terry. *A Million and One Nights.* New York: Simon and Schuster, 1926.

Randall, Richard S. *Censorship of the Movies.* Madison: University of Wisconsin, 1968.

Ray, Man. *Self Portrait.* London: Andre Deutsch, 1963.

Reed, Rex. *Conversations in the Raw: Dialogues, Monologues, and Selected Short Subjects.* New York: World, 1970.

Renan, Sheldon. *An Introduction to the American Underground Film.* New York: Dutton, 1967.

Rhode, Eric. *Tower of Babel: Speculations on the Cinema.* New York: Chilton, 1967.

Richardson, Robert. *Literature and Film.* Bloomington: Indiana University, 1969.

Richie, Donald. *The Films of Akira Kurosawa.* Berkeley: University of California, 1970.

————. *George Stevens: An American Romantic.* New York: Museum of Modern Art, 1970.

Ringgold, Gene (with DeWitt Bodeen). *The Films of Cecil B. De Mille.* New York: Citadel, 1969.

Robinson, David. *Buster Keaton.* Bloomington: Indiana University, 1969.

————. *The Great Funnies.* New York: Dutton, 1968.

————. *Hollywood in the Twenties.* New York: Barnes, 1968.

————. *Hollywood in the Twenties: A Complete Critical Survey of Hollywood Films from 1920–1930.* New York: Paperback Library, 1970.

Robinson, W. R. (ed.). *Man and the Movies.* Baltimore: Penguin, 1969.

Rondi, Gian L. *Italian Cinema Today.* New York: Hill and Wang, 1965.

Rosenberg, Bernard, and Harry Silverstein. *The Real Tinsel.* New York: Macmillan, 1970.

Ross, Lillian. *Picture.* New York: Rinehart, 1952.

Ross, T. J. (ed.). *Film and the Liberal Arts.* New York: Holt, Rinehart and Winston, 1970.

Rotha, Paul. *Rotha on the Film.* New York: Oxford University, 1958.

Roud, Richard. *Godard.* New York: Doubleday, 1968.

Ruesch, Jurgen, and Weldon Kees. *Nonverbal Communication: Notes on the Visual Perception of Human Relations.* Berkeley: University of California, 1969.

Sadoul, Georges. *French Film.* Falcon, 1953.

Salachas, Gilbert. *Federico Fellini.* New York: Crown, 1969.

Samuels, Charles (ed.). *A Casebook on Film.* New York: Van Nostrand, 1970.

Sarris, Andrew. *The American Cinema: Directors and Directions.* New York: Dutton, 1968.

————. *Interviews With Film Directors.* New York: Avon, 1967.

———— (ed.). *The Film.* Indianapolis: Bobbs-Merrill, 1968.

Scheuer, Stephen H. (ed.). *Movies on T.V.* 4th ed. New York: Bantam, 1968.

Schramm, Wilbur, with Philip H. Coombs, Friedrich Kahnert, and Jack Lyle. *The New Media: Memo to Educational Planners.* Paris: UNESCO, 1967.

Schrelvogel, Paul. *Films in Depth* (separate booklets for study, including the following titles: *An Occurrence at Owl Creek Bridge, No Reason to Stay, Overture—Overture/Nyitany, The Language of Faces, Orange and Blue, Toys, Timepiece, Night and Fog, Sunday Lark. Flavio, The Little Island, A Stain on His Conscience*). Dayton: Pflaum, 1970.

Schumach, Murray. *The Face on the Cutting Room Floor*. New York: Morrow, 1964.

Sharp, Dennis. *The Picture Palace and Other Buildings for the Movies*. New York: Praeger, 1969.

Shelby, H. C. *Stag Movie Review*. Canoga Park, Calif.: Viceroy, 1970.

Sherman, Eric, and Martin Rubin. *The Director's Event: Interviews with Five American Film-Makers*. New York: Atheneum, 1970.

Shipman, David. *The Great Movie Stars: The Golden Years*. New York: Crown, 1970.

Sitney, P. Adams (ed.). *Film Culture Reader*. New York: Praeger, 1970.

Snider, Robert L. *Pare Lorentz and the Documentary Film*. Norman: University of Oklahoma, 1968.

Sohn, David A. *Film: The Creative Eye*. Dayton: Pflaum, 1970.

Solmi, Angelo (tr. Elizabeth Greenwood). *Fellini*. New York: Humanities, 1968.

Spottiswoode, Raymond. *A Grammar of the Film: An Analysis of Film Technique*. Berkeley: University of California, 1950.

Springer, John. *The Fondas*. New York: Citadel, 1970.

Stack, Oswald. *Pasolini on Pasolini: Interviews with Oswald Stack*. Bloomington: Indiana University, 1969.

Steene, Birgitta. *Ingmar Bergman*. New York: Twayne, 1968.

Steiger, Brad. *Monsters, Maidens, and Mayhem: A Pictorial History of Hollywood Film Monsters*. Chicago: Camerarts, 1965.

Stephenson, Ralph, and Jean R. Debrix. *The Cinema as Art*. Baltimore: Penguin, 1965.

Stewart, David C. *Film Study in Higher Education*. Washington, D.C.: American Council on Education, 1966.

Strick, Philip. *Antonioni*. Loughton (Essex), Eng.: Motion Publications, 1965.

Sussex, Elizabeth. *Lindsay Anderson*. New York: Praeger, 1970.

Swindell, Larry, *Spencer Tracy*. New York: World, 1969.

Tabori, Paul. *Alexander Korda*. London: Oldbourne, 1959.

Talbot, Daniel (ed.). *Film: An Anthology*. Berkeley: University of California, 1966.

Taylor, John Russell, *Cinema Eye, Cinema Ear: Some Key Film-makers of the Sixties*. New York: Hill and Wang, 1964.

Thomas, Bob. *Selznick*. New York: Doubleday, 1970.

———. *Thalberg: Life and Legend*. New York: Doubleday, 1969.

Thorp, Margaret. *America at the Movies*. New Haven: Yale University, 1937.

Truffaut, François. *Hitchcock*. New York: Simon and Schuster, 1967.

Tyler, Parker. *Classics of the Foreign Film: A Pictorial History*. New York: Citadel, 1962.

―――. *The Hollywood Hallucination*. Introduction by Richard Schickel. New York: Simon and Schuster, 1970.

―――. *The Three Faces of the Film*. New York: Yoseloff, 1960.

―――. *Underground Film: A Critical History*. New York: Grove, 1970.

Verdone, Mario. *Roberto Rossellini*. Paris: Editions Seghers, 1963.

Walker, Alexander. *The Celluloid Sacrifice: Aspects of Sex in the Movies*. New York: Hawthorn, 1967.

―――. *Stardom*. New York: Stein and Day, 1970.

Ward, John. *Alain Resnais, or the Theme of Time*. New York: Doubleday, 1968.

Warshow, Robert. *The Immediate Experience*. New York: Doubleday, 1962.

Weaver, John T. *Forty Years Of Screen Credits*. Metuchen, N.J.: Scarecrow, 1970.

Weinberg, Herman G. *Joseph von Sternberg*. New York: Dutton, 1967.

―――. *The Lubitsch Touch: A Critical Study of the Great Film Director*. New York: Dutton, 1969.

―――, with preface by Fritz Lang. *Saint Cinema: Selected Writings 1929–1970*. New York: Drama Book Specialists, 1970.

Weise, E. (ed. and tr.). *Enter: The Comics—Rodolphe Topffer's Essay on Physiognomy and the True Story of Monsieur Crepin*. Lincoln: University of Nebraska, 1965.

White, David Manning, and Richard Averson (eds.). *Sight, Sound, and Society—Motion Pictures and Television in America*. Boston: Beacon, 1968.

Wilde, Larry. *Great Comedians Talk About Comedy*. New York: Citadel, 1969.

Willis, John. *Screen World 1949–* . Annual, 21 vols. New York: Crown, 1970.

Wollen, Peter. *Signs and Meaning in the Cinema*. Bloomington: Indiana University, 1969.

Wood, Robin. *Arthur Penn*. New York: Praeger, 1970.

―――. *Hitchcock's Films*. New York: Barnes, 1965.

―――. *Hitchcock's Films: A Complete Critical Guide to the Films of Alfred Hitchcock*. New York: Paperback Library, 1970.

―――. *Howard Hawks*. New York: Doubleday, 1968.

Wood, Tom. *The Bright Side of Billy Wilder, Primarily*. New York: Doubleday, 1970.

Youngblood, Gene. *Expanded Cinema*. New York: Dutton, 1970.

Zalman, Jan. *Films and Film-Makers in Czechoslovakia*. Prague: Orbis-Prague, 1968.

Zinman, David. *Fifty Classic Motion Pictures: The Stuff That Dreams Are Made Of.* New York: Crown, 1970.

Screenplays and the Process of Filmmaking

Agee, James. *Agee on Film.* Boston: Beacon, 1964.

Agel, Jerome (ed.). *The Making of Kubrick's 2001.* New York: New American Library, 1970.

Alton, John. *Painting with Light.* New York: Macmillan, 1949.

Antonioni, Michelangelo. *Screenplays of Michelangelo Antonioni.* New York: Orion, 1963.

Baddeley, W. Hugh. *The Technique of Documentary Film Production.* New York: Hastings House, 1963.

Beckett, Samuel, and Alan Schneider. *Film By Samuel Beckett.* New York: Grove, 1969.

Bellocchio, Marco. *China Is Near.* New York: Orion, 1969.

———. *Viridiana, The Exterminating Angel, Simon of the Desert.* New York: Orion, 1969.

Bergman, Ingmar. *Four Screenplays of Ingmar Bergman.* New York: Simon and Schuster, 1960.

Bobker, Lee. *Elements of Film.* New York: Harcourt, Brace & World, 1969.

Boyer, Deena (tr. by Charles Lam Markmann). *The Two Hundred Days of 8½.* Afterword by Dwight Macdonald. New York: Macmillan, 1964.

Burder, John. *The Technique of Editing 16MM Films.* New York: Hastings House, 1968.

Capote, Truman, with Eleanor and Frank Perry. *Trilogy.* New York: Macmillan, 1969.

Carrick, Edward. *Designing for Moving Pictures.* New York: Studio, 1947.

Carson, L. M. Kit. *David Holzman's Diary: A Screenplay.* New York: Noonday, 1970.

Cassavetes, John, and Al Ruban. *Faces.* New York: New American Library, 1970.

Clair, René (tr. by Piergiuseppe Bozzetti). *Four Screenplays: Le silence est d'or, La beauté du diable, Les belles-de-nuit, Les grandes manoeuvres.* New York: Orion, 1970.

Cocteau, Jean (ed. by Robert Morris Hammond). *Beauty and the Beast.* New York: N.Y.U., 1970.

———. (tr. by Lily Pons). *The Blood of a Poet.* New York: Bodley Head, 1947.

———. (tr. by Carol Martin-Sperry). *Two Screenplays: The Blood of a Poet, The Testament of Orpheus.* New York: Orion, 1968.

Cross, Brenda (ed.). *The Film Hamlet: A Record of its Production.* London: Saturn, 1948.

De Sica, Vittorio. *Miricale in Milan.* New York: Orion, 1968.

Dreyer, Carl (tr. by Oliver Stallybrass). *Four Screenplays.* London: Thames and Hudson, 1970.

Duras, Marguerite (tr. by Richard Seaver). *Hiroshima Mon Amour.* Picture editor Robert Hughes. New York: Grove, 1961.

Eastman, Charles. *Little Fauss and Big Halsy.* New York: Pocket Books, 1970.

Eisenstein, Sergei M. *Ivan the Terrible.* New York: Simon and Schuster, 1962.

Eisler, Hans. *Composing for the Films.* New York: Oxford University, 1947.

Eliot, T. S., and George Hoellering. *The Film of Murder in the Cathedral.* New York: Harcourt, Brace, 1952.

Fellini, Federico (tr. by Howard Greenfield; ed. by Tullio Kezich). *Federico Fellini's Juliet of the Spirits.* New York: Ballantine, 1965.

———. *La Dolce Vita.* New York: Ballantine, 1961.

——— (tr. by Judith Green). *Three Screenplays: I Vitelloni, Il Bidone, The Temptations of Doctor Antonio.* New York: Orion, 1970.

Ferguson, Robert. *How to Make Movies: A Practical Guide to Group Film-Making.* New York: Viking, 1969.

Fielding, Raymond. *The Technique of Special Effects Cinematography.* New York: Hastings House, 1965.

Fonda, Peter, with Dennis Hopper and Terry Southern. *Easy Rider.* New York: New American Library, 1969.

Foote, Horton. *The Screenplay of To Kill a Mockingbird.* New York: Harcourt, Brace & World, 1964.

Fry, Christopher. *The Bible.* New York: Pocket Books, 1966.

Gassner, John (ed.). *Best Film Plays of 1943/44.* New York: Crown, 1945.

———. *Great Film Plays.* New York: Crown, 1959.

——— (ed. with Dudley Nichols). *Best Film Plays of 1939/40.* New York: Crown, 1941.

Geduld, Harry M. (ed.). *Film Makers on Film Making: Statements on their Art by Thirty Directors.* Bloomington: Indiana University, 1967.

Gelmis, Joseph. *The Film Director as Superstar.* New York: Doubleday, 1970.

Godard, Jean-Luc. *The Married Woman.* New York: Berkeley, 1965.

Goode, James. *The Story of The Misfits.* Indianapolis: Bobbs-Merrill, 1963.

Gordon, George N., and Irving A. Falk. *Your Career In Film Making.* New York: Julian Messner, 1969.

Herman, Lewis. *A Practical Manual of Screen Playwriting: For Theater and Television Films.* New York: World, 1966.

Higham, Charles. *Hollywood Cameramen: Sources of Light.* London: Thames and Hudson, 1970.

———, and Joel Greenberg. *The Celluloid Muse: Hollywood Directors Speak.* New York: New American Library, 1970.

Hopper, Dennis. *The Last Movie.* New York: New American Library, 1970.

Isaksson, Ulla. *The Virgin Spring.* New York: Ballantine, 1960.

Kantor, Bernard R., with Irwin A. Blacker and Anne Kramer (eds.). *Directors at Work.* New York: Funk and Wagnalls, 1970.

Larson, Rodger, Jr. *A Guide for Film Teachers to Filmmaking by Teenagers.* New York: Cultural Affairs Foundation, 1968.

Leyda, Jay. *Films Beget Films.* New York: Hill and Wang, 1964.

Livingston, Don. *Film and the Director.* New York: Macmillan, 1953.

Maddux, Rachel, with Stirling Silliphant and Neil D. Issacs. *Fiction Into Film: A Walk in the Spring Rain.* Knoxville: University of Tennessee, 1970.

Madsen, Roy. *Animated Film.* New York: Interland, 1969.

Manoogian, Haig P. *The Film-Maker's Art.* New York: Basic Books, 1966.

Manvell, Roger. *Three British Screenplays: Brief Encounter, Odd Man Out, and Scott of the Antarctic.* London: Methuen, 1950.

Mascelli, Joseph V. *The Five C's of Cinematography: Motion Picture Filming Techniques Simplified.* Los Angeles: Cine/Grafic Publications, 1965.

———— (ed.). *American Cinematographer Manual.* Hollywood: American Society of Cinematographers, 1966.

Maysies, Albert, and David Maysies. *Salesman.* New York: New American Library, 1969.

McGowan, Kenneth. *Behind the Screen: The History and Techniques of the Motion Picture.* New York: Delacorte, 1965.

Mercer, John. *An Introduction to Cinematography.* Champaign, Ill.: Stipes, 1970.

Miller, Arthur. *The Misfits.* New York: Viking, 1961.

Miller, Merle, and Evan Rhodes. *Only You, Dick Darling, or How to Write One Television Script and Make $50,000,000.* New York: Bantam Books, 1964.

Montagu, Ivor. *With Eisenstein in Hollywood.* New York: International Publishers, 1969.

Naumburg, Nancy (ed.). *We Make the Movies.* New York: Norton, 1937.

Nilsen, Vladimir. *The Cinema as a Graphic Art.* New York: Hill and Wang, 1959.

Nurnberg, Walter. *Lighting for Photography.* New York: Hastings House, 1956.

Oringel, Robert S. *Audio Control Handbook.* New York: Hastings House, 1956.

Osborne, John. *Tom Jones.* London: Faber, 1964.

———— (ed. Robert Hughes). *Tom Jones: A Film Script.* New York: Grove, 1964.

Pennebaker, D. A. *Bob Dylan—Don't Look Back.* New York: Ballantine, 1968.

Petrow, Mischa. *Efficient Film-Making Practices: Rules, Forms & Guides.* New York: Drama Book Specialists, 1970.

Pincus, Edward, and Jairus Lincoln. *Guide to Filmmaking.* New York: New American Library, 1969.

Provisor, Henry. *8MM/16MM Movie-Making.* New York: Chilton, 1970.

Pudovkin, V. I. *Film Technique and Film Acting.* New York: Grove, 1960.

Quigley, Martin, Jr. (ed.). *New Screen Techniques.* Quigley, 1953.

Rattigan, Terence. *The Prince and the Showgirl.* New York: New American Library, 1957.

Reisz, Karel. *The Technique of Film Editing.* New York: Hastings House, 1968.

Renoir, Jean. *The Rules of the Game.* London: Lorrimer, 1970.

Rilla, Wolf. *A–Z of Movie Making.* London: Studio Vista, 1970.

Robbe-Grillet, Alain. *Last Year at Marienbad.* New York: Grove, 1962.

———. *L'Immortelle.* Paris: Editions de Minuit, 1963.

Serling, Rod. *Patterns.* New York: Simon and Schuster, 1957.

Shoman, Vilgot (tr. by Martin Minow and Jenny Bohman). *I Am Curious (Blue).* New York: Grove, 1970.

———. *I Am Curious (Yellow).* New York: Grove, 1968.

———. *I Was Curious—Diary of the Making of a Film.* New York: Grove, 1968.

Skillbeck, Oswald. *ABC of Film and TV Working Terms.* New York: Focal, 1960.

Smallman, Kirk. *Creative Film-Making.* New York: Macmillan, 1969.

Sontag, Susan. *Duet for Cannibals: A Screenplay.* New York: Farrar, Straus & Giroux, 1970.

Southern, Terry. *The Journal of The Loved One: The Production Log of a Motion Picture.* With photography by William Claxton. New York: Random House, 1965.

Souto, H. Mario Raimondo (ed. by Raymond Spottiswoode). *The Technique of the Motion Picture Camera.* New York: Communications Arts Books, 1967.

Spottiswoode, Raymond. *Film and Its Techniques.* Berkeley: University of California, 1951.

Taylor, Theodore. *People Who Make Movies.* New York: Doubleday, 1967.

Trapnell, Coles. *Teleplay.* San Francisco: Chandler, 1966.

Truffaut, François, with Helen G. Scott. *Hitchcock.* New York: Simon and Schuster, 1966.

Vadim, Roger. *Les Liaisons Dangereuses.* New York: Ballantine, 1962.

Vardac, A. Nicholas. *Stage to Screen: Theatrical Method from Garrick to Griffith.* New York: Blom, 1949.

Visconti, Luchino (tr. by Judith Green). *Three Screenplays: White Nights, Rocco and His Brothers, The Job.* New York: Orion, 1970.

———. *Two Screenplays: La Terra Trema, Senso.* New York: Orion, 1970.

Wanger, Walter, and Joe Hyams. *My Life With Cleopatra.* New York: Bantam, 1963.

Warhol, Andy. *Blue Movie.* New York: Grove, 1970.

Wexler, Norman. *Joe.* Introduction by Judith Crist. New York: Avon, 1970.

Wilder, Billy and I. A. L. Diamond. *Irma La Douce.* New York: Midwood-Tower, 1963.